The Records of
The Court of Sessions
of
Suffolk County
in the
Province of New York
1670–1688

Transcribed by

Thomas W. Cooper

HERITAGE BOOKS
2013

HERITAGE BOOKS
AN IMPRINT OF HERITAGE BOOKS, INC.

Books, CDs, and more—Worldwide

For our listing of thousands of titles see our website
at
www.HeritageBooks.com

Published 2013 by
HERITAGE BOOKS, INC.
Publishing Division
5810 Ruatan Street
Berwyn Heights, Md. 20740

Frontispiece: Antique map of Long Island by Robert Ryder,
courtesy of Brown University

International Standard Book Numbers
Paperbound: 978-1-55613-799-0
Clothbound: 978-0-7884-6834-6

TABLE OF CONTENTS

INTRODUCTION

After the English seized New Netherland in 1664, they organized a large portion of their new colony into a jurisdiction which they called Yorkshire. This new Yorkshire, like its English namesake, was divided into administrative units called ridings. All of Long Island east of Oyster Bay fell into the East Riding. This volume contains the records of the Court of Sessions of the East Riding from 1670 to 1688.

After 1683, New York was reorganized into counties, and the East Riding was renamed Suffolk County. Suffolk County was made up of six towns: Southampton, Southold, East Hampton, Brookhaven, Huntington and Smithtown. The first five towns had been part of New England before they were absorbed by New York. English people from Massachusetts had begun to settle on Long Island in 1640, three years after the Pequot Indians had been crushed and their control over the Long Island Sound region had been destroyed. When this record begins in 1670, the first generation of English planters on Long Island had begun to pass away and those who survived were beginning to compose their last wills and testaments.

For the most part, this volume consists of probate records. It also contains records of court cases and copies of deeds. But its chief value is as a collection of wills and estate inventories of an entire generation. Enmeshed in the stylized formulas used when drafting wills can be discerned the thoughts, feelings and beliefs of the ordinary men who lived on Long Island in the latter half of the seventeenth century. The inventories, compiled over a period of eighteen years, provide thorough documentation of their material wealth. For many of them, these wills and inventories constitute the principal enduring expression of their lives.

It should be kept in mind that this is a transcription of a collection of 17th century transcriptions. The original wills, deeds, and inventories were brought in to court and copied by the clerk of the court into the record. Sometimes copies made by the various town recorders were brought in. This helps to explain why the format and spelling vary from entry to entry.

The wills could be either written or oral. Often they were dictated to the local schoolmaster who would consult a form book to find the correct format. On page 13 is an excellent account of how wills were drawn up in the seventeenth century. John White of Southampton had a written will drafted in May 1662, shortly before his death. In 1670, when White's son died, John Laughton, the teacher to whom White had dictated his will, testified in court that White had made oral stipulations that differed slightly but significantly from his written will.

More valuable for historians than the wills are the inventories. An inventory of each man's estate was taken shortly after his death so that his estate might be administered and distributed in an equitable fashion. Because they were compiled by different men, the inventories vary widely in their detail, coverage and orthography. Despite these inconsistencies, the inventories, when they are taken as a whole, offer an incomparable view of life on Long Island during the latter half of the seventeenth century. Frequently, these lists provide us with what, in many respects, appears to be a more objective, less self-conscious perspective than that found in other contemporary official records. The inventories contain an enormous amount of unsifted data covering such varied interests as textiles, domestic animals, kitchen utensils, bedding, furniture, business relationships, tools, crops, food, arms and ammunition, tableware, liquor, clothing, books, whaling and slavery. The reader might wish to consider the inventories as if they were the work of an anonymous *Seicento* genre painter who managed to capture these Long Island households on the day their owners passed away.

Omissions from the record speak as eloquently of the values once held by a society as matters which have been scrupulously preserved. The reader should remain alert to those aspects of contemporary life which the records ignore completely or to which they award only cursory mention. Sometimes, it is a silent witness who has the most significant evidence.

These court records are the work of two men. Henry Pierson (1615-1680) became clerk about 1668. Pierson filled the first 100 pages of the book. Working from the back of the book, he entered the estate of Alice Stanborough. The inventory of Pierson's own estate was copied into the record by his successor beginning on page 103. John Howell Jr. (1648-1693) filled the remaining leaves of the book. He is not to be confused with his father, Major John Howell, who served as one of the court's justices.

This transcription is an attempt to duplicate the original volume as nearly as was technically and practically possible. The pagination is the same as in the original document. For this reason, there are two page 200's. Each line of text represents one line of handwriting. However, pages where the writing appears upside-down, have been transcribed right side-up. Also, the majority of zeros in the inventories have been rendered as dashes. For instance, where the clerk would have represented ten shillings as 00 10 00, the transcriber has taken the liberty to represent it as - 10 - in order to make the value of items more readily apparent to the reader.

Seventeenth century orthography presents certain challenges to the modern reader. For instance a letter resembling a "y", equivalent to our "th", and called a thorn, meant that the words "the", "them" and "that" were written as ye, ym and yt. This has been duplicated in the transcription. Other writing practices have been ignored. Superscriptions have been brought down to the line. Words with u's and v's have been given their modern spelling. If the clerk wrote "aboue", it has been transcribed "above".

Crossed p's could not be crossed on the transcriber's computer, so the reader is expected to deduce that they were from their context. For example, Cooper was often spelled Coop with a crossed p. Frequently, the clerk ended a transcription with the Latin formula, "A true copy per me". This will appear in this transcription as "p me" and the reader is expected to infer that the p was crossed. This also applies to double consonants. In the seventeenth century, "son" was spelled sonne. The double consonant could be rendered by placing a hyphen over a single "n". In this case, it would be transcribed here as sone. The transcriber would like to express his gratitude in advance to the reader for the patience which may sometimes be required in order derive the full meaning of the text.

The reader is reminded that, in the seventeenth century, the English still adhered to the Julian calendar and that, therefore, the year began for them on March 25. When they wished to avoid confusion, they would write the year in the period between January 1 and March 25 thusly; 1671/2. If the text is not explicit, the reader may assume that the Julian year is intended. The first date which appears in the text is March 4, 1669. This was in 1670 according to the Gregorian calendar. And because the date had been adjusted when the new calendar had been adopted, countries using the Gregorian calendar were ten days ahead in the seventeenth century. The same day would have been March 14, 1670 in France and Italy. This is important to keep in mind because the court often met in early March.

The transcriber would like to express his appreciation to Dr. Raymond Hillis, Mr. Randall Lewis, Mr. Jeff McNally, Mr. Henry Hoff, Mr. Robert Steen, Miss Monika Maciejowski and my parents, Mr. and Mrs. Thomas W. Cooper, for their advice and encouragement.

CAUTION:

For the convenience of the reader, the transcriber has added maps and an index to the text. In compiling the maps and index, he has made assumptions which may or may not be found to be correct. The reader is therefore cautioned not to consider them or the assumptions on which they are based as being in any way authoritative statements of fact.

INVENTORIES OF SUFFOLK COUNTY ESTATES

TOWN	# OF ESTATES	AVG	MEAN	LARGEST ESTATE
Southampton	55	361	177	2349
Southold	28	158	123	477
East Hampton	24	181	113	1463
Brookhaven	11	92	61	202
Huntington	9	165	195	306
Smithtown	1	143	143	143
SUFFOLK COUNTY	128	£244	£123	£2349

This table does *not* represent an even playing field. There are not any inventories for blacks or native Americans and only three women are represented. Some inventories include real estate while others list only the moveable goods. In many cases, the individual distributed large portions of his estate before his death. This table is useful only in determining the relative size of the estate itself. Although there is often a correlation between the size of a deceased person's estate and that individual's social position in the community, it is the transcriber's opinion that the relationship is *not* sufficiently reliable and that further reference to other factors and to the inventories themselves would be advisable if determining the social standing of an individual is the reader's principal objective. (The rate lists for 1675 and 1683 are especially useful for this purpose. They may be found in Volume II of *The Documentary History of New-York*) The figures below are gross amounts. Liabilities against the estates have not been subtracted from the totals.

		£	s	d	*Page*
1	Robert Fordham	2349	2	0	*76*
2	Lyon Gardiner	1463	7	10	*
3	John Cooper Jr.	1370	18	0	*73*
4	Henry Pierson	1256	1	5	*103*
5	Ellis Cook	1154	12	10	*82*
6	Daniel Halsey	994	7	0	*118*
7	Joseph Raynor	938	19	8	*124*
8	Arthur Howell	887	15	5	*139*
9	John White Sr.	887	8	0	*
10	Thomas Topping Jr.	703	14	6	*110*
11	Joseph Fordham	701	16	3	*309*
12	Thomas Halsey Sr.	672	9	2	*89*
13	Josiah Stanborough	643	19	1	*
14	Anthony Ludlam	598	14	6	*119*
15	Thomas Cooper, Southampton	492	17	3	*151*
16	Joseph Youngs	477	9	0	*§*
17	Lieut. Thomas Cooper	420	16	4	*317*
18	Joseph Taylor	406	18	8	*126*
19	Barnabas Horton	405	16	0	*102*
20	Richard Stratton	399	12	3	*58*
21	Samuel Clark, North Sea	384	3	0	*86*
22	John Cooper Sr.	374	15	0	*

		£	s	d	Page
23	Thomas Cooper, Southold	368	7	0	*§*
24	John Fordham	342	0	0	*140*
25	Jonas Bower	339	0	0	*16*
26	John Topping	326	2	6	*228*
27	Matthias Curwin	308	11	6	*§*
28	William Purrier	307	15	0	*51*
29	Thomas Sayre	307	7	0	*23*
30	Thomas Brush	306	12	0	*56*
31	Thomas Wicks	286	5	6	*19*
32	Edward Tredwell	285	0	0	*#*
33	William Russell	273	7	0	*116*
34	Thomas Halsey Jr.	248	15	0	*314*
35	Roger Smith	246	17	3	*52*
36	Stephen Coppock	243	18	10	*68*
37	John Herbert	241	19	0	*§*
38	Richard Shaw	240	2	6	*143*
39	William Salmon	227	5	8	*§*
40	Richard Terry	222	12	0	*55*
41	William Fithian	215	4	6	*114*
42	Alice Stanborough	210	1	7	*283*
43	James Neighbor	206	11	0	*25*
44	John Jenners	202	13	0	*95*
45	Francis Munsey	201	0	0	*48*
46	Thomas Jones	195	0	0	*2*
47	William Hedges	193	12	6	*40*
48	Jacob Wood	190	18	6	*122*
49	William Hallock	188	17	0	*159*
50	John Youngs	185	18	0	*178*
51	Thomas Jessup	182	17	0	*160*
52	John Hand	181	14	6	*&*
53	Thomas Hutchinson	180	18	0	*63*
54	John Woodruff Jr.	177	7	0	*9*
55	John White Jr.	170	5	0	*14*
56	Cornelius Vonk	164	8	0	*121*
57	William Browne	160	0	8	*@*
58	William Edwards	157	9	0	*177*
59	Obadiah Palmer	148	9	½	*105*
60	Thomas Terry	147	8	6	*34*
61	John Stratton	145	14	6	*223*
62	Obadiah Smith	143	0	0	*118*
63	George Harris	139	18	0	*154*
64	James Haynes	123	8	4	*§*
65	John Elton	123	0	0	*44*
66	Nathaniel Bishop	113	17	0	*180*
67	William Williams	111	16	0	*108*
68	Benjamin Haynes	105	7	0	*275*
69	John Mapes	104	0	6	*136*
70	Joseph Youngs	103	15	2	*45*
71	John Post	99	8	0	*304*
72	Zerubbabel Phillips	98	18	0	*299*
73	Thomas Chatfield	98	3	10	*299*
74	Isaac Hedges	98	1	0	*61*
75	Thomas Reeves, Southampton	97	18	6	*191*
76	Richard Curtis	97	14	0	*28*
77	John Youngs	97	0	0	*47*
78	Anne Rogers	95	17	3	*5*
79	Joshua Garlick Jr.	95	6	0	*80*

		£	s	d	Page
80	John Annings	93	14	0	*307*
81	Philemon Dickerson	93	0	0	*36*
82	John Mappham	88	0	6	*187*
83	Christopher Fowler	86	4	9	*144*
84	Robert Gouldsbury	84	8	6	*145*
85	Thomas Reeves, Southold	84	3	0	*135*
86	David Howell	83	2	0	*163*
87	William Fancy	83	0	0	*99*
88	John Jennings	77	0	6	*243*
89	James Herrick	74	12	0	*233*
90	Peter Payne	74	5	0	*§*
91	John Osborne	72	2	0	*300*
92	Matthew Lum	71	8	0	*20*
93	Christopher Lupton Sr.	69	14	0	*246*
94	John Parsons	69	12	6	*203*
95	Samuel Wheeler	66	0	0	*#*
96	Nathaniel Norton	61	5	0	*181*
97	John Bennet	61	0	10	*162*
98	John Laughton	56	17	0	*316*
99	Nathaniel Baker	53	10	0	*291*
100	Evan Owen	53	5	0	*163*
101	Thomas Prickman	51	4	0	*294*
102	Joseph Marshall	50	18	0	*188*
103	Thomas Smith	48	16	0	*180*
104	Edmund Shaw	48	5	0	*65*
105	William Hakelton	46	17	0	*188*
106	Barnabas Wines	46	7	0	*97*
107	Isaac Overton	45	2	0	*311*
108	John Corey	43	3	6	*240*
109	Josiah Bartholomew	41	15	7	*306*
110	Jeremiah Vail	35	10	0	*298*
111	Nathaniel Dominy	33	12	0	*291*
112	John Brooks	33	0	0	*204*
113	William Segrave	31	1	0	*155*
114	[-] Frost	29	1	0	*§*
115	Thomas Travally	28	3	6	*282*
116	Elizabeth Payne	26	19	10	*§*
117	Christopher Foster	25	17	0	*271*
118	William Mulford	25	9	0	*240*
119	John Mulford	25	2	0	*232*
120	Samuel Mills	19	1	0	*193*
121	Christopher Lupton Jr.	17	1	0	*312*
122	Richard Brooks	16	16	0	*308*
123	Caleb Dayton	15	14	2	*311*
124	John Thomas	15	14	0	*39*
125	[-] Squires	11	7	11	*206*
126	Henry Lewis	8	3	0	*@*
127	John Finch	2	18	9	*193*
128	Thomas Hilton	1	15	0	*@*

** Southampton Town Records, Vol. II; § Southold Town Records, Vol. I; # Huntington Town Records, Vol. I; & East Hampton Town Records, Vol. I; @ Southampton Town Records, Vol. I*

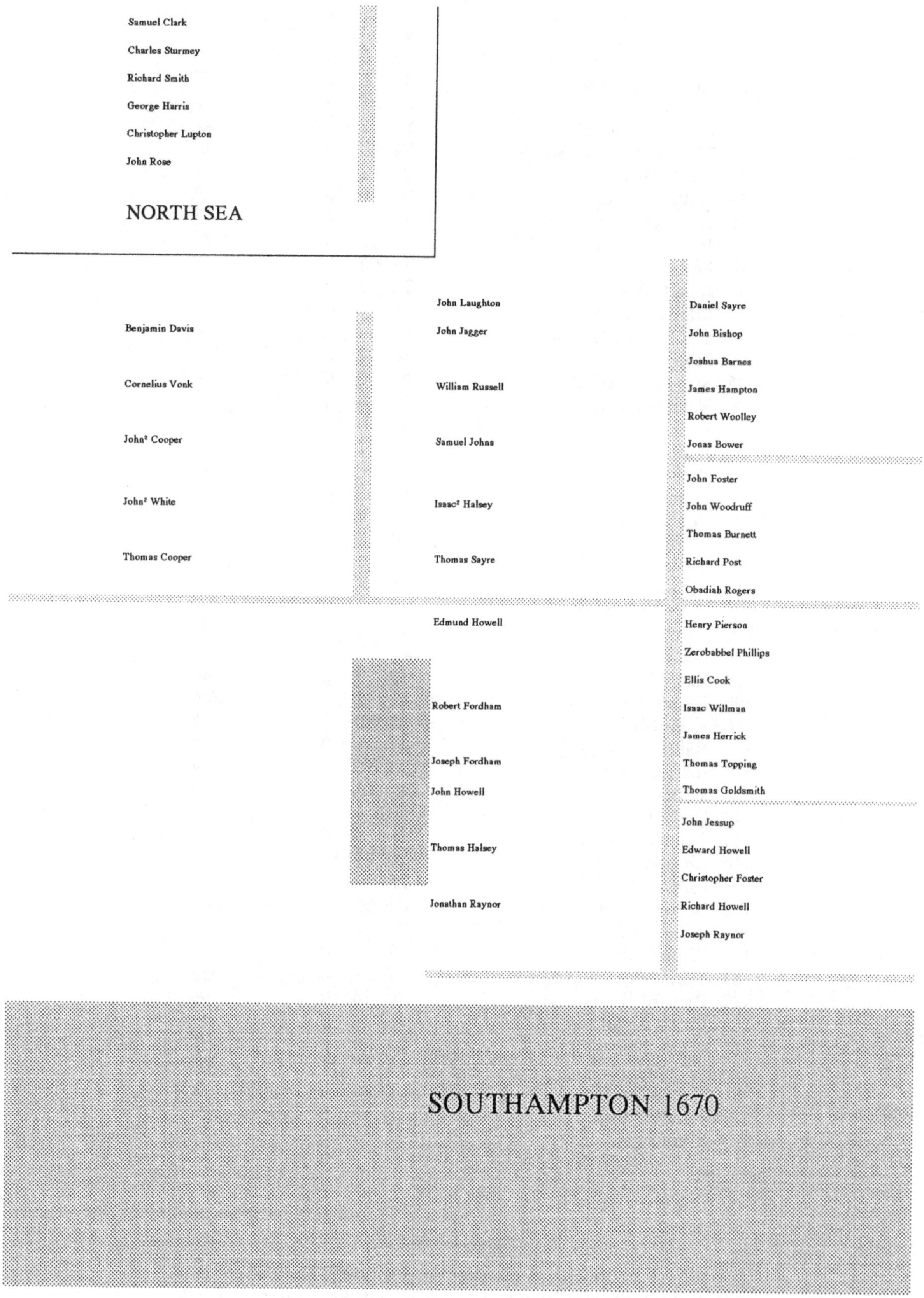
Samuel Clark
Charles Sturmey
Richard Smith
George Harris
Christopher Lupton
John Rose
NORTH SEA
Benjamin Davis
Cornelius Vonk
John[2] Cooper
John[2] White
Thomas Cooper
John Laughton
John Jagger
William Russell
Samuel Johns
Isaac[2] Halsey
Thomas Sayre
Daniel Sayre
John Bishop
Joshua Barnes
James Hampton
Robert Woolley
Jonas Bower
John Foster
John Woodruff
Thomas Burnett
Richard Post
Obadiah Rogers
Edmund Howell
Robert Fordham
Joseph Fordham
John Howell
Thomas Halsey
Jonathan Raynor
Henry Pierson
Zerobabbel Phillips
Ellis Cook
Isaac Willman
James Herrick
Thomas Topping
Thomas Goldsmith
John Jessup
Edward Howell
Christopher Foster
Richard Howell
Joseph Raynor
SOUTHAMPTON 1670

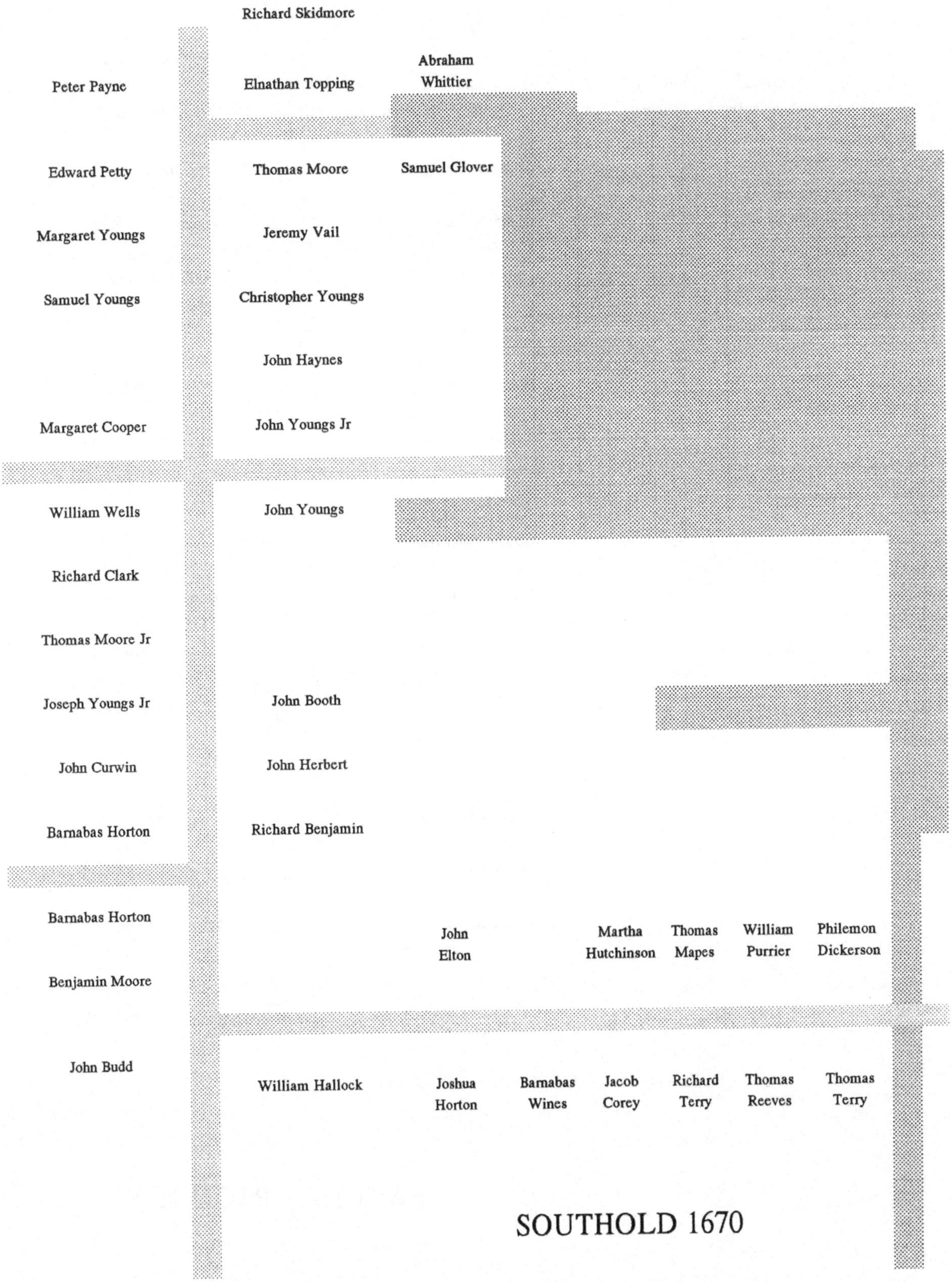

SOUTHOLD 1670

EAST HAMPTON 1670

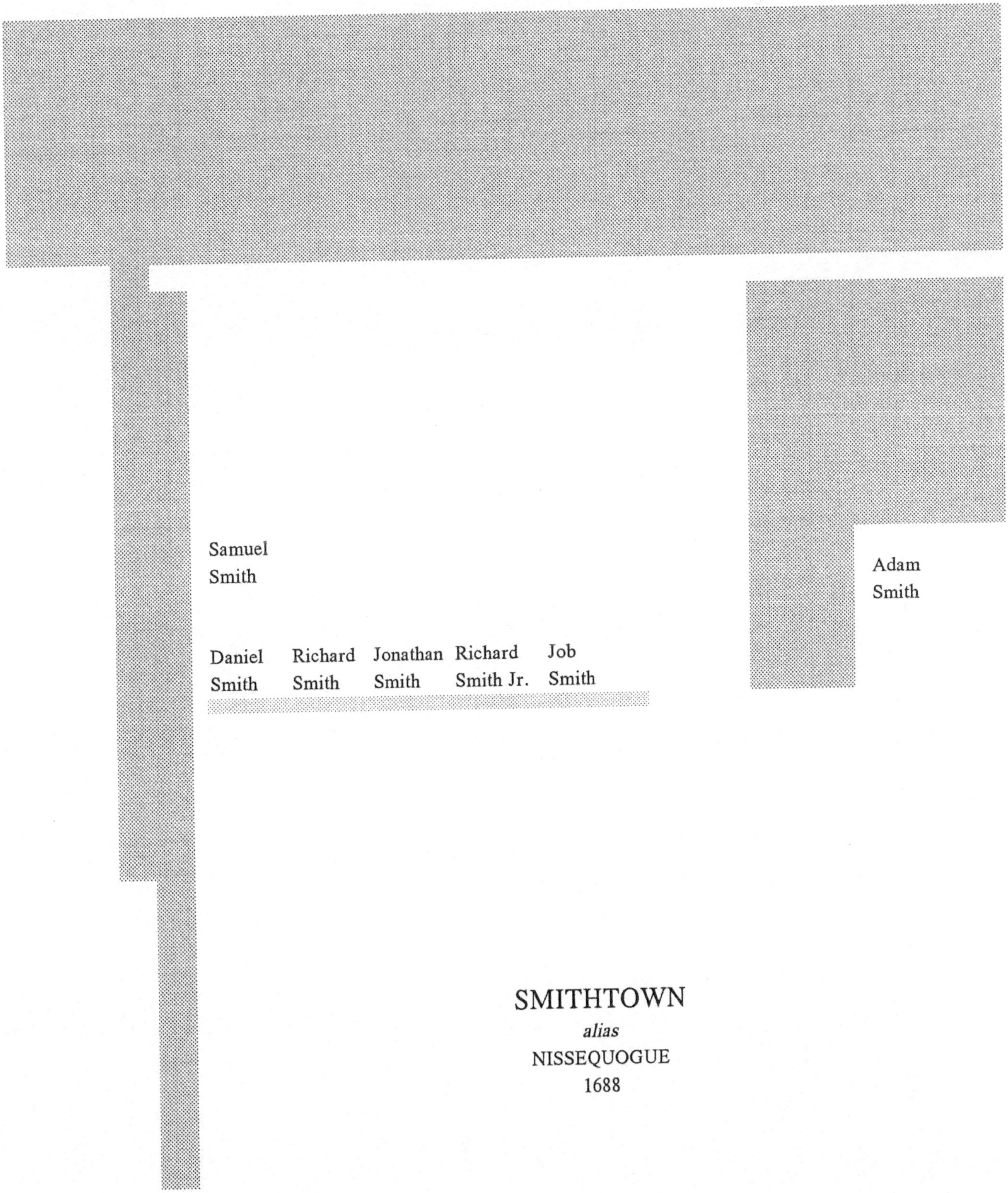
Samuel Smith
Adam Smith
Daniel Smith
Richard Smith
Jonathan Smith
Richard Smith Jr.
Job Smith
SMITHTOWN
alias
NISSEQUOGUE
1688

[first leaf]

at Southampton
At ye within Sd Co:rt of Sessions held March:4th:1669
^

Mr: Jonas Wood of Huntington Enters a complaint
against Jonathan Smith of Neeceaquake, for his
takeing up, and keepeing in his hand neere three
quarters of a yeare, a horse belonging to ye Com=
=plainant and for ye Sd Jonathan his new mark
=ing branding and Dorking of ye Sd horse.
The Sd Complaint to bee prosecuted at ye
Co:rt of Sessions to bee held at Southold next
June.

The abovesd Complaint was prosecuted At
ye Co:rt of Sessions held at Southold June
the first 1670 By Mr: Wood his Attorney
namely Thomas Skidmore.
Richard Smith Junr: as Attorney for his
brother Jonathan, made answer:

The plea on both Sides heard by ye Co:rt and
all the testamonies presented, duely con=
=sidered, the Co:rt adjudg that the Said
horse rightly belongeth to mr Wood the
Sd Complainant And doe order that the
Defend:t Namely Jonathan Smith Shall
pay to the plf: thirty shillings in Currant
pay, And costs of Suite with 25s unto
ye Sd Thomas Skidmore, attorney in the
case, besides his Charges: And if ye Sd
horse die before ye Sd Mr: Wood is Discharg
=ed of him, then hee the Sd Jonathan is
to Satisfy unto Mr: Wood the value of ye
Sd horse with Such further costs as may
arise thereby: - - -

1st: page

A Court of Sessions held at Southampton the fourth Day of March By his Ma:ties Authority in the 22th yeare of the Reigne of our Sove= =raigne Lord Charles the Second By the Grace of God of Great Brittaine ffrance & Ireland King Defender of the Faith &c. And in the yeare of our Lord Christ 1669.//

Samuell Titus of Huntington prsents to the Co:rt ye under written Testamt, w:ch the Cort give order to record: As followeth:

The Last Will & Testament of Thomas Jones of Huntington, haveing his memory and understand= =ing: his will is that his three youngest Sonnes may have Six poundes each of them. And I Doe give to my two eldest Sonnes twenty shillings - each of them. And ten poundes to my Daughter Martha. And I doe give my eldest Sonne Thomas my best cloak, and to my Sone John - my worst. And all soe I doe make my wife my executrix in witness whereof I have Sett to my - hand this 16:th of february 1669:

his marke

Thomas C Jones

Samuell Titus
Thomas Powell:

These two witnesses Samuell Titus & Thomas Powel have given theire oaths to the truth of this will this 26th of february 69.

Huntington: before me Jonas Wood

A true Coppy of ye originall p me
Henry Peirson Cleark
of the Sessions of ye East Riding

The abovesaid Will and Testam:t of Thomas Jones being prsented to this Co:rt of Sessions &c: the Court doe approve of the abovesaid proof of the Said Will: And according to the Will of the Testator this Co:rt doe appoynt that his wife namely Catherin Jones bee law= full Executrix of the Sd Will. And further the Co:rt doe order and appoynt that w:th all

con=

convenient Speede, Shee the Said Executrix doe cause
A true Inventory to bee made according to law
of all the estate the sd Testator Dyed Seized
of, And to send the Sd Inventory into ye hand
of ye Cleark of the Sessions, or at furthest to
Deliver it in to the Co:rt of Sessions at South
=hold to bee there held next June &c:

Huntington May) A true Inventory of all ye goods
the 28:th 1670) and Chattells of Tho: Jones deceased

Imprs: his weareing apparell	5	–	–
It one fether bed, a payre of blankets and two pillowes, & five Curtains	5	–	–
It one Small fether bed, and a payre of Blankets and koverleed	3	–	–
It one Small flock bedd, a blankett and two old ruggs	1	10	–
It for 13£ of sheeps wooll	1	–	–
It for 8 payre of Sheets	7	10	–
It for 6 pillibars 3 tables cloes and eight Napkins	3	–	–
It 1 payre of Blankets	1	12	–
It for Brasse and pewter	8	–	–
It for three Iron potts	1	10	–
It for 3 Iron posnits		10	–
It for two old frying pans		3	–
It for 2 payre of fire=tongues 3 tramells 2 spits 2 payre of pothookes and two smoothing Irons	1	5	–
It for 3 guns and two Swords	3	–	–
It for 4 old Chests	1	–	–
It for an old bible and other Bookes		10	–
It ould lumber in the Chamber	2	–	–
It old lumber in the Cellar	2	–	–
It for an old Charte and wheeles	1	–	–
It for 4 oxen	24	–	–
It one Steere come 5 yeare old	4	10	–
It for 7 Cowes	28	–	–
It for 2 Steeres come 3 yeare old	7	–	–
It for			
	112=	00=	00

		£	s	d
	It for Seaven yearlings	7	–	–
	It for 6 Calves	3	–	–
	It for 13 Sheep and 4 lambs	7	–	–
	It for 15 young Swine	12	–	–
	It for one horse and one mare	13	–	–
	It for one yeareling horse	2	10	–
	It Accomodations of howse and lands	35	–	–
omitted in its place before	It 3 Chaines	1	10	–
	It 2 axes 4 old howes, boult Cleaves – –)		–	–
	Sheare and Coulter and other Small Iron things)	2	–	–
		83	–	–
	on ye other Side –	112	–	–
		195	–	–

Apprized by us whose names is here Subscribed

Samuell Titus
Thomas Scudder
Joseph Bailye Re: §
Thomas Brush.

Attested upon oath before Mr: Wood:
A true Coppy p me Henry Peirson:

This Inventory was Delivered in to the Co:rt of Sessions held at Southhold the 2 of June 1670. And accepted by the Co:rt /

The last Will and Teastament of Ann Rogers, late of Huntington, made ye 22:th of November An:o Dom: 1669.

Imprs: I give unto my sone Obadiah 10s: and 40s: to his oldest sone. Item, I give unto the rest of my Sones – six pound a peece. Item, Speaking about Sheep: Shee Said that John should have his owne; And I give unto Noah two ewes: And I give unto – Samuell and my Daughter Mary 3 sheep: goeing in his lott: Item I give unto my Sone Samuell one cow and one heyfer: Item I give unto my Daughter Hannah 3 Cowes and my Mare & foale and young horse: Item I give unto my Daugh= =ter Mary and Hannah my pewter brasse – howseholdstuf and weareing Cloathes to bee De= =vided betweene them: Item, I give my swine to bee Devided amongst my Children: Shee Said all the rest after shee had Expressed her minde

con

concerning Obadiah:

November 22th
Ano: Dom: 1669

Witnes my hand
Wm: Leverich

Mr: Leverage hath Sworne to the truth of this will
before mee Jonas Wood
Mary Jarvis

ffebruary 21: 69
Huntington

Catterne Jones have sworne to the truth of this will
before mee Jonas Wood / marke of Catterne Jones

A true Coppy p me Henry Peirson /

By the Co:rts appoyntment: endorsed on the back side of ye originall of the said will, as followeth: - - -

The within written Will being prsented to the Co:rt of Sessions (held March 2: 1669 at Southampton) the Co:rt Doe accept of the proof thereof, and are fuly satisfyed therew:th And at the request of Divers of the Legatees under their handes Expressed, ye Co:rt: Doe constitute and appoynt Samuell Titus of Huntington to bee the lawfull Executor of the Sd Will and Testam:t whoe is ordered by the Co:rt not to impropriate to his owne use, or disspose to any pson any of ye estate of the within mentioned Ann Rogers Deceased untill hee hath caused to bee taken accord =ing to law a true and iust Inventory of ye Said Estate: which Inventory hee is to send Downe in =to the handes of ye Clearke of Sessions, or at fur= =thest to deliver in to the Cort at South hold to bee there held next June. And when the estate is apprized and ye Legacies and Debts payed & diss= =charged, the overplus (if any) shall bee Equally Devided amongst all the Children of her the Deceased:

Samuell Titus ingaged to the
Co:rt to pforme & execute
what the Will requireth./

A Record A true Coppy &c: /

Huntington

Huntington March ye 10th: 1669/70
A true Inventory of ye goods and Chattells of Anne
Rogers Widdow Deceased./

		£	s	d
Imprs_	her weareing Apparrell	7	4	-
	pewter 35s 6d one glass 2s 6d one gugg 15d	1	19	3
It	Small things, as Sessars come & box		3	2
It	for holland 31s 8d a cape & neckcloth 18d	1	13	2
It	a payre of Shoes 6s Bookes 4s		10	-
It	for Searge 7s for a remn:t of holland 47s 8d	2	14	8
It	for a Small linning & Silke	2	1	-
It	for a hatt 6s for 3 aprons 9s		15	-
It	for a wastcoat & other Small things		14	-
It	for A sheits and other things	4	7	6
It	for a rugg and Blanket	4	12	-
It	a bed boulster and pillowes	2	6	-
It	1 Chest 2s a churne 3 garrs 8s		10	-
It	a Smoothing Iron & tosting Iron		2	6
It	Brasse and Iron	5	-	-
It	4 Cowes and one heifer	20	5	-
It	1 mare 1 Coulte one 2 yeare old horse	13	-	-
It	3 small Swine	3	-	-
It	6 accres of meadow & comonadg	5	-	-
It	Due uppon Bond	20	-	-
	Sume -	95	:17	:03

Prized by us whose names is subscribed - - -

Attested upon oath before Mr: Wood:

John Ted
Joseph Whetman

Due from the Deceased

		£	s	d
Imprs:	to Mr: Leverich		12	-
	to Thomas Skidmore		4	-
	to Caleb Wood		3	-
	to Joseph Baiely		2	6
		01	:01	:06

This Inventory was Delivered in to the
Co:rt of Sessions held at Southhold -
June 2: 1670
Ordered by ye Co:rt to bee recorded
And a True Coppy p me
Henry Peirson &c. /

March 4th 1669: At ye Co:rt of Sessions afforesaid:

A Complaint is presented to the Co:rt against Mr: John Laughton for his missdemeanour in Saying to Mr: John Howell that hee was a traytor to ye State, and hee would prove him Soe. / / /

Mr: Laughton being called, appeares, & being questioned by ye Cort about it, hee owned yt hee called Mr: Howell Soe. And confesseth yt hee had noe Just cause Soe to call him - - -

The Co:rt adjudg Mr: Laughton to pay a fine of 3 £ to the Cuntry: & costs of Co:rt in currant pay without further trouble: /

M:ris Alce Stanborough Entereth Complaint - - against Wm: Edwards of theire Towne of Easthamp =ton for his turning a water course upon her Land & howseing to her great inconveniency, and damage to the value of 5 £-10s. / - - - - -

The Sd Complaint beeing prosecuted at this Co:rt and ye witnesses on both Sides Duely considered the Cort Doth give theire Judgmt, and order as followeth:

That the plf: Sueing for 5 £ 10s Damage But not proveing it, this Cort Doth Judg & Determine accord= =ing to Law in that case provided that the plf: Shall Lose her Suite or Plainte, And pay unto ye Defend costs of Suite. And for prevention of any fur =ther trouble betweene the plf: & defend:t concern =ing the turning of a flux of water into ye plfs: ground, (wch is ye ground of ye prsent Difference): - This Co:rt doth order That the Constable of Easthampton and 3 of theire overseers Namely Steeven Hand Nathaniell Bishop, Steeven Hedges Shall veiw the ground belonging to the plf: and Defend:t And Set downe order and Disspose of that occation: (as may bee most convenient for both the plf: & Defend:t) wth the assistance of Mr: Mulford; And what those 4 men Doe Determine concerning the

pre

premises, as to what provission the plf & Defend:t
shall make and maintaine for turning of ye water
and where it shall run &c shall bee a small con=
=clusion betweene the plf: & Defend:t therein; they
beeing to Satisfy the Sd 4 men for what paines
they shall bee at. /

Edward Avery the Smith at Easthampton being brought
before the Co:rt to answer for his comission of -
fornication wth her hee now calls his wife -
Hee acknowledging ingenuously the fact or offence
and undertakeing for his wife therein alsoe
The Co:rt give Sentence that hee shall pay -
3 £ as a fine to the Cuntry, & costs of Co:rt
all which hee promiseth to satisfy &c. /

A complaint being prsented against Thomas - -
Diment of East hampton for formeing a warrant &
fixing a Justices hand to it, and makeing Some -
use of it, The Complaint appearing to the Co:rt
to bee iust, hee is Sentenced by the Co:rt to pay
10s fine to the Cuntry. And noe more because
hee pleads & affirmes it was done in merrym:t
and hee is alsoe to pay Co:rt Charges:

Mr: Jonas Wood by his order entereth complaint
against Jonathan Smith of Neeceaquake for takeing
up, and keeping in his hand neare 3 quarters of a
yeare a horse belonging unto him the Sd Mr Wood
as alsoe for ye Sd Jonathan his new markeing
and branding and Dorking of the Sd horse. - -

Whereupon the Sd Jonathan was called &
appeared, and was bound by the Co:rt in
the Sume=Sett of 10 £ to answer the Said
Complaint at ye Cort of Sessions to bee
held at South hold Next June.

See the first leaf of this book -
concerning this last Complaint //

At a Co:rt of Sessions held at Southold June 1st: 1670
Was prsented the will and Testament of John
Woodruff of Southampton: w:ch is as followeth.

\- In the Name of God Amen: To All Xipian people
Know yee That I John Woodruff Senior of South=
hampton in ye East Rideing of Yorke=sheire on -
Long Island Being in pfect Strength of Memorie
Blessed bee God: Although weake in body: And
not knowing the time of my Decease, Doe make
and ordaine this presents to mee my last will &
Testament:/

Imp - I freely Give and bequeath my Soule to God yt gave
it mee, And my Body to ye earth from whence it
2: was taken. - 2ly: I give unto my Eldest
Sone John Woodruff of Elizabeth Towne, one
halfe Crowne peece of Money In full of all por
=tions and Pattrimonies whatsoever to bee ex
=pected from mee, or out of any pt of my Estate

3ly - I Give and bequeath after mine and my
my wifes Decease unto my Daughter Anne
Wooley, and to hers Twenty poundes out of my
Estate, to bee paid, tenn poundes imediately
and 10 £ at two yeares after. - - - - -

4ly - I Give and bequeath in like Manner unto my -
Daughter Elizabeth Dayton and to hers, the
like Sume of Twenty poundes out of my Estate
to bee paid tenn poundes Imediately, & 10 £
at two yeares after: - - - - - -

Lastly- I By this, make my wife Anne Woodruffe and
my youngest Sone John Woodruffe Joynt Exe=
=cutors of this My Last Will & Testament, to See
the Said abovesd: Legacies Disscharged, viz, the
halfe Crowne imediately upon Demand after
my Decease, And the halfe of each other Legacy
after mine and my Said Wives Decease, and the
other halfe that time two yeares after ye former
All the rest of my Estate both lands & Chattells
& cattell and howsehold Stuffe, to bee to the only proper
be=

behoofe and benifit of my Said Executors: In Witnes
whereof I have hereunto Sett my hand and fixed
my Seale this 4th of May An:o Dom: 1670

his
John J Woodruffe
marke

Signed Sealed and
Delivered in ye prsents of
Christopher ffoster
John Laughton

Know all men by these prsents That this above=
=written will is my owne hand writeing, And I saw
the Said John Woodruffe Sett to his marke, & take
off the Seale or Stampt from the wax As -
witnes my hand John Laughton:

This Attestation of John Laughton is alsoe
upon oath before the Co:rt of Sessions held at
Southold June ye first 1670

A true Coppy p me Henry Peirson

Southampton May 24: 1670
Wee the Subscribed being required: Doe according to
our best Judgments & Skill apprize of ye Estate of -
John Woodruffe Deceased as followeth

		£	s	d
Imprs:-	4 oxen at 25 £ 1 old cow 3 £ 10s	28	10	-
	1 Young cow 4 £ a heifer & calfe 3£ 15s	7	15	-
	a Small 4 yeare old Steere	3	15	-
	2 Steeres of 2 yeare old 1 yearling	6	15	-
	one Steere and a little yearling	3	10	-
	More w:ch are abroad: one 3 Yeare old)			
	Sagg: 1 Steere of 3 year:old & 1 yearling wch)			
	upon credible information was apprized at)	8	5	-
	alsoe a mare & a very poore yeareling	9	-	-
	alsoe 17 sheep & 7 young Lambes	9	18	-
	alsoe 4 Swine 3 £ 10s & 4 Shoats in Sight 26s 8d	4	16	8
	Yoakes Chaines, carte, & plow w:th apurtenances	4	10	-
	1 fether bed bowlster, pillowes, 1 rugg)			
	2 blankets a pr of Sheets & curtaines)	8	10	-
	a Small rugg blanket & Sheete	1	10	-
	an old flock bed 3 old blankets and a)			
	remnant of trucking cloth)	2	5	-
	3 Sheets 15 Napkins 2 towells 3 pillow)			
	beares 2 tableclothes. 1 chest & old trunk)	5	8	-
	4 pewter dishes 2 little ones, 4 plates)			
	2 candlesticks 2 poringers 2 Saltsellars)			
	1 lamp, 2 tunells, 2 pewter potts, a tin pot)			
	4 earthen platters 5 Spoones and)			
	3 earth potts)	3	-	-
		107:	07:	8

a brasse

		£	s	d
It: a brasse pott=mettle kettle 2 Small	)			
brasse kettles, & 1 old one	)	1	15	–
1 Chaffin dish a morter & skimer		–	5	–
2 Iron potts. 2 kettles & morter & pestle		2	5	–
2 AndIrons, tongs, fire shovell,	)			
a pott hanger and grid Iron	)	1	15	–
an ax, hoes, and other od tooles	)			
as Syeth Sickles &c	)	1	5	–
A table, 3 chests, a cupboard	)			
and other lumbar at 3£ 10s	)	3	10	–
2 Driping pans an old chamber pot	)			
an howre glasse: 2 pr: Sheep Sheares	)			
& an old brasse skellet, a bible &c:	)		15	–
weareing apparell		3	10	–
one half of the land howseing & accomodati=	)			
=ons, is already clearely by Deed of	)			
guift Dissposed to his Sone John	)			
the other halfe if it bee to bee aded	)			
to the Sume of ye estate wee aprize att	)	55	–	–
		70:	00:	00
	on contra	107:	07:	00
	£:	177:	07:	00

Witnes our hands this 24:th of May 1670

John Howell:
Henry Peirson
Edward Howell
John Jennings:

A true Coppy./

The Co:rt being Satisfied w:th the proof of ye Said will and accepting and allowing of ye Sd Inventory &c Doth grante unto the Sd Anne Woodruff & her Younger Sone John That they Shall bee, and are Lawfull & Joynte Executors of the Sd Will and testam:t according to the minde of ye testator therein expressed: – –

At the Co:rt of Sessions held at Southold June ye 1st: 1670
was prsented the Will and Testament of John White Deceased
w:ch the Co:rt ordered to bee recorded; and is as followeth. - - -

In the name of God Amen, I John White of Southampton
in the East Rideing of Yorke=sheire on Long Island, Sick but in
whole minde Doe make this my last will and Testament - -
wherein first I bequeath my Soule into the hands of Almighty
God from whome I received it, And my body to the earth from -
whence it came. And my goods, My funerall charge being first
expended, to bee Dissposed of as followeth.

Item- I give unto my only Sone John All my right title & interest
unto All and every pt and percell of Lands that is mine whe=
=ther in possession or reversion, with all buildings Edifices &
appurtenances whatsoever thereunto belonging, to him and
his heyres forever: And in case my Sone die without issue
then my lands before mentioned shall returne unto my Daugh=
=ter Elizabeth and to her heyres begotten of her body: and if
Shee die without issue alsoe, then my Loving wife Hannah -
Shall enjoy the Sd Lands dureing her life and then to -
returne unto the Eldest Sone of my brother James:
And if hee alsoe die without issue male, then the
one Moity of the lands before mentioned shall bee
devided betweene my two Nephewes John Topping
and Thomas Topping. And the other Moitie -
thereof to bee Devided amongst my fowre young
=er Sisters. Provided alwayes that my loving
wife Hannah Shall enioy the use and profit
of my Said lands and howseing untill my Sone
come to the age of one and twentie yeares, And
thence forward to enioy the third parte thereof
Dureing her life: ffurther I Doe give unto
my loveing wife Hannah the one Moitie of
my estate psonall and the other Moity or -
halfe thereof, I Doe give unto my two children
abovesaid to bee Devided between them as -
followeth Namely two thirds thereof unto -
my Daughter Elizabeth, And the other third
thereof unto my Sone John. ffurther I doe
hereby Constitute my Loving wife Hannah
my Executrix of this my Last will & testam:t
ffurther I Doe hereby Ordaine constitute and
appoynt My Loving friends Daniell Saers, &
my brother in law Thomas Topping to bee -

over

Overseers of this my last will and testament, &
guardians of my Children, to Disspose of my children
abovesaid and theire estate dureing theire -
minority, And to See this my last will Duely ex=
=ecuted according to the premises: Given under my
hand and Seale this ninth Day of May in ye year
of our Lord one thousand Six hundred & seaventy

In ye prsence of us John White : -
Thomas Cooper
Thomas Cooper Junr:

endorsed on the back side /

Thomas Cooper Senr: and Tho: Cooper Junr:
whoe are the above witnesses Doe now this
30th of May 1670 witnes upon oath that
this within written &c is the true will and
testam:t of the Sd John White Deceased -
before us Henry Peirson
John Jessupp
Richard Howell
Isack Halsey:

A true Coppy /

Thomas Topping of Southampton deposed
before the Cort of Sessions held at Southhold
June the 2st 1670 Saith that ye w:th in written
is and was the very will of John White De=
=ceased, & that hee this Depon:t wrote ye
Sd will for him, and see him Signe & Seale
the Same as is alsoe testified by ye other
above Sd witnesses.
The Co:rt are fully Satisfyed with, and doe
accept of the above Sd proof of the with in
and before written testament &c:
Henry Peirson Cleark
of ye Sd Co:rt of Sessions:

A true Coppy p me Henry Peirson - - -
The Cort Doth finde Hannah White the late wife
of the Sd Testator, and Doe adjudg [her] and admit
her to bee Sole Executrix of her Sd Deceased hus=
=Band his Sd Will & testament; Allsoe Daniell
Sayre & Tho: Topping mentioned to bee Super=
=visors: the Co:rt well approve of them both for
that end & purpose. //:

At ye Cort of Sessions held June ye 2: 1670
The Deposition of John Laughton.

This Depont testifyeth that about eight or nine - yeares agoe, Sometime in the month of May - hee being Schoole Mr: at the Town of Southamp= =ton, And John White lying on his Sick or - rather Death bed, Did Send for him to make his will, which accordingly hee Did: And after the reading of the Sd: will, hee this Depon:t would have written over the will againe, by reason of Something that hee then Saw in it vizt: that it was short in the respect of settle= =ment of the Land upon the heyres Males of - both his Sonnes: And hee then being in pfect Strength of Memory Soe far as this Depon:t could pceive, Said it was noe matter, and bid him bring it to him, for hee feared hee should not have his Sight to Signe & Seale it, for his Eye Sight failed him much: Soe hee this Depon:t called, or Desired to be called in to witnes the Said Will Mr: Thomas Topping Junr: and hee asked him or Desired to witnes it. And hee this Depon:t Said to goodman White you had better let mee write it out faire again and I will enlarge to them and to theire - heyres, for interlineing in a will is not usuall. and hee said he would it were in, or words tending to that purpose, But hee found - his Sight to faile, Soe that it would bee too late to write it over againe: But that was the will of the testator that it should bee to them and to theire heyres: I doe here= unto Attest as witnes my hand the Day and yeare and place first above written

John Laughton

This Deposition was taken before the Co:rt of Sessions held at Southhold the 2 Day of June 1670 and ordered by the Cort to bee recorded.

A true Coppy p me Henry Peirson
Cleark of ye Sessions:

Southampton May 24: 1670

Wee the Subscribed being hereunto required Doe apprize of ye goods & chattells of John White Deceased as followeth.

			£	s	d
Imprs	2 oxen of 5 yeare old		13	10	–
	3 Cowes 13 £ 10s 2 heifers of 3 year old 6 £ 10s		20	–	–
	2 Steeres of 3 yeare old		8	–	–
	4 of 2 yeare old		9	10	–
	4 yearlings & one very poore one		6	10	–
	a mare that is lame		4	15	–
	1/3 of 3 young horse kinde as ptner	)			
	with Jonas Holdsworth	)	4	–	–
	2 Sowes and 3 Shoats		2	12	–
	Due to him by Bill on Substantiall Debts		9	–	–
	3 barells of oyle Sent to ye Bay		7	10	–
&	12£ of whale bone 8s 1 hide 11s		–	19	–
	one fether bed. one boulster. 3 pillows	)			
	2 pillow beares. one rugg, & blanket	)	13	6	–
	1 pr: of Sheets 1 pc: of broad cloth	)			
	2 Iron potts a little Iron kettle	)			
	& a brass Skellet w:th pothooks	)	1	10	–
	3 axes, a Spade & other tooles		3	–	–
	2 pewter Dishes. 1 Basin. 2 poring:rs	)			
	1 quart pott. & a Small bottle wth Spoones	)	10	12	–
	1 fine Saw. Smoothing Iron; frying pan	)			
	and pot hangers & a lamp	)	–	14	–
	one gun and Sword		1	17	–
	a chest & bowles & chaires & Lumber		1	–	–
	1 bagg of fethers and a Syeth		–	15	–
	weareing apparell		3	–	–
	the howse & a 50 £ Lotm:t		55	–	–
	an Iron kettle & 1 brass kettle		2	15	–
			£170	05	00

John Howell
Henry Peirson
Edward Howell
John Jennings:

This Inventory was prsented unto, and accepted By the Cort of Sessions held at Southhold June the first 1670

A true Coppy
p me Henry Peirson. /

At the Co:rt of Sessions held &c: in South=
=hold June the 7th 1671: By Mr: John
Mulford and Mr: Jonas Wood Justices
of the peace:
Was presented the Will and Testament
of Jonas Bower Deceased wch ye Co:rt
Order to bee Recorded. And is as follows:

November 13th: 1670:

The last will and Testament of Jonas Bower
of Southampton is as followeth./

Imprimus: I give my Soule to God that gave it, and
my body to bee decently buried./

1 I give unto my Sonne Joseph Seaventeen
Accres More or less lying at the flying
poynt, and three accres more in the last
Devission, to take it at the east end next
Robert Wooley: further I give the Said
Joseph halfe my meaddow at the Beach;
and halfe my Meadow at Quaquanantuck
with a fifty pound Comonidg, and a fifty
in the ox=pasture. And all the abovesd: land
and Meadow to be valued at a reasonable rate
by indifferent men, And the rest of his portion to
bee made up in Cattle, if any bee wanting. /

2ly: ffor my Sone James, My will is that hee Shall have
his portion paid in Cattle according to ye prises
mentioned in the Bond. /

3ly:/ And for Jonathan, I leave it to my wifes liberty
to pay him his portion as Shee Shall See meete: /

4ly:- My Will is That My wife Shall have my howseing
and land untill my Sone Jonah bee at age, and ye
rest of ye Stock of cattle, And if my Sone Jonah -
should Die before hee bee at age, or after, without
ishue, then the howseing and land to bee my Sone Isaccs
My wife the thirds to enjoy as long as shee liveth:
and then to returne to Jonah, or Isaac as before men
=tioned: But if Jonah liveth then Isaacc Shall have
that thirty one accres lying by Thomas Halseyes:
But if my Sone Isaack Should Die without ishue, the
Said land to return to my Sone Jonah: And if please
god my Daughters live whilest they come at age, then
my

my wife to alow them Somthing out of the stock as Shee Shall finde her Self able: ffurther my will is that my wife Shall have liberty to dwell in the howse as long as Shee liveth. / And Lastly I Doe make my wife Soale Executrix of this my Will: And alsoe that my Cousen John Howell, Richard Post and John Jessup Senr: to bee over seers of this my Will, to See it performed: To the verity of what is above written I hereunto sett my hand Jonas Bower. /

In ye presence of
John Howell.

marke
John + Jesup /
his

Capt: John Howell and John Jessup whoe are ye above= =Said witnesses Doe now this 6th of June 1671. further witnes upon oath that this within and above written is and was the true will and Testam:t of the Said - Jonas Bowre Deceased:

Deposed Before us:
John Cooper
Henry Peirson
Edward Howell. /

A true Coppy of ye Originall./

The Co:rt Doth finde Hannah Bower the late wife of - the Sd: Testator and Doe adjudg and admit her to bee Sole and lawfull Executrix of her Sd Deceased husband his afforesaid will and Testament: And the Co:rt well approve of the forementioned Capt: John - Howell, Richard Post and John Jessup Sen:r to bee overseers: &c:

Southampton May 29: 1671.
Wee the Subscribed beeing hereunto required by vertue of Justice Mulford his warant Doe Apprize of the goods & Chattells of Jonas Bower Deceassed, accord =ing to our best Skill & Judgm:t As followeth: /

		£	s	d
Imprs–	6 Cowes, one w:th another 4 £: ps:	24	–	–
	3 of 3 yeare old: and one yeare 3 £: 5s	13	–	–
	4 of 2 yeare old at 45s: ps:	9	–	–
	5 of one yeare old att 25s: ps:	6	5	–
	6 oxen abroad valued att 6 £ : ps	36	–	–
	more by information abroad one Steere of 5 yeares: three of fowre)	20	–	–
It:	1 horse, and one mare of 3 yeare	12	–	–
It:				

	£	s	d
It: 7 Sheep 3 £	3	–	–
It: 4 Small Swine	2	–	–
howseing and 200 £ lotmt	160	–	–
weareing Apparell	3	–	–
5 yrds of Searge at 6 s p yrd:	1	10	–
2 fether beds & what belongs to them) as tick and bowlster)	10	–	–
9 payre of Sheets	9	–	–
2 yrds of holland at 4s p yrd	–	8	–
4 yrds of course Linen at 3 s p yrd	–	12	–
5 yrds of home=Spun at 3s p yrd	–	15	–
9 pewter platters, basin, pot & poringers Spoones &c:	2	8	–
8 brass kettles, and one Skellet	6	10	–
4 Iron potts, & 3 Small kettles & a frying pan	5	–	–
4 Chests, a trunk, 3 boxes	2	10	–
2 guns, and two Swords	3	–	–
one warming pan	–	17	–
an ax, Drawing knife, and other tooles	1	–	–
milke vessells and lombar	2	–	–
an olde loome and geeres	1	10	–
cart, plough, Irons to them yoaks & 2 Chaines	2	10	–
grindestone and bookes	1	5	–
Sume is –	339	:00	:00

Witnes our hands the Day and yeare above written

John Cooper.
Henry Peirson.
Edward Howell
Thomas Topping.

A true Coppy. /

To the aforesaid Co:rt of Sessions held June 7 1671
was presented the Will & Testament of Thomas
Wickes: which ye Co:rt ordered to bee recorded
and is as followeth./

The Last Will and Testamt of Thomas Wickes
of Huntington: Being in pfect memory and -
understanding Doth Despose of his estate as
followeth: ffirst my will is that my wife Shall
have a third parte of my accomodations I
now live one, During the time of her Life, and
at her Decease to leave it to my Sone John;
and alsoe the bed with what belongeth to it
that I now ly on, and a Cow, which Shee Shall
chuse. And in case Shee Dislikes liveing w:th John
then John Shall provide her a howse convenient
for her to live alone in: Secondly I doe give
to my Sone Thomas the lot that was John Lume
with all the accomodation thereto belonging,
together with the alotment of Meadow that I
bought of Noah Rogers, and alsoe two Cowes,
a Iron pot, a frying pan; and a bed & fur=
=niture to it as my wife Shall See fit, and also
Nailes to fit up his howse. And to my Sone John
I Doe give at present the other two thirds of my
accomodations I Now live on; And to my
Daughter Rebecka I doe give forty shillins, and
to her three children, twenty Shillins each of
them. And to my Daughter Martha I doe
give fouer poundes and twenty Shillins to her
child. And what ever my estate amounts to
more, my will is that it Shall bee devided equal
betweene my wife and fouer of my Children,
w:ch is John, Elizabeth, Mary, Sarah: and yt things
may bee carried comfortably an end I have made choice
of Isack Platt and Thomas Powell to bee overseers: In
witnes hereof I have Set to my hand and fixed my Seal
this 13th of June 1670.

his marke
Thomas T Wickes

Test: Samuell Wood
Caleb Wood

These two above Specifyed witnesses have given theire oath to
the truth thereof before mee Jonas Wood. /

A true Coppy /

An Inventory of the estate of Thomas Wicks Deceased, Taken by Samuell Titus and Joseph Whitman, being chosen by Samuell Wood Constable of Huntington

		£	s	d
Imprs:	2 accomodations	60	-	-
	In Cattell	84	2	-
	in horse=flesh	21	-	-
	in Sheepe	18	-	-
	in Swine	30	16	-
	in Cart and plough tackleing	4	9	-
	in puter brasse and Iron	6	18	-
	in edg tooles	2	-	6
	in bedding	24	5	-
	in graine	11	10	-
	in his weareing Cloaths	6	3	-
	in wheeles cards, chests, tables sives and other lumber	5	7	-
	in wool & flax yarne and bookes	9	18	-
	in a gun and Sword and other Small things	1	17	-
	£	286	=05	=06

This Inventory was taken by us
Samuell Titus
Joseph Whitman. /

The widow of the Deceased together with her Sonne John Desires the Co:rts approbation to administer upon the Estate, they Doeing what the Law provides in that case: as witnes our hands:

marke
the T of
Rebeka Wicks /
John Wickes /

A true Coppy /

Widdow Wicks and her Sone John Wicks (upon theire abovesaid request and engagemt) are app= =ointed and ordered Joyntly to administer on ye Estate of ye fore=mentioned Tho: Wicks Deceased And the Cort Doe impower them to execute and Doe in all things according to the intent, & con= =tents of his Sd Will and Testament. And ye Co:rt Doth well approve of ye Sd Isack Platt and Thomas Powell to bee overseers:/

At ye Co:rt of Sessions held in Southampton
March the first 1670.

Was prsented the proof of ye Will & Testament
of Mathew Lum Deceased, as followeth./

Joseph Rainer upon oath before ye Co:rt saith
That Some certaine Dayes before Mathew Lum
Dyed, which was in May last, hee this Depon:t
was wth him, and pceived (to this Depon:ts
best apprehension) that hee was in good un
=derstanding. And then hee this Depon:t heard
the Sd Mathew Say, that if it pleased God
to take him away by Death, hee Did be=
=queath what hee had in Southampton to his
brother Samuell Lum: onely all Just Debts
to bee paid out of it.
Jonathan Rainer upon oath before the Co:rt
attests ye Same.
Whereupon the Co:rt doth order that ac=
=cording to the Intent of ye Sd Will hee the
Sd Samuell Lum shall take into his posses=
=sion all the lands, goods; & Chattells, which
hee the Sd Mathew Lum Dyed Seized of.

An Inventory of ye Estate of Mathew Lum De=
=ceased as followeth./

	£	s	d
1 horse of 3 yeares old	6	-	-
1 Cow: & a heifer of 2 year old	8	-	-
his Smiths tooles as bellowes &c.	6	10	-
Soe much English goods as came to:	7	10	-
1 gun & 1 narrow ax	1	-	-
his wearing apparell	2	5	-
1 Chest and 3s in mony	-	13	-
the howse & land & fenceing that was in ye possession of Mathew Lum whiles he lived wee value at	39	10	-
	71	=08	=00

apprized by us appoynted
Edward Howell
Thomas Topping

This Inventory was presented to the Co:rt of Sessions
held March 2: 1670 and by the Co:rt allowed
and approved

A true Coppy /

In the Name of God Amen: I Thomas Sayre off –
Southampton on Long Island in Comt: Nova Yorke
Being in pfect Strength of Memory (blessed bee the
Lord for it) but weake of body, And not knowing ye
Day of my appoynted change; Doe make this my last
Will and Testament, in manner following. – –
Imprs:- I Give and freely bequeath my Soule unto God
that gave it, And my Body unto Earth from whence
it was first taken: 2dly: I Give unto my Sone ffran=
=cis Sayre, two Accres of land lying next unto his
owne in Capt: Neck, in ye great plaines. And two
accres more of land lying in the Eight accres lotts in
the Sd: great plaines: A pewter flaggon, a pewter
Bole, and great pewter platter. / – – – –
3d:ly: I Give unto my Sone Daniell Sayre, two accres of
land lying next unto the abovesaid two accres in
in the Eight accres lotts & three accres more of land
lying in the tenn accres lotts, and one great pewter
4th:ly: platter.//. 4th:ly: I give unto my Sone Joseph
Sayre, fourty pounds Sterling, to bee paid to him
by My Executor, tenn pounds p An: to begin w:th=
=in five yeares next after my Decease, to bee paid
in good Mchtable Shoes, or other pay that will -
procure hides, towards his Setting upp of Tanning. /
5th:ly: I give unto my Daughter Damaris Atwater forty Shill:
6th:ly I give unto my Daughter Mary Price forty Shillings:
7th:ly I Give unto my Daughter Hannah Sayre – –
twenty pounds to bee paid at her Day of Marriage
or when Shee Shall be Eighteene yeares of age;
which Shall first happen. And that my Ex=
=ecutor Doe keepe her Cow and calfe & theire
encrease for her, untill Shee bee either mar=
=ried, or in Some other capeable way to main=
=taine them: – – – – – – – – –
8th:ly: I give my howsehold goods to bee equally De=
=vided betweene my Sone Jobe, & Joseph, and
Hannah: And that when they bee Devided – –
Hannah have her first choice of the parts./

Lastly:

Lastly- I By this my last will & Testament have made my Sone Jobe Sayre My Sole Executor, to receive all my wordly Estate, both of howseing, lands, goods & cattle & Debts Due to mee from any pson or psons: and to pay all Debts Due from mee, And All Legacies above Specifyed: In witnes where =of I have hereunto Sett my hand and Seale this 16th Day of Sept:ber 1669

Signed Sealed and Delivered in ye prsence of
Obadiah Rogers
John Laughton. /

Thomas Sayre:

A true Coppy of ye Originall w:ch was presented unto the Co:rt of Sessions held in Southampton March the first &c 1670: and proved by the Testimony of ye Sd Obadiah Rogers & John Laughton: And ye Cort finde, order & im =power the Sd Job Sayre (mentioned in ye Will to bee Sole & lawfull Executor: whoe is to doe in all things according to the tenure and con =tents of the Sd Will & Testament.

An Inventory of the Estate of Thomas Sayre Deceased, Apprized by us whoe are hereunto Subscribed, and were hereunto appoynted: As followeth: this 16th Day of June 1670

	£	s	d
one horse 10 £	10	-	-
4 oxen	26	-	-
4 Cowes and a calfe	16	-	-
2 Steeres of 3 years, in ye woods	7	10	-
2 heifers w:th one calf: & 1 Stear of 3 ye:r old:	7	10	-
3, yearlings	4	10	-
2 hoggs, 7 shoats	5	10	-
1 fether bed, bowlster, bedsteed:)			
3 pillowes: curtaines: 3 blankets)			
& a remnant of trucking cloth)	9	-	-
1 fether bed, bowlster, an old blanket)			
curtaines, and a Sheete)	5	10	-
5 Sheets at	2	7	-
4 old pillow beares	-	16	-
6 Napkins 1 old table cloth 4 towells	-	15	-

Six

		£	s	d
Six pewter platters		1	-	-
3 basons, a flaggon a quarte pot: a pinte pot	)			
a bowl w:th Some other Small pewter 2 tin lamps	)	1	15	-
3:old brass kettles, a Small Iron pot	)			
2:old brass skellets	)	2	15	-
1 bedsted, rugg, Sheets, flock bed & bowlster		4	10	-
3 bushells of Salt		-	12	-
a peece of old flock bed and winowing Sheet		-	5	-
3 old blankets, 2 old pillows and Sheete		1	5	-
1 firkin of Sugar		1	15	-
in hides; by estimation		34	-	-
Spit, pot hangers 2 old Syeths, Grid Iron				
tongs and a paire of bellowes		1	-	-
Axes & other tooles, & tanners knives		-	18	-
cart, plough, yoaks & chaines		4	-	-
Spade & hoe		-	3	-
wearing clothes of all Sorts		2	10	-
the howseing and land and tann fats		150	-	-
It the lumbar		2	-	-
3 Chests, and milk vessells		1	15	-
1 brass pot at 16s bookes & a pr of Scales 20s		1	16	-
		307	-07	-00

John Howell
Henry Peirson
Thomas Cooper
John Jennings

A true Coppy of the Originall p me

Henry Peirson &c:

And ordered by ye Co:rt to bee Recorded. /

At ye Cort of Sessions held at Southampton the 6th 7th of March 1671 By Capt John Manning ^ high Shereif Mr: John Mulford, Capt: John Howell, & Capt: John Youngs Justice

Was prsented (by Mr: Joseph Bayly of Huntington), the Will and Testament of James Naibor, wch the Co:rt order to bee recorded, and is as followeth:

In the Name of God Amen: I James Naibor Of Huntington - upon Long Island in Yorksheir Cooper Being Sick In Body But of pfect me =mory have made this my last Will and testament in manner & forme following: ffirst I bequeath my Soule to God my maker and redeemer: My body to the Earth from whence I came /

Imprimis: I give and bequeath unto Martha my youngest dafter my great trunk and best Cheast with all my Lining and wool =ing, sheits, pillibars, and all wareing apparell of her mothers and mine, except one paire of my best sheits & a paire of pillibars which I give and bequeath unto - Marcie my grandchilde, and alsoe I give to my grand =childe ten poundes to bee raised out of my howse at Boston, which howse I give equally betweene my ffive Dafters when this ten poundes is raised, Mary Sarah: Elizabeth Rachell and Martha equally to bee devided amongst them: If my other goods will pay my debts besides what I have given unto my dafter Martha, if not, then what is wanting to bee raised out of my howse: and what is left, to bee equally de= =vided as afforesaid; And the ten pounds that I give to my grandchilde Marcie with the Lining to remain in the hand of my Daughter Martha untill Marcie accomplis the adge of twenty one yeares or bee maried And if either of my daughters chance to Dy whilest the howse is undevided, then that parte to remaine equally amongst the rest: All the rest of my goods and Chattels; after my debts bee paid, and all other lawfull charges defraid I give and bequeath unto my Daughter Martha, whome I make My Sole - Executrix: Alsoe I doe desire and appoynt Mr: William Barthelmew, and goodman Sundall booth of Boston to bee my executors in trust to See this my Will & Testament ful= =filled: And alsoe I Desire Thomas Scudder and Joseph Bayly

Bayly, both of Huntington to bee helpfull to my Dafter
Martha for the getting in of my Debts in Huntington and
Oyster Bay, and alsoe to help Ship those goods for Boston
Witnes my hand this 27th: of January In the yeare
of our Lord 1671 James Nabor

Signed and published
In the presents of
marke of
the M
Martha Owen
the marke of Peter P ffloyd
Joseph Bayly:

A true Coppy p me Henry Peirson /

Joseph Bayly of Huntington upon oath affirmeth
That ye above & before written is the true Will &
Testam:t of the Sd James Nabor, And that hee
the Depont Did write ye Sd Will for him. /

The Co:rt being well Satisfyed wth ye proof of ye affore=
=Said will of James Nabor Deceased, And the affore Said
Joseph Bayley Entring obligation to this Cort for the
pformance of what the law requires according to ye
Tenure of ye Sd Will and to Save the Cort harmeless
This Co:rt Doth order and impower the Sd Martha -
Nabor mentioned in the Sd will to bee ye lawfull ex=
=ecutrix of the Sd Will & Testament of ye Deceased
according to the minde of ye Testator therein ex=
=pressed. /

A Just and true Inventory of the goods & Chattells of James
Naibor. Apprized the 22th: of ffebruary: By Thomas - -
Shidmore and John Cory, and taken by Joseph Bayly
Re:r

		£	s	d
Imprs:-	an old fether bead a flock beed and two boulsters, a little pillow & two ruggs	5	10	-
It	4 blanketts, a kefferlid & hammoke	3	-	-
It	2, old beed Sacks fowre old pillowes	1	-	-
It	3 old boulsters 2 hammokes, a little pillow & 2 old Cushings	2	19	-
It	2 yeards of trucking cloth	-	18	-
It	an old Rugg, and Blanket	1	5	-
It	6 payre of Sheites & a half Sheite	8	18	-
It	6 payre of pillibors & a boulster case	2	5	-
It	4 table cloaths & 2 dozen of Napkins	4	12	-
It	an old hammoke & two towells	1	2	-
It	one Dram Cup	-	8	-

It:

			£	s	d
It	thrid and ffilliting		–	8	–
It	a wasket & a payre of Drawrs		1	11	–
It	a great trunke		2	10	–
It	4 neck hand kerchers 12 dressings	)			
	and two apperens	)	4	6	–
It	20 Cooifes. 7 pocket handkerchers		1	12	–
It	2 stock neck cloths. 20 forehead clothes	)			
	and 6 Small peeces of lining	)	1	12	–
It	a Tinn Candlestick		–	2	–
It	11 forad cloaths & 2 pr of gloofs		1	7	–
It	a warming pan		–	15	–
It	2 Iron potts & pothookes		2	–	–
It	2 tramells. 2 And Irons. a Small pot		1	6	–
It	a pr of tongs. a skillet 3 candle sticks		–	18	–
It	a Spitt. frying pan: pestell & Morter:		–	11	–
It	a quart pot. 3 pinte potts. 3 poring:rs		–	14	–
It	a box: a belles. Bedsack & earthen pott		–	18	–
It	4 Small earthen potts. & a bottle		–	4	–
It	a Smooting Iron & a fire Iron		–	10	–
It	a Sword. belt. Musket & bandalears:		2	2	–
It	4 bookes & a wooden platter		–	18	–
It	6 barrells of Salt		5	4	–
It	a grindston and Spindle		1	–	–
It	2 gounds & a petticoat		8	–	–
It	a cloak. hatt. & pr of gloufs		5	5	–
It	2 Setts of Curtens and Vallons		3	2	–
It	a Carpit black Lace & Small Scales		1	8	6
It	2 old casks		–	10	–
It	for a case of knives		–	16	–
It	for 4 pd of yarne & hat brush		–	14	10
It	2 payre of woosted gloves		–	8	–
It	for thrid and Buttons		–	9	–
It	for 14 bands and Neckcloths		1	16	–
It	a great Cheast		1	10	–
It	5 hatts. 3 payre of Shows		2	9	–
It	for 2 Curtens. a valen & a few buttons		–	12	–
It	for a coat and pr of breeches		2	10	–
It	a pr of bodice. an old coat & wastcoat:		–	18	–
It	an old Sarge Sute		1	5	–
It					

		£	s	d
It	a Cheast	1	-	-
It	pr of And Irons tongs. a fire Shovell	1	3	-
It	a cros cut Saw and 2 fiels	-	18	-
It	pr hand Screws	-	3	-
It	2 cow hides & 9 deare skins	4	2	-
It	a N[-] 7 pd of Sheepe Wooll	-	11	6
It	a percell of brood hoopes	-	10	-
It	17 bushells of wheat & 9 bush: of peas	6	1	-
It	3 bushells of Indian corne	-	9	-
It	2 fleeches of bacon 92 pd: wt	2	6	-
It	92 £ of tallow & 8 pd: of candles	2	11	-
It	a pewter platter. a bason. 2 chamber pots	[-]	-	-
It	a payre of Stillars	-	15	-
It	a Set of Curten rods	-	4	-
It	5 barels of beif. a barell of porke	16	-	-
It	a cotten blanket & 2 wheeles	1	4	-
It	3 shirts & a paire of drawrs	1	5	-
It	4 pillow bars & a paire of Sheeits	1	8	-
It	a Sheet. 2 pillow bars & 8 neck cloos	1	12	-
It	2 old towells, an old Napkin	-	2	-
It	50 weight of hoogs fat & an Iron kettle	1	15	-
It	an old chest with trifleing things	1	-	-
It	an old flask & 2 keelars	-	13	-
It	a womans old Clooke	-	5	-
It	a bushell of Salt & 7 barells	1	1	6
It	a pcell of old tooles & old Iron	1	12	-
It	a Brikoven: 2 Coopers cross hoopes tunel	[-]	-	-
It	2 Joynters. a Sett of Coopers tooles	2	9	-
It	pt of an other Set. 2 other Iron tooles	2	3	6
It	a trundle bed sted & cord. & ax	-	9	-
It	old Drwars and a Samp pestle	-	3	-
It	a paire of pattens	-	4	-
It	2 guns. 2 old Swords & Bandeleers	2	12	-
It	2 old Spades & a half bushell	-	3	6
It	10 old barrells and a funnel	1	6	-
It	2 bowles and an Iron Shoot	-	4	-
It	Debts by Book	49	10	-
	in all -	106	:11	:00

Thomas Skidmore
John Cory: /

A true Coppy p me Henry Peirson
but is 206£-11s- sumd //

At ye Co:rt of Sessions held at Southampton
ye foresaid 6:7: of March 1671.

Thomas Mapes Constable of Southold presented to the Co:rt the Inventory hee and two of the Over= =Seers tooke at theire Towne of the Estate off - - Richard Curtis, whoe of late there Dyed In= =testate. And Caleb Curtis, the Eldest Sone of the Sd Richard, Alsoe presenting himself to the Co:rt and requesting that hee might bee im= =powered to Administer of the Sd Estate, The Co:rt referr the Disposition of the matter at - prsent unto Capt: John Youngs, And Doth Order that all the Children of the Sd Deceased pty or Some one in theire behalf, appeare at ye Co:rt of Sessions to be held at Southold next June then to call on the Sd busines and give an ac= =compt of ye proceed therein That Soe ye Co:rt then may make Disposeall of ye estate according to law in yt behalf. And Record may bee made thereof

An accompt of ye Estate of Richard Curtis Lately De= =ceased: of cattell horses & Swine febr:20th:1671/72

1s horse kinde	13	-	-
2- in neat Cattell	34	16	-
3- in Small Swine	3	15	-
4- ye bed & bedsted & yt belongs to it	7	15	-
5- a trundell bed & that belongs to it	5	-	-
6- an other bed and that belongs to it	3	-	-
7- an other bed and the furniture	-	10	-
8- 4 Chests and 2 k[?]ettles	2	-	-
9- in brass & puter	7	10	-
10 Iron ware	1	10	-
11 other Lumbar	2	17	-
12 Armes and Amunition	4	-	-
13 for cloathes	7	4	-
14 for plough Irons: & other implemts about husbandry	3	15	-
15 for a cannoo, a cart rope & pitchforke	1	2	-
£:	97	:14	:00

Thomas Mapes
Barnabas Horton
John Conklin

A true Coppy
p me Henry Peirson:

At ye foresaid Co:rt of Sessions held March: 6:7:71.

The will & Testam:t of Thomas Terry of Southhold
Deceased being presented to the Co:rt the Sd will
being witnessed by Divers knowne and substantiell
men yet not upon oath; The Cort being moved there
=unto, Doe order that in regard the Testator omitted
that necessary Circumstance in his will as to appoynt
an Executor, And his sone Daniell Terry is willing
to bee Executor thereof, And forasmuch alsoe as the
Co:rt is informed that pt of the Estate may Suffer
Detriment if not Disposed of in Short time, The Sd
Daniell Terry Shall bee, to all intents and purposes
the lawfull Executor of the Sd Testament & Estate
provided that hee forthwith legally prove the Sd will
before Justice Youngs at Southold by the oathes of at
least two of the Sd: witnesses and ye Inventory of
ye Estate alsoe bee confirmed according to law, and alsoe
put in Security to pforme what the law requires con=
=cerning the Sd will, and Send both ye will & ye Invento=
ry wth ye obligation of Security into the hands of ye
Cleark of ye Sessions to bee recorded and kept: - -

At ye Sd Co:rt held in Southampton &c:
Whereas the Trying of oyle Soe neare the Street
and howses is Soe extreme noysome to all passers=
=by, especially to those whoe are not accustomed
to the sent thereof, and is conceived hurtfull to
the health of people And in respect it is very
Dangerous (if the oyle should fire) for fire=
=ing howses or hay=stacks: This Cort Doth -
therefore Order, That noe pson whatsoever -
After this present yeare Shall try any oyle in
this Towne nearer than 25 poles from ye main
Street of the Towne upon penalty of paying five
poundes fine every pson that shall at any -
time thansgress therein.

Moreover the Co:rt Doth Determine &
appoynt that this order is to bee pub=
=lished and in force in Easthampton alsoe:

At a Co:rt of Sessions held March:6: 1671/72

Mr: Richard Smith of Neeceaquake enters Com=
=plaint against Isack Willman & Henry Ludlam of
Southampton for theire holding of land belonging to
the Complainant, more than what he sould them:
It Being ye Complainant prosecuted ye Sd complaint
onely against the Sd Henry Ludlam, and makes
nothing appeare to ye Co:rt to prove his Complaint
The Co:rt Doth award or Sentence the Complain
=ant to pay Costs of ye Complaint./

John Cooper, as Attorney for Mr: James Mills of Vir
ginia: Enters an action of Debt against Hackaliah
Bridges on w:ch accompt Some goods of his were attached
The Jurymen were: Joshua Barnes. Joseph Rainer. Richard
Howell. Tho: Topping. Tho: Goldsmith. Robert -
Dayton. and Ensigne Bayly of Huntington. - -
The plf: produced his lre of Attorney from Mr: Mills:
Alsoe a Bill of Debt from ye Sd Hackaliah to ye
Sd: Mr: Mills / Alsoe ye plf: produced Severall
writeings knowne to bee Signed by ye Sd Hackaliah
which were compared wth ye Sd bill to confirme
to ye Cort the reality thereof.
The Jury finde for ye plf: wth Costs of Suite. /
The Co:rt give Judgment according to ye Juries verdict
The Co:rt grant execution to ye plf: to bee Served
upon ye Sd goods Attached.

Mr: Thomas Backer of Easthampton plf:
Against Tho: Skidmore of Huntington defefendt
In an action of the case concerning Debt & Damage
or not accompting.

It appeareing to the Co:rt that by reason of Sickness
the Defend:t is necessarily hindred from makeing his
appearance: The Co:rt referr the tryall of this - -
Action to ye Co:rt of Sessions to be held at Southhold
next June

The Constable & Overseers of Easthampton enter
Complaint against Reneck Garison and his
wife for being guilty of fornication before

they

they were marryed: It being sufficiently proved
The Co:rt give Sentence that they both shall have cor
=porall punishm:t publickly. viz w:th five stripes
a peece: But John Tenison And Cornelius Vonke
Engageing to ye Justices to pay 40s- to ye Cuntry -
for ye Sd Reneck & his wife, as a fine, ye Sd Sen=
=tence is by the Justices reversed

The Constables of Easthampton enters Complaint a=
=gainst Mr: Thomas Backer for takeing goods into his
possession and Detaining them, Not withstanding the
Sd goods lay under Arrest or attachmt:
The Co:rt Doth finde yt Mr: Tho: Backer tooke a
barell of Oyle illegally into his possession: And doe
award or Sentence him to returne the Same unto ye
Constable of Easthampton from whose custody it was
Soe taken. And alsoe to pay as fine -10s- to ye poore
of the Parish: And Cort Charges. /

A Complaint Entered against Henry Rogers of -
Seatauk for his Selling pt, and likelyhood of imbe=
=zelling the rest of the lands Sometime belonging
unto his predeceassour Namely Georg Wood, And
Settled by a Cort of Sessions held at Southhold in June
1668. for his surviveing children theire mainten=
=ance & bringing up: Henry Rogers confessing
hee hath Sold pt of ye Sd lands, and it appearing
alsoe that they were settled or Dissposed to ye childrens
use as afforesaid, The Co:rt Doth Order That noe
pson whatsoever shall henceforth buy any pt
or pcell of the Sd lands upon penalty of loseing
what they shall pay for it: And ye Sd lands -
Shall always remaine for the use of ye children
as aforesaid they were appoynted: and this Co:rt
Doth further Determine that this order bee alsoe
recorded & published at Seatauk that Soe here=
after none may plead Ignorance hereof:/

Capt. John Youngs enters Complaint against Thomas
Diment for his missdemeanour towards him.
This Co:rt Doth Order that Tho: Diment shall finde
prsent Sufficient Security for his good behavior:
till ye Next Co:rt of Sessions: and pay the cost
of this Complaint:

M:rch 7: 1671/2

A Complaint entered against Peeter Whitteere for
his abusive cariage towards Justice Mulford.
The Co:rt doth Order or Sentence, that ye Said
Peeter Shall make acknowledgm:t of his evill and
abusive carriage, Next Lords Day come Seaven=
=night at ye publique Meeting in Easthampton
to the Satisfaction of Mr: John Mulford. - -
And hee is to pay the costs of the Complaint
as alsoe his former fine imposed. /

Mr: Tho: Backer of Easthampton Enters Complaint
against Tho: Osburne for Mollesting him in ye
quiet possession of his goods, to his great damage.
The Co:rt referre the heareing & Determineing
this Complaint &c to ye Next Co:rt of Sessions
But if the pties agree before; then they are
to enter theire agreemt & pay ye charges.
Mr. Backer wth=Drawes ye Sd Complaint /

At ye Court of Sessions held at Southhold June 5th:1672
By Capt: John Manning High Shereif & Capt Jo: Youngs:

Concerning the Estate of Richard Curtis Deceased an Inven=
=tory whereof was presented to the Last Co:rt of Sessions, &
is recorded in page 28. And Capt: John Youngs in=
=forming that Caleb Curtis hath left in his hand
obligation to Competent value for payment of the
rest of the Children theire portions or propor=
=tions of the Sd Estate according to an agreement
made amongst themselves before Capt Youngs or
to his knowledg: This Co:rt Doth Admitt him ye
Sd Caleb to be Administrator of ye Sd Estate -
And order that hee Shall have Letter of Ad=
=ministration: /

Southold this 26th: of November 1671.

I Thomas Tery Senr: of Southold in the County of Yorke being
very Sick & weak, yet in perfect memory: Doe make this my -
last Will and Testament as followeth: I Doe give unto my be=
=loved wife fiveteene bushells of corne yearely to bee paid unto
her: ten bushell to bee paid by my sone Daniell Tery, and five
bushells to bee paid by my Sone Thomas Tery, and this to
bee done yearely by them dureing my wifes life; or widowhood:
And alsoe I give unto my wife my bed, and all that belongs
to the Same, with all the howsehold goods within Dores, these
Doe I give to my wife as her owne proper goods for ever. alsoe
I Doe give unto my wife foure bushells of apples dureing her life
or widowhood yearly: And if my Sone Daniell doe marry
and like not to live together, then my Sone Daniell Shall build
my wife a convenient howse for her comfortable being, dureing
her life or widowhood. Alsoe I give unto my wife the Milke
of one Cow as long as Shee lives or remaines a widow. I
give unto my Daughter Elizabet Tery, one Cow to bee
paid to her at the Day of Mariage, or when Shee comes
to age. And alsoe I give to my Daughter Ruth Terry
one Cow at the Day of Mariage or when Shee comes of age
I give to my Daughter Mary Reves one Cow or a Steere.
Alsoe I give to my sone Daniell my howse with all ye
accomodations belonging thereunto within the owld -
boundes, & I give alsoe to my sone Daniell half
my land at Accabauk: I give unto my sone - -
Thomas

Thomas Tery all my land at Curchauk, with half my land at Accaback. /

Allthough two of us whose hands are to this will can=
=not remember all the pticulers, yet what they can=
=not remember, the other that were present Doe remember

Barnabas Wyndes
Barnabas Horton
Thomas Hutchinson
ye marke of O Martha Hutchinson:
John Elton. /

At ye Co:rt of Sessions held at Southold June ye 5th: 1672 Barnabas Wyndes, John Elton and Martha Hutchinson upon oath doe affirme that the above written is & was the reall Will of Thomas Tery Deceased, although his hand is not Set to it

A true Coppy p me Henry Peirson Cleark &c:

		£	s	d
1671	An Inventory of ye estate of Tho: Tery lately deceased./			
	The howse & land apprised	50	-	-
	the lands and meadow at Corchake	20	-	-
	ye land & meadow at Accobock of both Sides ye river	15	-	-
	It 3 horse kinde	15	-	-
	It 3 Cowes	10	-	-
	It 2 oxen 9£: 4 Steeres 8£ 10s	17	10	-
	It the bed in the howse & yt belongs to it	4	10	-
	It ye pot & hooke & skellet	1	-	-
	It ye frying pan and the hake	-	12	-
	It a woollen wheele, a linen wheele & a pr of cardes	-	15	6
	It a chest and box	-	5	-
	a barell, a tub, a bowle, & firkin	-	9	-
	in pewter 4s	-	4	-
	a pale, & a meale Seave and Dishes	-	10	-
	2 axes and a bill	-	10	-
	a gun	-	16	-
	an old Sythe & wedges, a Sickle 2 Augers 2 chissells) a hooke & hand Saw)	1	3	-
	other lumbar 4s	-	4	-
	a carte & plow & cart rope	2	10	-
	cloathes 2 £ 10s: a Steere prized at 4 £ is	6	10	-
	£:	147	-08	06

Thomas Maps
Barnabas Horton. /

A true Coppy

Abraham Whitteere of Southold engageth himselfe (before the Co:rt held this 5th of June 72:) to bee Security for Daniell Terry that hee Shall Satisfy and pay all the legacies mentioned and bequeathed in his fathers will

and

and Testament, And that hee Shall Doe & execute therein
according to whatsoever the law requireth. /
Whereupon ye Sd Co:rt doth admitt him the Sd Daniell Terry
to be Sole & lawfull Executor of ye forementioned will of his
Deceased father. /

At ye Sd Co:rt held June ye 5th 1672
was presented the Will & Testament of
Phelemon Dickerson: and is as followeth

Phelemon Dickerson of Southold in the Jurisdiction of New=
=yorke being in pfect Memory Maketh this my last Will &
Testament in manner following: That is to say I will and
bequeath unto my beloved wife, my howse and home lott, with
all the accomodations belonging thereunto, that is within the
owld Towne bowndes both up=land and Meadow, with all ye
appurtenances thereunto belonging Dureing her life or widow=
=hood: And after that to bee disposed to my Children equaly
Alsoe I give unto my wife four Cowes and all my goats, wth
all my moveable goods that is within my howse, and alsoe my
Cropp of Corne. and my Swine. this I give my wife for
Ever. And the rest of my cattell to be Desposed of to my two
Daughters Elizabeth Dickerson and Mary Dickerson when -
they come of the age of one & twenty: Alsoe my will is yt:
my two oxen and my two Steere, That my sone Thomas and
my Sone Peeter shall have them, provided that my wife -
have the use of them dureing her life or widdowhood, and
after that, then to bee devided betweene them. I give to -
my Sone Thomas fourteene ackers of land at North Sea w:ch
I bought of John Bayly: Alsoe I Doe give all ye rest of my
land at North Sea and at Cuchack to my three Sones, as
alsoe my howse & home lot after my wifes decease, or in
case Shee mary, then to bee Devided equally to my three
Sones: I Doe alsoe make my wife Mary Dickerson Sole
Executor of this my last will, In witness hereof I have
here unto Sett my hand: Dated this 20:th day of June
1665.

the marke of Phelemon
Dickerson #

witnes:- Barnabas Wyndes Senr. /
John Youngs Past:r
Thomas Hutchinson

A true Coppy p me Henry Peirson /

Barnabas Wyndes and Thomas Hutchinson doe
affirme upon oath before the Co:rt that the above=
written is the true and reall will of Phelemon -
Dickerson Deceased.

Whereupon the Co:rt Doth admitt Mary Dickerson, ye widow
of ye Sd Phelemon to bee Sole & lawfull Executrix
of her husbands Said Will & Testam:t /

March the latter end 1668. Deceased

An Inventory of the Estate of Phylemon Dickesun lately ^

	£	s	d
Imprs:- The Howse and land	30	-	-
the outlands at Corchauk Occobauck & elsewhere	20	-	-
4 Cowes	15	-	-
in goats	2	-	-
in Swine	2	10	-
one poore ox: & 2 Steeres	8	-	-
4 young Steeres	5	-	-
a bed & what belongs to it	2	10	-
an other bed & what belongs to it	2	10	-
in pewter & brasse	1	10	-
in Iron ware	1	10	-
in Bookes	-	10	-
Armes	1	-	-
2 old Chests & other Lumber	1	-	-
£:-	93	-00	-00

Thomas Mapes, Constable

(Barnabas Horton
Overseers: (Charles Glover
(Tho: Hutchinson

A true Coppy /

January ye 14: 1672.

Mr: John Tompson of Seatuk plf: enters an action of Sclander or deffamation against Richard Mintorne Defend:t to bee tryed at ye Next Cort of Sessions./

The Sd Plf: & Defend:t are agreed;

Bee it knowne to all men whom it may concerne that Richard Minttorne of Southampton Doe acknowledg that I have Spoken ffoolishly and unadvisedly to the Dissparagement of Mr: John Tomson of Seatauket, and that of my knowledg I know nothing of it. And this I give for - - publique Satisfaction, as witnes my hand

Witnes Richard Mintorne
Job Sayre.

A true Coppy of ye Originall
p me Henry Peirson

January 14th: 1672
Mr: John Tomson of Seatauk plf: Enters an action of Sclander or Deffamation against John Beswick Defend:t to bee tryed at ye Next Co:rt of Sessions:

The Sd Plf: & Defendt are agreed. /

Know all men whome it may concerne that whereas I John Beswick have taken upon evill reporte - against Mr: John Tomson, w:ch I made not of my - Self, but took it up of an other man, in Saying yt: I was never banished from Stanford as hee was Which I acknowledg that I know noe Such thing of him of my owne knowledg; By which I acknow= =ledg that I have Done the afforesaid John Tomson much wrong, and am very sorry for it as witnes my hand this 16:th of January 1672:

his
John O Baswek
marke

A true Coppy of ye Originall
p me Henry Peirson &c: /

Georg Harris as Attorney for Mr: Edmond Batter of Salem plf: enters an action of Debt to the value of nine poundes od mony according to bill wth costs of Suite against Peeter Whitteere Defendt to bee tryed at ye Co:rt of Sessions to bee held ye 5:th of March: 1672/73

The Sd pties, Namely Georg Harris for ye Sd Mr: Edmond Batter - and Peter Whitteere are agreed as followeth:
The Sd Peter ownes the Said bill of 9 £-2s-6d. whereby hee became Duely indebted to the Sd Mr: Batter, that value, but alsoe avoucheth that hee hath paid in pt thereof to ye Sd Batter or- his order - 6 £-8s. wherefore and for other considerations hee ye Sd Peter is to have liberty of time untill the 29th of Sep= =tember next to make proof thereof. And if legall proof hee produceth, of ye Sd pretended payment; then hee is to pay the remainder according to the Said bill; But if hee makes not - Such said proof of ye Said pretended payment by the Said 29th: of Septeb:r Then hee ingageth him self to pay the Said 9 £-2s-6d. according to the tenure or purport of ye Said - bill unto the Sd Batter or his Said Attorney: and ye Sd: Peter oblidgeth himself to pay to the Marshall his fees of 6s-8d and to ye Cleark 5s &c. /

p me Henry Peirson /

At ye Co:rt of Sessions held By his Ma:ties Authority
in Southampton the 5.6.7. Dayes of March 1672/73

Thomas Benedick and Henry Whitney plfs:
against Mr Richard Smith of Neeceaquake Defendt
in an action of Defamation.

The Jury finde for the plfs: Costs of Suite and that the
Defendt: Shall make publique acknowledgment that hee
hath Done goodman Benedick and Whitney wrong in
Saying they were perjured psons, or to pay the Said
Benedick & Whitney the Sume of fifty poundes, the
place where the acknowledgemt is to bee
made wee leave to the Co:rt

The Co:rt give Judgmt: accordingly, And ye place of
acknowledgm:t to bee in open Co:rt and ye acknow
=ledgmt to Stand upon record.

Whereas I Richard Smith of Neeceaquaak have Spoken
words to severall psons and in severall places tending
much to the Deffamation of Mr: Benedick & Whitney
in Saying they were forsworne or perjured psons, and
this fully Evidenced against mee in Co:rt I Doe
acknowledg my great evill therein, Desireing ye pties
whome I have thus wronged to forgive mee, hopeing
it shall bee a warning to mee hereafter, of offending
in ye like nature.

The abovesd is A true Coppy of ye acknowledgmt made by
Mr: Richard Smith in open Cort.

In the name of God Amen: I John Thomas of Broo[k]
=haven Al:s Seatawcot on Long Island Mariner
beeing weak in body but Sound in minde and memory
Doe make and Ordaine this my Last Will & Testam[t]
as followeth: First I bequeath my soul to God
my Creator, hopeing in the merits of Christ alone for
everlasting life: Alsoe I bequeath my body to bee
decently buried in the usuall burying place at Brook
=haven by the care of my Executor: And for my world
=ly Estate, My will and Meaning is that upon my De=
cease Mr: Daniell Lane of Brookhaven abovesaid -
Shall claime and take into his possession whatsoever
is now belonging to mee in the Towne afforesaid, -
that is to say my howse and land, as well upland and
meadow as alsoe all rights perquisits and priviledge
belonging to my Single Allotment in ye Towne afore[sd]
Likewise my goods and Chattells, that is to Say my apar
=ell, furniture & Implements, All whatsoever per
=tain

tayning to mee, together wth all the Stock I have, whether my horse beasts, Neat cattell or Swine. For and in Order to the paymt of my Debts, as well for my Dyet keeping & Expenses Dureing my long Sicknes, As alsoe towards the care and Charge of my funerall. And whatsoever else I Stand indebted for to all others - whomesoever Soe farre as my estate will extend And of this my last Will & Testamt I Ordaine my approved friend Mr: Daniell Lane abovesaid my Sole Execut:r as witnes my hand and Seale this 26 Day of June In ye yeare of our Lord God 1672

Witnesses
Nath: Brewster
Richard Waring
Sarah Brewster

John Thomas
his marke +

A true Coppy p me Henry Peirson Cleark

The Sd Will & Testament of John Thomas, wth ye Inventory of his estate being prsented to the Sd Co:rt held the 5th &c of March: 1672/3: ye Co:rt approve of both, appoynt them to bee recorded and adjudg & admit Mr: Daniell Lane to be ye Testator therein Expressed:

An Inventory of John Thomas Estate lately Deceased in Brookhaven taken this 7: December 1672 p the - - Constable and Overseers of Brookhaven:

Imprs:	chest. 1 Suite carsy half worne wastcot & hatt:	2	5	-
	p outher Lumber to the value	1	10	-
	for a house and land Sould: Due	11	-	-
	pr a toe blankit & kitell	-	19	-
		15	:14	:00

This is a true list given to the Constbl and Overseers p me Daniell Lane. /

A true Coppy p me Henry Peirson Cleark:

The last Will and tesstemnt of William Hedges of Eastthampton

Imprimis: I give my Soule to god who gave it and my body to the Dust whenc[ ]
it Came and my Estate as followeth

and I desire Tho: James and Robert dayton to bee over Seers of this my estate

2 To my Eldest Sonne Steeven I give one halfe of all my upland
and medow In Esthampton towne and my meddow at the head
of the hook pond to bee wholly his and the other half of all
my upland I give to my Son Steeven After the deceas of Rose
my wife: and I give to my Son Steeven half my Commonage
both here in the towne and at Montauckit:

3 To my son Isaak besids what land I have allredy given him
I give half my meddow land that any where lyeth A
broad from the towne and half my Commonage both here and
att Mentaukut

4ly To my four Daughters I give ten pounds to bee equally di
=vided after my deceas fifty shillings to Each of them

lastly = I give to my beloved wife Rose what houseing is mine and half the upland
to bee improved by my son Steeven for her use what shee shall need and
after her deceas to bee disposed as aforesd and I give to her all my
stock in Cattle Sheep or hors kind what is mine & at her Deth to be
disposed as Shee Sees Cause and do give to her all my household goods
and I do make her Executrix of this my estate and will witnes my hand
witnes Tho: James March ye 17: 1672/73 William H hedges mark

November ye 11 1674 this will being prsented to the Court: is Aprooved by the Courte and
they order and Apoint Rose Hedges Sometime the wife of william
Hedges lately Deceased to bee the Executrix of his the Sd william Hed[ges]
Estate according as it is expressed in the will
by order of Court
p mee John Howell register

An Inventory of the Estate of william Hedges deceased ap=
=prized September 29:1674:

Imprimis 4 Cowes at 4 £ a peece: 1 Steer 4 year old: 4 £: 10s:	20	10	–
2 Steers 3 yearold vantag	8	–	–
1 Steer 2 heifers 2 yearold vantag :2 £:15s:p:	8	5	–
1 heifer Calf this year 18s	–	18	–
1 Mare 3	3	–	–
2 Horses 4 yearold: 3 £ p horse	6	–	–
1:2 yearold at	2	–	–
19 Sheep at 8s per	7	12	–
6: or 8 lambs more or less at 5s p lamb	1	15	–
his part of the House	6	–	–
7 acres home lott	35	–	–
15 Acres of plaine land 2£–10s p acre	37	10	–
16 acre woodland	16	–	–
8 acres meddow	8	–	–
3 acres more of meddow at Hooke pond	4	10	–

1 bed and boulster 2 pillows	3	5	-
3 pair of Sheet	4	4	-
4 blanketts	2	15	-
1 Coverled	1	-	-
3 pillow beares	-	15	-
3 peices of Cours linnen	-	12	-
1 napkin 2s:6: 2 Shirts 12s	-	14	6
2 yards of kersey 15s: 1 new short Coat 1£:15s:	2	10	-
2 Coats 1 p of breeches	3	-	-
his other wearing Cloaths	1	10	-
1 hatt 10s . 2 Cushones 3s	-	13	-
2 paers of Stockings 4s: Iron old potts and hook 10s	-	14	-
1 Iron Chafing dish	-	3	-
1 brasse kettle 10s : 1 brasse scellitt 4s:	-	14	-
1 old brasse kettle 10s : 3 pewter dishes 1 £ 4s	1	14	-
2 poringers 4s: 2 saucers 5s	-	9	-
2 pewter potts & 2 Spoones :9s: 1 tin puding pan 2s	-	11	-
1 Earthen plater 1s:4d: 11 peices of wooden ware 11s	-	12	4
1 Chamber pott 8s: & 1 keeler 3s	-	11	-
1 old Churn 2s-6d: 1 tramell 4s-6	-	7	-
1 pair of old tongs 1s-8 :1 tin lamp 2s	-	3	8
1 Cream pott 2 other Earthen potts	-	3	6
1 table frame 2 fourmes 1 Chaire	-	14	-
6 milk vessels :1 wooden Cann	-	9	6
4 old books 1 pr of spectacles Case	-	8	-
	193	12	6

Apprized by us Tho: Backer
John Strathon

A true Coppy p me John Howell Jur Clarlk:

I Lattimer Sampson of Oyster Bay upon Long Island, being Intended (God permitting) to travell to the Barbados, And well knowing the casualty of mans life and certainty of Death Doe make constitute and appoynt this to be my last will & Test= =ament in manner and forme following, that is to Say, I Give Will and bequeath all my Estate both reall and psonall on Long Island, Shelter Island or elsewhere in New England (and the gaines or advance (the principle being repaid in England - with in two yeares after my Decease) of all such goods, as shall be Sent to mee (within one year after the Date hereof) upon my proper accompt, Unto Grizzell Sylvester, Eldest Daughter of Nathaniell Sylvester of Shelter Island & to her heyres and Assignes forever: And I doe hereby - constitute and appoynt the said Nathaniel Sylvester, and the Said Grizzell Sylvester to bee my Executor, and - - Executrix of this my Said will in testimony whereof I have hereto Set my hand and Seale. Dated in Shelter= Island the Sixteenth Day of the month called ffebruary in the yeare one thousand Six hundred Sixty eight 1668/9

Lati:r Sampson

endorsed on ye Back Side

(Sealed Delivered and published by the
(within named Latimer Sampson to bee
(his last will and Testament.

In prsents
Christopher ffoster
John Young
Isaac Arnold

A true Coppy p me
Henry Peirson Cleark:

The above written Will beeing presented to the Co:rt of Sessions held By his Highnes James Duke of Yorke his Authoryty in Southampton the 3.4. Dayes of March: 1674/5, was there proved to the Satisfac =tion of the Co:rt by the Evidence of Capt John Youngs, and Mr: Isack Arnold whoe are two of ye witnesses to the Said will, and made oath before ye Cort to the truth thereof, Whereupon the Cort Doth adjudg that Mr: Nathaniell Sylvester And his Daughter Mris: Grizzell are & are to bee reputed to all intents & purposes the true and Lawfull Ex= =ecutor & Executrix of the estate of the Said Latimore Sampson Deceased

A true Coppy of ye will; & Recorded as above written
p me Henry Peirson Cleark of ye Co:rt of Sessions

At a Co:rt of Sessions held in Southhold June 1st:1675

Was presented the Will and Testamt of Mr John Elton of Southhold: and is as followeth:

In the name of God Amen: I John Elton of Southhold on Long Island being very weak in body but of Sound - memory Doe Declare this my last will & Testament: ffirst I comit my Spirit into the hands of Jesus Christ - my blessed Saviour & redeemer, and my body Decently to bee buried

Item- My Just Debts and funerall charges being payed, I Doe give all my moveable Estate, the on half to my Deare wife, the other half to Isaack Overton to bee had possessed and Injoyed by them Severally and - theire heyres for ever.

Item- I Doe give unto my Deare wife afforesaid the one halfe of all my lands howses & buildings to bee at the only use and Disspose of my Said wife Dureing her natu= =rall life and noe longer.

Item- I Give unto Isaack Overton my Sisters Sone All my lands and appurtenances thereunto, and unto his heyres for ever. That is to Say the one half as Soone as my Executors Shall have cleared my Debts, And the other halfe at Eight months end after ye Decease of my wife

Item- I give to my Daughter in law Anna Nicolls tenn poundes to bee paid her in cattell as Soone as my Executors Shall think it convenient.

ffurthermore I Doe Denominate and appoynt my trusty and well beloved friends Mr: Joshua Hobert & Mr: Thomas Hutchinson to bee the Executors of this my will & testam:t Impowering them to use all Discreet meanes and wayes to promote the wellfare of my estate, and to Counsell and Direct my deare wife and kindsman as may bee most to Gods glory and theire good, to the best of theire Skill and Discretion. Signed with my hand at Southhold this 29: Day of Aprill in the yeare of our lord 1675.

Witness present
Mary Wells
Elizabeth EC Clark
her mark

A true Coppy p me Henry Peirson Cleark:

The Sd: two witnesses Deposed to ye reality & verity of the above written Will before the Co:rt of Sessions held at Southhold the 3 Day of June 1675.

May ye 2: Ano:1675
An Inventory of the goods, Lands, Cattle & Chattells
of Mr: John Elton of Southhold lately Deceased - -
made by us undernamed.

		£	s	d
Imprs–	2 pewter potts 2 puter Cupps	–	12	–
	1 brass Cettel 1 brass Skillet	–	12	–
	1 Iron pott	–	10	–
	glass bottles and earthen ware	–	12	–
	1 warming pan	–	10	–
	in barells tubs & other wooden Ware	4	–	–
	one frying pan 3s. in armes and amunition 20s	1	3	–
	on whell. 3 Chaires	–	8	–
	in weareing clothes woolen and linen	5	15	–
	in Iron tolles	1	18	–
	one carte & wheeles Spanshakell & bolts	4	–	–
	1 plow & Irons & 1 chaine & yokes	2	–	–
	his Share of cattell w:th Anna Nicolls	5	–	–
	5 oxen 20 £ 5 Cowes 12 £	32	–	–
	3 three yearlings 6 £. 6.2 yearlings 9 £	15	–	–
	4 yearlings 4 £ Calves 10s	4	10	–
	7 piggs 35s. 8 Swine 8 £.	9	15	–
	2 horses 8 £. 2 mares 5 £.	13	–	–
	30 Sheep	15	–	–
	the Dwelling howse barne & 4 accres of land	45	–	–
	4 accres more lying South of ye Dwelling howse	22	–	–
	one accre and a half at the reere of the the howse lott	3	–	–
	21 accres of land at North Sea	12	–	–
	3 accres in the old feild	5	–	–
	3 lotts Comonage	5	–	–
	21 accres in hog neck	5	–	–
	2 accres of meadow in pine neck	5	–	–
	1 accre of meadow at goose Creek	1	10	–
	1 accre of meadow in hog neck	2	10	–
	3 accres of meadow at Corchaug	3	–	–
	the moty of pissapruk meadow at Corcaug) & 30 accres of upland at ye aforesaid place)	4	–	–
	180 accres of woodland at Corchaug	20	–	–
	Sume is–	123	-00	-00

Richard Terry
John Budd
Thomas Mapes
Joshua Horton

A true Coppy p me Henry Peirson Cleark &c
The aforesaid Will and testament of Mr: John Elton - -
being

being proved in Co:rt by the testimony upon oath of the two witnesses to ye Sd Will Namely Mris: Mary Wells and Elizabeth Clark of the Sd Southhold, the Cort Doth alow of ye Sd Will, And Doe finde and adjudj that according to ye minde of the testator therein exprest Mr: Joshuah Hobart & Mr Thomas Hutchinson are and are to bee reputed to all intents the Lawfull Executors thereof, And the Cort Doth Order and impower them, or either of them to act & Doe in all things, respecting the Sd Will, according to ye contents thereof and ye lawes of this Governmt in yt behalf: And alsoe that letters of Executorship bee given – them to that effect:

The Inventory of Joseph Youngs of Southhold prsented to the Co:rt held the Sd 1.2.3 dayes of June 1675, & is as followeth:

The 12 of Aprill 1675. ye Inventory of Joseph Youngs

	£	s	d
his apparell	3	–	–
in potts and kettles	3	15	–
3 Shets & a Shurte	2	–	–
1 feather bed & boulster. one rugg & blanket	6	–	–
one other bed & 3 pelues & 3 blanketts	3	–	–
in pewter w:th 4 earthen dishes 16s wooden ware 8s	1	4	–
payles and churne and other things	–	15	–
Chayers and Cradles	–	10	–
2 tables & one wheele & a chest & 2 bedsteds	2	–	–
a gun & Sword powder and bulletts	1	8	–
tooles & axes wth other tooles & things	2	–	–
a frying pan and hooke	–	3	–
plow & carte coulter & shear. 3 wedges & yoke Irons	2	–	–
2 howes & a cart rope & 2 Syeths & Siccles	1	2	–
cattell & horse & 3 Swine	30	15	–
the howse and accomodation	40	–	–
Sume is –	99	:12	:00

John Elton | Barnabas Windes
Jacob Core | John Bud
Josuah Horton

A true Coppy

Endorsed on the back of ye Sd Inventory.

	£	s	d
Due from Isaac Arnold to Joseph Youngs)			
from Capt: Nathaniell Sylvester) to-	–	17	4
Joseph Youngs Indepted to Barnabas Windes	–	15	10
Due for Rates from Joseph Youngs Junr: to John Elton	1	11	10
Due from Joseph Youngs to Simon Benjamine	–	15	–
Due from Joseph Youngs to Josea[–] Horton	–	7	6
Due from	3	:10	:2

Due from Joseph Young to Samuell Wind for his coffin	-	5	-
Due to Richard Terry from Joseph Youngs -	-	8	-
	00	:13	:00
Sworne before me by John	3	:10	:00
15 2 mo: 1675. Elton Constable	4	:03	:02

Isaac: Arnold. /

A true Coppy of ye Originall

The Sd Joseph Youngs Dying intestate, and his wife or relict M Sarah Youngs Desireing liberty and power from the Cort to administer of the Estate of her deceased husband, And the Co:rt findeing noe Impediment therein, Doe admit her the Said Sarah to bee Sole Administratrix of ye Sd Estate. And the Co:rt Doth order that Shee Shall have letters of Admini==stration given her to that effect, Shee first giveing in Se==curity to the Co:rt as the law requires:

In the name of God Amen: I John Elton of Southhold on Long=Island beeing very weak in body but of Sound memory, Doe Declare this my last will & testament: ffirst I Committ my Spirit into the hands of Jesus Christ my blessed Saviour and Redeemer, And my body Decently to bee buried

Item- My Just Debts and funerall charges being paid, I Doe give all my Moveable Estate: the one halfe to my Deare wife, ye other halfe to Isaack Overton to bee had possessed & enjoyed by them Severally and theire heyres for ever.

Item- I Doe give unto my Deare wife afforesaid the one halfe of all my lands howses & buildings to bee at the onely use & Disspose of my Said wife Dureing her naturall life and noe longer.

Item- I Give unto Isaack Overton my Sisters Sone all my land and appurtenances thereunto, and unto his heyres for ever, that is to Say, the one half as Soone as my Execut:rs Shall have cleared my Debts, And the other halfe at - eight months end after the Decease of my wife

Item- I give to my Daughter in law Anna Niccolls tenn poundes to bee paid her in cattell as Soone as my Executors Shall thinke convenient

ffurthermore I Doe Nominate and appoynt my trusty or well beloved friends Mr: Joshua Hobert And Mr: Thomas Hutchinson to bee the Executors of this - my Will & Tesytament, impowring them to use all - Disscreet meanes and wayes to promote the wellfare of my estate, & to counsell and Direct my deare - wife and kinsman as may bee most to Gods glory and theire good, to the best of theire Skill and -

Disscre=

Discretion. Signed with my hand at Southhold this 19th Day
of Aprill in the yeare of our Lord 1675.

Witness present John Elton

Mary Wells

Elizabeth EC: Clark
her marke

The Said two Witnesses Deposed to ye reality and verity of the above written will before ye Co:rt of Sessions held at Southhold the 3 day of June 1675.

Henry Peirson Cleark

A true Coppy p me Henry Peirson Cleark of ye Sess:s

The last Will of Mr: John Elton
is before entered : - - - -

The Inventory of Pastour John Youngs Deceased his-
Estate as followeth:

	£	s	d
in wooden ware & 2 old bedsteds & old chest- & 3 chayers. 2 tables & a forme & boule & tray	2	-	-
2 kittles 2 potts hake & pot hock	3	-	-
in peuter	2	-	-
2 old beds & boulster & blankets one rugg and Curtaines & vailing	4	-	-
lyning & Sheets and pillowbeares	2	10	-
5 oxen & 1 lame steere & 1 Cow & 2 of 2 yeare old & one half share of one yearling	27	10	-
one horse	3	-	-
24 Sheepe 12 £ 3 Small Swine 2 £	14	-	-
3 Chaines . plow Irons & Cart Irons	4	-	-
howse and land	30	-	-
Old books by Mr Hubard prized at	5	-	-
	97	:00	:00

Barnabas Windes
John Corwin
A true Coppy Joshua Hortom
Jacob Core

Wee Doe teastify that wee heard Mr: John Youngs pastr to the Church in Southhold resolve and Declare that if God Should take him out of this life before hee had made a will concerning his estate, that then hee would leave it all to his wife, And that Shee Should Doe with it - - what Shee pleased: And further wee testify that very neare to his Death, hee Said hee had Done Nothing as to a will but left all to his wife and to her Disspose

Barnabas Windes Sworne before mee this 5:th of Aprill
Barnabas Horton 1675. Isaac Arnold /

/ A true Coppy. /

M:ris Mary Youngs the widdow and relict of Pastour John Youngs Deceased, upon her request is admitted by the Court

to bee Administratrix of the estate of her said husband & de=
=ceased, shee putting in Security to the Court according to law in that behalf. And In as much as the Sd: Mrs: Mary Youngs her Sd Security is not at hand in time of Sessions, the Court doth Order That upon her delivering in her Said Security unto Justice Arnold and hee Sending it to the Cleark of the Sessions, upon his receipt thereof for the Courts use, - Shee Shall have letters of Administration Sent, and Signed by him in the name of this Cort

Accordingly Lettrs of Administration was Signed & Sent to Mr: Arnold for M:ris Youngs

At the foresaid Cort of Sessions held in Southhold the 1st.2.3. dayes of June 1675. Was presented the Inventory of the estate of ffrancis Munsey of Seatauket alias Brookhaven whoe dyed Intesta[te] an accompt whereof was formerly given to the Court of Sessions held in Southampton in March last

A Record of the Sd Inventory is as followeth:

An Inventory of the estate of ffrancis Muncy lately Deceased dying without will, Mr: Odell and Henry Pery and Wm: Satarly and John Tompson Did take an - Inventory of the estate, this being the first of Septem[ber] in 1674:

	£	s	d
4 oxen	24	-	-
2 Steeres, ye one 3. ye other 4 yeere old	7	-	-
5 Cowes	18	-	-
2 Steeres 3 yeare old & vantage	7	-	-
3 three yeare olds and vantage	8	-	-
1 two yeare old	2	-	-
3 yearlings	3	-	-
3 Calfs	1	10	-
1 black mare & coult	3	-	-
1 py bald horse 3 yeare old	2	-	-
1 howse & 1 barne. 1 lott & half & 60 accres of land	100	10	-
with lumber in the howse . cart & cart tackleing. plow & plow tackleing	10	-	-
hoggs in the woods. corne & flax	15	-	-
	201	:00	:00

Debts that was due in the deceaseds time:

	£	
To Mr: Bryan	27 - -	
and cattell that dyed Since ye Inven= =tory was taken 1 Cow 1 three year= =old heifer	6 10 -	37 :10 :00
1 two yeare old Steere. 1 year old horse	4 - -	
	37:10:00	
		163 :10 :00

And whereas Hanah Munsy the widow or re=
=lict of him the Said ffrancis Munsy, desireing

to

to Administer on the Sd Estate of her deceased husband, and it being Soe long time hath passed and ye Court Seeing noe reason to the contrary, And it beeing alsoe that Justice Wodhull is become Security - for the Sd Hannah according to law to the Co:rts sa= =tisfaction. This Co:rt Doth adjudj that Shee the Sd Hannah is, and is to bee reputed to all Intents and purposes Sole Administratrix of the Sd Estate, and doe grant unto her to have lettrs of Administration. Shee being to pay - all Just Dues out of the Sd Estate and ye remaine thereof to bee to her and hers: - - - -

---

At the Court of Sessions held in Southampton By his Ma:ties Authority in ye 27th yeare of his Reigne Annoq Dom: 1675, and March: 1 . 2 . 3 was presented the will and Testament of William Purrier deceased: and is as followeth:

I, William Purrier of Southhold in the East Rideing of York=sheire upon Long Island being (through gods mercy) in perfect health of body, and of Sound minde and memory, doe make this my last Will & testament in manner and forme following

First I bequeath my Soule to god whoe gave it, trusting in the merrits of Jesus Christ to bee received into the armes of his mercy, and my body to Christian burial &c:

2ly- My will and desire is that my Executor (hereafter named) Doe take his mother, my eldest Daughter Mary Reeve (if Shee Survive mee) imediately - after my Decease into his family, and provide for her comfortable Subsistance, Dureing her life. w:ch if Shee refuse, then my will is that my Sd Execut:r Shall pay unto her in leiu thereof twenty Nobles yearely: the three first yeares after my Decease.

3ly- Thirdly I give and bequeath unto Sarah Mapes and Martha Osman my two youngest Daughters twenty poundes each of them, to bee paid by my Said Executor within three yeares after my de= =cease, to bee made by three equall payments, of the Said yeares in land or cattell at Comon rates But in case they or either of them Shall happen to Die before mee, that then the Said Sume to bee e= =qually Devided amongst the Children of Such of my Sd: Daughter or Daughters Soe Dying in my life time, as afforesaid.

fourthly

4ly- ffourthly: I give and bequeath unto Isaak Reeve (whoe now lives
with mee) two working cattell, and one horse out of my cattell
and what the Sd Cattle & horse Shall bee Judged less in value
then twenty poundes by Indifferent prizers, Shall bee made
up to him, by my Sd Executor when hee Shall attaine to ye
5ly- age of twenty and one yeares. ffifthly I give & bequeath
to my Grandchilde Mary Windes one Cow to bee Delivered
6ly- her within one month after my Decease./ Sixtly, I
give and bequeath unto Thomas Terrill, that married my
grand Daughter Mary Reeve, two accres of land neare or
adjoyneing to his now Dwelling howse (provided the high
=way bee left as now it is) to him and heyres for ever,
But in case hee make Sale thereof, then my Will is that
my Sd Executor have the refusall thereof before any othe[r]
7ly- pson. 7:ly My will is that my abovesaid three Daughters
viz: Mary Reeve, Sarah Mapes, and Martha Osman,
Shall have each of them one payre of theire Mothers Sheets
which my Executor Shall Deliver them (as equall in value [ ]
they admit) within one month after my Decease: Also yt
my Grand daughter Mary Winde Shall have one payre of
8ly- the Same Sheets at the time abovesaid: 8ly and lastly I
make Institute and Ordaine James Reeve my grandsone
now liveing with mee my whole and Sole Executor of this
my last Will & Testament, to whome I give all my
Dwelling howses, out howses Lands Erable, Meadowes Pasture
Common & Commons of Pasture, Woods, Underwoods & all
Allotments whatsoever to mee the Sd William Purrier be
=longing within the boundes of Southhold abovesaid, with all
goods and Implements of household and husbandry, to him
the Sd James Reeve, and to the heyres of his body lawfully be=
=gotten, or to bee begotten for ever more: Provided that hee
the Sd James Reeve or his Assigne, pay or cause to bee paid
all Such Debts or legacies as above Specified: And if in
case the Sd James Reeve Shall happen to dye without law=
=full issue, then my will & meaning is that all my abovesaid
lands and goods whatsoever with every Pt and Pcell
thereof, Shall bee equally Devided amongst all my grand=
=Children then living: In Witnes whereof I ye Said
William Purrier have hereunto Set my hand this 13th day
of December in the yeare of our Lord God 1671.

Signed Sealed & published / William M Purrer
In the presence of / his mark
John Youngs /
Nich: Eedes / A true Coppy p me Hen: Peirson Cleark

Capt John Youngs and Mr: Nich: Eedes upon oath before ye Cort
doe attest that the afforesaid, is the true & reall will & testament
of Wm: Purrier of Southhold deceased. // the

of Wm Purrier deceased
The last Will and testament ^ being presented to ye Court of Sessions held as beforesaid March the 1 . 2. 3 : 1675. and proved by the testimony of Capt: John Youngs and Mr: Nich. Eedes The Court Doth adjudj and order that according to ye minde of the testator in ye Sd will Ex=pressed James Reeve therein mentioned is, and is to bee reputed whole & Sole Executor thereof, and to that effect is to have letters of Executrship given & granted to him./

July the 26th 1675. An Inventory of the estate of William

Purrier deceased, as followeth.	£	s	d
in bedding and furniture	6	-	-
in weareing clothes	6	10	-
5 pr of Sheets and other lining	7	-	-
in brass and pewter and in Iron potts	7	-	-
one chest and other wooding wear	2	-	-
1 cart & wheeles and other Implements	4	10	-
in Sithes and Sicles	2	-	-
in tooles	1	10	-
in armes and amunition	2	-	-
in horse kinde	8	-	-
10 oxen	50	-	-
9 cowes	22	10	-
5 of 3 year old	10	-	-
5 of 2 year old	7	-	-
3 yearlings and a calf	2	5	-
in Swine	15	-	-
in Sheepe	1	-	-
the howse & accomodations at the Towne	50	-	-
the farme at Mattituck & the meadow at accaboak	100	-	-
in lether 50s. in baggs 20s	3	10	-
	307	:15	:00

A true Coppy of the In=ventory, Saveing that ye Originall is wrong Sumed up at 317-15-00:

Thomas Mapes
John Corwin
Joshua Horton

Entred p me Henry Peirson Cleark

The Inventory of the goods of the Deceased Roger Smith of Easthampton in ye East Rideing of York=sheire: January ye 20th: 1671/2

	£	s	d
Imprs: In the fire roome. pothooks & hangers & lamp. 10 pewter ^Spoones	–	7	–
3 pewter Dishes. 1 pewter platter 1 ps: pewter)			
1 qt: pott. 1 pt. pott. 1 Candlestick. 2 pewter porengrs)	1	–	–
2 earthen pitchers	–	1	3
in a box upon the Shelf. 1 pr holland Sheets	1	10	–
6 wooden trayes & other Dishes	–	7	–
1 bible and other bookes	–	5	–
his wearing aparell & a Chest & one ps: read cloth	3	4	–
1 bead. 3 pillowes. 1 pr Sheets & 2 blanketts	3	15	–
one cradle & 2 pillowes. 1 pillow Coat & 1 blanket	–	14	–
2 wooden kellers. one old anchor. 1 paile	–	3	–
2 brass kettles	2	–	–
4 Iron potts, & 1 pr hooks, & 1 frying pan	2	6	–
one old musket & 3 ps: of Dryed meat	1	6	–
in the Inner roome ½ a bushell of Salt	–	2	–
2 bar: poark & 1 barrell of beef	9	6	–
2 flitches backon & other meat	1	10	–
3 earthen potts with fatt in them	–	8	–
a bed a bolster a sheet a blanket & a rugg	2	6	–
Sheep Skins and other lumber	–	5	–
In the Chamber the wooll	2	–	–
In Indian corne	4	10	–
1 bushell of Salt & 3 tubs	–	6	–
2 Sythes 5s in tallow 8s 1 bagg & hops 4s)			
1 hand Saw 3s 6d)	1	–	6
2 Sicles wth old wheele & lumbr 3s. 2 Stooles 3s	–	6	–
1 pade. 1 Stubing hoe. 2 hooes. 1 ax. 2 wedges)			
one beetle ring)	–	16	–
1 Coulter. 2 Shares and a ring	–	16	–
a cart clevis & pin. 2 yoaks & 2 chaines	3	10	–
1 grindestone 8s- 5 loade of fodder 2 £	2	8	–
Corne in the barne 2 £ 10s. 2 hides 16s	3	6	–
the whale Craft	3	–	–
9 Swine	7	–	–
37 Sheep 15 £. 4 oxen 20 £	35	–	–
6 cowes: 3 heifers & 1 bull with other young Cattell	52	–	–
the howse and land 100 £. 1 pr Sheep Sheeres 3s-6d	100	3	6
	246	:17	:03

Apprized by us whoe are here underwritten, appoynted by the Constable & Confirmed by oath before mr: Mulford.

Thomas Chatfeild
Jeremiah Conckling

A true Coppy p me Henry Peirson Cleark of ye Sess:s

the Debts

The Debts of Widow Smith March 4th: 1671

		£	s	d
Imprs–	To Phillip Leake	–	14	–
march ye 4th.	167½ Reconed with Widow Smith)			
	and Due to mee Tho: Backer)	8	8	–
	Due to Mr: Tyng	14	–	–
	Rebeca Smith			
4	Due to Mr: Thomas James	4	4	8
	Reconed and Due to John Hopping	20	–	–
	Reconed and Due to Wm: Brookes	1	–	–
	Due to Joshua Garlick Jur	–	9	–
5	Due to Wm ffithing	–	10	–
5	Due to Samuell Mulford	–	12	–
5	Due to Mr Tyng for warps	1	1	–
	Due to Joseph Osburne	–	10	–
	Due to Samuell Bushnell	–	9	–
	Due to Jeremiah Conckling	–	1	6
	Due to Isaack Hedges	–	2	6
	Due to Joshua Garlick, Senr	–	2	6
	Due to Wm: Edwards	–	6	1
	Due to Wm: Mulford	–	6	4
	Due to Richard Stratton	–	3	9
	Due to Nathaniell Bishop	–	1	6
	Due to Renick Garrittson	–	13	4
	Due to Thomas Diament	–	7	–
	Due to Mr: ffordham	–	3	–
	Due to Mr: Chatfeild	–	7	–
	Due to Mr: Tho: Trowbridg	1	10	–
	Due to the Constable	–	2	6
	Due to ye Marshall	6	–	–
	The totall Sume of debts due is – £:	62	-04	-08

A true Coppy p me Henry Peirson Cleark &c: //

And the Court Doth appoynt Thomas Osburne Senr: and Thomas Osburne Junr: to bee guardians to the Sd widdow and her children and to devide ye Sd Estate amongst them according to law &c: //

The afforesaid Inventory & accompts concerning the estate of Roger Smith of Easthampton Deceased being presented to the Court of Sess:s held the aforesd 1 . 2 . 3 . of March 1675. and noe exceptions found against the Same, at the Desire & request of Rebecca Smith ye relict of him the Sd Roger Smith, by her brother Thomas Osburne, the Court Doth admitt her the Sd Rebecca to bee Administratrix of all the Estate her Sd husband Died Seized of, and Doth adjudg and Order her to have letters of Administra =tion: provided her Sd brother give in bond of 180 £: to save ye Court harmeless according to law &c: //

July this 6th: 1675.

I Richard Terry of Southhold in the East Rideing on Long Island being weak in body but Sound in understanding, blessed bee God, Doe make this my last Will and Testament in manner and forme following: ffirst I bequeath my body to the Dust from whence it came, And my Emortall Soule to ye Lord Jesus Christ whoe purchased it with his most precious blud, by whome alone I hope for eternall Salvation: And touching the outward Estate God hath lent mee, I Despose thereof as followeth: I give and bequeath to my beloved wife Abigall Terry for her life time the accomodation in Towne, the howse and land that properly belonge to that howse in Towne. That is to Say with foure accres of land that Joyne to the howse with the orchard and fences about the Same, And eight accres of land that lye at the North Sea, and 100 in the Calves Neck, and one in ye ould feild, and 100 accres of meadow in the great meadow at Catchacke: I give unto my Sone Gurshom Terry half my woodland at Catchacke; and my Sone Samuell the other halfe: Alsoe a peece of Meadow that was my brother Tho= =mas Terry which I had by vertue of Exchange: - -
I give unto my Daughter Abigall twenty accres of land more or less, lying in the ffort Neck; I give it to her & her heyres for ever, thats to Say Thomas Riders heyres & on Cowe: I give alsoe to my two Sonnes Nathaniell & my Sonne Richard my howse and land which I live upo[n] here at Squash Neck: with all the meadow that Doe be= =long unto it lying in the fresh Meaddow. And this to possess when my Sone Richard comes to the Age of one and twenty. I doe alsoe give unto my Sone John after his mothers Decease the howse and the accomodations in Towne with the rest of the accomodation belonging thereunto as is formerly expressed: I give unto my Sone Gurshom a yocke of young Steeres and a young mare one yeare ould and the Vantage, and two Sowes:
I Doe alsoe leave all my children to bee at my wives Comand, to bee educated and brought up, both for the good of theire Soule and body, tell they come unto - theire respective Age, that is to Say, my Sones at the age of one and twenty, and my Daughters at eighteene.
I give unto my Sonne Nathanell, and my Sonne Richard a yock of oxen, and to have them when they - come to possess the farme, with one Cow for milke. - -
Alsoe I give my Sone John one Cow when hee come to age. And for all the rest of my Cattle that is not

exprest

Exprest. I leave to my wife for her Selfe and for the -
bringing up of my Children tell they come of age: and foreage:
I give unto my Sone Samuell 100 accres of meadow lying
at Accabacke: And I make my Sone Gurshom my
Executor, and my wife Execketreckes of this my Last
Will and testament. And for all my Debts which I
owe, it Shall bee paid out of that estate that is not -
Disposed of, that is left in my wives hand: In witnes
whereof I have hereunto Sett to my hand and Seale
the Day and yeare above written:

Witnes Barnabas Windes
the marke N
of Sarah Windes

Richard Terry

Postscript:
Memorandum it is to bee understood that
when my wife Sees cause to live in the
Towne, my three Eldest Sones Gersom
Nathaniell & Richard Terry Shall Fitt
and repaire her howse in a habitable
& Comfortable measure. /

A true Coppy /

The before written Will of Richard Terry is allowed
and approved of by ye Court of Sessions held the a=
=foresaid 1 . 2 . 3 . of March 1675 and ye Court
doth finde & adjudg that according to the minde of
the testator in the Sd teastament expressed, his
Sone Gershom Terry; and Abigall Terry the wid=
=ow or relict of him the Sd Richard Terry de=
=ceased are, and are to bee reputed to all Intents
and purposes Joynt Executor & Executrix of ye
Said Will, and are to have lett:rs of Execut:rship:

July the 26th 1675. An Inventory of ye
Estate of Leiften:t Richard Terry deceased

	£	s	d
one beed with the furniture	4	-	-
5 blankets	1	15	-
1 pot . an Iron kettle. a frying pan . one skellet	1	-	-
in pewter	-	12	-
in weareing cloathes	5	-	-
1 carte, wheeles, and a plow, plow Irons and cart Irons	3	15	-
in wooden ware	1	-	-
in tooles	2	5	-
Armes & amunition	2	10	-
3 horse kinde	8	-	-
Six	29	:17	:00

	£	s	d
Six Oxen	30	-	-
five Cowes	12	10	-
4. of three year old	8	-	-
5. of 2 year old	7	-	-
5 yearlings . one calf	5	5	-
18 Swine and 5 piggs	20	-	-
the howse & land with land belonging	30	-	-
the farme at paquash neck	50	-	-
the land and medow at Corchaug & at Acaboack	30	-	-
	192	:15	:00
brought from ye other Side	29	:17	:00
ye totall	222	:12	:00

A true Coppy p me Henry Peirson Cleark

At a Court of Sessions held at Southhold the first Day &c
of June 1675.

An Inventory of the estate of Thomas Brush off - -
Huntington Deceased was presented to the Court
and is as followeth:

		£	s	d
Imprs:	2 gownes 6 £. 1 Coat & wastcoat 40s	8	-	-
	1 Childes blanket & 2½ yrds Searge	1	10	-
	1 hatt and coat	3	10	-
	in puter & earthen ware & glass bottells	6	-	-
	in beding	18	-	-
	in Chests bedsteds & Cubbards wth some other lumb:r	4	-	-
	in tramells and Irons. tonges. pothooks	2	3	-
	Iron pots & kettles 7 £:6s in lumber 2 £:10s	9	16	-
	in bookes 20s: in armes 3 £ 7s	4	7	-
	in bridle bitts & Sithes & Sickles & other Small things	1	7	-
	in tooles	2	1	-
	in Carte & wheeles & tackling for ye Same	5	6	-
	for 6 workeing Cattell 40 £. 7 Cowes 34 £	74	-	-
	in one Steere & 1 bull	8	-	-
	in 6 young Cattell	13	10	-
	in Sheep 10 £ in horse flesh 20 £	30	-	-
	in Swine 24 £. one Smoothing Iron 4s	24	4	-
	in pillow beares	-	18	-
	in land & howseing and all appurtenances) thereunto belonging)	90	-	-
		306	:12	:00

A true Coppy

The Said Inventory being as afforesaid presented to the -
Court by Thomas Brush and his grandfather John -
Conkling. The Court approves of the Said Inventory
& accompt, and at the request of him the Sd Thomas
Brush (and it being the Said John Conkling hath put
in Bond according to law to the Courts Satisfaction)

the

the Court Doth adiudg that hee the Sd Thomas Brush is and is to bee reputed to all intents and pur= =poses lawfull and Sole Administrator of ye goods and Chattells belonging to his father Deceased, to= =gether with whatsoever Debts were Due unto him And to pay whatsoever is Due to bee paid out of the estate: And out of what remaines hee is to have a double portion (according to law) with ye rest of the Children: And that which remaines is - equally to bee Devided amongst the rest of the Children by even proportion, for whome, hee ye Said John Conckling voluntarily is content to be Overseer. And the Court Doth well approve thereof. / - - - - - - -:

The last Will and Testament of mee Richard Stretton Senr: of Easthampton being in my perfect minde and understanding.

ffirst I give my Soule to god whoe gave it, and my body to the Dust from whence it came. And - - mine Estate as followeth:

1 - To my Eldest Sonne Richard I give my two Six accre home lotts of the 2d: devission lyin next Thomas Osburn Junr: on the South, & Leiftent Talmage upon the North:

2 - To my Second Sonne Thomas I give Six accres of land out of my home lot, at the reare of its ad= =dition, the whole breadth, fronting upon the lane, one Side, and Willm ffithean on the other Side: And I alsoe give him my Six accre lot w:ch belonged to my owne allotment, lying the farthest Lott beyond Abraham Hauke.

3 - I give all my land both east and west to my two Sonnes abovesaid to bee equally devided be= =tweene them after the Decease of my wife - Elizabeth Stratton, excepting my land at the - little plaine, and six accres more lying at ye two mile hollow

4 - I give to my fowre Sonnes all the meddow belongs to mee and all the Commonage, and what land may bee laid out to mee hereafter with all the priviledges belonging to ye Said land to bee equally devided amongst them.

5 - I give my home lotts, and my howseing & buildings upon the Same to my wife Elizabeth, Dureing her life and after

after her Decease to my my two youngest Sonnes Isaack and
Benjamine, together with all my land at the little plaine
and my Six accres of land neere the two mile hollow. -
My will is alsoe that if any of my Sonnes Decease with=
=out issue my other children Surviveing Shall have theire
part of land afforesaid, Shall have it parted equally a=
=mongst them. /

6 - I give to my Daughter Elizabeth twenty poundes to bee
paid her by my Executrix (whome I appoynt to bee my
wife Elizabeth) out of my Moveable Estate, when Shee
comes to age, or if Shee live to bee married, to bee then
paid her:

7 - I give to my Eldest Sonne Richard Thirty poundes to bee
paid him when hee comes at age of 21 yeares by my executrix

8 - The Overseers of this my will I Desire to bee my father
in law William Edwards, and my brother John Stretton
Senr: Witnes my hand and Seale

In presence of us — Richard Stretton
Tho: James
William Edwards Aprill 7th - 1674

A true Coppy of the Originall p me
Henry Peirson Cleark. //

Easthampton April ye 27th: 1676

An Inventory of the Estate left by Richard Stretton lately Deceased

	£	s	d
one alotment next the high way wth accomodations) thereto belonging, and house)	60	-	-
the other alotment	60	-	-
8 oxen	34	-	-
6 Cowes	18	-	-
5 . three year olds	12	-	-
7 . 2 year olds	12	5	-
6 yearlings	6	-	-
to cattell not knowing theire age	25	-	-
in horses	5	-	-
the Sheep	4	14	-
the Swine	7	-	-
Cart plow and tackling belonging	4	4	-
Axes adds & Stubing howes	1	5	-
howes & Spade	-	8	-
Sieths & Sickell	-	13	-
wedges & rings	-	6	-
tramells and hooks	-	11	-
fier shovell & tongues	-	10	-
Spit	-	2	-
one bedsted and beding	9	-	-
20 pewter Dishes	7	6	-
8 beasons of pewter	1	4	-
17 poringers	1	4	-

pewter

	£	s	d
pewter flagings and potts	2	2	–
pewter bottles	–	7	6
Small pewter cupps Spoones	1	5	–
chamber potts	–	9	–
6 brass kettles	11	–	–
5 Skillits & morter	2	–	–
1 warming pan & Scimer	–	15	–
6 Iron potts & frying pans	5	10	–
tin weare	–	8	–
earthen weare	–	10	–
2 pewter Dishes	–	10	–
one box Iron and grd Iron	–	8	–
Some bottles	–	3	–
1 payre of Stillyards	1	5	–
1 looking glass	–	8	–
1 peece of canvase	2	8	–
2 remnants of Searge	1	7	6
1 remnant of Cotton	–	7	–
peniston	1	7	3
Cersey 4 yds 3/4 at 10s	2	7	6
broadcloth	2	–	–
Searg 9 yds at 6s	2	14	–
broadcloth 2 1/2 yds at 16s	1	16	–
peniston 2–3/4 at 4s	–	11	–
Cersey 22 yds at 7s	7	14	–
lining cloth – 10 yds at 2s–6d	1	5	–
lining cloth 8 yds at 3s–6d	1	8	–
lining cloth 10 ½ yd at 2s	1	1	–
Diaper 4 yds at 6s	1	4	–
Diaper 10 yds ½ at 2s–6d:	1	6	3
lining cloth 10 yds at 9d	–	7	6
Curting stuff 1 yd ½ at 6s	–	9	–
Stockings 8 payre	–	12	–
blue ling at 1s–6d	–	7	6
	328	:05	:00
Siller cup and 6 Spoones	5	3	–
5 yds of taffity	2	5	–
thred	–	2	6
one chest at	–	4	6
one chest at	–	10	–
1 civerlid . 2 blankets	1	15	–
2 yds of tradeing cloth	–	14	–
1 peece of Manchester	–	4	–
lockram 2½ yds at 2s–6d	–	6	3
5 yds of canvas at 3s	–	15	–
1 yd of flanill	–	3	–
7 yds of dowlis at 4s	1	12	–
6 yds of hollon at 5s	1	10	–
4 yds of Scotchcloth 3s	–	12	–
2 yds of dowlis at 4	–	8	–
7 ½ of lining at 4	1	10	–
2 yds			

	£	s	d
2 yds of callicoe at 2s	–	4	–
2 yds of searge at 6s	–	12	–
2½ yds of flanill at 3s	–	7	6
bed ticking	2	10	–
1 yd 1/4 of hollon at 8s	–	10	–
1 yrd ½ of hollon at 5s	–	7	6
3 yds of hollon at 6s	–	18	–
2£½ of thrid	–	8	–
2 peeces of tape	–	3	–
1 yrd ½ of hollon at 4s	–	6	–
3 yrds of Searge at 6s	–	18	–
galloome & Silke	–	10	–
2 Cobbert locks	–	3	–
4 yds of Searge at 6s	1	4	–
1 case and bottles	–	15	–
10 yrds of Sackcloth	1	–	–
cotten wooll	3	–	–
fflax	–	12	–
3 yrds of fustin at 2s	–	6	–
4 paire & 1 Sheet . tablecloth	5	–	–
Nayles	–	6	–
2 barells of Salt	1	10	–
Dry Cask, tubs firkin	–	15	–
Shuger	1	–	–
1 bed and all belonging to	6	10	–
Sacks and Cushings	–	18	–
lining & woollen yarne	2	–	–
1 Carpet & table	1	–	–
1 bible & howre glass	–	6	–
the Credle and what belongs to	–	15	–
chains	–	10	–
boales . dishes . chesfats	1	5	–
pailes & Sives	–	10	–
	55	:02	:09
the Armes and Cloas which hee)	328	:05	:00
gave to bee equally Devided be=)	383	:07	:09
=tweene his two Eldest Sonnes)	016	:04	:06
the totall Sume	–399	:12	:03

A true Coppy of ye Originall p me Henry Peirson Cleark
At the Court of Sessions held in Southhold June
the 6 . 7 . &c 1676. The afforesaid Will and –
Testament of Richard Stretton Deceased being
proved by the testimony (upon oath before ye Court)
of the two psons Subscribed as Witnesses to the

Said

Said Will, Namely Mr: Thomas James and William Edwards; The Court Doth ffinde and adjudg the now widow or relict of the Said Richard Stretton, Namely Elizabeth Stretton, to bee Sole Executrix of the Sd Will and Testament; And Doe alow & admit her Soe to bee, to all intents & purposes. alsoe ye Court Doth approve of the Said William Edwards and John Stretton mentioned in the Sd Will, to bee Su= =pervisers thereof, according to the minde of ye testator therein Specifyed. /

Southampton March 5: 1672.

Thomas Mapes and John Bud of Southhold being en= =gaged by oath, to apprize two thirds of a pcell of land in the lower Neck at the Oyster Ponds, which is within theire Towne Boundes, which Sometime appertained unto John Herbert: They the Said Depon:ts haveing Maturely Considered the Matter Doe apprize and value the Sd: Land at the Sume of Seaventeene poundes: In Witnes whereof they have hereto Sett theire hands the Day abovesaid

Thomas Mapes
John Budd

The Court of Sessions held at Southampton the 6th of March 1672/73 Doth approve and allow of the abovesaid Apprizement:

Signed p me Henry Peirson Cleark
In the Name & p the Order of
the Court.

A true Coppy of the very Originall: entered as above this 18th of february 1676. p me Henry Peirson
Cleark of ye Sess:s

At a Court of Sessions held in Southampton March 7th.8th.9th: 1676/77 was prsented the Inventory of ye Estate of Isaack Hedges of Easthampton (whoe Dyed Intestate) Which the Court approved of, and appoynted to bee recorded & is as followes

Easthampton: A list of the Estate of Isaack Hedges apprized according to the rate of wheat fowre shillings p bushell by us under written

	£	s	d
Imprimus. the howse and 29 accres of land with the appurtenances thereto	60	–	–
Item 3 Cowes	7	15	–
Item 6 Sheep	2	5	–
Item 2 mares and 2 mare Coults	2	–	–
Item 2 Swine	–	10	–
Item 2 brass kettles one skillet & warming pan	2	15	–
Item 2 Iron pots & pot hooks one frying pan & an Iron= =hanger over the fire one grid Iron a pr of tonges–	1	6	–
Item	76	:11	:00

	£	s	d
Item: Some Carpenters & Coopers tooles & 3 Iron wedges	3	4	–
Item: Some pewter	–	16	–
It:– Some tyn & earthen ware	–	7	–
It:– Some wooden ware	–	15	–
It:– 2 Spining wheeles . one howre glass & 2 glass bottles	–	6	–
It:– one bedd & beding thereunto belonging	8	16	–
It:– one gun and cutlash	1	12	–
It – one little peece of Searge & an old coat	1	–	–
It – the Chests & boxes & little tables & chaires	1	2	–
It – Some cotten wooll & flax	1	15	–
It – 2 bookes	–	6	–
It – 2 Seeves & one wicker basket	–	4	–
It – 3 hanbaskets . & an old Sadle & bridle	–	10	–
It – Sett of boxes & hoopes for a little pr of wheeles for^ a cart	–	12	–
It – 2 Smoothing Irons & a pr of cards	–	5	–
alsoe Some Sugar and Mollasses formerly In the howse but now Spent	21	:10	:00
and 6£ of yarne formerly upon accompt but now in cloth.–	76	:11	:00
Thomas Talmage/ all £:	98	:01	:00

A true Coppy p me Henry Peirson Cleark:

The afforesaid Inventory beeing presented as before is incerted and noe exceptions found against ye Same At the desire & request of Johanna the widow or relict of the Sd Isaack Hedges (by her father Josuah Barnes) the Court Doth admit her ye Sd Johannah to bee to all Intents & purposes Sole Administratrix of all the estate her Said husband Dyed Seized of And Doe adjudg & Order her to have letters of Ad= =ministration to that effect , Provided Josuah – Barnes according to his promise to ye Court, put bond of Security according to law, to Save the Court harmeless in granting her the Said Johanna Such Said admittance to administer: And the Court doth allow of, and appoynt him the Said Joshua Barnes (being father to the Sd Johanna) to bee guardian to his daughter Johanna & her children and to See that the Estate bee Devided amongst them, or diss= =posed of for theire use according to law:

At the afforesaid Court held march.7.8.9: 1676.
Was presented an Inventory of the Estate of Mr: Thomas Hutchinson of Southhold (whoe Dyed Intestate) ye Court Doth approve of the Sd Inventory and appoynt it to bee recorded. and is as followeth:

Taken the 25:th of September 1676.

	£	s	d
Cloathes	7	-	-
Sword and guns	3	-	-
Chest and lock	-	5	-
wooll & flax, rotten wooll	1	-	-
beding	8	-	-
3 old barrells	-	8	-
wheeles Cart: plow, chaines, Spade, ax w:th other Iron:	6	-	-
pot, kittls, skillet, pewter, table Cradle) pailes Sive 45s: Churne bowls 30s)	3	15	-
Dishes and Spoones	-	5	-
flake	-	5	-
4 oxen	20	-	-
6 Cowes	18	-	-
2 Steeres 4 yeare old	8	-	-
2 Cattell 3 years old 5 £ 2 cattell 2 year old 4 £	9	-	-
3 yearlings	3	-	-
2 Calfs	1	-	-
8 swine 1 yeare½ old . 10 Sumer piggs	12	-	-
horses 4	10	-	-
howseing land and meadow	70	-	-
	180	:18	:00

Joshua Horton Constable
Barnabas Horton
Benj: Yo: overseers:

A true Coppy of the Originall
p me Henry Peirson Cleark. //

At the Desire and request of Martha Hutchinson (the widow or relict of him the Sd Mr Thomas Hutch =inson) presented by her brother in law Isaac Wilman of Southampton, the Court Doth admit her the Said Martha, to bee to all intents and purposes, Sole Administratrix of all ye Estate her Said husband Dyed Seized & possessed of, and Doe adjudg and Order her to have letters of Administration to that effect: pro= =vided that the Sd Isaac Wilman according to his engagement or pmise Doe give in bond (according to law in that behalf) to Save the Court harmeless, and the Court doth allow of and appoynt him the Sd Isaac to bee Super vizer of the Sd Estate and ye Cildren of the Sd Mr: Hutchinson that the estate may not bee Imbezeled but improved to the use of ye Sd widow & her children

At the Said Court held March the 7.8.9: 1676/77
The peticon of Joshua Garlick Junr: being pre=
=sented; the Court takeing the Same into Considera=
=tion, as alsoe the bodily infirmity and impotency
of the peticoner which was testifyed to, by divers
of his Neighbours of Easthampton present, In
answer of the Said peticon, The Court Doth -
Judg that the Sd peticoner Shall bee free, &
exempt from all publique traineings

At a Cort of Sessions held at Southhold June 6: 1676
The Court takeing into Serious Consideration the peticon off - -
Abraham Whitteere of ye Sd Southhold, Doe adjudg his
request therein reasonable; And Doth Determine & Order
that the Childe mentioned in the Sd petticion, Shall bee and
remaine (God pmitting life) with him the Said Abraham
and his wife , or which of them Surviveth, As an appren=
=tice, untill it come to bee one and twenty yeares of age.
they affording to ye Childe ^ and theire Apprentice ^ at all times competency of food
and rayment with Instructions, & if need bee, due correct[ion]
and all things necessary for theire Said Apprentice. /

In answer unto the Petticon of Abraham Whitteere of
Southhold: The Court Doth adjudg and Order that the
peticoner, according to the Injunction already upon him
Shall pay next killing time the Summes (which by
former Court hee was enjoyned) in fatt Cattell as in
=Different men Shall apprize them, or any other
good pay at price currant: Alsoe this Court doth
adjudg, Order and determine, that whatsoever was
alleadged against him hitherto (for ought that is
come to the Courts Sight or knowledg) Shall bee noe
barre or lett to the petticoner in being a witnes
or giveing testimony, as other men, in any case
whatsoever.

At the Court of Sessions held at Southhold by his Mat:ies Authority June 5.6.7: 1677
Was presented to the Court the Inventory of the estate of Edmund Shaw Deceased and is as followes

		£	s	d
Imprs:	two mares	6	10	-
	4 Cowes	16	-	-
	12 Sheep	4	-	-
	2 paire Loomes: and tackling	8	-	-
	his wearing cloathes att	1	-	-
	a rugg & 2 blanketts & Sheets	3	-	-
	a Cheast	-	10	-
	a gun 1 £ 5s	1	5	-
	4 barells of oyle	8	-	-
	the totall is -	48	:05	:00

The Estate is equally devided amongst us the under written, being the psons concerned, and all legacies faithfully pformed, and Debts truely paid, as ever hath beene or is demanded: In witnes whereof wee have hereunto Set our hands this 8th Day of June 1677

Thomas Shaw
Henry Ludlam:

A true Coppy p me Henry Peirson Cleark

Whereas the Court of Sessions held June 1676 at Southhold Ordered, according to the Will of Edmond Shaw, then presented, That Thomas Shaw should Administer of the Estate of the Said Edmond Shaw and bee Executor of the said Will provided hee gave in a true Inventory, unto Mr: Justice Topping or any of his Ma:ties Justices of the peace, to theire Satisfaction; And give his bond to Save the Court harmeless in granting Administration or executorship unto him; theise are to Certify that wee Subscribed accept the above Inventory of 48 £-5s & according to the minde of the Said Court of Sessions, and Order thereof, Doe thereto consent, and doe appoynt That the abovesaid Inventory bee recorded and letters of Administration or Executorship bee given unto him the Said Tho: Shaw (hee giveing in bond as beforesaid) Given under our hands this 9:th of June 1677.

Tho: Backer
John Topping:

A true Coppy p me Henry Peirson Cleark &c.

The last Will and Testament of Edmond Shaw Senr: May the 3d: 1675.
ffirst I give my Soule to God whoe gave it and my Body to the Dust whence it came. And my Estate as followeth:

1st- To my Sonne Thomas Shaw, fourteene poundes
2- To my Sonne Richard Shaw I give fourteen pound.
3- To my Daughter Ludlam, wife of Henry Ludlam I give fourteen pounds
4- I give to my Daughter ffoster wife to John ffoster eight pounds
5- What is over and above that is not mentioned of my Estate, My Will is, it Shall bee equally Devided be= =tweene my two Sonnes, Thomas and Richard, and my Daughter Ludlam: And that my Sonne Tho= =mas Shall have the land which I have given him and hee is possesse; besides what I here Express-
Alsoe that my two Sonnes Tho: & Richard bee Executors of this my will
in this my will & Testam:t ^ In Confirmation of this, Will and testament I Sett to my hand & Seale

Edmund S Shaw
his mark & Seale

In presence of us
Thomas James
Jeremih Conkling

the 31, May 1676.
This attested by Jeremih Conkling
before mee Tho: Backer

The above written will was further proved in Court of Sessions held at Southhold June 6th- 1676. By testimony of Mr: Tho: James then Deposed:

A true Coppy p me Henry Peirson
Cleark

Know all men by theise presents that wee Samuell Blagge of Stratford in New England merchant & Capt: John Howell of Southampton in the Collony of New York, are held and firmely - bound unto our Soveraigne Lord the King in the Sume of two hundred poundes, to bee paid unto o:r Said Soveraigne Ld: the King his heyres or Suc= =cess:rs To which payment well and truely to bee made, we binde our Selves Joyntly and Se= =verally; for and in the whole, our heyres Execu= =tors & Administrators and every and either

of

of them firmely by theise presents, Sealed with
our Seales, Dated the seaventh Day of June in ye
twenty ninth yeare of his Ma:ties Reigne - - -
Anno 1677.
The Condition of this Obligation is Such that where=
=as the above bounden Samuell Blagge Comenced
an Accon of an acc:t agst Samll Edsall & Andrew
Gibb, at Southampton at the Court of Sessions held there
in the Month of march last past; in wch action the Said -
Samuell Edsall and Andrew Gibb were cast, and ye Judgmt:
of Court was That the Sd Samuell Edsall and Andrew Gibb
Should render a Just and honest acct: to the above bounden
Samll Blagge: ffor Compleatm:t of which Judgment, an
acct: hath beene produced to the Worp:l Court, which
acct: the Court Judges Doth accomplish the Said Judgmt:
ffrom which the Said Blagge Appeales to the next
Court of Assises to bee held at the Citty Hall of New
Yorke in October next: If therefore the above - -
Bounden Sam:ll Blagge Shall duely & legally pro=
=secute his Said Appeale Then the above written
Obligation to bee voyd, else to remaine in full
force and vertue

Sealed & Delivered — Sam Blagge
In the prsence of — 1677
Henry Peirson — John Howell /
John Laughton /

A true Coppy recorded p appoynt=
ment of the Court p me

June 11th: 77) — Henry Peirson Cleark:

At the Court of Sessions held &c: June 5:6.7: 1677.
The present Constable and Overseers of the Towne of
Southhold are impowered Ordered and required by
this Court and the Authority thereof (In answer of ye
Pettition of Christopher Youngs of the Said Southhold)
wth all convenient Expedition, to lay out a highway
in or through the nine accres of land which Pastour
Youngs Deceased Sometime gave to the Sd Christopher
and two of his brethren namely Joseph & Benjamine
and they the Sd Constable & overseers are to lay out
the Said high way for widenes and place as may bee
in theire best Judgments most convenient for the whole
that the Sd Christopher may come to make improvement
of his pt without becomeing tresspasser. wch highwa[y]
Soe

Soe laid out, shall remaine and continue for ever a comon high way unto the Said pties concerned, except the Said three brethren to whome the Sd nine accres belongs, mutually a= =gree Soe to Devide the Same, as that each & every of them may come to his & theire pper pt conveniently without beeing trespassers unto any.

At the Court of Sessions held in Southampton March ye 6. &c: 1677/78

By	Capt: Matthias Nicolls	Mr: John Topping	)
	Capt: Thomas Willet	Mr: Isaac Arnold	) Justices
	Mr: Thomas Backer	Mr: Richard Wodhull	) of ye peace

It being represented unto this Court That Stephen Coppock whoe had beene an Inhabiter in Southampton for about two or three yeares was Drowned the last Spring, left an Estate behinde him in theise pts But hath noe relations that are knowne here, It is Ordered, And the Court - Doth adjudj That the Officers of the Townes of this Riding whome any of the Said goods or Estate of the Sd Coppock Shall bee knowne to bee Due They are hereby Impowered to take the Same into theire charge & Custody untill the next Court of Sessions. When and where they are to render an accompt of the Same, haveing in the mean time power to pay Such Just Debts of his, but of the Sd Estate, as shall bee made appear by his Book, or before Some one of the Justices of the peace. The Said Officers are alsoe hereby impowered to make Sale of perishable or leaky goods they - Shall receive as pt of the Sd Estate, for money or very good pay; And bee accomptable to the Sd Court in June next, for the perticulers.

Southampton May the 19th: 1677 An Inventory or accompt of the vissible Estate of Stephen Coppock. Taken by us John Jagger Constable; John Jessup & Edward Howell Overseers, As it appeares to us, By Credit in his booke of accompt, and Bills of Debt: And goods belonging to him undissposed of. And firstly, as wee finde by his book as followeth:

	£	s	d
Due unto him by Book acco:tt ffrom Job Sayre	-	2	6
ffrom Thomas Cooper Junr:	1	5	10
Oliver Norris	-	12	-
Mr: John Laughton	3	6	-
Jacob Wood	-	6	-
Enoch ffithian	-	12	-
James Heldrith	-	12	-

Richard

		£	s	d
ffrom –	Richard Howell p: 7:	1	15	–
	Samuell Cleark	–	3	–
	Wm: Russell	–	16	–
	Edmond Cleark	–	4	–
	John Woodruff	–	13	–
	Isaac Mills	–	11	–
	Robert Norris	–	13	–
	Josiah Laughton	1	10	6
	Darby Murfeild	–	10	6
	Charles Sturmy	–	12	–
	Sam: Barnes	–	2	10
	John Davis	–	5	6
	John Mulford Junr:	–	6	–
	Hen: Ludlam	1	1	6
	Joell Burnet	–	12	–
	Joseph Rainer	–	12	–
	John Cooper	3	1	–
	Samuell Lum	–	12	–
	Gershom Culver	–	14	–
	Isaac Willman	3	1	2
	Mr: Meppam	–	15	–
	Thomas Halsey Junr	1	12	–
	John ffoster	–	15	6
	Joseph Marshall	–	16	–
	Edmond Howell	1	–	9
	Rich Minthorne	–	3	6
	Robert Kellam	–	5	–
	Ben: Gold	–	2	8
	John Larrison	–	12	–
	Ben: Morgan	–	15	–
	Arthar Howell	–	10	–
	Andrew Davis	–	3	–
	John Hoppin	–	7	2
	Tho: Osburne	–	2	–
	Wm: Barnes of Easthampton	–	13	8
	Arthar Cressy	–	12	–
	John Edwards	–	4	–
	Benony fflint	–	2	4
	James Topping	1	5	10
	Elnathan Topping	3	10	7
	Ben: Hand	–	13	6
	Thomas Rose	–	14	–
	Mr William Brinly	1	10	–

James

	£	s	d
James White	1	7	–
Shamgar Hand	1	9	9
James Right	–	8	–
Southampton Towne	–	12	–
Anthony Ludlam	–	7	1
Mr: John Tomson of Seatauk	3	–	–
Thomas Diment	1	7	6
Ebenezer Leeke	–	6	–
Christopher Leamyng	–	10	–
Mr: Justice Arnold	–	3	–
Ben: Davis	1	16	–
Robert Kellam	–	9	11
Thomas Trevally	5	1	11
John Beswick	–	12	–
John Lupton	–	9	–
Timothy Laskin	–	14	–
John Osburne	–	2	6
John Tennison	–	12	–
Leiften:t Post	–	6	–
Daniell Halsey	1	3	–
Samuell ffithin	–	6	–
John Cook 17s	–	17	–
Peter Norris	1	1	–
John ffithin	–	3	–
John Miller	1	7	–
Anthony Kelly	–	2	–
Anthony Tomson	1	4	–
Wm: Perkins	2	–	–
Wm: Parker	–	2	–
Mr: Tho: James	–	17	–
Christopher ffowler	3	3	6
Jonathan Heldrith	–	12	–
John Rose	–	3	–
John Wade	1	15	–
Ben: Hand	1	8	–
John Johnes	–	10	–
John Richardson	–	10	–
Edward Johnes	–	7	–
Jonas Stephens	–	10	–
Tho: Reeves	2	7	10
Thomas Topping	1	1	–
James Herrick	–	16	10
Richard Smith page 65	–	4	8

John

	£	s	d
John Else	–	5	–
Mr John Topping	–	7	–
Sumd up in all	84	:14	:04
More Due to Stephen Coppock –) from Joseph Marshall by bill) 66 barrells of Oyle merchtble)	132	:00	:00
The Totall – £:	216	:14	:04

By us Subscribed whoe were hereunto – –
appoynted by Mr John Topping Justice
of the peace.
Witnes our hands – –

John Jessupp
John Jagger
Edward Howell

A true Coppy

An accompt of the Constable and Overseers of Southampton of what Moveable goods they finde belonging unto – Stephen Coppock Deceased: as followeth.

		£	s	d
Imprs:–	46 hatt=blocks	1	10	–
It.	1 Iron kettle. 1 Iron pot in ye furnace)	1	10	–
It.	1 pr of bellowes . 2 water payles	–	6	6
It.	1 empty barell . 2 earthen potts	–	1	6
It.	1 Small glass bottle . a Small Jugg	–	1	–
It.	a round brush . a pr of sheep sheares	–	1	4
It.	1 chaire . 1 hatt	–	7	6
It.	2 Iron tooles to trim hatts with	–	4	–
It.	1 gun . pr bandeleeres . a Sword, belt	2	6	6
It.	a Small glass bottle . 3 round high hatts	–	12	8
It.	1 Curry combe . Some galls for dying	–	4	6
It.	1 pr of Stilliards . a hone	–	9	–
It.	Some Mackerill line . a pr of Scales	–	6	–
It.	5 Sacks . pr of wooll cardes	–	9	–
It.	15 Small Skins of furr . good for nothing	–	–	–
It.	1 logg of dying wood . 3 great Skeines of Silk	–	9	–
It.	2 Small baggs with powder in them	–	4	–
It.	1 curbbit bridle, to goe with ye horse one truell 12d)	–	1	–
It.	a booke titled ye fuell of content	–	5	–
It.	1 paper of Dying Stuff	–	1	–
It.	a book of ye new disscovery of ye old light	–	1	–
It.	2 old hoggsheads . one goose of Iron	–	7	6
It.	1 whetstone Some Coppers is in an anker 2 bowes for a hatter)	1	6	–
	one chest			

			£	s	d
It:-	1 chest. 2 pr of howlsters		-	12	-
	a Small bagg of feathers		-	3	-
	1 Square brush		-	-	6
	[ ] the chest & 7 Skins of raccoone an fox a lookingglass	)	-	13	8
	3 Small bookes. w:th covers		-	6	-
	2 Small printed paper bookes		-	1	6
	of linen, ½ Sleeves, a neckcloth, one handchercheif, 2 pr of shoes	)	1	11	-
	1 wastcoat. 1 great coat		3	-	-
	2 pr plate buttons. & 9 d in Silver		-	5	-
	1 pr of trowses 1 shirt		1	8	-
	1 Castor hatt 34s . 7 mussquash Skins ye Skins good for nothing	)	1	14	-
	1 pr of Stuff=half=sleeves		-	3	-
	1 pr of Drawers		-	5	-
	put a board in Joseph Marshalls chest . 1 Dowlas Shirt				
	2 Cambrick Neckclothes & 1 of linen		-	10	-
	3 pocket handcherchers		-	4	-
	1 pr of thrid stockings		-	6	-
It:	Delivered aboard the vessell Symon Grover Mr: 13 brlls of oyle. It. 1 bar:ll of porke: & 3 bundles of whale bone.		4	10	-
	an howreglass & a bible in ye hand of ye wife of Thomas Topping	)	-	12	-

The above said & goods Apprized by us Subscribed being -
Appoynted thereunto and Sworne by Mr: Justice Topping
Witnes our hands this - - - - John Jessupp
21th day of March 1677/78 Edward Howell

A true Coppy

The Business concerning the Estate of Stephen Coppock whoe dyed Intestate being represented unto the Court of Sessions held at Southold June the 4th: &c 1678. The Court Ordered and adjudged That - John Jessupp and Thomas Topping both of Southampton Shall take into theire Cognizance and custody the estate of the Said Stephen Coppock deceased for the preservation thereof. and receive what debts they can finde due to him and pay out of his Estate whatsoever appeares to them to bee due from him, as Shall bee lawfully demanded; And give acco:tt of the whole unto the Court of Sessions to bee held at South= =hampton in March next: And if any pson indebted to the Said Stephen Shall upon lawfull demand refuse

to

to make payment then the Sd John Jessup & Thomas Topping are hereby impowered to Endeavour the recovery thereof by Suite of law or otherwise, as the case shall require: They to bee competently satis= =fied out of the Said Estate:

At the afforesaid Court of Sessions held at Southampton the 6th Day of March 1677/8

The business relating to the widdow Sarah Cooper of the Said Towne of Southampton, And ye Estate which be= =longed to her husband John Cooper Deceased, (and Intestate) being Considered; the Court Doth appoynt five men, Namely John Jessupp, Edward Howell, Thomas Cooper Obadiah Rogers and Thomas Topping to apprize the Sd Estate, and to make a pfect In= =ventory thereof.

The Oath of Apprizers was Administered unto them before, or in presence of the Court. /

March the 8th 1677/8. An apprizall of the Estate of the late Deceased John Cooper: Taken this Day out of the accompt formerly taken by ye Overseers and now apprized by the five men chosen and appoynted to it by the present Court of Sessions: is as followeth.

	£	s	d
by 6 brass kettles at	4	19	-
by 24 poringers	2	8	-
by 3 peuter plats	-	7	-
by one quart bottle	-	3	-
by one pinte pott	-	4	-
by 17 whisks	4	4	-
by 2 yeards of Silke	-	14	-
by 7 bibells	3	3	-
by one Coile of warpe 200 l weight	15	-	-
by 5 gros of hooks and eyes	-	5	-
by 9 pr of Small bodies	1	7	-
by 1 pair of belos	-	3	-
by 28 l of Iron	-	9	4
by 17 yeards of Cotton	3	8	-
by 17 yeards of Duffells	8	13	-
by 51 yeards Dito in remnants	22	19	-
by 23 bunches of Small twine	1	7	6
18 Small Deare Skins used in ye family:			
by 4 1/4 of red Cotton	-	17	-
by 6 yeards ½ of course hollon	1	6	-
54 weight of tobaccoe Smoked out.			
by 11 Small Sickells	-	10	-
by one Small Iron pot	-	10	-
by 6 Dozen of pipes	-	4	-

			£	s	d
	By	one payre of Stilirds	1	4	–
	by	one pr of fishing hooks	–	15	–
	by	6 pound of Candles	–	3	–
	by	36 of Indian Corne & 16 of wheat./			
	by	47 fleeces of wooll not now extant - - -			
	by	17 harping Irons	8	10	–
	by	3 old boats	10	–	–
	by	4 old warps	10	–	–
	by	3 handwarps old ones	1	–	–
	by	3 old Chests of ye childrens			
	by	3 fether beds & 1 chaffbed & 1 Small bed)			
		wth Coverlid Sheets, ruggs & blankits, all)	30	–	–
in ye Originall	by	1 bed given to her Daughter - - -			
sum:d at	by	2 pr of old Curtaines	3	–	–
£ s d	by	3 guns 3 £ 3 old Swords, 1 case 3 bottles 42s	5	2	–
143 -01 -10	by	1 old Cask, and 5£ of fethers all	–	7	–
	By	175 weight of Tallow	4	7	6
	by	8 bouls & trays 3 keelers. 3 earthen vessells all	1	8	–
	by	4 Sithes. 2 Spinning wheeles.1 Can. 1 tin pot. 2 doz: trench:rs	1	11	6
	by	4 Cutting knives. 4 whale hooks. 3 old brass pans	4	2	–
	by	1 Small brass kettle. 24 Napkins	3	14	6
	by	13 pound of wooll - - -			
	by	2 tin cups.1 tin pan.1 pinte glass bottle. 1 warming pa:	–	18	8
	by	one great bible	–	10	–
	by	1 pr old Scalls. 6 plaine Coshins. 1 pr of Small Skalls	1	11	–
	by	4 old pistolls. 1 great Scall beame & weits. 1 old beam:	5	–	–
	by	56 weit of pewter & 10 poringers. 2 basons	9	15	–
	by	2 Chamber potts. 1 great flagon. 2 quart pots)			
		and 1 Candlestick)	2	1	–
	by	6 earthen Dishes. 2 gill potts. 1 quart pot			
		more Small things	1	9	–
	by	his wearing clothes both woollen & linen	12	–	–
	by	14£ of lead. 1 two q:rt bottle. 1 pinte bottle	–	10	–
	by	1 plaine Cubard. 6 old chaires. 1 old Stock lock	1	15	–
	by	1 bed pan. 7 old platters. 1 tin pan. 1 tin pan more	1	13	–
	by	1 pinte pot. 1 tin funell. 1 Chaying dish	–	5	–
	by	7 Spoones. 1 Skimer. 1 choping knife. 6 Iron potts	4	16	–
	by	8 brass kettles. 1 pestell & Morter	10	10	–
	by	one wooden Can. Coopers tooles & Grindstone	3	12	–
	by	one chaffindish. 2 Skellits. 4 Sives)			
		3 baskits.3 Sickles)	2	3	–
	by	one Iron peal. 3 tramills. 2 tin lamps & 4 pailes:	1	16	–
	by	earthen pans. 1 glass bottle. 1 Driping pan	–	10	–
	by	one frying. 4 keelers. 4 chesfats. 3 matocks	1	8	–
	by	2 wooden platters & 1 tray. 1 old saw. 1 cheespress	–	16	–
	by	one ridell. 3 weges. 1 beetle. 4 hows. & old barills	1	6	–
	by	old barills & tubs and other lumber	12	–	–
	by	4 Iron kettles. 1 Coper & 4 Cooling Cask	15	6	–
	by	4 Cask for oyle part of them in 4 hoops	8	–	–
	by	2 Small Cask: by 4000 staves. 1 harrow	25	6	–
	by				

			£	s	d
	By	Carts, plows Chaines, yoaks & 2 augers	12	15	-
	by	one pillian. one Sadle. 3 axes 20 barells	7	6	-
	by	2 forks. 1 old Cask. 14 planks neare 200 foot of plank	1	8	-
	by	2 Neigros, & 2 children	90	-	-
	by	2 old grinstones. by 4 doz: of old hurdles	2	14	-
	by	24 Skeines of linen yearne	1	4	-
	by	80 boshells of wheat. 3 Chests. 1 trunck. 1 lookinglass	20	-	-
	by	one barll of porke. 3 barlls of beef	9	-	-
in ye Origin	by	3 table cloths 2 old table	1	14	-
=all	by	2 oxen. 6 Cowes. 4 Steeres. 3 younger. 5 2 year olds	79	-	-
sum:d at	by	4 come too yer olds. 4 yearlings. 28 sheep	21	4	-
£ s d	by	6 Swine. 10 piggs. 6 horses, 4 mares	51	-	-
445 :11 :2	by	3 of to year old. 3 yearlings	9	-	-
	by	10 bushells of oats	1	5	-
	by	the land at North Sea	50	-	-
	by	the Last Devission at Meacocks	60	-	-
	by	ye Close in the great plaines 40 £	40	-	-
	by	Severall pcells of land & medow at Shenecock:	40	-	-
	by	10 accres of land by ye Ox pasture gate	50	-	-
	by	12 accres laid out North of John Jaggers close	20	-	-
	by	150 accres of land at Southhold	40	-	-
	by	ye howse. home lott. barn and all buildings and fences about it	380	-	-
	by	the Commonage belonging to all	100	-	-
	by	1 pr of Andirons	1	-	-
	by	one bed of Maryes given her by her father:			
			782	05	00
			445	11	02
			143	01	10
		Errours excepted in Casting up: In all -	1370	-18	-00

The Apprizemt being made at the value of Cuntry pay

Matth: Nicolls: / - - -

This Apprizemt made by us Chosen thereunto:
There is alsoe a Considerable quantity of bluber and Bone now in being, but not all come home that wee have not Apprized, which is esteemed to bee such a quantity as may Satisfy a Debt of 50 £: now to bee forthwith as Soone as may bee tryed out and payed.

Edward Howell
John Jessup
Thomas Cooper
Thomas Topping
Obadiah Rogers /.

there

There is alsoe other Debts that the widow owns Shee is in= =Debted as to Ellis Cook 8 £ in money: To Henry Peirson 8 or 9 pounds by his owne accompt as hee claimes, And Severall book= accompts Not yet pused exactly.

A Coppy of this taken this 11th Day of March 1677/8 to bee entered in the Office of Records

Matthias Nicolls, Secr – :

A true Coppy p me Henry Peirson Cleark. //

Widow Sarah Cooper is by this Court admitted to Administer upon all ye Estate of her husband Deceased, Shee and her Sonne John Giveing in theire Bond according to Law for ye Courts Security: And Shee thereupon to have lett:rs of Administration

The peticon of Mr: Joseph ffordham being Considered by this Court: The Court Doth adjudg that the Agreemt men= =tioned in ye Sd Peticon, made mutually between ye peticoners mother (m:ris Elizabeth ffordham) and the peticoner, together with the rest of ye relations con= =cerned, touching the Devission of ye Estate of Mr: Robert ffordham deceased is to stand, and is by this Court allowed of. And alsoe this Court Doth admit ye Sd Mrs: Elizabeth ffordham, and her Sonne Mr Joseph ffordham to bee lawful Executors or Administrators, of the Said estate, And they are to Doe & Pforme ac= =cording to ye Said Agreement, and what is re= =quired by the law in Such cases to bee observed.//

Southampton October the 26th: 1674

An Inventory of the Estate of Mr: Robert ffordham lately Deceased: as followeth:

		£	s	d
By:	howseing and land with the devissions appertaineing thereunto is apprized at	1164	–	–
by	pt of a Catch	30	–	–
by	books 53 £-7s-6d by hay & corne 80 £-7s-6d is:	133	15	–
by	a bed and furniture	12	–	–
by	3 wool beds wth Sheets & blankets to them	11	–	–
by	a fether bed and boulster pillow & Sheets	8	–	–
by	a Coverled & home made rugg	3	10	–
by	a paire of Sheets & 5 yrds of home Spun cloth	2	10	–
by	3 yrds of home Spun cloth & a pr of sheets	1	12	–
by	a Coverled & a bed tick with 2 bits of ye Same and Carpet	5	5	–
by	14 yrds of home Spun & a peece of fustin ticking	4	6	–
by	2 peices and a remnant of linen	9	15	–
by	Some Small remnants of cloth & Stuff	2	6	–
by	a trunck & Cubord & a Set of old Curtaines	13	10	–
by				

	£	s	d
By 2 pr of Sheets & a Single Sheet	2	10	–
by 13 yrds ½ of Duffles	6	15	–
by 5 quoshens & remnant of home Spun cloth	1	15	–
by cheese. cob Iron & tongs & fire shovell	12	17	–
by 2 leather chaires & 2 Stooles & 15 yrds of osunbrigs	4	5	–
by Mr: ffordhams wearing clothes	6	6	–
by 5 chests linen yarne & oatmeale wth other lumber	4	15	–
by hopps and old lether Skins	3	10	–
by 9 lether Skins & an Indian bagg & peaz with lumber & a Still	3	15	–
by feathers and Candles & 4 barlls of Salt	6	19	–
by Some other Lumber & 2 pr of Sheets	2	15	–
by pewter. 2 Cettles & two guns	15	15	–
by 3 old Cettles & 2 skellets & 4 Iron potts and two Iron kettls	7	8	–
by 2 tramells . 4 pr of pothooks. Spit dripping=pan. Cob Irons	3	5	–
by a Skimer, a pewter Dish a peele & 2 barells of porke	6	14	–
by 2 pailes Dishes cheese fatts & a can	1	–	–
by a frying pan, churne and fan, brass morter & pestle	1	6	–
by tallow & Suet. a pt of a hogshead of Sugar & lumber	12	–	–
by a Sadle 5 Shovells & cream pots & trays w:th other lumb:r	3	–	–
by a Cettle tunell tramell Smoothing Iron & tongs	1	17	–
by a lanthorne Stillyards & chest with Some Small things in it	2	–	–
by 2 Chests and a Jugg	–	15	–
by Gold and Silver money	13	14	–
by a Cubbord a box 5 chaires & a table	2	–	–
by a lookingglass 2 brushes, bellowes & howre glass	–	12	–
by 2 payre of hollon Sheets 5 table cloths & pillowbears	7	–	–
by plate 7£ by Scales & weights & a bottle 24s	8	4	–
by 2 ploughs. cart. & harow, & 4 Chaines	8	–	–
by axes wedges, rings, Shovells a Spade, mattuk, howes & sieths	3	10	–
by 7 Sickles. 3 yoaks. 4 forks	1	13	–
by two old Swords and a payre of bandileers	1	10	–
by Suger, warming pan close=Stoole Some Sower wine and other things	7	–	–
by woolen yarne a basket of flax, bags & old bedsteds	3	14	–
by a grindstone & pipe staves and sheeps wool	30	2	–
by 567 foot of board & backen	4	5	–
by 6 payre of shoes, & 1 old share & 9 hives of bees	11	5	–
by a dozen of Spoones and trenchers	–	8	–
by horse kinde 113 £ by Swine 15 £	128	–	–
by 5 oxen. and 9 yearling cattell	109	–	–
by eight 2 year old cattell. and 7 fowre year olds	48	–	–
by five 3 year olds and 2 two year olds and fourteene Cowes	83	–	–
by 9 cowes & a bull	13	–	–
by 260 Sheep	91	–	–
by a Servant Neigre	40	–	–
by			

			£	s	d
By	one Neigro boy 10 £ by one English boy 10 £		20	-	-
by	one English boy more		10	-	-
by	book Debts and rates		200	-	-
by	a Jak		2	-	-
		in all:	2349	-02	-00
	Debts and charge being Subtracted)		£	s	d
	the whole is)		2052	-05	-00

Apprized by us whose names are here under written. /

John Howell
John Jessupp
John Howell Junr:

All goods and chattells and Estate
whatsoever was apprized
except the phisick -

And Mr: Joseph ffordham was Sworne
in Court to the truth of this Inventory.

A true Coppy taken of that w:ch was transcribed by the -
Cleark of the Writs in the yeare 1674: viz:t of ye Inventory:
and Recorded p me Henry Peirson Cleark of ye Sessions

At a Court of Sessions held March 6th: 7th: &c: 1677/8
The will of Josuah Garlick of Easthampton Deceased being presented to this Court, But Since it could not bee proved, by reason the witneses to the Sd will were absent, Soe that the business could not be settled; The Court Doth adjudg and Order That when the Sd will is proved by the testimony of the witnesses before any of the Justices of the peace, The Inventory of the estate Duely made, And Bond given to Save the Court harmeless, Then Letters of administration or executrship Shall bee given unto Elizabeth ye widow or relict of the Sd Josuah Deceased according as the value of the Sd estate by the Inventory re= =quires, The Apprizers of the Sd Estate to bee those that made the list of the pticulers thereof and Signed it. Mr: Justice Backer to Administer ye oath to them, and to take the oversight of this matter.

August the 24th: 1677.
The last Will and Testament of Joshua Garlick - Junr: ffirst I doe give my body to the Dust, and my Soule to god that gave it. & my estate as followeth
2ly- I doe leave my home lott being twelvve accres of Land and the Mill to my wifes use untill my Sonne Joshua come to bee twenty one yeares old. And then hee is to have the Mill. And on - thair comeing to bee twenty one yeares of age, I

doe

Doe give them towe thirds of the home lott to bee equally devided
and my wife the other third: And if either of the boyes dye
3ly- before 21 yrs: the other is injoy his part: Thirdly I doe
give my Sonne John five accres and half of land lying be yond
the Indian well, and three accres of medow at Accoboneck:
4ly- I give my Sonne John one towe year old horse: and my
daughter Hanah one mare:
5ly- I Doe give my tooles to my Sons Joshua & John
equally to bee Devided between them, when they are
capable to use them.
6ly- I Doe give my Sheep to my Daughter Elizabeth.
Lastly- I Doe leave the rest of my estate, not above mentioned
to my wife Elizabeths Disspose: Capt Talmage
Mr: John Mulford Overseers:

Witnesses I G

John Miller
Samuell Mulford

By Order from the Court of Sessions
held at Southampton ye 6.7.8, of
this Instant this will attested be=
=fore mee this 16th: of march 1677/8
Tho: Backer Justice of ye peace.

The last Will and Testament of Joshua Garlick Junr:
ffirst I doe give my body to the Dust, and my Soule to God yt
gave it. And my Estate as followeth:
2ly- I doe leave my home lott being twelve accres of Land
and the Mill to my wifes use untill my Sonne Josuah
come to bee twenty one yeares old, and then hee is to
have the Mill, and at thair comeing to bee twenty one
yeares ould I Doe give them towe thirds of the home lott
to bee equally Devided, and my wife the other third.
And if aither of the boyes Dye before hee is twenty one
yeares old, then the other is injoy his parte.
3ly- I Doe give my Sonne John five accres and half of land
lying beyond the Indian Well, & three accres of -
meadow at Accaboneck.
4ly- I give my Sonne John, one towe year old horse,
And my Daughter Hannah one Mare.
5ly- I Doe Give My tooles to my Sonnes Joshua & John
equally to bee Devided betweene them when when
they are capable to use them.
6ly- I Doe give my Sheep to my Daughter Elizabeth:
Lastly: I Doe leave the remainder of my estate, not above men=
=tioned to my wife Elizabeths Disspose: Capt: Talmage
Mr: John Mulford, and Samuell Mulford Overseers of
the will: Whereas the will above written is
enterlined and Some is put out, this above written below
the Seale is the true intent of the will above: by mee
Samuell Mulford:

A true Inventory of the Estate of Joshua Garlick
Deceased, being apprized by us underwritten
May 31th: 1678.

		£	s	d
Imprs:	The dwelling howse & land belonging to him	35	–	–
2ly–	the Wind mill	30	–	–
3–	his horse flesh	5	–	–
4–	3 Small cattell 4 £ 10s 4 Sheep 20s	5	10	–
	two Swine 20s ye beds and beding 7 £ 10s	8	10	–
	the brass and pewter 30s	1	10	–
	Iron ware in the howse	2	–	–
	1 gun and Sword 20s: wooden ware in ye howse 20s:	2	–	–
	a bible 6s. ye Joyners Tooles 15s	1	1	–
	4 turning tooles 4s & ye Coopers tooles 15s	–	19	–
	the Carpenters tooles. & 1 Spade & stubing hough	3	16	–
		95	-06	-00

The above written Estate is prized under oath by us

(John Stretton
(Thomas Chatfeild
(Jeremiah Conckling
(Benjamine Conckling
(Benjamine Osburne

The widow Garlick Doth Say that shee is indebted about 45 £ of this Estate. //

A true Coppy p me
Henry Peirson § Cleark &c

This was finished at the Court held in June 1678

At ye Court of Sessions held at Southampton By his Ma:ties Authoritie the 5th: 6th &c Dayes of March 1678/9:
The Will and Testament of Ellis Cook Deceased is proved by ye Testimony of the three Witnesses Namely Henry Peirson: Tho: Diment and Georg Harris whoe were Sworne in Court: And Martha the widow or relict of the Said Ellis Cook is admitted Sole Executrix of the Sd Will and testam:t upon this terme and Condition, that Shee pforme what by ye Sd will is required and alsoe give in Sufficient Bond for Security: concerning those Children of hers, which were borne Since the makeing of the Sd Will, and have Noe portion allowed them therein That they Shall have truely paid unto each of them the full Summe of fourty poundes, by her the Sd Martha Cook (now Executrix) when, or as they the Sd Children or any of them shall marry, or at farthest as they come to bee twenty one yeares of age. Alsoe shee is to Doe and pforme all things ^ respecting the Said will that the Law of this Governmt requires of – – Executors: And the Court Doth aprove of Thomas Cooper and Job Saire (insted of John Cooper deceased) to bee Supervisors:

In

In the name of God Amen
The last Will and Testament of Ellis Cook
Made this 5th: of Sepb:r Anno 1663.

I Ellis Cook of Southampton being by Gods providence Sick and
weak in body, But in pfect memory doe make this my -
last Will and Testament as followeth:
1 - I doe Comit my Soule unto the hand of Almighty god yt gave it &c:
2 - I Give and Bequeath unto my Sonne John Cook one -
feather bed and furniture thereunto; my owne wear=
=ing apparell; My Carpenters tooles; one mare; and
two Cowes. All to bee Delivered unto him when hee is
at the age of one and twenty yeares: And if hee behave
himself well to his Mother, and live Civilly in con=
=versation in the Judgment of my friends whome I
make Overseers of this my will, then I give unto him
more, either my howseing and Land at Meacocks, or
my howseing and accomodation at the Towne afforesd:
which may bee most meet in the Judgment of my
Wife: with this proviso, That what Land shall bee
Soe Dissposed of, unto him my Sd Sonne, hee shall not
make Sale thereof, or any pt thereof without the
Consent of the Sd Overseers, or Some whome they
shall appoynt and Authorise in theire sted. - - -
3: I Give and bequeath to my Daughter Martha thirty
poundes, and one feather bed w:th furniture thereto. - -
4- I Bequeath unto my Sonne Ellis the other pt of my
land or accomodations Which shall bee undissposed
of by the abovesaid, to enjoy the Same after my wife
her Decease, if hee bee at the age of one & twenty
yeares. But hee shall not Disspose of any pt thereof
without consent of the Sd Overseers or those they
Shall appoynt in theire sted. Alsoe I give unto him
fifty poundes, to bee paid unto him when hee is one
5 - and twenty yeares of age. I Give and bequeath unto
my Daughter Elizabeth thirty poundes and one fether
6 - bed with furniture thereunto. I Give & bequeath
unto my Daughter Mary thirty poundes, and alsoe
I give unto her one feather bed if my wife can Spare
it, if not then then tenn poundes insted thereof: All my
Sd Daughters to have theire Sd portions paid unto
them when they marry, or at the age of twenty one
yeares pticulerly which shall bee first: And if
any of my Sd Children die before they receive theire
Sd portions, My Will is that then my wife disspose

that

that unto the rest that Survive as shee shall see occation.

7 - Moreover if my wife bee with Childe, and that it live, I doe Give and Bequeath unto it fourtie poundes to be paid as unto my other Children in respect of maner & time as afforesaid. - - -

8 - I give unto my Servant Thomas Stevens one heifer of about one yeare old to bee Delivered unto him at the expiration of his Apprentisship - provided hee carry himself as hee ought in his place dureing his time of Service &c: - - -

9 - I doe make my wife Martha my lawfull execu[trix] of this my Will and testament. And my Brother[s] John Cooper and Thomas Cooper Overseers thereof And soe I commit my Body (in Gods appoynted time) to bee decently buried in the earth from which at first it was taken: Witnes my hand the Day & yeare first above written.

Ellis ⌐ Cook

In presence of us
witnesses
Henry Peirson §
Thomas Diment
Georg ŀ Harris
his marke

A true Coppy of the very Originall
p me Henry Peirson Cleark

An Inventory of the Estate of the late deceased Ellis Cook of Southampton Apprized this 26th of ffebruary 1678/9 as followeth

		£	s	d
Imprs:	the ould home Closease that is Judged twenty acres more or less with the howseing upon it apprized at)	230	-	-
Item:	the little Close next Arthar Howell	21	-	-
It:	the two former Devissions by estimation forty five acres)	120	-	-
It:	250£ Commonage with twenty acres already laid out)	80	-	-
It:	land at the Towne: the home lott wth the land in the plaines & ye meadow wherever)	100	-	-
It:	4 ould Oxen & 4 younger	54	-	-
It:	11 cowes	47	-	-
It:	6 3 year ould cattell and a bull at	22	-	-
It:				

It:	8, two yeares ould	18	-	-
It:	11 yearlings	18	10	-
It:	30 young Swine and shoats at	30	-	-
It:	2 Riding horses	10	-	-
It:	13 horse kinde old and young	36	-	-
It:	1 yrd of broadcloth 26s 5 yrds of curtaine stuf 50s	3	16	-
It:	13 yrds of Callicoe 21s 8d 6 yrds of holland 48s	3	9	8
It:	3 Small remants of linen		13	-
It:	18 yrds ½ of Dowlis	3	14	-
It:	Pt of a peece of Camlet	5	10	-
It:	17 yrds of Searge	5	2	-
It:	5 yrds of Searge	1	10	-
It:	20 yrds of course kersey	7	-	-
It:	5 yrds of course half thick	1	2	6
It:	20 yrds of blew linen	2	10	-
It:	5 yrds of Swanskin	7	5	-
It:	stramering 3 yrds		3	-
It:	a remnant of Cambrick and a remnant of Silke	2	10	-
It:	a grosse of gimp buttons & some bengall	2	3	6
It:	a prcll of Silke galloone	1	7	-
It:	a prcell of colored threed . 2 peeces of filliting		13	6
It:	3 hatts & a peece of Manchestr	1	4	-
It:	a pr of wosted stockings		8	-
It:	2 Cushions 8s 4 pr of sheets 4L 10 s	4	18	-
It:	9 pr of sheets more	12	-	-
It:	2 duz of Napkins and 3 table cloaths	4	12	-
It:	12 pr of pillow beares	3	-	-
It:	a bed and what belongs to it	8	10	-
It:	another bed and furniture	9	-	-
It:	8 deal planks	1	-	-
It:	a little table and 2 deal planks	1	5	-
It:	another bed & furniture	9	5	-
It:	a bed & boulster and furniture	9	-	-
It:	2 other beds worse	11	15	-
It:	55£ of puter	7	6	8
It:	32 poringers	4	-	-
It:	2 Drinking potts and Salt Seller		15	-
It:	flagin, driping pan & some old puter & a new lanthor	1	9	-
It:	a pcell a brass kettles, wth tallow in one of them	16	10	-
It:	7 small Iron potts	7	-	-
It:	4 barrells of beef and one of porke	11	-	-
It:	a warp new, and hand warpe	5	-	-
It:	4 barrells & ½ of Mallasses	6	5	-
It:	a cask of Nayles	7	-	-
It:	8 Dear skins at	1	14	-
It:	a firkin of butter and a pcell of cheese	5	5	-
It:	43£ of Cotten wooll:	2	13	-
It:	a Chest and a pcell of glass	3	14	-
It:	a small quantity of wine	1	10	-
It:	Spanish Iron 249£	6	4	6
It:	a Castor hatt	1	15	-
It:				

		£	s	d
Item–	a parcell of Dale board	1	10	–
It:	a pcell of flax unswingled	1	10	–
It:	a pcell of lime & brick	1	2	–
It:	5 bushells of salt	1	–	–
It:	5 chests	2	–	–
It:	7 yrds of Duffles & a pcell of yarne	3	8	–
It:	2 chaines & a pcell of Iron Implemts	2	5	–
It:	Axes and augers & other Implemts	3	10	–
It:	Sawes and Cuttink knife	1	5	–
It:	4 Sacks & a sadle & pillion & bridles	1	15	–
It:	cloathes, wearing apparell	5	–	–
It:	49 sheep	20	–	–
It:	a gun. a warming pan & other Iron necessaries	3	–	–
It:	3 Sives. frying pan, lamp & other things	1	–	–
It:	cart tackling wth plough & Irons	2	–	–
It:	a pcell of Sugar. Jer of oyle w:th other things	3	–	–
It:	a 150 bushells wheat and 60 bushells of Indian korne w:th the hay)	62	–	–
It:	Shingles and other lumber	5	16	–
It:	powder and shot and pailes	1	14	6
It:	in Debts	32	–	–
It:	a bed & boulster and furniture	8	–	–
It:	A debt forgotten	30	–	–

John Howell
John Jessupp
Tho: Topping
Edmund Howell

A true Coppy p me
Henry Peirson Cleark &c /

The totall sume of the Inventory
Amounts to – 1154£–12 s–10 d
errours in summing up excepted. //

At the afforesaid Court of Sessions held March the 6th.7th.1678/9. The Will and testament of Samuell Cleark of the North Sea Deceased was prsented and proved by two of the witnesses to the Sd Will Namely Capt: John Howell & Mr. John Laughton whoe were sworne in Court, and witnessed to the reallity of ye Sd Will: where=uppon the Cort doth finde and adjudg that the Widow or relict of ye Sd Samuell together with her two Sonnes Samuell and Edmond are Joynt Executrs of the Sd Will: & are by the Court admitted soe to be to all Intents & purposes.

The Sd Will is as followeth:

In the Name of God Amen: I Samuell Cleark of South=hampton in the East Rideing of Yorksheire on Long Island being now in my pfect memory though weak in Body and

not

not knowing the time of my change, Doe Make this my last Will and testament, as ffolloweth: Imprs: I freely give and bequeath my Soule to God that gave it mee and my Body to the earth from whence it was first taken. And for my worly Estate I give as followeth: ffirst my will is that after mine and my wives Decease, That all my Land and Meadow bee equally Devided betweee my two Sonns Samuell and Edmond Cleark; Only what I have Given unto my Sonn Samuell by Deed of gift is to bee onderstood to bee pt. of his halfe of the Sd Land
my Sonne Samuell
and medow, only when they devide ^ is to have all my - whome lott and houseings and Orchards that is thereupon. and my Land called by the Name of whomses I Give unto my Sonn Edmond for his whome lott, And if my Sonn Edmond Settle heere, That then my Sonn Samuell Shall allow him towards his building either in worke or pay as will hire Such worke, the Sume of fifteen poundes And my Mill to bee Devided between the Said Edmond and Samuell: and for my other fifty poundes Commonage that is not given to my Sonn Samuell, I give it to my Sonn Edmond and his heyres. Secondly I give unto my Sonn Samuell a couple of steeres of three yeares old and the brown heifer of the Same age: Thirdly I give my Sonn Edmond a bead and beading, And to my - - Daughter Sarah a bead & beading. And all the rest of my howsehold goods, I leave it to the Dissposeing of my - wife, for her to give unto Edmond and Sarah as Shee shall See cause: And for my tooles, I give them to my two Sonns Samuell and Edmond to be equally Devided - betweene them: 4thly I give unto my Daughter Susanah a Sheep, and to my Daughter Mary a sheep, and to my Daughter Martha a sheep, and to my daughter Hanah a sheep; And to Sonne Edmond my black horse, and to my Daughter Sarah a three year old maare, and one Cow & heifer Which my wife Shall See cause to give: And for all the rest of my Cattell & horses and mares & sheep yt: are not already Dissposed of, I leave them all to my wife to Dispose of as Shee Shall See cause amongst her children, Namely Edmund and Sarah and the rest Lastly I make my wife My Sonn Samuell & Edmond Joyntly Executors of this my last will and Testament to See it fulfilled. In witnes whereof I have hereunto Set my hand and fixed my Seale this 11th Day of May 1675.

Samuell Clarke

Sighned and Sealed
in the presence of
John Howell
Charles Sturmy
John Laughton.

A true Coppy of the Originall
p me Henry Peirson Cleark

Southampton febr: 24 : 1678/9.

An Inventory and apprizement of the Estate of the late deceased Samuell Clarke of the North Sea: by us under written Chosen by the Justice & Constable & Overseers to that purpose.

			£	s	d
1 -	ffirstly the old howse, half ye barne and halfe the home=lott at	))	40	-	-
2 -	the Meadow adjudged at 14 accres at		30	-	-
3 -	at Cow=neck 16 accres of old land at		20	-	-
4 -	a home lott of 4 accres of land lying at Homeses at		6	-	-
5 -	at the clay pits 4½ accres of land 2 of Sowed with wheat	))	15	-	-
6 -	part of pcells of land lying neare ye Tow valued at 12 accres at	))	18	-	-
7 -	at Maicocks 1/3 of 20 accres and the hal of about 3 accres at	))	14	-	-
8 -	a 50 £ commonage at 20 £: and half of t Small peces of meadow of 4	))	24	-	-
9 -	2 old mares. 3 young ones & 1 poore old horse all		13	-	-
10 -	2 oxen at 12 £ 6 Steeres at 28 £ 6 Cowe two at 6 £ 4 two yrs old 8 £ 5 Cafs 5 £	))	83	-	-
11 -	12 Sheep at 7s p head		4	4	-
12 -	4 Swine		3	10	-
13 -	part of a carte plow Irons chaines and yoaks		4	15	-
14 -	all the Carpenters Tooles at		10	4	-
15 -	a Spade Stubing ho 1 gun . 1 Sord: 1 pr of Stiliards		2	6	-
16 -	one chespress & 1 Churn . & 2 brlls wth other lumb:r at		2	-	-
17 -	3 old brass Cettells and one Skellet		2	10	-
18 -	2 Small Iron potts 1 Small kettle & hangers & pothooks		2	-	-
19 -	for pewter Dishes and pes & basons & other old vessells		3	-	-
20 -	36 boshells		9	-	-
21 -	6 boshells of Indiam		-	15	-
22 -	10 boshells of oats		1	5	-
23 -	1 fether bed . rugg . bolster and pillow		7	-	-
24 -	5 yrds of Searg at 6s p yrd . 2 yrds of peniston at 4s-6d		1	19	-
25 -	by 5 worne Sheets at 8s p a Sheet		2	-	-
26 -	by 8 yrds of new linen		1	12	-
27 -	1 Chest at 16s. by 8£ of corse yarn at 18 d p £		1	8	-
28 -	by 8 old hogsheads at 3s p a pes		1	4	-
29 -	by 50 weight of tallow		1	5	-
30 -	by one blankit . 1 old fan . 4 old barlls. 1 old blankit		2	-	-
31 -	by 6 old baggs and one old rope		1	10	-
32 -	by one bed at 50s by 6£ of linen yarn at 18d: p £		2	19	-
33 -	by one paire of wooll Cards 1 warming and Sadle and bridle	))	-	16	-
34 -	By two Beds at 8 £ a ps:		16	-	-
35 -	By one chest: 3 Sheets and his wearing c two remnants of cloth	))	6	16	-
36 :-	By:				

			£	s	d
36	-	By one Cobard at 10s. 2 books at 15 s. 2 barlls of beef & porke and more 5 £)	6	5	-
37	-	by milk bouls, bottles and other lumber at one chest at)	2	-	-
38	-	by 3 old hatts 2 old Sickles. one chaire stooles and other lumber)	1	-	-
39	-	By the Sale of the water mill	20	-	-

Obadiah Rogers
John Jessop
Thomas Cooper
John Jagger

A true Coppy p me Henry Peirson Cleark:

	£	s	d
The Sume of the Inventory erors excepted in accompting)	384	-03	-00

At the afforesaid Court of Sessions held March ye 6th:7th:&c 1678/9
The Will and Testament of Thomas Halsey Deceased is presented: And the truth and reality thereof proved by the testimony of one of the witnesses to the Sd Will Namely John Else whoe was Sworne in Court, The other witnes to the Sd Will namely Richard Barret, being Deceased: And the Court Doth finde (according to the Said Will) & adjudj Tho. Halsey, and Isaac Halsey to bee the lawfull - - Executors of the Said Will and Testam:t and are by the Court admitted Soe to bee Joyntly, They being to observe the rules and directions of the Law of this Governm:t and to pforme what in the Sd Will and testament is required.

The Sd Will is as followeth:

Southampton In Yorkesheere: ye 28 Day of June 1677
The last Will and Testament of Thomas Halsey Senr: being in a right minde and Sound Judgment is as followeth.

Imprs- I give and bequeath my Soule to god that gave it and my body I bequeath to the Earth Decently to bee buried. And my woorly goods as foloeth

2ly- I Doe give unto my wife one woolan Wheele: & one linan Wheele, and my little Iron poot, and a yelow rugg, and one white Duch Blanket, and foore bushells of wheat to bee paid yearly as long as Shee liveth: the first to bee paid within one Moonth, and foore ewe Sheep

3ly- I Doe give and bequeath unto my Sonne Thomas my howse & howseing and home lott with all the appurtinances there unto belonging and ye Beech loot, & the littel plaine Clooase, and the litel Clooase

one

one the Southside of Ms: Rainers Comonly called Trouble=
=some, & the Cloase at ye Millneck Comonly knowne
by the Name of Peeters Clooase: And I Doe give
to my Sonn Thomas the loot that I had this last
Devission at Meecokes: & the table in the parler, &
the fife Joynt Stooles: & the Bedsted & Curtins in
the poorch Chamber. -

4ly I Doe give and bequeath unto my Sonn Isaack my
Cloas at the head of the creeke: & five Eakers - -
ajoyning thereunto: & five Eakers in the greet plain
in the tenn Eaker Lotts: and three Eakers lying
at the Toune ponnd: & tenn Eakers in the ox=
paster: And I doe give unto my Sonn Isaack
the ginn loot with foore Eakers & a halfe in ye litel
plaine: And I doe give unto my Soon Isaack of the
next Devison twenty Eakers, and hee is to have his
Coyse out of my three hundred in lue of the land
at Sagaponack: and the remainder of all Devisons
whatsoever hereafter thay are to devide it equally
betwixt them all three, & the rest of that devision
hee is to have his equall part with Thomas & Danell
and hoog Neck is to bee devided betwixt them E=
=qually also: And I doe give unto my Sonn Isaack
that Loot of meedo that is in Seeboonack one the
South Side: & one Eaker in Halseyes Neck, and halfe ye
meedow on the South Beech, and the other halfe to Danell

6ly- I Doe give and bequeath unto my Soone Danel one lot
of meedoe lying one the North Side of Seeboneck, and
the home loot that I booht of Mr: Smith, and my loot
at Sagabonack: & too Eakers in the litel plaines, tha[t]
is the Estermost too Eakers that I have there: And
I Doe give Danel one horse one mare & too oxen: -

7ly- I Doe give & bequeth unto my Daughter Elizabeth
the wife of Richard Howell twenty pound to bee payed
in goods or Cattell according as too men Sall pries them

8ly- I Doe order that my three Soones Shall Devide
all Quagonantuck, and all the North Side towards
Southhold and all hoog Neck betwixt them equally.
I Doe Will and appoynt my Soones Thomas and
Isaack to bee the Exseketors of this my last Will &
Testament to See that it bee Justly and truly pformed
And what shall remaine of the Estat not here menshoned
in my Will, that they devide it equally betweene them my two
Exseketors: In Witnes where I have heere unto Set My -
hand the Day & yeere before mentioned

In the presence of us — Thomas Halsey

Ri: Barret — A true Coppy of the Originall.

John Else — p me Henry Peirson Cleark:

Southampton

Southampton September the 2th: 1678.
An Inventory of the Estate goods and Chattells of the late Deceased Thomas Halsey as followeth:

			£	s	d
Impr	4 Miltch Cowes at		19	–	–
Item:	the howseing and home lott		120	–	–
It–	the Beach lott 18 accres more or less		30	–	–
It–	the little plaine Close at		35	–	–
It–	Troublesome 3 accres within fence		15	–	–
It–	20 accres at Kellyes pond		20	–	–
It–	20 accres of the next devission and 100 £ Comonage after the Devission bee laid out & finished	))	20	–	–
It–	the close caled the head of the Creek 15 accres		40	–	–
It–	at the tenn accre lot 5 accres		10	–	–
It–	ye three accre lot by the pond		15	–	–
It–	10 accres in the ox pasture		20	–	–
It–	the land at the Jinn and the little plaine		20	–	–
It–	40 accres in the next Devission with a 100 £ Comonage after the Sd Devission bee laid out	))	45	–	–
It–	2 lotts of Meadow at Sebonack, and a lott upon – beach w:th an accre in Halseyes Neck & Quaquanantuck	))	5	–	–
It–	Smiths Lott		25	–	–
It–	20 accres at Sagaponack wth 20 accres more in this next devission, wth a 100 £ Commonage after this – Devission bee finished	)))	45	–	–
It–	the Close called Peters		40	–	–
It–	a table and 5 Joyne Stooles		1	10	–
It–	an ould gun		1	–	–
It–	13 paire of Sheets that are worne		18	–	–
It–	2 Doz: of Napkins		1	15	–
It–	4 table cloathes & 3 paire of pillow beares		2	15	–
It–	an ould featherbed, bolster & 3 pillowes		4	10	–
It–	a Coverlid and 4 ould blanckets		2	5	–
It–	a paire of Curtaines and valaines		2	–	–
It–	a feather bed Coverlid and bolster		5	–	–
It–	1 blanket and Coverlid		1	–	–
It–	wearing Cloathes		4	–	–
It–	Curtaines vallaines & 2 bedsteds		1	10	–
It–	2 ould Chests		–	6	8
It–	peuter dishes and other Small things		5	12	6
It–	a remnant of Duffles a coverlid & ould blancket		2	15	–
It–	2 brass kettles a brass pot and skillet		3	10	–
It–	on Iron pott and a little Iron kettle		1	10	–
It–	2 tramells an Iron Morter a Spit, & other things		1	–	–
It–	table . pte of a barell of mallasses & other lumber		5	–	–
It–	3 Shoats 30s 5 Steeres 25 £ 2 Cowes 7 £		33	10	–
It–	4: 3 year olds 12 £. 4: 2 year olds 10 £ 3 yearlings 6£		28	–	–
It–	5 Sheep 30s. 2 horses & 2 mares & 1 yearling 14 £:10s		16	–	–
	6 load of hay		6	–	–
			672	–09	–02

Apprized by us, appoynted By two Justices of the peace vizt: Mr Arnold and Mr: John Topping – –

John Howell
John Jessupp
Joseph Rayner
Thomas Topping

A true Coppy p me
Henry Peirson Cleark &c:

Dated this 6th Day of March 1678/9 at Southampton

Whereas I Benjamine Horton of Southhold have greatly Sclandered and reproached Capt: John Youngs & Mr: Joshua Hobart Minister of Said Southhold in affirming & Declarring before Mr: Justice Arnold and others, That theire Depo= =sition as Evidence, in a case Depending in this Court Be =tweene John Conckling and my Self, was a libell, there= =by aspersing these psons as Libellers, and be punishable by law: ffor which Notorious Sclander and abuse they have taken out process against mee in theire legall vin= =dication: Yet findeing them willing to pass it by; upon my acknowledgment of my fault herein in open court which fault I doe now Desire this worp:l Court and all psons here present to take Notice off. That I Doe here voluntarily owne and acknowledg the Said Sclanderous words, And that I have thereby greatly wronged them both, of whome I here crave pardon. And that Said action may not be prosecutrd against mee: And what charge Shall come hereby, I Doe promise to pay forthwith to content and alsoe I Desire that this my acknowledgmt may bee recorded as Conviction and Evidence against mee if I offend them at any time hereafter in this thing, which if I shall Doe: that - then they may prosecute mee as the law Inables them for this my Sclander, As if this acknowledgment had not been made. Witness my hand &c:

Testr: Jos: Hobart. Benjamen Horton.//

A true Coppy of ye Originall p me Henry Peirson Cleark and ye Sd Acknowledgmt was read and made in open Court of Sessions held Sd 6th: m:rch: 1678/9

Southampton this 16th Day of May 1679.

Whereas Martha Cook the widow or relict of Ellis Cook Deceased is admitted by the Court of Sessions held last March to bee Executrix of the Will and Testament of her Said husband, By vertue, or occation whereof Shee be =comes Engaged to pay unto her children theire distinct, and Severall portions according to the Said Will: Whereupon this Day, the Sd Martha as Ad= =ministratrix Doth make over Designe pay and Deliver unto her eldest Sonne John Cook, ye neck of land lying on the East Side of the Creek wch is East ward of her now Dwelling howse at Mecock which Neck lyeth by Estimation for thirty - accres; bee the Same more or less: And the litle Closease accompted fowrteene Accres bee

the

the Same more or less, lying and being at the Said
Meacocks, betweene the two wester more closes
belonging to Arthar Howell: And twenty accres
of land lying on the west Side of the hollow, that
comes downe to Mr: ffordhams close at Meacocks
The land of Arthar Howell lying on the South -
Side thereof; Alsoe in like manner shee ye Sd:
Martha Doth make over unto him her Said Sonne
John tenn accres of land more, In or belonging
unto this present Devission, the Same to bee
disspposed unto him the Said John Cook, as shall bee found
most Suitable and convenient for him and his brother
or whoe is to have it hereafter, by the Judgment of
the Overseers of the Sd Will, Namely Thomas Cooper
and Job Sayre; Alsoe a fifty poundes Comonage
with the benifits and privilidges thereof for time
future after this Devission of land before Mentioned
is finished: All wch lands and Commonage Shee the
Said Martha Doth give or pay or Designe unto her
Sd Sonne John Cook his heyres Executors, Administratrs
and Assignes forever; To have & to hold and
quietly to possess and enjoy the Same & every pt
thereof quietly ffor all, or notwithstanding any
thing Shee the Sd Martha or any one in her name
Shall Doe or cause to bee Done; as his full pro=
=portion of land and good allowance out of ye
lands, Now in her hands which her Said husband
dyed Seized off. And hee the Sd John Cook Doth
acknowledg to receive the Sd lands and Commage of
his Sd Mother as being therewith fully Satisfyed
and contented, as his full portion, or proportion of
land, out of his Said Deceased father's Estate of land
And this is, and is to bee accompted the very full
end, & ulimate Agreem:t about the Said matter be=
=tweene them the Sd Martha Cook, and her Sonne
John Cook: The which by mutuall agreemt alsoe, they
committ to Record the Day and yeare first above
or before written:

At a Court of Sessions held at Southhold By his
Ma:ties Authority &c: the 3.4.5. Dayes of June 1679.

The last Will and Testament of Thomas Hilton of Seatauk was presented and the proof thereof accepted by ye Co:rt And the Court Doth finde and adjudg according to ye Said Will, Zachery Haukins of ye Sd Seatauk (and upon his request) to bee Sole and lawfull Executor of all the Estate of him the Sd Thomas Hilton deceased, vizt: both that Small matter (as by ye Inventory) is in hand, and what= =soever else any maner of way, any where belongeth unto him the Sd Thomas Hilton, or which may belong unto him And the Co:rt Doth appoynt him the Said Zachery - - Haukins to have letters of Executorship given unto him:

A Certificate of the Sickness and death of Thomas Hilton lately deceased at Setawcott ^ as alsoe of his last will and testament humbly represented to the next Court of Sessions to be holden for the East Riding on Long Island as followeth: The Sd Thomas Hilton arived att Seatawcet in winter last, Being imployed as Ship Carpenter & Marriner, by one Mr: Blagg of New Yorke, but was left Sick at thehowse of Zechary - Hawkins in the Towne abovesaid and there remained till his death except dureing a Journey to and from New =Yorke: When at length lying under a constant langwish =ment, But very sound in his understanding and memory, hee expressed this his last Will and testament, before us - whose names are Subscribed:. I apprehend my Death - Drawing on, and noe care for this world, that lyes neere my heart, as the makeing amends for the long charge and trouble I have brought upon this family - - meaning Zechary Hawkins and his wife, whoe hee Said had done by him more like a father and mother then Strangers in a Strang land, Therefore (Said hee) I will and bequeath all I have to ym: whether here or else= =where, And to that end desire that Mr: Blagg aforsd: may bee impowered by letters of Attorney to require & recover all that belongs to mee in virginia for the use of the Sd Zechary or his Assignes: Complaineing that his abillity was noe more to make ym amends according to his Desire.

Signed for information of
Authority. June 2: 1679
by Nathaniell Brewster
John Biggs
the marke of P peter ffloyd

Sworne to before mee
this 2th: of June 1679
Richard Wodhull.

A true Coppy p me Henry Peirson Cleark &c:

the Inventory:

The Inventory of the goods of Thomas Hilton Deceased
and taken the next morning after buered, hee dieing
in Zakery Hawkins howse of Brookhaven upon Long
Island.

Imprs: two hatts and a cap
a Straght bodycoat . a wascoat . 2 pr of ould drawers
one pr of ould briches . a ould coete
two ould neckcloths . & a Sash . & 2 pr of Shoose
2 pr of wodmill Stockings . a Small discrien glass
a Chest . & a payre of ould gloves
two Combes, and a case one combe
a broad ax . a broad chissell . a plaine Iron
a glass bottle

This Invetery taken before us
Richard ffloyd Constable
John Geners)
John Tooke) Overseers:

May the 7th:1679 . The goods of Thomas Hilton were prised
by John Smith: Petter ffloyd: Simon Alefax
at thirty five shillings. before mee
Richard ffloyd Constable
By Justice Wodhulls order

A true Coppy of the Inventory and apprizement
p me Henry Peirson Cleark.//

At the fore Said Court June 3.4.5. 1679.
John Jenners of Seatauk Deceased, his Will and testament is
produced & presented in Court . his Inventory sworne to by
the apprizers namely Richard Wareing & Thomas Thorpe.
And the Court Doth finde and adjudg by the Sd Will that
the widow or relict of the Sd John Jenners, and his Sonne Thomas
Jenners are lawfull Executors of the Sd Will and are by
the Court admitted Soe to bee, to all Intents & purposes
when the Reverend Mr: Nathaniell Brewster and
his wife, ye Witnesses to the Sd Will (and whoe at this
Court are not present) have given theire oaths before
any of the Justices of the peace for this East Riding
for Confirmation of the truth of the Said will.
And when Certificate is sent into the hand of ye Cleark
of ye Sessions under the hand of the Sd Justice of the peace
that Soe Administers the oath unto the Sd Witnesses
Then The Cleark is to enter upon Record That the Said
Widow and her Sonne Thomas are admitted as Lawfull ex=
=ecutors of the Said Will and testament.

In

In the name of God Amen: I John Jenners of Brookhaven -
Alias Seataukcott, on Long Island being weak in Body but
Sound in minde & memory, Do ordaine and make this my
last Will & Testament as followeth: ffirst I bequeath my
Soule into the hand of God my Creator, in the hope of Ever=
=lasting life by the merits of Jesus Christ my Redeemer
And for my Worldly goods I will and bequeath as followes
ffirst I give and bequeath unto my faithfull well be=
=loved wife Alice Jenners my howse and all my whole
accomodation of Land in the Said Towne to have & to -
hold (wth all the previlidg thereto belonging dureing
the tearme of her Naturall life: And alsoe my Will
and meaning is, that in case my Sd wife Shall Judg it -
fitting hereafter, Shee may Disspose, make Conveighance
or allienate all my Said accomodation at her Discretion
Yet Notwithstanding the premises, It is my Desire and
Intention That my Children may hereby Stand the more
oblidged to carry themselves, Dutifully to theire mother
And that in theire Soe doeing Shee may bee induced of her
motherly affection to preserve and Manage the Said Ac
=comodation for theire future good. That is to Say, that
my three Sonnes Thomas, John, & Joseph may after their
mothers decease, have and enjoy the Sd accomodation equally
shared amongst them, for them and theire heyres for ever
And for prevention of strife in laying out the Said Shares
I appoynt the Same to bee equally devided into three portions
by Indifferent psons chosen by my three Sonnes aforesd
provided and alwayes to bee remembered that the Sum of
twenty poundes shall bee paid unto my daughter Elizabeth
Jenners within two yeares after her mothers decease and
for that end I Will and Ordaine by these prsents that
my said howse and land Shall remaine engaged by way
of Security. Moreover it is my will and meaning that in
case either of my Sonnes Should Dept this life under age
then his portion of my Said Lands shall bee equally -
Shared betwixt the Survivers: Alsoe I give and bequeath
unto my Sonnes Thomas and John, each of them one Cow
to bee delivered Within two yeares after my decease
as alsoe one Mare to each of them within the Sd tearm
and to my Sonne Joseph I give my horse called Button
to bee delivered at the time of my Decease, and one mare
three yeares after. Alsoe my Sorrell Mare I bequeath
to my daughter Elizabeth to bee delivered two yeares
after my decease, And the encrease of the Said mare yt
may arize in the meantime. Moreover I give & be=
=queath unto my daughter Mary Now the wife of William
Satterly of the Towne of Seatawcott one Cow of fowre
yeare old, to bee Delivered two yeares after my decease - -
ffinally

ffinally Whatsoever remaines of my estate beside ye pre=
=mises, whether in the Towne aforesaid or else where I give
and bequeath to my beloved wife aforesaid towards ye pay=
=ment of my debts and the future Support of her life; onely
excepted, Notwithstanding any thing herein before espressed
That my will and meaning is, That whatsoever rights or
priviledg Shall bee found Due to mee in the Plantation
of Stratford in the Colloney of Hartford, I give and be
=queath the Same to bee equally Devided betwixt my Sd
wife and my Son John Jenners: As alsoe that if either
of my Sonnes should hereafter make Sale of his Share of
the Land herein bequeathed. That Such Sale shall be first
tendred to one of my other Sonnes and not Sould to any
other without both the brothers (if living at the time) re=
=fuse the Same. And of this my last will and testament
I Ordaine and make my Sd wife and my Sonne Thomas
my true and lawfull Executors: As witnes my hand &
Seale this Seventh Day of March in the yeare 1674

John I Jenners
his mark

Memorandum that before ye Signing
& Sealing hereof two words were
blotted out of the Eight line of the
former page. and one word out of
the twenty Sixth line

Witnesses
Nathaniell Brewster
Sarah Brewster

A true Coppy of the originall
p me Henry Peirson Cleark:

The prisement of the Inventory of John Jenners
Senr: Deceased the 10th: of may 1679:

	£	s	d
The howse and accomodations	100	-	-
five oxen at	25	-	-
three cowes at	10	10	-
won tu year ould 30s: won yearling 16s	2	6	-
5 horse kinde	15	-	-
7 Swine	8	-	-
his wearing close	5	-	-
Tooe beads with furniture	12	-	-
Tooe Iyron potes	1	10	-
won brass Cettell	-	10	-
to pewter	2	-	-
Tooe Chistes	-	10	-
won bibell	-	15	-
Cart and plows wth all tacklin	10	-	-
axes and hoes and other ware	1	12	-
woden	194	13	-

	£	s	d
Wooden ware belonging to the howse	1	–	–
the crop upon the ground	7	–	–
(	8	:00	:00
(brought from contra	194	:13	:00
A true prisemt of evantary is £:	202	:13	:00

his marke)
prised by us: Rich: R Wareing)
Thomas Tharpe)

At the Court of Sessions held at Southhold June the 5th: 1679. Richard Wareing and Tho: Tharpe the above apprizers, gave oath to ye above ap= =prizemt, according to the tenure of the oath of apprizers:

A true Coppy of the Originall, Recorded as before written.

p me Henry Peirson Cleark

Memorandum That the two witnesses to the foremen= =tioned Will & Testament of John Jenners Deceased Namely Nathaniell Brewster & Sarah Brewster have made oath to the truth & reallity of ye said Will Before Mr: Justice Wodhull at Brook= haven as appeares by his Subscription under ye Sd will, dated June the 20th : 1679. whereupon by the Courts order before recorded, they two psons - Namely the widow of ye Sd Deceased and his Sonne Thomas are admitted Joynt Executors of the Sd Will & Testament. //

At the Court of Sessions held at Southhold By his Ma:ties Authority the first. 2d & 3d dayes of June Anno Dom: 1680 The last Will and Testament of Mr: Barnabas Windes of Southhold in the East Rideing of Yorksheire upon Long Island, was presented. And ye Sd Will haveing been formerly proved By the testimony of Jacob Corey and Abraham Corey, at the Court of - Sessions held at Southampton March ye 4th: 1679/80: to ye Courts Satisfaction; here followeth a Coppy of the Sd Will & Testament: vizt:

Barnabas Windes of Southhold senerd In the - Jurydicktion of New Yorke being in parfet memo= =ry: macketh this my last will & testimony in manner as followeth: That is to Say I give unto my youngest Daughter Prudence Wyndes all my moveable goods within dores, Except those things w:ch I give unto my Sonne Samewell, That is one fflockbed and Boulster, on Coverlet and Blancket, with the rest of my waringe parrill, except my best hate and my best tropers Coote, which I give unto my Sonn Bar=

Barnabas Windes: I give alsoe unto my Daughter Prudence all my shepe, and all my Swyne: I give unto my Sonne Barnabas my Dwelling howse and Loate, withall the accomodations be= =longing thereunto, & goose Creek medow: & Cutchack, with one hundred accres more or less that lyeth at Quacs Neck, Joyneing to my Sonn Samewell; This I give to my Sonne Barnabas and his heyres forever, and this to possess within Six Monthes after my Decece: And all the rest of my Cattell I give unto all my Children alycke, equally devided; My Just Debts being paid:

Alsoe I Doe teastify By this - my hand that their is fowre Cow= =kinde that are my daughter Prudence Windes her owne to disspose of as she please: and I make my - daughter Prudence Windes my Sole Exsectetor of this my will. In witnes hereof I have Seat my hand
Dated this 23th: Day of November: 1675
Barnabas Windes

Witnes
Thomas Hutchinson
Jacob Core.

A true Coppy:

This Court before mentioned herein held June the first , 2d , & third dayes 1680. doe admitt the Sd Prudence (Now wife to John Goldsmith) to bee Sole and lawful Executrix of the Sd will & Testa= =ment of her father Sd Barnabas Windes, and - - doth grant unto her, to have lres of Administration or Executrixship: - - - - - -

Southhold the 10 day of December 1679

Whereas an Inventory of the goods & Estate of - Barnabas Wines late of Southhold Deceased, being taken by the Constable and Overseers of the Sd Towne, according to theire Estimation thereof amounted to the Sume of ffourty Six poundes Seaven shillings

A true Coppy:

Samuell Glover Const:
Abraham Corry
John Corwin - - - - - - - -

Memorandum: That upon the Backside of the last foremen= =tioned Coppy, In the Originall thereof, is endorced as followeth: At the Court of Sessions held at Southhold the 3: of June 1680. Samuell Glover being sworne saith that the Inventory of Barnabas Windes deceased, his Estate was - Committted unto his keeping, But hee can not finde it yet hee knowes that the Sume in all of the Sd Inventory was noe more but as is within Said fourty Six poundes & - Seaven Shillings : & the Depont saith he was Constable that yeare. a true Copy p Henry Peirson Cleark:

At a Court of Sessions held at Southhold
and begun the Second Day of June 1680.

The last Will and Testament of William ffancy of Seatauk Deceased w:ch was proved at the Court of - Sessions held March ye 8th 1677/78: was at this Court produced, and alsoe an Inventory of the Estate under the hands of two Apprizers, Namely Nathaniell Norton, and Wm: Jayne Sworne the 31th of may 1680 Before Mr: Justice Wodhull Justice of the peace At the request of the widow Katherine ffancy (expressed to this Court under her hand by Peter Whitteere) She the Sd Katherine is admitted by this Court, to all Intents and purposes Sole Execu= =trix of the Said Will, And Estate of her Said - Deceased husband: Shee being to pforme what an Executr ought to Doe, according to the lawes of this Governm:t in that case provided. /

Brookhaven June 17: 1675

I Wm: ffancey being very Aged, and a Cripple Doe make this my last Will and Testament. ffirst I bequeath my Soule to God in Jesus Christ, and my body to bee decently buried in the buriall place in Brookhaven: My Will and meaning is That my Sonne Samuell ffancey shall have half my ac =comodation, That is on halfe of my home lott and Seaven ackers in the ould feild, and one halfe of all the out land Devided and undevided, and one half of all my meadow at the ould mans, and all my pt of medow and upland in ye ould pur= =chase at the South; All this one halfe I bequeath to my Sonne Samuell ffancey after my Decease except onely all my meadow at Conscience I reserve wholly for my wife. All this I be= =queath to my Sonne Samuell upon Condition that is, my Sonne is not to Sell any pt or pcell of the Same, But my Will and meaning is That this land Shall bee for my Sonne Samuell and for his heyres for ever. Secondly I doe bequeath the other half of my accomodation and all my medow at Conscience to my beloved wife Katherine ffancey, my will and meaning is that my wife shall have the whole Dissposeing of all ye rest of my whole Estate within dores & without except twenty Shillings I bequeath to my Sonne Joseph ffancey. Alsoe my will and meaning is

that

that my Sonne William ffancey Shall receive his
posion after the Decease of my wife Katherine -
ffancey. I alsoe bequeath to my Daughter Hanah
ffancey too Cowes or tenn poundes to bee paid her
when Shee comes to age or marry. As for my Daugh=
=ter Rechell She hath received all her posion all=
=ready. I now being very weak in my - -
limes, yet thanks bee to god fresh in Sences and me=
=mory, Desireing that this being my last will and
testament may stand and bee brought forth to
light, when it please god to call mee; To his pro=
tection I Comit my poore Soule, and poore wife
and all my Children to the protection of ye Al=
=mighty God in Jesus Christ whose able to Save
all that come unto him. my desire is alsoe that
my Nebar widow Martha Smith Shall keep
this my last will as long as I live.

This will was made Signed - and delivered in the prsents of us Witnesses:
The marke of
Martha ꝭ Smith widow
John Thomas.

his
Wm: /\ ffancey
marke /

A true Coppy of ye Originall

Brookhaven Aprill ye 10th: 1677.

The Inventory of the goods and Estate of Wm: ffancey of the Sd Towne Deceased taken by the Constable and Overseers & apprized as followeth:

	£	s	d
Impr: an accomodation of land	60	–	–
three Cowes 12 £. one mare in ye woods 50s	14	10	–
7 Swine 4 £ - 3 blankets 28s. 1 ax 5s	5	13	–
1 iron wedg 3s. 1 chest 5s. an Iron pot 10s	–	18	–
2 Spinning wheeles 7s. 1 pewter plater 4s	–	11	–
1 bible 5s. an Iron Skellet 5s	–	10	–
1 paile 18d. 1 tub 18d. 1 Sive 18d	–	4	6
2 barells 6s. 1 broad how 4s	–	10	–
1 frying pan	–	3	6
	83	:00	:00

Nathaniell Norton)
& William Jayne) Sworne before me
Apprizers)

Richard Wodhull
the 31th of May 1680

A true Coppy of Sd Will & Inventory
p me Henry Peirson Cleark:

[This page is the last entry in the hand of Henry Pierson.
The handwriting on the following pages is that of John Howell Jr.]

Att a Court of Sessions held at Southampton
and Begune ye 2nd Day of March 1680/1

The last Will & Testament of Barnabas Horton of Southold Deceased was produced at this Court as also the Inventory under the hands of the Apprizers Namley John Corwin, Jacob Corey, Benja Youngs Att the Request of Mary the Widdow & Relict of the sd Barnabas deceased (presented to the Court by Mr Joshua Hobart under her hand) And the Evidences appearing & Sworne in Court the will was proved and the sd Mary Admitted Executrix to all Intents and Purposes of the sd Will, & Estate of her sd Deceased Husband She being to performe what an Executrix ought to doe according to the Lawes of this Governmt in such Case provided.

May the 10th Anno 1680

I Barnabas Horton of SouthHold in the East Riding of
the uncerta[inty]
Yorkshire upon LongIsland Calling to Remembrance ^ of this Temporall Life; And finding sundry Distempers dayly - growing upon me Doe now make this my Last Will & Testamt And thereby Dispose of my Earthly Estate in manner ffollowing - And first of all I give unto my Eldest Sone Joseph Horton Ten Sheepe Kind to what he formerly had for his full Porcon, also I give unto Benja: Horton my Second Sone ten Sheep kinde, to what he had formerly for the full porcon, also I give to my Eldest Daughter Hannah Trevally Ten Sheepe kinde as her -full Porcon, also I give to my Daughter Sarah Conclynes Sone vizt. Joseph Conclyne five Sheepe kind for her full Porcon also I give unto my third Daughter Mary Budd five Sheepe as her full Portion, also I give & bequeath to Caleb Horton my third Sone One Horse kinde and the one halfe of all my Right in Accobauge after my wifes decease to what he had in Possession at Cochauge for his full Portion also I give to Josuah Horton my fourth Sone all the House, Lands, Meadows, Orchard, and Common of Pasture wch was mine & is now in his Possession and the one halfe of all my Meadows and Upland within the Bounds of Accobauge and all my meadow at Oyster Ponds - and one Horse kinde for his Porcon also I give & bequeath

to

To my Youngest Son Jonathan Horton all my dwelling Houses
Barne, out housing, Home-Lotts, Areable-Lands, Meadows -
Allottmts & wtsoever else of Right belongs to my possession which
is neither before nor after in this my Last Will and Testamt be=
queathed or disposed of with this provisoe and Exception that the
New House Remaine Soley to my wife for her use during her Life
also that she have the use of the Barne and OutHouseing as need shall
require, also that she have the third Bushell of all that Grain wch
ariseth & Groweth yearly upon my Lands paid her by my Sone Jonat
han and also that he Winter & Sumer her foure Cowes Constantly
but the Increase shall be his, And further I give unto my Sone
Jonathan two Bullocks, also I give & bequeath unto my
Youngest Daughter Mercy Youngs three Cowes & one Heifer
But if there be not soe many left undisposed of Then she
have the worth of those that shall be found wanting paid
to her in some other good pay that shall be Equivalent
to them, also a ffeather Bed wth Bolster & Pillows one
Coverlid two Blanketts and foure paire of Sheets and
also one great Brass Ketle, one Iron pott & foure pewter
Dishes, ffinally I give unto my well beloved Wife Mary
Horton all the Rest of my Estate undisposed off, And
doe make and ordaine her Sole Executrix of this my
last Will & Testamt for the full Confirmacion whereof
I the abovesd Barnabas Horton doe hereunto sett my Hand
and Seale the day and yeare first above written

Signed & sealed in prsence
of us Jonas Houldsworth
Richard RB Benjamine
his marke

Barnabas Horton

Memorandum that the words
lyned in the 14th lyne was do
the signing & sealing hereof a
are to be understood as is exp
in the Margent.

It is to be understood that my Sone Jonathan possess & improve the
one halfe of all my Right wthin the Bounds of Occabauke during the
time of my Wifes Naturall Life, but at her death it is to become
my Sone Calebs for him to Enjoy Everafter.
A true Copie the Wittnesses being Sworne in Court

The Inventory of the Estate of Barnabas
Horton Deceased

	£	s	d
Land & houseing	200	–	–
Oxen Seaven	30	–	–
ffive Cowes	12	10	–
Three three yearlings	6	–	–
ffoure two yeare olds	5	6	–
ffoure yearlings	3	15	–
Three Calves	1	–	–
Sixteen Horse kinde	24	–	–
Sheepe Nynty	35	–	–
Swine ffourteen	10	–	–
Pewter	2	10	–
Brass	8	–	–
Iron pott Ketle Driping pann hookes Spitt	3	–	–
Wooden Ware Tubbs Bowles Dishes Churne &c:	4	–	–
Tinn Candlesticks	–	10	–
Three Chaines And Irons for fire	2	–	–
ffoure Chests	1	5	–
Table fforme Chaires kneadtrough	1	15	–
Three ffether Beds & Covering to them & Bedsted	25	–	–
Linning	15	–	–
Wooling Cloathes	13	–	–
Cushings	–	10	–
Barrells Bags Measures & other things	1	5	–
Summa Total £	405	16	00

John Corwin
Jacob Cory
Benjamine Youngs

Att a Court of Sessions held at SouthHampton
Begune the 2nd day of March 1680/1
Was Presented to the Court by Mary Peirson Relict
& Widdow of Henry Peirson of South Hampton deceased
an Inventory of her sd Husbands estate
^ Aprized by Mr John Howell, Edward Howell, John
Jessupe, Thomas Cooper who were Sworne by Mr John
Tapping Justice of the Peace wch Inventory and

Aprizemt

Apprisemt was allowed by the Court & Ordered to be Recorded; being as ffolloweth.

SouthHampton November ye 8th 1680

An Inventory of all & Singular the Goods & Chattels and Lands of Mr Henry Peirson Deceased Apprized by Capt John Howell Jno. Jessupe, Mr Edward Howell, and Tho= Cooper as ffolloweth.

		£	s	d
Item	his wearing Apparell	21	16	0
Item	his Bookes	6	19	-
Item	his Houseing & ffencing & Land adjoyning	350	-	-
Item	the Close at the old Towne	100	-	-
Item	the Close at Litleworth	120	-	-
His Land at the Great & Litle plaines		66	-	-
Item	his Land at Hogge neck besids Joseph 1/3 pt is	13	6	8
Item	his Bedstedd Bed & furniture	12	-	-
Item	a pr sheets a pcs Manchester	2	5	-
Item	a Remt kersy & a Remt penistone	3	6	-
Item	4 yds Red kersy at 10 s p yd 7 yds more at 9 s	5	3	-
Item	2 remts: bro:Clothe 6 yrds kersy	5	8	-
Item	a yd Red Bro:Clothe & 4 1/2 yds Red Searge	3	-	-
Item	a Remt of Cambrick & a Coverlaid	1	4	6
Item	a Chest & Cupboard 2 Candlesticks & 2 Cushins	5	5	-
Item	3 yrds Cushing stuff & warming pan 1 ounce silk	1	5	-
Item	an Old ffetherBed Coverlid Blanketts & Sheets & Bedsted	5	-	-
Item	an old Chest & pr of Sheets	1	16	-
Item	3 Sheets 2 table Cloaths a pillow 16£ Cotton Yearne 4£ flax	6	18	-
Item	17£ ffethrs 14£ flax 20£ Cotton woole	3	8	-
Item	Linning & Cotton yarne a fether bed wth Covering			
Item	a pr Sheets & Bolster	11	6	-
Item	Curtaines Valents Napkins a Sheet & pillows	5	10	-
Item	Sheepes woole a Brass pott & Iron pott	2	6	-
Item	3 1/2 yds Searge & 3 1/2 yds Duffalls 44£ of Iron	4	2	-
Item	Kersy & 7 yds Kersy more	4	-	-
Item	4 yds of Kersy homespun & 4 yds Coarse Kersy	2	16	-
Item	7 yrds Linning 4 of ffustian a yrd of Holland	3	6	-
Item	4 1/2 yds of lino 9 yds of ticking a Sheete	5	1	6
Item	a Chest & a Bed & furniture wth Curtaines Valants	15	4	-
Item	his meadow at North Sea Shinacock Sepannock hogneck	37	-	-
Item	his Meadow at Quagonantock	12	-	-
Item	5 yd Drugett 4 yds lino & a Rmt of Diaper	1	10	-

Item	4 yds peniston 1 Remt of ticking	1	9	–
Item	Buttons Napkins a Chest 5 yds Holland	3	19	–
Item	Carpet stuff & a pr holland Sheets	4	5	–
Item	a bed tick and a Single Sheet	4	5	–
Item	a fether Bed & Bedstedd & Beding	9	–	–
Item	2 Chest 3 Gunns & a Sword a lookeing glasse	6	4	–
Item	14 yds Duffalls 7£ a bed & furniture	14	–	–
Item	4 yds homespunn a small old bed & furniture	4	8	–
Item	a parcell of Sylkes new & old 14 bushells of salt	3	18	–
Item	20 plates & a Small plate	10	10	–
Item	2 Basons 4 plates 4 drinking potts & old pewter	2	6	–
Item	21 porringers 3 platers a Tankard & a saltser	3	8	–
Item	3 Brass ketles a Smaller ditto 2 skilletts	16	15	–
Item	3 Iron potts 2 Skilletts & a ketle wth some broken ware	5	16	–
Item	3 Iron ketles & a posnett & a dripping pan & 2 potts	7	14	–
Item	1 Iron ketle a Chamber pott & a lanthorne	1	16	–
Item	4 Chaires 2 tables 6 Cushings 4£	4	5	–
Item	a Smoothing Iron Tosting Iron & Grid Iron		10	–
Item	a Spitt pole 2 trammels 4 axes Wedges & Beetles	2	4	6
Item	2 China dishes a tunnell 3 milk pans		7	–
Item	12 Bowles a Churne a 1/2 bushll a Seeve other Lumbr	3	10	–
Item	12 Spoones 12 trenchers Baggs tongs	1	2	–
Item	2 ploughs Harrowteeth 3 Chaines 3 Yoakes	6	2	–
Item	Cart & wheeles hoopes boxes Clevis 100 foote of Board	3	7	–
Item	his Catle £185:10:0d 10 Horses 39 £	224	10	–
Item	wheate Hay & oates	35	10	–
Item	Sheepe Hoggs & Indian Corne	32	5	
	Total is £	1256	:01	:5

John Howell
Edward Howell
John Jessupe
Thomas Cooper

Upon the Peticon of the sd Mary Peirson for Liberty to Administr upon the aforesd Estate as alsoe to Ascertaine her third of the whole estate according to Law The Cort doth Admitt her the sd Mary Peirson to be sole Admini= stratrix of the whole Estate she performing the same according to Law as also her third pt of sd according to her peticon

Att a Court of Sessions held at Southampton
by his Maj:ties Authority the 2: 3 & 4th dayes of March
1680/1

The Inventory & Aprisemt of the Estate of Obadiah Palmer who was Drowned & Dyed Intestate being presented to this Cort by John Palmer & Will:m Barnes in behalfe of themselves and the rest of the Brothers of the Decedent as also a Peticon for Liberty to the sd Jno: Palmer & Will:m Barnes to admi= nister upon the aforesd Estate The Cort takeing the same into Consideracon did allow the sd Inventory & Aprizmt and ordered Mr Jno: Laughton to Peruse & Settle the Accos of the Decedent and make Returne thereof to the Cort and to Record the Same by the aforesd Inventory being both as ffolloweth

An Inventory of the Estate left by Obadiah
Palmer Deceased
EastHampton March ye 1st . 1680/1

	£	s	d
4½ yds Searge at 7 s	1	11	6
2 prs of Stockins at	-	12	-
4 pr of Gloves at	-	10	-
2 Bunches of Galloome at	-	3	-
One Rapier	1	-	-
One Tunnell	-	1	-
2 Coates one 50s	3	10	-
4 yds Ossenburgs	-	10	-
one pcs of Cotton Ribon	-	4	6
one Booke	-	3	-
one pr of Trowsers	1	-	-
one yd 3/4 of Linning blue	-	3	6
One Gunn & 2 Locks at	2	-	-
2 Gilt buckles	-	1	6
One Marking Iron	-	1	-
One Razor & Hoone	-	3	-
One Powder Horne	-	-	6
One Inke horne	-	1	-
3 Knives	-	2	6

2 paire of Sizers	-	1	-
one yd blue Linning	-	2	-
one hatt	-	5	-
One paire of Shoes	-	9	-
6 Gemletts	-	2	6
4 heele Spurs	-	2	-
6 peeces of sealing wax	-	2	-
2 pr of Dovetailes	-	1	-
2 yds of Girt webb	-	1	-
5 pr of Shoo buckles	-	2	6
2 Candlesticks	-	4	-
One Bed & Coverlaid	1	-	-
2 Combes	-	-	6
One Chest & Box & other Small things	-	10	-
Tobacco & 20 Pipes	-	2	6
One Lance	-	10	-
Money	82	17	-
Part of a Boate & Craft	1	19	4
A Cutting knife	-	4	-
One Wooden Botle	-	2	-
100£ of whalebone being Damnified	2	10	-
£	102	16	4
By us Stephen Hand	82	17	-
Thomas Osborne £	19	19	4
Jeremiah Conclyne			

Stephen Hand Objecting in Co:rt That (being in hast when they Counted the Money) there might be a mistake in their Reconing; There being only 82 £ placed upon sd Palmer his bookes; The Cort Judged it might possibly be a mistake in telling the money

March ye 4th 1680/1 Whereas I was Ordered to State & View the Bookes & Bills Delivered to me that are due to Obadiah Palmer Late Deceased

		£	s	d			£	s	d	
	Tho: Mulford	–	9	–		Brought over	33	11	8	½
	Benj:n Mulford	1	4	–		Jno: Lawrisons	2	10	–	
Thes Debts	Wid.w ffifer	–	12	–		Tho: Hickhams	–	16	–	
are by ye	Elnathan Tapping	–	3	8		Jno: Crugo	–	7	–	
Booke &	Jno: Squire	–	3	–		Jno: Richardsone	–	12	–	
are uncrost	Joseph Osborne	–	15	6			37	:16	:8	½
or Ball-	Mrs: Margarett Hobart	–	4	10	½	By 135 yds Ossenburgs	7	:15	:–	
anced	Jeremiah Miller	–	6	–		In the Inventory	102	:16	:4	
	Tho: Dom Junr	–	4	–			148	:9	:½	
	Robt. Kedg	–	4	–						
	Stephen Stratton	–	4	–						
	Tho: Stratton	–	8	–						
	Jonathan Rose	2	2	8						
	Will:m Whiple	–	4	–		Credit				
	Will:m Barnes	–	13	4		Tho: Stephens	1	9	1	
	Mr Thrope a firkin Butter					Jno: Wheeler	–	–	9	
	Jno: Morehouse	–	11	–						
	Mr Sam: Mullford	2	9	–						
	Tho: Stephens	2	5	4						
	Benja: Gayler	–	1	4						
	James Hildreth	–	8	6						
2 places	Benj:n Palmer	3	–	6						
	Sam:ll Mills	–	8	6						
	Edward White	–	5	–						
	Thirston Raynor	–	2	4						
	Jno: Mullford	–	7	6						
	Sam:ll Brookes	3	10	–						
	Jno: Dimon	–	10	–						
	Jno: Osborne	–	1	4						
	Jno: Brookes	–	1	–						
	James Hand	–	10	2						
	Eliz: Diament	–	2	8						
	Rodger Earle	–	13	9						
	Benj:n Osborne	–	1	1						
	Joseph Stratton	–	4	–						
	Nat: Talmage	–	–	8						
	Carryed over	33	:11	:8	½					

The above is a true Copie of Mr: John Laughtons Returne to the Court pursuant to an order to peruse the Bookes Bills & accos of Obadiah Palmer deceased Compared wth Orriginall
Cr

The aforesd Inventory & Returne being allowed by the Co:rt Upon the Peticon aforesd The Co:rt did Admitt the Aforesd John Palmer & William Barnes adminis trato:rs of the whole Estate aforesd to all Intents and - purposes they giving Sufficient Security for the - performance thereof according to peticon & the Lawes of this Guvernmt.

At A Court of Sessions: held at Southold June the 7 1681: was Presented A peticon of Jane Williams Relict and widow to William Williams of brook haven. Late Deceased with and Inventory of her Said Husbands Estate Aprized by & Sworne to before Justice wodhull wch Inventory and Ap prizmt is Allowed by the Court: and ordered to be Recorded being as followeth.

An Inventory of the goods and Estate of Mr Williams Marcha[nt]
Deceased as followeth Vizt the 2d Day of July 1680:

The Said Estate being Aprized	£		
the house and accomadacons at	80	-	-
three Horse kinde at	5	10	-
Three Swine at	1	10	-
Beds and beding at	11	9	-
wareing Cloaths	8	-	-
household good or Nessesaris for house keeping	5	7	-
£	111	=16	=00

Brookhaven this Sworne before Richard Wodhull June ye 3 : 1681

The Aforsaid Jane Williams upon her Petistion is Admited by this Court to be Administratrix of her Said husbands Estate Shee puting Security to this Court according To Law on that be half and in as much as the Said Jane Williams her Security is not at hand the Court Doth order her to Deliver in her Security and Send it to the Clark of the Sessions for the Courts use that then Shee Shall have leter[s] of Adminstration Delivered to her in the Courts name

A true Coppy of the Inventory and Record by me John Howell Junr:) June 13: 1681

At A Court of Sessions held at Southold June ye 7: 8: 9
Annoq Dom: 1681 was presented the will and testa
ment of willm wells of Southold Deceased or Als: a
Deed of givft: with a petistion of the willm wells
his widow or Relict now wife to Thomas Maps
that her Son willm Wells might might be Impower
ed by this Court to Administer upon his fathers Estat
A long and with her: the Will or Deed is as followeth

November the 13: 1671
These presents witneseth that I willm wells of
Southold in the East Rideing of yorkshire in Long
Doe for good and Serious Consideracons me hereunto
Moveing give and grant all my Right title and
Intrest of in and unto all my houses Land tennemts
Allotments and Meadows with in the bounds of South
hold with all my goods and Chatels unto my well beloved
wife Mary Wells for her Comfortable Subsistance &
Education of my Children: but not to Dispose of Any
pte or pcell there of otherwise but for portions
to the Chilldren as Shee Shall See Cause haveing re
Spect to my Eldest Sonne as wittnes my hand and
Seall the Day and year first Above written
Signed Sealed and Delivered in prsts of) Wm Wells
us Barnabas windes
Richard Terry

A true Coppy p me
John Howell Clarke:/

June 7:1681 At A Court of Sessions held at Southold was ^ presented A peticon
of Mary Mapes Late Wife to Willm Wells of South
hold Deceased: requesting her Sone william might be
with her Directions impowered to act and performe -
Executry: upon his deceased fathers Estate :

Itt is ordered that william Wells the Sonne of Wm
Wells late of Southold Deceased is by this Court
Authorized and Impowered to act and perform all that
Trust that was reposed in Mrs Mary Wells his
Mother as to the Disposall of the Estate left by
his father with his Said Mother for the Ends and
purposes in the act and Deed of his
father

now in this Court as more particulerly in Said deed doth Apear the Said William Wells to act and Execute all the Said power that was given to his Mother to all Intents and purposes as Shee her selfe might or Could have done by virtue of Said act of his fathers to his mothe[r] as fully and Amply as Shee her self Could have Done if Shee had not remarried In all wch his acting he is to be regulated and directed by his said mother and not to doe or act any thing in any Case Contrary to ye minde of his mother: but in all things accord =ing thereunto all which his such acting accord =ing to this order with the Restrictions and Limitat[ions] herein Contained this Court Doth Ratifie and con - firme: &c: -

p order of Court: A true Coppy
Attest John Howell Clark: -

An Inventory of all & Singuler the Lands goods and Chatels of Mr Thomas Topping Deceased May ye 3d: 1681 Aprized may. the 6th: 1681 p John Jessup Edward Howell Samuell Johnes and John Howell Junr as followeth: Sworne to ye - Aprizmt by Justice Toping &c.

		£		
Item	the home Lot being 20 Acres at	100	-	-
Item	the houseing 70 £ and Seven Acres in ye great plains 14 £	84	-	-
Item	6 acres of Land in Capts neck	21	-	-
Item	6 acres ½ in halseys nek and one in Capts neck:	37	-	-
Item	3 acres in Coopers neck 10£=10s & 1½ in ye litle plains	14	-	-
Item	40 acres at Sagabonack	70	-	-
Item	25 acres at litle worth	62	10	-
Item	his part at hog neck & meadow at quaqua & Sebon	23	-	-
Item	5 Steers 20 £ 5 Steers 3 year old 16 £=5s	36	5	-
Item	1 mare 50s: 4 oxen 26 £ one Steer 5 £	33	10	-
Item	5 Catle 2 year old 10£: 7 Catle one year old 7£	17	-	-
Item	9 Cowes 36 pound one Steer 3 year old 3£	39	-	-
Item	30 Sheep 12£ Swine 4£=10s - a table 12s	17	2	-
Item	a bedsted bed and furnyture 12£ one Small bed 2£)	14	-	-
Item	2 Chests 32s (chayres 10s) 20 pound fine yarn 3£: Sword & belt 20s)	5	2	-
Item	one hour glass 1s one Smoothing Iron 5s	-	6	-
Item	2 bibles and other books 28s: 2 pares of Cards 4s	1	12	-
Item	botles and Jugs 14s: 2 beds 2 blankets & rug 6£	6	14	-
Item	2 boxes 3s one barrill of Rum 6£: a looking glass 4s)	6	7	-
Item	10 pewter plates 4£ 10s: 12 poringers 24s	5	14	-
Item	2 Cups 8s: 7 pewter pots 24s 3 old pewter platers 6s)	1	18	-
Item	2 basons 6 Spoons with some other Small things	-	15	-

Item	Tin ware 5s) 3 ketles 2 bras one Coper 8£ 10s)	8	15	-
Item	3 Iron pots & ketle 50s frying pan 10s	3	-	-
Item	poole and tongs 12s the haters Shop 18£	18	12	-
Item	2 Iron pots 50s a gun: fleshfork and tramell 37s)	4	7	-
Item	9 bowles 19s:6 wooden plates and a tunell 8s	1	7	-
Item	a straining dish 3 pails with other wooden ware	-	11	6
Item	3 Seivs 7s a ridle 18d Earthen ware 6s 2 chamerpots 4s	-	18	6
Item	an old brass pot 5s 3 barills of meate 5£ Baken 10s	5	15	-
Item	oyle 7 gallons 10s a bedsted bed and beding 11£10s	12	-	-
Item	a bed and beding 10£: 9 bushills of wheat 45s)	12	5	-
Item	6 baskets of Indian Corne 24s) 6 pound of flax 10s a botle	1	14	-
Item	silk and linen 3£=8s) a pr of Sheets 40s) 2 Chests 33s)	7	1	-
Item	his wareing Aparrill 7£) 3 Spining wheels 20s)	8	-	-
Item	2 Churns 2 boxes an old Chest a meal trough	1	2	-
Item	flax 30s) one box 4s) 2 bushels ½ of Salt powder & led 12s	2	6	-
Item	a Sadle and bridle 12s Lumber in the house 20s)	1	12	-
Item	12 napkins 24s) 4 table Cloaths 18s) 5 pillow Dra)	3	2	-
Item	a paire of fine Sheets 30) 5 Course Sheets 3£	4	10	-
Item	a Spade 9s a how 5s) 2 Sieths 10s) one Sicle 18d: 2 axes 7=6)	1	13	-
Item	cart & wheels boxes hoops Clevis lince & entry pins	4	-	-
Item	3 yokes 12s) Chains 20s Share coulter boult & Coller 26s	2	18	-
Item	a pitch fork & 3 pillow Drawers	-	11	6
	Totall	703	=14	=6

This Accompt taken as it was Aprized p John Howell Junr

A true Coppy of the origanall Inventory of the Estate of
the Said Deceased Thomas Topping p me

John Howell Junr Clark

At a Court of Sesions at Southold June ye 7:8:9 days was presented the Aforesaid Inventory by hanah Topping widow and Relict to said Thomas Topping Deceased: with a pitistion to administer upon Said Estate: She haveing given In securyty according to Law: the Court Doe Admit her to all intents and porposes Sole Administratix of Said Estate She perform ing the Same in all Respects acording to Law:

Brookhaven December ye 10: 1679
An Inventory of the Estate of Wm Williams Deceased the 9th of this Instant Dying Intestate: Imprimus
A house and home Lot Containing ten Acres of Land lying over Against Leifnt Floyds Swamp near to John Combs his home Lot and Eight Acres of land lying near Willm Sallyers in New Towne
Item 2 M ½ of brick 24 Deale boards

Credit William Salyer	3	8	6
Credit by Thomas Smith 20s	1	-	-
Credit by Thomas Geners 30s	1	10	-
Credit by Samuell Barber	2	17	-
Credit by John Jeners	1	16	8

his

his wareing Cloaths vizt one pr of Trousers one Coat one hat
two Shirts a bed & boulster and blanket and Coverled one
wascoat one musquet

		£	s	d
	Credit by Jacob Longbotham	4	5	-
	Credit by Mr Brewster	-	17	6

The Aprizmt of the goods or Estate of William Williams
Deceased December the 11: 1679

		£	s	d
Impr–	A bed and boulster at	-	12	-
	Item A blanket at	-	7	6
	A Coverlet at one pound	1	-	-
	A wastcoat at	-	6	-
	A hat at 6s - a Shirt at 4s a Coat & trusers 30s	2	-	-
	A Musquet at	1	-	-
	8 Acres of Land at New Towne	6	-	-
	10 acres of Land near John Combs where ye house Stands	5	-	-
	The house at	7	-	-
	20 boards at	2	-	-
	2 Cord ½ of bricks at	2	-	-

By u Thomas Holmes
Samuell Edsall
John Tompson Clark
The mark of Wm WI Joanes) A true Coppy p me Henry Peirson

March Court 1680/1) Mr Joseph Lee Requesting the Court for Liberty to Ad
minister upon the Estate of the Aforesaid William williams
Bricklayer Deceased; he giving in Security to performe
the Same According to Law The Court takeing the
Same Into Consideration In Regard none of the -
Decedants frinds or Relacons prayed for Administracon
and the Creditors being unpaid Doe Admit the Said Joseph Lee to all in
tents and purposes Administrator of Said Estate hee brin[g]
ing in A true Inventory into this Court performeing
the Same acording to Lawe:

William Williams Debts

	£	s	d
To Abram Dayton for worke left undone	-	5	-
To Mr Thomson upon the ballance of accots	-	11	2
To Serjent Bigs for Drink	-	11	6
To John Thomas his for makeing lining	-	1	6
To Ralph Dayton for Rum	-	16	-
To Ralph Dayton for goeing to ye old mans	-	5	-
To Samuell barber for 3 pints of	-	3	-
to Samuell barber for Atending him	1	-	-
to Thomas Helmes 1£ money & 1£ of flaxe	-	2	-
to ballance accompts with John Davis	2	4	6

A true Coppy p me Henry Peirson Clarke to Court
of Sessions &c -
A true Coppy of the Coppy p me John Howell Junr
Clark to the Court of Sessions -

The Last will & testement of Willm fithian of
East hampton In the East Rideing of newyorkshire
being In perfect minde and understanding as followeth

first I give my Soule to god that gave it and my body to the dust form
whence it Came & my Estate as followeth all debts paid
Imprimis to my beloved wife Margaret I make her Executrix of my
whole Estate I shall leave Dureing her life; and After her deseas
my will is what is left bee thus Devided:
To my Eldest Son Enoch (I haveing Done formerly for him more
then the Rest of my Children the males that are surviveing)
I Doe give my Close Lying Eastward from the towne Lying next to
will Barnes Lott also my 7 acres lott Lying upon the Easterne plaine
by Hookpond Alsoe I give him my lott at the Indian well: also the third pt
of my Last Devission of Land Lying northwest from ye towne be=
=ing woodland Alsoe I give my Sonn Enocke my peece of meadow at ye
northwest and one peece of meddow lying at accobanak John
Hoppin Lying on one side of it & goodman Bishop upon ye other side
Also I give my Aforesd Enoke halfe Commonage belongs to me both at
the Towne and at Meantaukutt my will also is my son Enoke have yt 7
acres of land lying Northwest for his present use and possession if hee See
Cause to Improve it; & hee to have uppon the Norwest Side of ye Sd devison

2ly: I give to my Son Samuell my home lott in the Towne where I
Live together wth the Addition & all the Houseing upon the Aforesd land
also I give him my Seven acre lott lying upon the westerne plaine
Also I give him fourteen Accres of Land being two third parts of
the Last Devison Lying north west from ye Towne and on the Southeast
Side of the Said lott also I give my Aforesd Son Samuell my peice of
meddow lying upon Accobanak neck also anothe peice of meddow
lying in the great meddow Lying South from that I give my A
foresd Son Enoch Also anothr peice of meddow Lying Eastward of ye
East Creek at akobonack alsoe I give him halfe my Comonage both
at the Towne and at mentaukut

3 My Will is yt all my moveable goods whether Cattle or housold
goods be my wives Dureing her life and After her Decease
the one halfe of my [?] Cattle I give to my Son Samuell: and ye
other half of my Stocke and housold goods to bee Devided to my
other Children: Enoch Sarah hanah and to my grandchild daughter
of my Child Martha Deceased if Shee Shall Continue wth my
wife till her Deceas to have a part with the rest also my Son
Samuell to have his proportion of the houshold goods with ye rest

4: My will is my Son Samuell be Executor of this my Testamt
After his mothers deceas if hee Survive her; but if god
take him away before her I will my Son Enoch to have
all my land & be Executor of this my will also

my

my Desire is [Thomas] Baker & Mr Thomas James of this
Towne be the overseers of this my will In Confermation
of this my will I Sett to my hand and Seale this 11th Dece[m]be[r]
Anno:quo: Dom 1678 his

Signed & sealed In presence of us William X Fithian
Thomas Baker marke
Thomas James

A true Coppy of the origanall will
p John Howell Junr Clark: to ye Court of Sessions

This under writeing is a true Inventory of william fithian
Lately Decease taken by us Constable and overseers

home Land & building	70	-	
out Land 48 acres 30£) 2 oxen 10£) 3 Cows 9£	49	-	
three 3 year olds 7£=10s) 4 two year old 8£) 4 yerlings 6£)	21	10	-
three Calfes 3£) ½ a horse 30s) 25 Sheep and lambs 7£)	11	10	-
one Sow and 6 pigs 2£) in beding & Covering 9£	11	-	-
In linen 7£:12s) a warming pan 10s) 3 brass Scellits 18s)	9	-	-
one great kettle 5£:10s) 3 little kettles 1£	6	10	-
Six Iron potts and pothoocke & hangers	3	15	-
A Smoothing Iron 2s:6d: a grid Iron and Chafingdish 4s)	-	6	6
fire Shovell & tongs plow Irons & Chaine	2	11	-
Six Small platters 26s) 2 plates 5s) 3 Small basons 7s)	1	18	6
one Chamar Pot: 5 old porengers 11s) 1 tin Candlestick: 1s)	-	12	-
4 poringer: 7s) 3 basons 20s) 2 plater 8s) a pewter cup 18d)	1	16	6
one tanker 7s) 7 Spoons 3s:6d) 3 bottles 2s) tin ware 5s)	-	17	6
one old Chamarpot 1s) an old lanthorne 2s:6d) in Chayres 10s)	-	13	6
4 Cushions 4s one Speet 3s:6d) 3 old Chests 20s)	1	7	6
12 bushell of Corne 30s) 30£ of tallow 15s) 3 old axes 6s)	2	11	-
4 barills of beef 8£) one hide 12s: a pcell of Loose meat 10s)	9	2	-
In other Lumber 20s) a Lookinglass & brush 2s:6d	1	2	6
This taken by us the whole Sum	215	:4	:0

Benjamin Conkling Constable Jeremia Conkling: Thomas osborne
John Stratten: overseers: A true Coppy p John Howell Junr

March At A Court of Sessions held at Southampton by his
ye 2th Majestyes Authority by his Majestys Justices: of the Peace for
168½) the East Ride of Yorkeshire) was presented the Aforesd
will and Inventory of the said William fithian Deceased of
Easthampton being proved In this Courte by ye testimony
upon oath of the two Psones Subscribed as wittnesses to the Said
will namely Mr Thomas Baker and Mr Thomas James the
Courte

Courte Doe finde & Adjudge the now widow or relict
of the Said Willm fithian Namly Margaret Fithian
to be Sole Executrix of the Said will and testement and
Doe allow and Admit her soe to bee to all Intents and
purposes Alsoe the Court Doth allow Aprove of the said
Thomas Baker and Tho: James (mentioned in ye said
will) to bee Supervissers therof according to th mind
of the Testator therein Specified:

At a Courte of Sessions held at Southampton

By his Majests Authoryty upon ye first 2th and third
Days of March 1681/2.
Was presented the Will and Inventory of Willm
Russell Deceased of Southampton which was prov
ed at this Courte by the Testimony upon of the two
psons subscribed as wittneses to the said wills namly
obadiah Rogers and Mr John Laugton: and the Court
doe apoint the said obadiah Rogers (Seing the widow
is since Deceased) to gether with Mr Job Sayre as
Executor In trust: to the said will and Inventory
of the said estate: to Dispose of it according to
the minde of the testator In the will underwritten

In the Name of god Amen I William Russell of Southampton In the East Rideing of Yorkshire

on Long Island being In perfect Strength of Memory blessed be
the almighty god for it though at present weake in body and not
knowing the day of my apointed Change Doe ordaine this my
1 Last Will and Tetament as followeth Imprimis I Give and
freely Bequeath my Soule to God my Creator whoe gave it
unto mee: & my body to ye Earth from whence it was first
Taken: and my Estate as is hereunder menconed
2ly I Give and bequeath unto my two Sonns Oliver Russell and
William Russell all my Land and meaddow in the bounds of South
hampton and A fifty pound Accomadations to Equally Devided between
them as my Beloved Brother Obadiah Rogers Shall See Cause
to Devide it; (3 ly) I make my Beloved wife Elizabeth Russell
my Executrix of this my Last will to have the Disposall of all
my Moveable Estate and to Dispose of it as Shee Shall See Cause
Amonst my other Children: Lastly I make the said obadiah
Rogers overseer of this my will and Testament and to see after
my Children and there land for them In wittnes whereof I have
hereunto sett my hand and fixed my Seale this 27th Day of August 1678

Signed sealed and Delivered in the pesence of us — his
Obadiah Rogers John Laughton. — william B Russell
mark

Octobr) The Inventory of the Estate of William Russell of Southampton
ye 14:1681) Late Deceased Inventoryed and Aprized by Mr Edward Howell
John Jessupp Job Sayre and John Howell Junr being all
Sworne to the Aprizemt thereof by Justice Toppyng - -

		£		
Imprimis	the Dwelling house and 20 Acres of Land Adjoyning thereunto with A fifty pound Comonage at	110	-	-
	Item 20 acres of wood Land 30s p acre	30	-	-
	Item a fifty of Land in hogneck with medow	6	-	-
	Item the meddow at Conoplace and Shinecok	8	-	-
	Item 4 Cows 15£) 2 Steers 3 yr old 8£) 3 Steer 2 yr old 7£:10s)	30	10	-
	Item 2:3 yearold heyfers 7£) 3 yerlings 5£:5s	12	5	-
	Item 18 Sheep & lambs 5£10s) 3 hogs 4£:	9	10	-
	Item 4 horse kinde 7£ bed bedsted and furneture 10£	17	-	-
	Item a trundle bed bedsted and beding 5£	5	-	-
	Item a paire of hollen Sheets 3£) 4 homspun Sheets 3£:15s	6	15	-
	Item A Duzen of Napkins and a table Cloath	1	10	-
	Item a hangup 20s) 9 pewter platters 4£:10s) 4 porin 12s	6	2	-
	Item 3 plates a bason cup quart pot 2 porengers	1	4	-
	Item 2 Drinking pots & 3 Sausers ½ duzen of Spoones	-	10	-
	Item a Lanthorne and Earthen ware	-	17	6
	Item glass bottle Smoothing Irone and heaters[?]	-	8	6
	Item 3 bibles 18s) 5 Iron pots & ketles 2 brass cetles and Scelit	10	1	-
	Item 6 bowles 13s a tin ketle 2s a frying 2 Sievs 9s	1	4	-
	Item 2 Spining wheels 12s) a Spit 8s) a tramell 7s	1	7	-
	Item a paire of pot hooks 18d, a Sword 15s: a gun 25s	2	1	6
	Item a Lamp 2s) 2 hatts 6s): a table 2 Chests 2 boxes 40s	2	8	-
	Item 3 Chayres 6s a Cradle 4s a Churne 3s	-	13	-
	Item barrill tubbs and other Lumber	-	15	-
	Item 2 mattuks a plowshare: 3 axes: 2 wedges	1	9	-
	Item 2 pr of taylors Sheers a lathinhamer candlestik	-	7	6
	Item two hows tenn Shilling: a Spade 4s	-	14	-
	Item a Chaine 8s a Cleves 3s	-	11	-
	Item things sould a pr of boxes a plowshare and Coulter yoke Irons beetle ring and wedges A boult and Coller for a plow	2	12	-
	Item old Sieths 3s) Indian Corne 4 bushells 10s)	-	13	-
	Item aboute 3 bushells of Rye Inthe Shefe	-	9	-
	Item 10 pound of woole 10s) 2 load of hay 2£	2	10	-
		273	:7	:0
	there is 23£ of this Estat never Come Into the hands of the Executors In trust: therefore to be Deducted	23	:0	:0
		250	:7	:0

A true Coppy of the Aforesaid will and Inventory of william
Russell Deseased p John Howell Junr Clark

An Inventory and Aprizment of all and Singuler ye Lands goods and Chattels of the Estate of Daniell halsey of Southampton Late Deceased februr ye 24 168½ Taken and Aprized by Capt John Howell Mr Edward Howell Mr John Jessupp Mr Samuell Johnes whoe were Chosen and appinted by the ptyes Concerned and Sworne unto ye Aprizment of the same by Justice Topping ffebruary ye 27:168½

Imprimis to his Land at home 52 Acres: 4£ p acre	208	–	–
Item ye house and barne at	140	–	–
Item ye wood Close towards Cobspond 20 acres at at 25s p acre	44	–	–
Item Smiths Lott at Towne	40	–	–
Item the Land at Saga.bonk 20 1/3 acres) 40s p acre	40	–	–
Item one Acre of Land In halseys neck 5£) 2 gin acres 4£	9	–	–
Item 25 Acres at Sevenponds 30s p Acre	37	10	–
Item 20 Acres at Skuttle hole Devison 20s p acre	20	–	–
Item a 100 at quaqua: his meadow at Sebonak & beatch	5	–	–
Item 4 Cattle Come 2 yearold 45s p peice	9	–	–
Item 5 Cattle Come 3 yearold	15	–	–
Item 5 young Cowes 18£) 2 steers at 9£	27	–	–
Item 4 oxen 24£) 8 Cowes 38£) 3 heyfer 11£) 5 two yearolds 10£	83	–	–
Item 11 yearlings 30s) p head: a old horse 2 mares & Colt 8£	24	10	–
Item 40: Sheep 16 £) his Swine at 12£	28	–	–
Item 14 bushels of Sumer wheat at 4s:6d p bushell	3	3	–
Item 3 bushels of Rye: 7s) a barrill of pork & a barrill beef	5	7	–
Item a flock bed with furneture	3	–	–
Item a linin wheele & 2 bushells of Salt	–	16	–
Item a feather bed bedsted and furneture	6	–	–
Item 8 pr of Sheets 35s p pr 2 pare of fine Sheets: 4£	18	–	–
Item 2 pr of Sheets: 35s p pr) 7 napkins 10s	4	–	–
Item ½ duzen of Napkins 14s) 3 table Cloaths 24s	1	18	–
Item his Aparrell 10£) 2 guns at 3£ woolen yarne 28s	14	8	–
Item a pr of Andirons 5s) 4 Chests an old Cubord 40s)	2	5	–
Item a table 20s: A Sword and warming p 20s	2	–	–
Item a feather bed bedsted and beding belonging	11	–	–
Item a trundle bed and furneture	3	10	–
Item 10 pound of Cotton and linin yarne	1	10	–
Item two tables & a box at 30s mallases at 40s	3	10	–
Item 2 wheeles 10s) Cheespres 5s) bouls tunell & Can	1	5	–
Item a Churne payles trays Cheesfats 15s) 2 deerskins 10s	1	5	–
Item 2 Sieths & & takleing) 10 bushell of Corne 4 of oats	3	–	–
Item 70 pound weight of new pewter 3s p pound	10	10	–
Item 23 pound of old pewter at 2s p pound	2	6	–

Item glass bottles box Iron pewter Saucers and Candle Stiks	-	18	-
Item a pint pewter pott with: ure pott	-	8	-
Item a frying pan & an old brass pot	-	16	-
Item a great brass kettle with 2 lesser & a Scellit	4	-	-
Item a Driping pan apeper box 4d) 4 bowls 8s	-	8	-
Item 4 payls 5s) 2 Iron pots 40s) a harping Iron & lanc 15s)	3	-	-
Item two tramels fire Shovell and tongs	1	-	-
Item book 6s:) a Scellit and a Iron pott 42s	2	8	-
Item 2 old Sieths a Cutting knik a Spade and how	-	10	-
Item boxes 2 pr of hoops Ex pins linc pins Cart & wheels	3	10	-
Item 3 yokes 12s Clevis 5s) 3 Chaynes 30s	2	7	-
Item the plow and plow Irons	1	4	-
Item 5 axes beetles & wedges and an ads:	1	10	-
Item 2 forks 4 Chayres and ye lumber In ye house	2	-	-
Item winter wheat 35 bushell 5 p bushl	8	15	-
Item hay at 4£) 2 negroes at 70£	74	-	-
	994	:07	:0
Debts to be subtracted	30	:00	:0
	964	:07	:0

A true Coppy of the aforsd Inven	John Howell	)	
tory of Daniell halseys Estate	Edward Howell	)	Aprizes
p Jno Howell Junr Clark:	John Jessup	)	Sworne as
	Samuell Johnes	)	Aforsaid

March
Court 81/2 The Afforesd Inventory was presented to this Court Aforesd where it was allowed &c: and Mr Richard wodhull In be behalf of his Daughter the Aforsaid Jemima Requ[est]ed this Court that his Said Daughter: might Administe[r] upon the Estate of her husband Aforesaid the Court haveing Considered the Same Doe Admit her the Said Jemima Halsey as widdow and Relickt to the said Daniell) as Adm ministratix to the Said Estate to all Intents and purposes Shee giveing Sofficient Secury to act therin as the Law Directs In such Cases and Saveing the Court harmles: mr richard woodhull and mr Edward Howell are bound for ye said widow

---

At the Aforsaid Court of Sessions March the 1: 2: 3 days: 168½ was presented) The Inventory of Obadiah Smith Son of Richard Smith: of Smithfield who Died Intestate August ye 20th 1680 apeareth to bee as followeth

Imprimis a farm on the west Side of Nessequague River Containeing 100 Acres Land	30	-	-
Item five Cowes & 2 oxen	22	-	-
Item five Steer & Six younger Steers:	31	-	-

Item four heyfers	6	-	-
Item three Horses	9	-	-
Item Sixteen Swine	16	-	-
Item 6 Swine more 3£) 4 acres of medow 4 £)	7	-	-
Item Debts Due from Mr Kingsland) two peice of penistone at 7£ p peice ½ a case) of knives in 10s. in Cloath Searg 3£:10s)	18	-	-
Item one Chest and his wereing Cloaths	3	-	-
Item one Sadle	1	-	-

the pticulars herof are vallued
according to Rule of money

Johnathan Smith
Daniell Smith

A true Coppy p me John How

The Aforesaid Inventory of Obadiah Smith being psent ed to this Court who Sued for Administration and alsoe Samuell Smith Sued for Administration but not granted to nether at present by reason they have nothing to Show from the proper heyre namly Daniell Smith the Deced =dants younger brother but thorow the Importunyty of the said Richard Smith he is In the behalf of his Son Daniell Admited together with the Sd daniell as Administrator to the Aforesd Estate and are to be re puted Soe to be to all intents and purposes he the Sd Richard Smith give Sofficient Security to be responci =ble to the said Daniell for the Same according to Law and Saveing this Court harmles Securyty given In to the Clark

---

At a Court of Sessions held by his Majestys Authority at Southold June the 6: 7: 8 days 1682 was presented the following inventory:

South=hampton March ye 22th 168½ An Inventory of ye Estate (vizst) of all ye Lands goods and Chattels of Anthony Ludlam Late Deceased Inventoryed and Aprized by Samuell Johnes Constable Mr Edward John Howell Junr: and Nicholas Eeds: who were Sworne thereunto by Justic Topping the Day and year aforesd

Impr	the Land at home being in all by measure 39½: at 5£ p acre	197	-	-
	Item the Dwelling house with all other Howseing	130	-	-
	Item the Land at keelys pond	30	-	-
	Item ye land in the oxpasture	3	10	-
	Item the Land at little hogneck	7	-	-
	Item his 50£ Comonage	5	-	-

		£	s	d
Item	24 Sheep 11£) 11 hog 11£) 13 pigs 3£:18s	25	18	-
Item	a Sow at 25s a white horse at 5£) another horse at 50s)	8	15	-
Item	the Rest of the Horse Kind by Estemation	6	-	-
Item	2 oxen 12£ 2 Steers 8£) 4 Cattle 3 yearold 12£	32	-	-
Item	6:2 yearolds 12£: 4 yrlings 5£ 3 Cowes 11£:5s	28	5	-
Item	a weak Cow & 2 yearold heifer	3	10	-
Item	a bed bedsted and furneture 8£: a trundle ditto 70	11	10	-
Item	a Cuberd fourty foure s shillings	2	4	-
Item	a Chest 8s: 2 pistalls 20s powder and shott 6s	1	14	-
Item	2 ridles 4s: 14£ of flax 16s) 9 pound of linin yarne 22s6d	2	2	6
Item	Catrage box: a doule bitt and stok: 4s hansow and baskit:2s)	-	6	-
Item	His wereing Aparrill at	7	-	-
Item	5 glas Botles 5s: a gun 30s 8 platers: 2 basons 38s	4	3	-
Item	½ duzen of porengers: and two old basons	-	18	-
Item	3 drinking pots 10s Earthen weare 2s:6d	-	12	6
Item	a Lanthorne grater and 2 tunells & a pper box	-	5	6
Item	a driping pan 2 lamps 4s:6d) 3 pr of old Cards: 4s	-	8	6
Item	a Chamer pott 4s a pr of Iron fetters: and cury come	-	9	-
Item	mallasses 30s 2 pr of tongs & a bill: 4s bridle & Sadle 20s	2	14	-
Item	a broad ax bettle rings wedges: and a narrow ax 14s	-	14	-
Item	2 wooden bottles 5s: the tramell and Hooks 5s	-	10	-
Item	5 pails 9s a bedsted 6s a tub 8s	1	8	-
Item	a barrill of meate 40s a tubbe and keeler 5s 2 bouls 3s	2	8	-
Item	an Iron kettle 40s) 2 tubs 5s) 3 Seives 4s	2	9	-
Item	2 Iron potts & one old kittle 40s tubb and Cheesfatts 4s	2	10	-
Item	three keeler a tray and 2 bouls 10s:6 dishes and spoons 8)	-	18	6
Item	pt of A barrill of porke a frying pan and a [ ]ying seive 5	-	5	-
Item	3 Sheets a shirt and a westcoat at	2	10	-
Item	a bed bedsted with furniture at	8	10	-
Item	2 Spining wheels 7s: Cart rope 8s) 6 bushells of wheat 24s	1	19	-
Item	a Chafe bed and beding 30s: a pr of Stok bands 6s	1	16	-
Item	horse geers 3s: 8 bushells of wheat 40s a quantity of oats 30s)	3	13	-
Item	2 Deer Skins 8s) 2 bushells of Indian Corne 6s	-	14	-
Item	2 old Sieths and takle 8s) 3 sicles another old Sieth 8s)	-	16	-
Item	the Lumber in ye house	1	10	-
Item	ye plow Irons Share and coulter boult Collor & Cleves	1	5	-
Item	ye Cart and wheels with ye Irons belonging	2	10	6
Item	2 Chains 20s: a yoke 5s 1000 of boards 5£	6	5	-
Item	hay at 30s) pitchfork 18d A negro Servant man: 40£	41	11	6
	totall	598	:14	:6

The Aforesd Inventory of Anthony Ludlam was presented
To the Aforesd Court of Sessions held at: Southold: June 82 by ye widow
and Relict of sd Anthony Late Deceased: with a peticon to Administer
upon ye sd Estate: and seeing Shee hath ready at hand Samuell Johnes
And ffrances Sayre who are ready to bee Come Suretys for her perform
=anc thereof the Courte Doe Admit her to all intents and purposes
Sole Administratix on Sd Estate shee performing the same acording
as the Law Dirrects her Securyty with suretys taken in Court:&c:

At the Aforesd Court was prsented the Inventory of Cornelious
Vonke: by madline: widow and relict to Sd Cornelious with a
petion to Administer upon her said husbands Estate: which wch
was granted her by the Courte shee giveing Security according to Law

An Inventory of the goods Lands and Chattells of the Estate of
Cornelious Vonke who Deceased: August ye 8th 1681: taken and
Aprized: the tenth Instant: by Samuell Johnes Constble frances
Sayre: and John Howell Junr overseers

		£	s	d
Impr	the Houseing and home Lott: at	70	-	-
Item	one horse 5£: one 2 yearold mare 40s:	7	-	-
Item	2 Cowes: 8£ one two yearold: 50s	10	10	-
Item	3 Swine 40s) a pr of hollon Sheets at 3£	5	-	-
Item	3 home Spun Sheets 40s	2	-	-
Item	a bed and bested: a rug boulsters and pillows	5	-	-
Item	8 blankets: 8£) a bedsted bed boulsters and pillows 3£	11	-	-
Item	9 pillow Drawers:30s) 9 yrds of osenbrigs:20s	2	10	-
Item	40 pound of flax:40s flax un Broke 5s a hetchell 10s)	2	15	-
Item	a gun 40s a Sword 16s) 8£ of linin yarn 20s	3	16	-
Item	ten napkins 20s: 4 yds Lokeram 12s) 5 yds of fine linin 20s)	2	12	-
Item	5 yds ½ of fine Calico 30s) 3 ramants: of blue and white 9s)	1	19	-
Item	his two hats 30s his wereing linin 25s wollen 50s	5	-	-
Item	6 pound of Linin yarne 12s) 2 Chests:15s	1	7	-
Item	a gun 30s a Coboard at 3£) 3 Iron potts:and a ketle 70s)	8	-	-
Item	a duzen of porrengers 20s: 9 platers:50s	3	10	-
	bason platers			
Item	4 beakers 24s: 2 Saltcellers & a Cup:6s: a Sucking botle 8s)	1	18	-
Item	Earthen were at 30s a Lanthorne 4s	1	14	-
Item	a tin pott & tunell 3 Lamps a botle Sauspan and Cullender	-	11	-
Item	wooden were:at 25s fire shovell tongs tramell grid Iron 9s)	1	14	-
Item	a box Iron 6s a frying pan and warming pan 15s)	1	1	-
Item	a Looking glass 1s: a bible and other books 30s	1	11	-
Item	a Small bedsted and Cradle 10s Chayres 20s	1	10	-

Item

	£		
Item 2 Sieves 4s) 1 bushell of Salt 8s) 4 wheels & a bedsted 20s)	1	12	–
Item 2/3 of a barrill of mallases:40s: a bedsted 8s	2	8	–
Item 3 Sides of Sole Leather 54s more leather:3s	2	17	–
Item 2 tubs: 4 gallons of oyle 8s to other Lumber 20s	1	8	–
Item Shoemakers Last 8s: more leather 25s	1	13	–
Item all blades and tacks 16s: alls 4s: knives:9s	1	9	–
Item nipers and pincers:8s	–	8	–
besides book Debts: Sum totall is	164	:08	:00

A true Copy p Jno Howell Clerk:to:ye sessions

An Inventory of the Estate of Jacob Wood Lately Deceased
Aprized by Samuell Johnes Elnathan Topping Shamger hand
and Henry Person Sworne Before Justice Topping:

		£	s	d
To	Six Swine at 3£ to 2 Cowes at 7£: 10s	10	10	–
To	2 Steers at 3£:10s to a horse at 4£	7	10	–
To	ye house and and 20 Acres of Land with ye fenceing	120	–	–
To	2 yearling heifers at 40s	2	–	–
To	an ould feather bed and bolster 2 blankets & coverled	5	12	–
I:tm	a Linin wheele a cradle and meal trough	–	12	–
To	a Table at 7s: a remnant of Cloath 7s	–	14	–
To	a wollen wheele at 3s a Churne 18d	–	4	6
To	a pcell of whalebone 3£:10s: for Lumber In ye chamber 5s)	3	15	–
To	a bedsted and Cord 12s: a trundle bedsted and Cord 14s	1	6	–
To	10 porengers at 20s: 5 platers 23s: 2 plate 5s	2	8	–
To	1 great bason at 8s: 2 Small basons at 4s	–	12	–
To	4 old Sieths:7s to a ax beetle and old tooles 8s	–	15	–
To	1 old chamber pot 18d: 7 Spoons 5s 2 Drinking pots 9s	–	15	6
To	tin ware all at 15s to a bible at 8s a can 12d 2 Earthen plates 5s	1	9	–
To	a cut lash 15s: 1 Sicle 4 pailes and ye Rest of ye) wooden at 32s 1 barrill of beefe at 40s)	4	7	–
To	2 Creame potts 2s: 4 Chayres and other Lumber 15s	–	17	–
To	a friying pan 5s: 10£ of wollen and linin yarne 12s	–	17	–
To	3 iron potts 2 ketles 3£:13s to 4 botles 4s	3	17	–
To	Napkins 29s 2 sheets 20s an handsaw 3s	2	12	–
To	2 Chests and a box 22s to curtaines and vallencs 12s	1	4	–
To	2 files a paire of Compasses:3s Cowbell & Chissell 2s:6d	–	5	6
To	a box iron 3s a pr of tongs 4s a razor 3s	–	10	–
To	a Square 4s a gun 15s his wareing Aparrel	6	15	–
To	Shot and Lead 3s) 2 Shirts and a Looking glass 14s	–	17	–
To	½ a whipsaw 6s	–	6	–
To	a fether bed Rug boulster and 2 pillows	5	10	–
		186	00	6

To	2 pr of Sheets 32s a flockbed 8s	2	-	-
To	2 Shirts 30s	1	10	-
To	a Share: Coulter Coller and bolt by informacon	-	12	-
To	a Sadle at 16s	-	16	-
	this Inventory wrong sumed up brought from)	4	:18	:0
	before Entered now rectified ye other side)	186	:00	:6
	Sum totall -	190	:18	:6

A true Coppy p me Jno Howell Junr § Clk:

At ye Aforesaid Courte of Sessions held at Southold June 1682 was prsented by mary wood widow to said Jacob Wood the afore Sd Inventory with a peticon to Administer thereon wch by ye Courte was granted her according to Law Shee giveing Security to perform the ye same acordingly=: and farther she declares that her two Sonns Shall have her pt of her husbands Land at her Decease wch She gave the Clarke order to Enter

p order of Courte p Jno Howell Clerk

At the Aforesd Court of Sessions held at Southold June 1682 widdow mary Rainer Relict to Joseph Rainer of southampton Decesed prsented to this Courte a paper as a will and the wittneses thereunto Subscribe were Sworne In Courte to the the trueth of the Same: that it was his act and deed: and the Court allow
she is also Admited as Sole Executrix returning an inventory to ye next/
of it soe to bee the disposall of the sd Joseph Rainers Estat as ffolloweth:

Know all men by these prsents that Joseph Rainer of Southampton In ye East Ride of Yorkhier on long Island being by gods providence at this time Bound off the sd Island to Boston In new England and not Certainly knowing how the Lord In his goodness may Dispose of me Doe Order and Dispose of my Land and Estate as followeth

Imprimis I give and order that my Eldest Sonn Thirston Rainer shall have after my Decease all my land In ye oxpasture and halfe my land in ye great plaines and all my meadow in shinecok great neck and a Quarter parte of my Comonage after the next Devisson is Laid out and this to him and his Lawfull heires for Ever and if he dye without any Lawfull heyre then to return to ye Rest of my Sonns to be Devided Amongst them //

2ly I give unto my two Sonns Isaac and John all my land at wee =Copauge and the Divistion that was Laid out last year at mea cocks and the next Divission that Shall be Laid out: and halfe my Commonage after ye next Divition is Laid out and this all to bee Equally Divided between them and there heirs for Ever

3ly: I Leave all the Rest of my houseing and Land to ye Disposall of my Loving wife mary Rainer Dureing her

Life and After her Decease to fall unto my Sonn Josiah Rainer
And to his heires for Ever

4ly: I make my Loveing wife ^ my Executrix of this my Dispossall of my land &
to give out all Such Legacys as I Shall after give as to
my two Dauters mary and hanah Rainer fifty pounds
a peece to be paid out of my Estate: and to my Daughter Elizabeth
Rainer two:Cowes all the Rest of my Estate to belong and
bee at the Disposall of my Executrix In witnes whereof
I have hereunto set my hand & Seale this 8th Day of may:
Anno quo: Dom. 1678:

Signed and sealed In ye prsence of — Joseph Rayner
Henry Person Junr
John Laughton §

a tru Coppy p Jno Howell Clerk

Southampton June ye 12: 1682

A Inventory taken this Day of ye Estate of Joseph Rainer
Lately Deceased and also aprized by us Chosen and Sworne - - -

		£	s	d
Imprimis	to 150 pound Comonage at	15	-	-
to	ye Land Adjoyning with the home Lott Adjudged 33 acres 5£ p acre	165	-	-
to	ye houseing and barne	90	-	-
to	7½ acres of land in ye little plaines	37	-	-
to	17 acres in ye great plaines	51	-	-
to	meadow at Shinecock great and little neck and Seponak	25	-	-
to	a hundred and fifty of medow at quaquanantuk	15	-	-
to	20 acres of land at the millstone brook & orchard Land	29	-	-
to	68 acres of land at weecopouk at	204	-	-
to	20 acres of land at mecox	30	-	-
to	20 acres of land above Scutle hole	20	-	-
to	20 acres of land at hogneck	20	-	-
to	six:oxen 30£: to 9 Steer 16£) to ten Cows:37£: 8 cattle of 3 yrold 24£)	107	-	-
to	9 of 2 yereold 18£: 6 yearlings 9£: to 7 Swine 3£:10s	30	10	-
to	cart harrow yok Irons Chaine and plow	5	10	-
to	1 ax 1 how 1 matuk 1 Stubing how 2 whaleing Irons: 1 ads	1	16	-
to	2 beds & bedsteds and furneture	18	-	-
to	a Cubord 1£.10s: to 2 Coats 1 hat and other werein Cloaths	9	10	-
to	2 pr of blankets 29s: 1 pr of Sheets 20s: 1 Coverled 15s: 1 Chest 10s	3	14	-
to	1 table 2 Chayres 1 warming pan: 1 Sadle	2	3	-
to	4 Coshions M of nailes led and powder 2 Chests	2	1	-
to	16 pound of Course woolle 8d p pound 1 botle 1 hat at 5s	-	15	8
to	3 ketles 6£:10s: 4 pots at 3£ 2 scellits 14s 2 old kettles 1£	11	4	-
to	a Scimer ladell Iron morter and tunell	-	15	-

to

	£	s	d
to 38 pound of pewter 4£ 15 other old pewter 1£:10s	6	5	–
To 1 Smothing Iron and Candlestick 5s: to Earthenpots & tunel 18d	–	6	6
to 1 bible and other Small books at 16s to 1 Shovell 3s	–	19	–
to 1 andiron and to tramel 1 flesh fork 14s) 1 fire pan and tongs 6s	1	–	–
to 1 keelers 4 bowles 1 tray: 1 payle 1 ridle 1 sieve & earthen were	1	–	6
to 1 old plater poringers and other pewter 5s: 6 old barrill 15s	1	–	–
to 1 barrill of meat at 2 pound: 1 frying pan & earthen ware	2	5	–
to 1 grinston: at 18s 2 beds and bedsteds at 12£: 20 bushells of wheat 5£	17	18	–
to more beding at 10s) to Sieths and Sicles 10s) 1 old kettle at 8s	1	8	–
to woole and yarne 30 pound at 12d p pound 30s) 1 pr stillyards 12s	2	2	–
to 3 pailes Churne and tubs old iron 1 beetle and 2 wedges) with all other Lumber all at)	1	10	–
Sum totall is	938	=14	=8

memarandum: 5½ acres of wheat on the ground
Also in Timothy Laskins hand 73: pound
Also and In John Earles hands 41 pound 15s
this Mrs Rainer Desires Shold be noted

Edward Howell
Obadiah Rogers
his
Christopher C Lupton
mark
Charles Sturmey

A true Coppy p mee Jno Howell Junr §: June ye 16: 1682

Be it knowne unto all whome it may Concerne that whereas
Mary Rainer widdow and Relect unto Joseph Rainer Late Deceased
hath given In an Inventory of the Estate of ye said Joseph Rainer which
is upon Record by her order In the Court Records) with a memaran
=dum under written by her order that there is In John Earls hands
fourty one pound 15s= which the Said John Earle Doth no ways acknow
=ledge but he doth here by protest Against the said memarandm
Inserted in the Aforesd Inventory
this Aforesd protest was Entered p order of the Said Earle
this 28 of february 1682/3 p me John Howell Junr Clerk

The Inventory of the Estate of Mr Joseph Taylor Late Deces
ed of Southampton Inventoryed and Aprized by John Jessup –
Mr Job Sayre John Howell Junr Isaac willman whoe
were Sworne to the Aprizemt therof by Justice Topping
May the ye 31:1682.

Imprs:	to ye 4 acres of Land at ye oxpasture gate at:	12	–	–
Item	4: acres more upon Divistion in ye oxpasture	8	–	–
Item	ye 20 Acres of land In ye South Devition: at Sagabonak	30	–	–
Item	20 Acres behind widow Cooprs lot:at:	20	–	–
Item	20 Acres yet to Lay out:	20	–	–
Item	40 acres of land in Scutle hole Divistion	40	–	–
Item	20 acres of land at hog neck:at	15	–	–
Item	150 of Comonage:at	10	–	–
Item	3 Cowes at 12£: 1 heifer: 2yearold 50s: 2 yearlings 3£	17	10	–
Item	4 Sheep and two lambs 30s two pigs and a Calfe 30s	3	–	–
Item	8½ yrds of Cotten and linin Cloath 4s p yards:	1	14	–
Item	his wereing Aparrell at	15	–	–
Item	pr of Sheets at 30s. a paire of sheets at 20s) 6 pr more 10£:10s	13	–	–
Item	1 Sheet 10s 2 paire of fine pillow beers 15s 1 pr Ditto 10s	1	15	–
Item	4 pr Course Ditto 20s) ten towels 20s 2 duzen of napkins 3£	5	–	–
Item	9 Ditto 14s To 5 table Cloaths 37s) 3 Cubord Cloaths 18s	3	9	–
Item	2 wollets 4s: 2 Cloke bags 4s: to½ Duzen of Diaper napkins 15s)	1	3	–
Item	a rug 3£:10s to a Case of bottles 10s a Sadle 20s	5	–	–
Item	bedsted bed and furneture 10£: a barrill of rum 4s p gallon 6£	16	–	–
Item	50£ of Suger 25s a peece of Sarg 7£:10s	8	15	–
Item	11 yards of Stuff 46s) a yrd red Sarg: 4 yards of lace & 4 of ribin 24s)	3	10	–
Item	22 yds of linin Cloath 55s) 13½ yds of fine Scotch cloath 52s	5	7	–
Item	8 yds½ of sleesy hollond at	2	2	6
Item	ten yards ½ of fine Dowlase at 4s p yrd	2	2	–
Item	5 yds ½ of osenbrigs: 10s 9 yds of fusten 22s 6	1	12	6
Item	a yard ½ of turkey mohare 9s: ten yds of black sarg 70s	3	19	–
Item	a yard of silk 12s 11 yards of Sarg 66s	3	18	–
Item	a remnant of blue linin 5s: ½ a pound of thrid 5s	–	10	–
Item	a pound Ditto Coarse 5s a pcell of tape at 8s	–	13	–
Item	tables at 40s: 2 Chests and a Cradle 35s	3	15	–
Item	3½ yards of homspon Cloath:14s: 2 3/4 of fine hollond 33s)	2	7	–
Item	3 remnts of fine linin 18s to a Carpit at 10s	1	8	–
Item	7 Small Chayres 20s: 2 Small Chayres and 2 Stoole all raught 8s)	1	8	–
Item	a worked-great Chayre 12s to 4 Small trunk 30s	1	2	–
Item	a Coberd 30s: to ye workt Cushions 40s	3	10	–

Item

		£	s	d
Item	a peece of Silke at 10s a pcell of Cotton woole 15s	1	5	-
Item	aboute 2 bushell½ of wheat and 1 bushell Indian	-	15	-
Item	a peece of Stuff 24 yds by Information	4	16	-
Item	2 duzen ½ of tretchers 2s:6d to 3 pewter Dishes 20s	1	2	6
Item	tin ware and Candlestick 6s: a Jug: & 2 glas botles 4s:	-	10	-
Item	fine porengers and a bason: 12s	-	12	-
Item	Silver plate 7£:10s to Cash 7:8: vallued at	15	18	-
Item	14 barrills of oyle 28£ to 3 bags 10s 8£ lininyarn 24s	29	14	-
Item	milk vessells 10s 6d a brass ketle 20s a Scellet 9s	1	4	6
Item	2 paile 4s a frying pan 5s a pot ten shillings	-	19	-
Item	a tramell and ledle 8s a pr of Andiorns one broke 10s	-	18	-
Item	a Seive at 2s aboute 220£ of whalebone 7£:6s:8d:	7	8	8
Item	a gun at 20s a pistell at 15s: a Sicle 2s	1	17	-
Item	mallases at 3£ 2 wheeles 12s washd lethern Skins:8s:	4	-	-
Item	2 Inkhorns a looking and a Razor 6s	-	6	-
Item	old Sieths:3s To a desk and a box at 10s	-	13	-
Item	the Lumber In the house at	1	10	-
Item	a Library of books: at	50	-	-
	Sum totall	406	:18	:8

By us - - - John Jessup
Isaac Willman.
Job Sayre

A true Coppy p John Howell Jur. Clerk

Anthony Brokholls Esqr Comandr in Cheife
and the Councell of the provinc of New Yorke To Mr Isaac
Arnold of Southold aturney to Mr Adam Winthrop
and mr John foster of boston Marchants and Heirs Creditors
to Thomas Harris late of Boston aforsd Deceased Whereas ye sd
Thomas Harris haveing while he lived and at ye time
of his Death goods and Chattels within this province
his widow and Relect refuseing to take upon her ye Admin
=istration of his Estate and the Sd Adam winthrop and
John foster In ye behalfe of themselves and the other
Creditors to ye Said Estate haveing Obtained Letters of
Administration in ye Mattachusets Collony and the Sd
Isaac Arnold In there behalfes Desireing the Same
here as there aturney I Doe by these prsents ordaine

Opointe and Depute him ye Sd Isaac Arnold aturney
as aforesd to be Administrator of the Sd goods Chattles and
Creddites of the sd Thomas Harris Deceased for and in
the behalfe of the Sd Creditors and to take in to his Costody
and possession and Dispose of the Same well and truly
and alsoe to aske gather Sue for and Recover all Debts wt
=Soever Due to ye Sd Deceased and to pay any Debts In wch ye
Sd Deceased at ye time of his Death stood Bound as far as his
goods and Chattles Can Extend and psueant to ye bond &
Security given: fully to Administer Rendering atrue
and A Just acompt thereof acording to Law Given under
My hand and Seale In New yorke this ninth Day of
January In ye thirty third year of the Raine of our
Sovereigne Lord Charles ye Second by the grace of God of
England Scottland France and Ireland King Defend
der of the faith & annoq Dom: 1681

Anthony Brokholls

Letters of Administracon on ye
Estate of Thomas Harris Late
of Boston Deceased Granted to
Mr Isaac: Arnold In behalfe of
his Creditors: past ye office &c.
John West Clk:
A true Coppy p Jno Howell Junr Clk

At a Courte of Sessions held at Southampton by his Majesties
Authority In the year of our Lord 1682/3 & on ye 7th
8. & 9: day of March was presented by Mr Thomas James and Mr -
Edward Howell Severall Deeds of giftes wherein was Expressed ye
minde and Will of Thomas Dyment of Easthampton Deceased
wherein he hath Disposed of his whole Estate: This Courte haveing per
rused them Doe aprove and Confirme the Said Deeds In Hand In full force
and to be Recorded according to the true Intents and meaning of them
also it is farther ordered that Thomas Dyment Junr of Easthampton
shall not have his Deed of Gifte Delivered to his possession untill hee
Deliver up Into the hands of Mr Thomas James or Mr Edward Howell
aformer Deed which he hath upon which this Last hath Dependance
that the Said Deed may bee both Recorded together: and they Doe
Admitt the Said James Dyment as Executor to the Said Estate and Mr Tho:
James of Easthampton and Mr Edward Howell of Southampton are Apro
ved of and allowed to bee as Supervisers with the Said Executor according
to the mind of the tastator:

Wheras there is a Contract of Maryage to be in Convenient
time Consumated between my Eldest Sonn James Diamond and
Hanah the Daughter of mr Thomas James therefore be it known
to all men by these psents that upon the said Consideration I
Thomas Diamond Senr doe oblidge my selfe to the said Thomas
James To give and bequeath unto my Son James Diamond to have
and Enjoy after mine and my beloved wifes Deceas as followeth
(viz) my now dwelling house with barne and twelve Acres of
Land next Adjoyning all the furneture in my great Roome (ye
beding only Excepted: alsoe Eleven Acres of my Close which Lyes
Between Willm Edwards on the on Side and Tho: osborne and Richd
Brooks on ye other Side also two third parts of my meadow at Na
peakg also the foure acres of Land in ye litle plaines wch I form
erly bought of John Stratten and a third parte of my Share of
Montauk: and a Duble Share of the Quickstock wch I Shall Leave
behinde me also my whipsaw my Cross=cut=saw and my hand=saw
also I doe Engage my Selfe that my Sonn Aforsd Shall bee
Sole Executor of my Last will and testament and fully freely
and Absolutely possess and Enjoy to him and his heirs for Ever
all the Above perticulers After my Death and the Decease of
my Beloved wife as witnes my hand and Seale this 21 day
of August 1677

Signed Sealed & Delivered in prsents of)

all ye Above perticulers was
Enterlinde before ye Signeing & Seal[ ]
and the Sd James Diamond is to
have one third part of ye Comon
age that is my Right in the
bounds of this Towne

Also its to be understood I doe hereby Engage that In Case I
Dye before my wife that then my Sonn James Aforesd Shall
take present possession of the one halfe of my Dwelling house
and one halfe of the twelve Acres of Land as also the use of
the barne Aforsd as wittness my hand the year and day Aforesd

Signed Sealed In prsents of)

Thomas Diament

Josiah Hubert
Peregrine Stanbrow

the truth of what is Above
written was acknowledged by Thomas
Diament Senr Aprill ye 27 1682 be
fore me John Topping Justice

the Above written was Entered into the Towne Records
the 29th of September 1682 p me Thomas Tallmage recordr
A true Copy p me John Howell Junr Recordr

Be it knowne unto all men by these prsents that I Thomas
Diament of Easthampton upon Severall Considerations knowne to my
Selfe Doe give and bestow and of my owne free and vollentary motion
Grant and bequeath to my Eldest Sone James Diament over and A
bove wt I have given him in a deed wch apeare baring date August 21
1677 I Say I give unto him my best feather bed (viz) that I usally lye
upon and all the furneture belonging to it after my Deceas and his
Mothers as Curtaines boulsters vallaines pillows Coverled blankets pillow
beers and a paire of my best Sheets together with the bedsted: also I give to
him after my Deceas my Long table In the bigger Roome with ye form
belonging to it and my greater looking glass and the Cobord In the room
Aforesd and one of my great Chests and three of my best Chayres and
my great wicker Chayre also a Chest of Drawers I have Agreed for
when it Comes also I give to him my great Iron kettle which is
used to try oyle in and two of my bigest pewter Dishes also a paire of
ballowes tongs and Iron tramell also the best of my wareing garment
if he will ware them: also I give him fourty Shillings in money if
I have too much Left at my Decease and I give him the one half
of my Intrest in takleing boats or Indians with respect to ye whale
Dessigne know yea alsoe I give to my Sonn James all the above men
coned perticulers to Desend After him to his Eldest Sonn Thomas my
grandchild and In Case he Die before age to be to the next heir or heirs
male proceed from him Successively and In Confirmation of ye prm
mises I Sett to my hand and Seale this 27th day of December Ano:
Domo: 1680

Subscribed Sealed and Delivered — Thomas Diament
in prsents of us
Edward Hare
Thomas Harriss

the truth of wt is above written was
aknowledged by Thomas Diament Senr
Aprill the 27: 1682 before me
John Topping Justice

this above written Enterd into the Records of East hampton
September ye 29: 1682: p me Thomas Tallmage Recordr

This Deed of gift made by me Thomas Diament Sen of East
hampton in New yorkshire upon LongIsland to my Sonn James -
Diament whome I make my heire I being of Sound understand
ing and Reason and upon good Considerations as followeth be it
knowne that whereas I have made Severall Deed of gift to this
my Son James and it hath pleased god to take from mee Since yt
time my youngest Son John whom I intended Som parte of
my Estate I doe give to this my sonn James After my Decease my
house and barne herein the towne together with the whole -
Allottment and Adition Containing Sixteen Acres or thereaboutes
also I give unto him my Close Lying by Willm Edwards upon ye
great plaine being aboute fifteen Acres also I give to him besides
what already he hath in possession upon the little plaines

I Entreat Mr Tho: James of this towne & mr Edward Howell of Southampton be pleased to take the over Sight of this Deed and ye other Deed of gift for ye true performance of them:

The four Acres of Land I bough of John Hand also I give unto
him all the meadow belonging to me at Napeak and one third pt
of my medow at ye Northwest alsoe I give to him two thirds of all
my Comonage both at the Towne and Mentauket: this Land above
Expressed I give to him and his hiers to have and To hold the
Same for Ever After the Decease of mee and my beloved wife
Mary upon Condition that hee Shall not sell nor Allinate ye Said
Land but it Shall Decend to his heires of his body After him also
I make my Son James Executor of my whole Estate After my
Decease and to Enter upon the possession of my whole Estate if my
wife See Cause to marry againe: and to have the use of it in ye mean
time: and to maintaine my wife mary honarably out of it Dure
ing her Life and at the decease of my beloved wife mary She Shall
have Liberty to Dispose of twenty pounds to whom Shee pleaseth
In ordinary pay and In such goods as my wife and Sonn Shall A
gree of: this farther Condition that my Sonn James and my wife
to give at her Decease to my Daughter Sarah Headly of new Jersey
A feather bed with furneture to it: my Daughter Aforesd to give ye
Said bed to which of her Children Shee pleaseth: also he shall give out
of my Estate to my Daughter Abygaile foure pounds after ye decease
of her Mother In Common pay and price alsoe to give out of my
in comom pay
Estate Aforesaid to my Daughter Hanah Bird fourty Shillings ^ also
to give to my Daughter Ruth Dayton as aforesaid out of my Estate
ffourty Shillings in Comon pay: also to give out of my Estate as
Aforesd to my Daughter Ellizabeth Miller forty Shillings all
these After the decease of my wife Mary to be paid without
prizall of my Estate also I give to my grandchild mary Daughter to
my Sonn James my great trunk now up in the Chamber and in
Ratification and Confirmation of the prmises I Sett to my hand
and Seale this 28th of July Ano: Domo: 1682

Thomas Diment

the Enter linde words (in the mean time was before Signeing)

Delivered Subscribed
& Sealed in prsence of us
Thomas James
Kather: James

The Above written Entered in ye Towne Records
29 Septr 1682 p me Thomas Tallmage recordr

A true Coppy of the Aforsd will & Deed
of Gift: p John Howell Clarke:

This Deed of Gift made by me Thomas Dyment Senr of Easthampton
In ye East Rideing of yorkshire upon Long Island I haveing my
Reason and understanding: To my younger Son Thomas Dyament have
ing formerly given him upon his Marryage the house and Land was
mine at Georgica: and that peice of Land Called the girdled trees upon
the Little plaine I doe Confirme the Same upon the Same Conditi
on Exressed In that Deed of Gift I Doe also farther give to this
my aforesd Sonn Thomas the Land was formerly Meechams lott
upon the Little plaine being my farther lott there from the Towne
also I give to him my other lott upon the little plaine Comonly
Called Brooks his lott which I bought: this After my Decease: also
I give to him two thirds of my meadow Lying at the north west
from this Towne to be Equally Devided After my Decease alsoe I
give to his first borne Son twenty pounds in Contry pay & price
of which he hath already received fourty Shillings and the rest yt
he shall not Receive before my Decease my Executor Shall
pay the Remainer: The Condicon of this Deed is that my
Aforsaid Son Thomas shall not at Any Time Sell nor Allinate this
Land Above Specified but it Shall goe or Descend to the hiers of
his body After him and upon the Same Condistion I give him ye
Third of my Comonage both at the Towne and mentauket
belongs to mee Know yea that whereas it is Expressed above After
after ye Decease
my Decease is to be understood ^ both of me and my wife Mary
Dyment and in Ratification and Confirmation of the prem
mises: I Sett to my hand and Seale this 28th of July Ano: Dom: 1682
Also I Entreat Mr Tho: James of this towne and Mr Edward
Howell of Southampton be pleased to take the oversight of
to my Son Thomas
this and my other Deed of gifte for the Due pformance of ym
Subscribed & Sealed in presence Thomas Dyment
of us: Thomas James
kather: James

A true Coppy of the origanall p
Jno Howell Junr § Clarke

Be it knowne to all whom these presents Shall Come: that wher
as there hath been Some Discontent in mee mary Diment of East
hampton widow of the deceased Tho: Diment with Respect to the
Disposall of the Estate of this my Deceased Husband which hath
ocassioned Some Controversy and debate at Last wee are Come to
a full and fine Agreement for the Settleing of maters for ye
future soe long as it Shall please god to Continue me in life
as followeth: Imprmis that where as the house I Live in -
was to be halfe my son Jamess it is ordered that I to have the
whole house at my Dispose During my life and then to returne

Returne to my Sonn James 2ly: that my Son James Shall from time to time During my Life maintaine for me both Sumer and winter feed four good milch Cowes also that I Shall have the use of two Oxen & a horse when I Stand in need of them for my owne use alsoe what land I Shall See Cause to make use of for ye supply of me of bread Corne for my Selfe or family that I Shall have it allowed for mee Dureing my Life I doe also further firmly bind and Engage my selfe to give in a true Inventory and accompt of all the moveable goods within doors is in my hands or hath been since the decease of my husband Aforsd and doe farther en gage and bind my Selfe that none of these goods that shall be Left with me for my use Dureing Life Shall bee any way Em bezzelled of wasted or disposed without the Consent of my son whom my husband left Executor of his Estate and his over Seers my Son James alsoe Shall provid firewood for me Every Year Dureing life only he Shall have allowance of help of the Indian Servant Soe long as he lives with mee also Every year to have a fatt beast allowed the said mary yearly and the sd James to grind what meale Shall be wanting for her Supply lastly that the said mary Diment Shall have thirty pounds allowed out of the Estate as Comon price at her death to despose of as Shee pleaseth and In Such goods as James & Shee agree of: be it knowne alsoe the Said James Diment Shall Cause the Land Aforesd to be plowed So much as Shall be found needfull for the Suply of his mother with bread Corne and to take Care of the threshing and In gathering of ye Same and the grinding of it to meale lastly it is agreed that if here after it please god to visitt the Aforesd Mary Diment wth Sickness or Lameness So that what is not already menconed Shall not be found Sofficient for her Comfortable lively hood or maintenance She Shall have a further Supply out of ye Estate as Shall be found need full in that Condition for Confirmation of the premises wee mutually Sett to our hands and Seals this nineth day of march Ano: Dom: 1682/3 it is also farther agreed upon that if James Dyment Shall Consent the Aforesd Mary Dyament Shall have that feather bed now Lying In the Chamber next the Chimney and the boulster and blankett and other furneture belonging to Sd bed at her owne Dispose and to bestow upon whom Shee pleaseth After her De cease &c:

her
mary marP Dyment
mark

Signed Sealed and Delivered
In presence of us us
Samuell Howell
Sarah Howell
John Hills

Tho: James
Edward Howell

A true Coppy p me John Howell Clark
March ye 15: 1682/3

These may Certifie that I James Dyment of Easthampton Doe Com
mit all matters Concerning the Declaration of the Last mind of my
honerd father Deceased: Inserted In Severall papers under his hand &
Seale Soe far as Concerning my Selfe into the hands of mr Thomas
James of this Towne and mr Edward Howell of Southampton who[m]
my father Lefte to be overseers for the Due pformance of his Ex
press mind and will to act to all Intents and purposes in my behalf
and to Stand In full force as if I myselfe did personally apeare
March: 1682/3 wittness my hand
Signed in presenc
of us James Dyment
Thomas Harriss A true Coppy p John Howell Clark 16:1mo
Ruth James:

May ye 31: 1683 meantaukett:
know all men by these presents that we true proprietors of
mentauket have given and Doe Give unto John Osborne
A Small neck of Land: Lying in the South west Side of ye
great pond to him and his heirs and assignes for Ever to have
and to hold without any Claime from us or any under
us: wee Say that necke of Land which is Called: wattuquasset
as wittness our hands &c. Seach[]

his	the mark	of Sachataka
young Sacham	the mark	of gentleman
mark	the mark of	Chechonoo
the mark of Sowan	the mark	of Obadiah
the mark of wampequamon)	the mark	I=ambussu:
the mark of panesso	the mark	of wabeton
the mark of Conkamosik	the mark	of keant
Dicks mark	Livewell	his mark
the mark of young wabeton)	nat Indians	marke
the mark of Scander bag	tom Indians	marke
the mark nahannks	ben Indians	marke
Thot nose marke		
ahnaman his mark		

Signed and Delivered
by turfe and twigge be
fore Benjamin osborne
Thomas osborne Junr:

A true Copy of the origenall:
Enterd this 11 day of June: 1683
p me John Howell Junr Clerk

Att a Court of Session held at Southampton vizt on ye 7: 8: 9 day of march 1683: was presented the inventory of Thomas Reeves of Southold with a petition by & In the behalfe of Agnes Reeves widow to Said Thomas reeves to Administer upon Said Estate: the Court doe Admitt ye said Agnes Reeves as Sole Administratrix to said Estate or Inventory which is as followeth

An Inventory of ye Estate of Thomas Reeves of Southold who Deceased the first Day of December in ye year 1682

		£		
Imprs	hous and Lands ten Acres at home forteen At north Sea four Acres of meadow and a first Lott Comonage	50	–	–
Item	two Oxen	8	–	–
Itt	3 Cowes 9£ one two yearold heifer 30s two yearling 40s	12	10	–
Itt	2 young Swine 10s	–	10	–
Itt	four blankets one bed one boulster two pillows	2	4	–
Itt	weareing Cloaths four pounds	4	–	–
Itt	two Chests one box:10s one warming pan 10s	1	–	–
Itt	pewter Seven peeces	–	16	–
Itt	one Iron pott 8s Itt woode trumperry	–	15	–
Itt	his armes 2£ wheat and Indian Corne 2£	4	–	–
	the totall Sum is	84	=3	:0

Thomas Rider and James reeves are Surety for the said widow Administration . –

A true Coppy p John Howell
Junr Clark to Court of Sessions

Thomas mapes
Benjamin youngs
Stephen Bayly:

At a Courte of Sessions held by his Majestys Authoryty at Southold upon the 5:Day of June 1683: was presented the Inventory and Aprizment of the Estate of John Mapes who Deceased ye 9th Day of October In ye year 1682:

Inventory of John Mapes

		£	s	d
Imprs	one bed one boulster and two pillows	7	–	–
Itt	one Sett of Curtaines and vallaints	3	–	–
Itt	3 pewter platers:15s 5 pewter porrengers 12s	1	7	–
Itt	one pewter bason 6s one pewter Chamberpott 7s	–	13	–
Itt	one pewter tankerd 6s: 8 occomee Spoones 8s	–	14	–
Itt	3 white Earthen plates 18d one Earthen Saltseller 6d	–	2	–
Itt	one brass ketle aboute 6 gallons	1	10	–
Item	one brass Scillett 8s one Iron pott and tramell 25s	1	13	–
Item	one frying pan 5s:one ring and Staple for a nobyoke	–	9	–

		£	s	d
Itt	one Ax and one how 10s one mosket a repion and belt	3	–	–
Itt	one pair of Carpenters Compasses 1s: 3 wooden boules 2 wooden dishes 8s)	–	9	–
Itt	one wooden plater 2 wooden trays 5s one bedsted 1 Small table 23s)	1	8	–
Itt	two payles 3 Chayres one halfe barrell	–	8	6
Itt	firken one Chest 12s 3 coats 3 p trowsers one Stufe weascoat 6£:8s	7	–	–
Itt	one Carsey Coate one Small Looking glass	–	9	–
Itt	two pa:re of Stokens three paire of Shooses	1	–	–
Itt	one paire of Sheets one Coverled	2	10	–
Itt	one table Cloath foure napkines four pillobeers	1	–	–
Itt	four neckcloaths one bible one horne of powder	–	13	6
Itt	3 pound bullets one deer Skin	–	7	–
Itt	one wheele Spindle one Razor and Case	–	5	–
Itt	one gimlett one sett of Silver buttons	–	5	–
Itt	one Earthen Chamberpott one paire of gloves	–	3	–
Itt	three parts of a barrell of mallases one foot Joynt rule	2	7	–
Itt	one Sithe with all belonging to it	–	10	–
Itt	1 bushell of peas 17 pound tobaco: one Sickle	–	8	6
Itt	40 bushells of Indian Corne	5	–	–
Itt	40 bushells of wheat	9	–	–
Itt	30 bushells of oats	3	15	–
Itt	1 horse bridle Sadle holter 2 mares	3	4	–
Itt	6 Swin 2 yearold 5 Swine one yeareold	12	–	–
Itt	2 oxen 4 Cowes 3:3 yearold one two yearold)			
Itt	3 yearling 3 Calves)	29	5	–
Itt	2 mares 3 hatts	3	5	–
		104	-00	-6

the Aprizers Abram Corey Stepen bayly
Jonat: Horton Joshua Horton

upon the peticon of martha Mapes widow and relict to ye Said John Mapes Shee Is Admited to Administer upon the Aforesd Inventory: and hath given In Security according to Law: her Surety are mr william Halliock and Thomas mapes:-

A true Copy of the Aforesaid Inventory p John Howell §

In the name of God Amen the twenty eight day of March 1683 I Arther Howell of Southampton In ye East Riding of Yorkeshire on LongIsland being now Sick and weake In body but good Sound and perfect memory praised be allmighty god And Calling to Remembrance the uncertainty of this transitory Life, doe make Constitute ordaine and Declare this my Last will and Testement In maner and form following first and principelly I Comend my Soule to god-Almighty my Creator and my body to ye Earth from whence it was taken

Item I Give and to my Eldest Son Elisha when he Shall Come to the age of one and twenty years the one halfe of my Dwelling House and barne with the other Houseing and the one halfe of all my land at home that is Adjoyning to my Dwelling house and the other halfe of all the Aforesd houseing and Lands I Likwise Give unto him my said After my wife hanahs Decease

2ly: I Give unto my younger Son Lemuell all that my percell of Land lying by and Adjoyneing Eastward to Ezekiell Sandford his home Lott and that peece of Land Lying at or neer unto hakers hole: and that percell of Land at Swan Creeke neck which my Son Arther Deceased gave unto this my Said Sonn Lemuell: I confirme unto him and alsoe I give unto this my Said Son all that my peec of land at meacox plaine After my wifes hanahs Decease:

All my Other Lands and meadows whersoever Lying and being that Doth or may of right belong unto mee that is not above Expressed with my Hundred pound Comonage and In Crease of Lands I give unto my two Sons Aforsd Elisha & Lemuell to bee In Every Respect Equally Devided between them also I give unto my two Sons aforesd ^ Each of them one horse a piare of oxen all which perticulers Soe given are to be De livered Into there possession when they Shall Come to ye age of twenty one years Except what is before Excepted to be at my Sd wifes Decease

3dly: Item I give and bequeath to my Daughter Ellizebeth Looper (Shee haveing had already the most part of her portion) five pounds to be paid out of my Estate which is to bee In full for her portion:

4thly: I give unto my Six Daughters namely Hanah abiah martha Eleanor Thamasen and Penellopee twenty pounds a peece to be paid to Them out of my Estate when they Shall Come to the age of Eighteen yeares or at the Day of there mariag

5ly I make My Loveing wife Hanah Executrix of this my Last will and testement to pay out ye Legacyes herin Contained and I give unto my Said Loveing wife for

her Comfortable Subsistance Dureing her Life the one halfe of
my Dwelling Howse and barne and other Howseing and the one
halfe of all ye land at home Adjoyning to my now Dwelling howse
and at her Deceas to be as aforsd to my Son Ellisha: and what
Else of my Estate Shall yet Remaine besides what is Disposed off
at ye Discreson of
I leave to ye use of my beloved wife to be disposed of ^ her and ye
overseers of this my will hereafter Named
Further it is to be under Stood that whereas my wife is now wth
Child and if it Shall please god that a Son Shall be borne unto me
my will and meaning is that hee Shall have ye Aforsd pcell of Land
which I have before given to Lemuell which Lyes near unto
hakers hole and I Likewise give him an Equall Share with his two
brothers In all ye land and medows that I before menconed to
be equally Devided Elisha and Lemuell and if ye Child that is ye[t]
to be borne Shall be a Daughter my will is that Shee Shall have
twenty pounds paid to her out of my Estate as the Rest of my -
Daughters have but if Shall please god that ye Child that is yet
to be borne Shall be a Son as aforesd and one of ye three Sons -
Shall hapen to Decease before he Comes to age then his part
or portion Shall Returne to ye other two Surviveing brethren but
then
if two of them Shall Decease before they Come to age ^ there port[ions]
to be devided Equally Amonst all my Children then Surviveing
nextly I apointe mr Job Sayre John Howell Junr and Mathe[w]
Howell to be Supervizers and overseers of this my Last will
and testement with my Executrix Hanah my beloved wife
also I give to my two Sons aforsd my winde mill they to
have Equele Right In it and my wife to have Equall Right
with them In ye Said Mill Dureing her Life: and for ye fur
ther Confirmation of this my will I have here unto Sett my
hand and fixed my Seale the Day and year first above writt
=en &c:

Signed Sealed and Delivered — Arther Howell
In presence of

Job Sayre
John Howell Junr §

A true Coppy of ye origanall p
me Jno Howell Junr Clark:-

The Aforsd will and following Inventory was presented to
this Courte of Sessions now Sitting at Southold this 7th day of
June 1683: by mrs Hanah Howell widow to mr Arther Howell
Deceased with a peticon for ye Confirmation and proofe there
of where upon the will was prooved In Courte and the witt
nesses thereunto Subscribed Sworne unto the trueth of ye Same -
and the Said Hanah Admited as Sole Executrix to ye Said will
and granted to have Letters of Admministration and the Said Job
Sayre John Howell and Mathew Howell are allowed and apro
ved of as Supervisers of the Said will according to ye
minde of ye testator therein Specified:

An Inventory and Aprizment of ye Estate (vizst) all the Lands goods and Chattells of Arther Howell of Southampton decesed By John Howell Junr mr John Jessup Job Sayre and mathew Howell who were Sworne unto the Same by mr John Topping Justice of ye Peace May ye 15th 1683

Imprs to 3 yoke of Oxen 12£ p yoke	36	-	-
to 3 yokes and 3 Chaines and Clevis and pin wth Apurtenance	2	-	-
to an old Cart and wheels and ye old boxes	1	2	-
to 4 Steers of 5 yearold:at 16£) 2 Steer of 4 yearold at 6£	22	-	-
to 15 Cowes and Six Sucking Calves at	60	-	-
to 9: 3 yearold Cattle at 22£: 9 Cattle 2 yearold:16£	38	-	-
to 5 yearlings at 4£ to a bull Stagge at 5£10s	9	10	-
to 30 Sheep at twelve pound to 2 Sadle Horses 10£	22	-	-
to 2 young horse at three pound 2 mares 4£: & a yrling mare 15s	7	15	-
to the Swine at 31£ 5s	31	5	-
to ye Land at home being 43:Acres at 3£ p acre	129	-	-
to ye Dwelling howse and Howseing at	140	-	-
to the barne 35	35	-	-
to ten Acres of Enclosed Land at meacox plaines at 3£ p ac	30	-	-
to 20 Acres by Ezekiells Land 40s p acres	40	-	-
to 28 acres by Sagaponak pond at 30s p Acres	42	-	-
to ten acres by hakers hole 25s p Acre	12	-	-
to fourteen Acres of land at Huntington	14	-	-
to 14 Acres of land at hog neck	10	-	-
to a hundred at quaqua: to a hundred of Comonage	9	-	-
to the wind mill at 20£	20	-	-
to a plow and plow Irons and harow teeth Iron 50s	2	10	-
to a paire of Carte wheels not finished	-	[-]	-
to his wareing Aparrill 12£: his Sword belt & Sash 30s	13	10	-
to 2 gunes ans a barrell of a gun at 3£ to 5 old Sithes at 10s	3	10	-
to a paire of Stillyards at 15s to 34£ of pewter at 3s 4d p pound 3-19=14	4	14	-
to 24 pound of pewter at 18d p pound 1£=16s	1	16	-
to hollow pewter and Some tinware	2	16	-
to his tooles 2 augurs a hand saw 9s Cury Come 10 axes at 4s a frow	2	10	-
to 3 Shovels 4 howes and a Spade	1	4	-
to hopples and horse lock 5s a Sledge 7s	-	12	-
to 4 old Sicles 3s: 3 led waights (vizst) all 7/8 of a hundred 33s	1	16	-
to a Chest and Carpenters tooles 2£=11s powder led and Shot 6s:4	2	17	4
to Nailes 6s; 5 glass bottles: 3s:9d Coopers Joyntes 2s to Shoemaker tooles 5s	-	16	9
to a Diaper table Cloath and a duzen of Diaper napkins	1	5	-
to a Cuboard Cloath 10s to a paire of fine Sheets 27s 6d	2	17	6
to a Long table cloath and 12 napkin 28s 2 Small table cloaths 10s	1	18	-
to a boulster Case 10s to a pair of Sheets 30s	2	-	-
to a great Sheet Containing 8 yards of Dowlas 15s	-	15	-
to a paire of fine pillowbeers 20s: a p Dito fine 16s	1	16	-
to 2 p Ditto 16s to one Single Ditto 5s	1	1	-
to 2 p of Sheets 4£: 5 p Ditto: at 30s a p: 7£= 10s	11	10	-

		£	s	d
To	a duzen of napkins and three table Cloaths	-	4	-
To	7 pair of pillow beers 45s to towells, and other linin 15s	3	-	-
To	3 boulster Cases 18s 5£ 6s ing	-	18	-
To	a bedsted bed and furneture to it at 10£ a trundle bested and bed	15	6	-
To	a bedsted beds and furneture at 9£ to 20 bus of sumr wheat 4£:10	13	10	-
to	another bed and furneture 9£: 1 Ditto 6=10s	15	10	-
to	6 Coverleds and other beding 10£: 40 bus of winter wheat 10£)	20	-	-
to	19 yeards of bagin 2s p yard 38s: a trundle bedsted & beding 3£	4	18	-
to	5 bags 30s to 11 foot of glass 22s to 7 bushells of mault: 24s:6d	3	16	6
to	a Croscut=Saw at ten Shillings 60 bus of Indian corn 7£=10s	8	-	-
to	½ a whip Saw 7s to 2 bras ketles & a pan 4£	4	7	-
to	more brase and Iron pots and kettles 7£: 10s	7	10	-
to	ye warming pan and ½ bushell	-	10	-
to	wooden ware tubs milke vessells payles and Dishes at	2	16	-
to	Earthen ware and a tin pan 10s to a pcell of Shingles 20s	1	10	-
To	a Chest & 2 boxes at 12s a harping Iron 10s	1	2	-
to	tramels tong grid Irons pot hooks and bellows	1	16	-
to	bridles Sadles & horse takleing 50s: 8 chaires 16s	3	6	-
to	bookes at 3£) 2 pitchforks 2s) 3 barells of beef & a barrell of pork 9£)	12	2	-
to	11£ of linin yarne 24s=6 more yarne 5s) 2 yrds of wolen 8s)	1	17	-
to	a grindstone 5s all ye Lomber In ye house at fourty Shillings	2	5	-
	Sum totall is	887	=15	=5

Aprized By us (John Jessup
(Job Sayre
(John Howell Junr §
(Matthew Howell §
1683

A true Coppy p me John Howell Ju § Clark

At ye Aforsd Courte of of Sessions was presented an Inven
tory of the Estate of John fordham (who died Intestae)
of Southampton In ye East Rideing of yorkshire: which is accord
ing to former aprizement as it stands upon Record In ye In
ventory of his father mr Robert fordham the property being
noe ways altered: this inventory taken may the 17 1683:

		£		
Imprimis	45 Acres of land at mecox 4£ p aacre	180	-	-
Item	a hom lott of 3 Acres more or less: at 8£ p acre	24	-	-
Item	a 100£ Comonage with Encrease of woodland 57 acre)	63	-	-
Item	75£ Corrant pay In Stock in ye hand of Josep fordam	75	-	-
		342	=0	0

The Aforsd Inventory is allowed and proved In the aforesd Courte
of Sessions: and mr Jonah fordham upon his Request the
Courte Doe Admit him as the proper heire to Administer upon
the Aforsd Estate and upon his Desire grant mr Edward Howell
to be Joynt Administrator with him :&c. haveing given bond
to performe the Same

The Deposition of Josiah Wigin aged aboute 20 years

Testifyeth and Saith that Some Time aboute ye 23 Of March Last
he beeing at the house of mr Arther howell Deceased and then
Arther Howell Junr being very Sick and weak: and aprehensive
of Death Aproching Did Call to ye people in ye house and to me
In pticuler to take notice that he Did give his Land (which
his grand father gave unto him) unto his brother Lemuell
which is ye Land that was Layd out to him In Swan Creek neck
and farther Saith not
Southampton June ye 12: 1683: taken and Sworne before me

John Topping

Hanah Howell widow and Relict to Arther Howell Deceased
Testifieth ye Same that the Said Josiah Doth being Present
at the Same time

Sworne before me John Topping

East=hampton September ye 7: 1680
The Last will and Testament of Richard Shaw Senr first I do
bequeath my Soule to god that gave it and my body to the
earth from whence it was taken and my goods as followeth:

1 My will is that my wife Remember Shall have my Hous &
Ten Acres of Land here at home and a percell of Land In ye
old Easterne plaines Containing aboute ten Acres and all my meadow
at north west Containg aboute foure Acres all which I Doe freely
Give unto my wife Remember to possesse or to Dispose
of Dureing the time that Shee Doth Live a widdow but if Shee
Doth marry then my House and Land to Returne to my Children
only my will is (if need Soe Require) that Shee Shall have Liberty
of ye hous one year after Shee is marryed allsoe my will is that
my wife Shall have all ye Moveables wholly at her Dispose that is
to Say all ye moveables belonging to ye house Exepting the Looms
and takling belonging to them and two musquits

2dly My will is yt my five Chilldren that is to Say my five Sons which
are now at home with mee that all my Land I have Either by
Gift or by perchase or any other ways withall privelledgs belong
ing there unto that they Shall have it all Equally Devided Amongst

3ly them: - my will is that if any of these my Sons Shall Dye be
fore they Come to age the Land to Returne to ye Rest equally

4ly my will is that if any of my Sons Shall Soe Cause to goe away and
not Settle here that they Shall Sell it to there Brethren there
part of Land: alsoe my will is that my Eldest Son Richard
Shall have the house and halfe my Land at home: that is to
Say as it Lyes. alsoe I give him two acres of meadow at acobonak
lying by mr James Ditch: also I give to him three Acres and a halfe
of Land In ye old Easterne plaines and three acres be it more
or less In ye Indian well plaine: also my will is that my

that

That my Second Son Edward Shall have my peice of Land ly=
ing by Samuell psons Close and my Lott in ye Easterne plaine -
knowne by ye name of John osbornes lott and 2 acres of medow
Att ackobonak by ye hamock Alsoe I give him my linin Loome
with halfe my takling belonging to ye loomes and my other
Loome with halfe the tackleing I give to my Son Richard: alsoe
my will is that my two Eldest Sons Shold Improve my Stock and
there time and not to Leave there mother In debt; alsoe my
will is that Richard and Edmond Shall be Carefull in Improov
ing & preserveing of my Stock untill my Son Richard Shall Come
of age and then it to be Devided Into three parts; as followeth
and my son Edmond and my Son Richard to have one third equaly
Betwixt them: and on third to be put out for ye use of my 3
youngest Sons william Joshua & benjamin alsoe my will is
that ye other Third my wife Remember Shall have and my
youngest Child and if a Son yn a heir with ye Rest alsoe
my will is that my Daughter Elizebeth Shall have given to
her when Shee is married or at Eighteen years of age twenty
pounds In good Currant pay my will is that my Son Richard
Shall pay the twenty pound to Elezebeth as for my Son John
I have given and bequeathed him to his grand father and gra
=nd mother garlick whoe hath promised to bring him up and
give him a portion also I Doe make my Son Richard Executor
of this my will: to ye Confirmation of this my will I Set
to my hand and Seale the Day and Date above written:

Assigned and Sealled in ye presents of us

Richard Shaw

John psons
Samell Terrill

Also further I Doe Request and
Constitute my well beloved friends
and Brothers Henry Ludlam of South
=hampton and John psons of Eastham
pton to be Overseers of this my will
Richard Shaw

A true Coppy of ye Origanall p me John Howell
Clark to ye Court of Sessions

Att ye Aforsd Court of Sessions Southold June 1683: was present
ed the aforsd will and testement of Richard Shaw Deceased
of East hampton: by his Son Richard Shaw: with apetion for
the proofe of ye same and for Leagall Admission to Administer
whereupon the will was prooved the wittneses thereunto Subscribed
were Deposed to ye trueth thereof and the Said Richard Admited to
Administer as Executor: to ye Said will: and the Said Henry Ludlam
and John Psons allowed and aprooved of as Supervisers thereof acord
ing to the mind of the testator he the Said Richard Speedyly re=
turning an Inventory of Said Estate to ye Clark of the Sessions

which is Returned to ye Clarke aprized by the men pointed by the Courte and is as followeth

Long Island Easthampton

A Inventory of ye Estate of Richard Shaw Deceased as it is Aprized by us whose names are hereunto subscribed as it

	£	s	d
To 2 horses	6	–	–
To one Cowe and a heffer and 2 Sucking Calves	6	5	–
To halfe a yearling heifer 15s to 9 Shoats 3£	3	15	–
To one 2 yearold Horse 30s to 3 ewes and on Lamb 24s	2	14	–
To house & 20 acres of whom Land	115	–	–
To 10 Acres of Land In ye old Eastr plaines	15	–	–
To 10 Acres Ditto toward the further End of ye Said) plaines at 30s p Acre)	15	–	–
To apeese of Land by Samuell persons Close	5	–	–
To 10 Acres in ye Nth west plaines	12	–	–
To four Acres of medow at ye Nthwest	6	–	–
To 4 Acres more at acobonacke	6	–	–
To meadow at nepeake	1	–	–
To a Cart 25s to ye plow and plow Iron and yoake 22s	2	7	–
To Beding in the Chamber	5	–	–
To bedsteds and beding below	10	10	–
To 2 Loomes and tackling belonging	8	–	–
To 2 musketts 40s to an old Sadle 5s	2	5	–
To 2 tramill a frying pan a grid Iron & a peile) and a percell of old Iron)	1	16	–
To Iron potts and kettles 3£:16s to 2 brass kettles 4£:18s	8	14	–
To pewter 34s:6d to tin ware 7s	2	1	6
To Candlestick and Stilliards	–	11	–
To a Chest 12s to a grindston and wooden trumpery 42s	2	14	–
To Indian Corne	2	–	–
	240	=2	=6

Benjamin Osborn Constable
Benjamin Conkling
Samuel Parsons
John Parsons Senior

A true Coppy Compared p me

John Howell Junr Clark

The Inventory of Christo: Fowler Deceased his Estate

	£	s	d
To: 1:Dwelling House and Whome Lott Contain= ing one Acre)	42	-	-
To: 10: Acres wood Land 20£	20	-	-
To: 1:Cow 3£ 15s and 1 heifer a year & vantage 20s	4	15	-
To 1 mare And Colt at 3£:5s	3	5	-
To 2 Pigs at 30s	1	10	-
To: 1 bead & bowlster 40s: 4 old platters 25s	3	5	-
To: 2 pr of Sheets at 40s to one small pr Ditto 12s	2	12	-
To: 1 old Small Patcht Bead and 3 pillows 12s	-	12	-
To 2: Iron potts 28s 2 brass kettles 35s	4	3	-
To 3 old poringers 18d & platters 15s: 1 plate 2s	-	18	6
To: 3 wooden Boules 2s: 3 Chayres 6s	-	8	-
To 1 quart pewter pott 5s to 1 neckcloath 15s	-	6	3
To a paire of Sarge trowsers 10s 2 Shirts att 10s	1	-	-
To: 2 Chests at 15s to one Sadle at 15s	1	10	-
Sum totall	86	4	=9

The Above menconed pticulers ware Aprized according to the best of our Judgments as our Oath binds us Severall things Specified in the Inventory Being Disposed off by ye widow Hanah fowler for the paymt of Severall Debts: mr John Laug =hton not being there with us: September ye 19th 1683/ wee all agreeing In Every pticuer as wttnes our hand

John Meppam
Benjamin Davis
Samuell Whitshead

At the Aforesd Courte of Sessions held at Southold June: 1683 the Said widow fowler was Admited to Administer upon her Said Husbands Estate Shee giveing in Security according to Law and the Said Estate not amounting to a hundred pounds the Said widow to have Letters of Administration from the Clark Signed in the name of the Courte.

((

Att a Court of Sessions held at Southampton upon ye 18th Day of March 1683/4 was presented by peter whitehere the will and In ventory of Robert gouldsbury of Brookhaven deceased: with a peticon for ye wido Hanah gouldsbury to Administer as Executrix Alsoe ye Said peter whithare had a Letter of Agency to act on her behalfe to procure the proveing of the will: and Letters of Administration is granted to ye Said widdow: upon the Said Estate to Administer accord ing and persuant to ye will and Inventory here upon Record as followeth.

The Last will of Robert gouldsbury In ye name of god

Amen: first I Comitt my Soule unto ye hands of god through whose mercy through the meritt of Jessus Christ I hope for Salvation and my body to be Decently buried first I give my wif and and Childe all my land and House namly five Acres in ye old feild and five In ye little neck and Seven in ye west Devition and 15 Acres by newtowne near to Richard Clarkes Home Lott and twenty five Acres to Layout which I had of Samell - Terrill: and a Share of meadow where it Can be found - and five Acres In the home Lott where the Howse Stands and 2 halfes of Comonage: with all moveables and a horse All which I give to my wife and Child to have and to hold to them and there heirs for Ever ffebruary ye 18th 1683 4

Tests:
Richard Smith
John Thompson — Robert Goos + burys mark

A true Copy p John Howell Clark

The Estat of Robert Gooldsbury deceased this 20th Day of Janu: 1683 4: Invitaried before the Constable or overseers as followeth			
A Dwelling House & Shop and home Lott with five Acres of land In ye feild more five Acre In ye little neck and 15 Acre at newtowne more 7 Acres In ye west Devition and 25 Acres of Land not Laid out and A Share of meadow wher it Can be found with one horse: more Due from Benjamin Smith as by Record	10	15	-
more from Joseph Davis	3	10	-
the house Shop and home Sted prised att	25	-	-
the 5 Acres In ye old field 7£=10s ye 5 Acres in ye neck 5£	12	10	-
the 15 Acres at New towne	11	5	-
the 7 Acres at ye west Devition at	4	-	-
the Land not Laid out	6	5	-
the horse prised at 3£10s	3	10	-
more 3 howes 2 axes 3 wedges and beetle Rings	-	16	6
A Chest with his wareing Cloaths and beding	2	-	-
an old plow 3s: 2 guns and a barill of a gun and Sword 3£: 15s)	3	18	-
	84	-8	6

Aprized by Peter Whiehear
Jacob Longbottom
Will= Saterly Constable

A true Copy p John Howell Clark

At the Aforesd Courte of Sessions held at Southampton upon the 18: 19th 20 days of march 1683/4 for ye County of Sufolk was presented the will and testament of John Conklin of Hun tington Deceased by Epenetus platt: which is as followeth.

The Last will and Testement of John Conklin Late of Hunting =ton Deceased february ye 23; 1683/4
I John Conklin bein in my Righ understanding and perfect - memory Doe bequeath my Soule to god and my body to ye earth and my goods as followeth (viz) to my Son John I Doe give ten Shillings and to my Son timothy I Doe give fifteen pound out of that which I was to Receive for my Land which my son John Sold for mee at oyster ponds alsoe I doe farther by these prsents Confirme all my meadow Lying In ye oysterpond neck unto my Son Jacob Conkling to him and his heirs for Ever: hee paying to Mr Silvester four pounds and ten Shilling Also I Doe give unto Walter noaks three pounds and all my wearing Cloaths Except my best Coat also I doe give unto my grand Child Rebekah Hubert one horse or mare Alsoe I doe give unto Mr Eliphilet Joanes twenty Shillings and I doe make my Daughter Elizebeth Wood my whole and Sole Executrix

Wittnes John Corey
Samuell Titus
Epenetus platt

John
ye mark - of
Conkling

The wittnesses Subscribed were Sworne to ye trueth of ye will Above written In Court of Sessions Aforsd and to all Intents and purposes Doe Admitt of ye Said Elizabeth wood Sole Ex ecutrix according to ye minde of ye testator therein Specifi[ed] and Shee to have Letters of Administration Signed by ye Clark to Administer upon the said Estate &c.

Att ye Aforesaid Courte of Sessions held at Southampton by his
Majestyes Authority upon ye 18th 19 & 20th Days of March In 36
year of the Reigne of our Sovereigne Lord Charles ye Second
By the grace of god of great Brittaine france and Ireland
king Defender of ye faith &c and In ye year of Lord Christ 1683/4
Was Presented the will and Inventory of Thomas Cooper
of Southampton Deceased: as followeth:

In the Name of God Amen I Thomas Cooper of
Southampton In ye East Rideing of Yorkshire on LongIsland
Husbandman being in perfect Strength of memory blessed bee
god for it and not knowing the Time of my Apointed Change do
make this my Last Will and Testament In maner following
first I Give and bequeath my Soule to god my Creator who
at first gave it mee and my body After Decent buryall to ye
Earth from whence it was taken at first and for my worldly
Estate as is hereafter written First I Give and bequeath unto
my well beloved wife Mary Cooper Dureing her Naturall Life
my house and Homelott and ye Cloase in ye great plaine Ly
ing in halseys neck Except ye five Acres I bought of mr fford=
hame: and twenty Acres out of my Cowe Cloase: ten Acres out
of Thomass part and ten Acres out of Ichabods part to bee
Joyned together and a fifty pound Commonage and after her
Decease to Returne as is under written 2dly I give and be
queath unto my Son Thomas Cooper and to his heires and
Assignes for Ever Eight Acres of Land Lying Northward of his owne
home Lott and the five Acres of Land I had of Mr fordham
in my Cloase In Halseys necke and Six Acres of Land Adjoyn
ing to ye west End of his home Lott out of my great Cloase
Called Cow close and my orchyard Land: and ten Acres more Adjoyning
to ye Said Six Acres In ye Said Cow Cloase after ye Deceas of his -
Mother and the Remainder of my Aforesd Cloase In halseys
neck After his Mothers Deceas also my will is that when hee
Shall possess the five Acres Abovesd then he shall Resigne ye
Eight Acres he now possesseth in ye north Side of my Cloase or tho=
mas Burnets Cloase in halseys neck: Into ye Quiet possession of
his brother Ichabod and his heirs for Ever: Thirdly I give &
bequeath unto my Son Ichabod Cooper and to his heires for
Ever

Ever A fifty pound Commonage with all After Increase of Land both
at home and Att Quaqua and twenty Acres of Land out of ye west
End of my great Cow Closae After my Decease and ye other ten Acres
his mother now possesseth by this my will After her Decease and what
Land I have In ye oxpasture both in ye north and South Devistion and
my Eight Acres and halfe of land my Son Thomas Cooper now possess
eth on ye north Side of Thomas Burnets Closae In halseys neck
and all my meadow at Shinecok and Seaponack & one heifer of
Come three yeares old and a Cow Calfe and that horse Commonly
Called Ichabods Horse and halfe a fifty Pounds Commonage with
Encrease of Land that Shall After his mothers Decease happen and to
Enjoy this Lands and meadows After he is Attained to one and
twenty yeare of age 4thly I Give unto my Daughter Martha Cooper
two Cowes to bee paid her by my Executrix within one month
next After my Decease. I haveing already Given and Delivered
Into her Possession her Portion 5ly I give unto my Daughter
Abigaile Cooper twenty Pounds to be paid her by my Executor on
her Day of Mariage or mothers Death In Some good Currant
pay also my will is that my Son Ichabod Cooper Shall within
one yeare After her Mariage pay unto her ten pounds more
of good Currant pay or Else to give unto her three Acres of
Land next unto ye high way out of his Land in ye Cow Cloase
which he seeth Cause to pay unto her 6thly I give unto my
Daughter Elizabeth Cooper twenty pounds of good Currant
pay to be payd her at her Day of mariage by my Executrix
Also my will is that my Son Benjamin Cooper Shall pay unto
her within one year After the Day of her mariage ten pounds
more of good Currant pay or Else to give unto her my house
and Home lott which hee Shall See Cause to Deliver unto her
7thly I Give unto my Daughter Mary Culver (Shee haveing
Received her portion all ready) fourty Shillings, to be paid
her by my Executrix: In Some good Currant pay 8thly I give
unto my Son Benjamin Cooper After his mothers Decease
my house and Home Lott with all buildings and fencing and
out houses Shall be thereon: and A fiftey pound Commonage
both at home and at Quaquanantick with all After Encrease
of Land and halfe a fifty pounds Comonage more After his
mothers Decease with all Encrease of Land and my forty acre
of Land Laid out to me by the hay ground and my hundred pound
Divition with Jonathan Rainer In the Skuttle hole Devition
be the Same more or lesse and my Lott at hog neck as
it fell to mee by Devistion of Lotte with all ye meadow and -
other Privelledges unto ye Same belonging: the out Land
and

and fifty pounds Comonage and A heifer Come three years old and a Cow Calfe to possess at his being at ye age of one and twenty years and the Rest at his Said mothers Decease and in Case Ichabod Cooper Shall Depart this Life without any Lawfull Issue of his body or before ye age of twenty one years then all his Land and Estate to be and Remaine unto his brother Ben jamin and his heirs: and In Case Benjamin Cooper should Dye and Ichabod Live then his to fall unto Ichabod and his heirs for Ever and In Case they both Should Depart this Life then both there Lands to fall unto my Son Thomas Cooper and his heires for Ever and there other Stocks or what Estate they have to bee Devided Equally to there Sisters as shall then bee Liveing Lastly I hereby Doe make and Ordaine my - well beloved wife Mary Cooper My Sole Executrix of this my Last will to have all of my Estate whatsoever I have not heretofore given or Disposed of and to Receive all Debts Due to mee and to pay all Debts and Legacyes: and I Doe Ap pointe my Son Thomas Cooper and my friend Job Sayre to bee overseers of this my Last will and Testament and do give them power to See that none of my Sons doe Dispose or Change any of ther Lands without there Consent: & for the Confirmation of this I have hereunto Sett my hand and seale In South Southampton Abovesaid this first Day of Sep tember Ano Dom 1683

his
Thomas T Cooper
marke

Signed and Sealed In ye presents of
Job Sayre
John Laughton §

A true Coppy p John Howell Clark

The Above written will of Thomas Cooper was presented to the Aforesaid Courte and the witnesses Subscribed were De posed upon there oaths in Court to ye trueth of ye Same and the Said Mary Cooper is Accepted and Approved as Executrix and the said Thomas Cooper and Job Sayre are Confirm ed as overseers and Supervisers to ye Said will: acording to ye mind of the Testator there in Specified: the In ventory is hereunder Ritten.

An Inventory of ye estate of Thomas Cooper of Southampton Late Deceased taken and Apprized by Mr Edward Howell Mr Obadiah Rogers William Hakelton and John Howell Junr whoe were all Chosen thereunto and Sworne by Capt Howell Justice of the peace. Aprized acording to money - Imprimis

	£	s	d
Impr first ye Dwelling house and barne and home Lott of three Acres	33	–	–
to ye Land above Thomas Cooper Jur his house 55 Acres	96	5	–
to 40 Acres In ye great plaines whereof 21 is ye Close vallued at 4 £ p Acres 84 £: ye other 19 Acres at 35s p acre at 33 £ 5s	117	5	–
the Land at ye hayground 73 Acres 73 £	73	–	–
to 20 Acres of Land at hog neck and meadow belonging	14	14	–
to all ye meadow at Shinecok and Seponack at	6	–	–
to 200 £ Allottment in quaqua purchase of medow	8	–	–
to 2 Acres of orchard Land to tak up at	2	–	–
to 4 oxen 14 £: to 5 Cows at 10 £ 1 two year old 20s) 4 year olds 40s	27	–	–
to 2 Steers 4 year old 6 £: 5 three year old 7 £ 10s	13	10	–
to one horse one mare one yearling	6	–	–
to 18 Sheep 4£ 10s: to 7 hogs and 2 pigs 4 £	8	10	–
the Cart and wheels 2 plows yokes Chaynes and horse) geers Iron harrow And grindstone)	6	15	–
to beetle: wedges & 3 Axes 15s a matuk and 3 brode hows 12s	1	7	–
to a Cheese press 5s: 1 Iron kettle 25s 2 bras kittles & Scillit 3 £ 10s	5	–	–
to 2 little Iron potts 5 £: 1 Iron kittle 18s: 2 Iron potts 40s	2	18	–
to A woollin wheele 3s a box Iron 2s:6 3 guns a cutlas & Sword 4 £	4	5	6
to 2 Sieths and takle 5s: to 2 Sadles 16s	1	1	–
to 55 £ of pewter at 15d p pound	3	8	9
to 12 poringers 20s: a Cup: flagon Saltselers and Sauser 11s	1	11	–
to A Drinking pott a poringer & bason 4s:6 a lanthorne 3s	–	7	6
to a tin pott Chafing Dish a tin Driping pan & tin tunill	–	4	–
to a Duzen ½ of trenchers a glas bottle 2s:) 2 wood bowles 2s:6d	–	7	–
to a paire of Large Stillyards 16s: 3 Small bowles 2s6d	–	18	6
to a Small brass kettle & brass Candlestick	–	12	–
to an old frying pan 3s a looking glass 5s	–	8	–
to a great Iron pott and A little one	1	4	–
to bedsted fether bed and all furneture at	6	10	–
to another: Ditto with a trundle bedsted and fether bed) and beding to them)	6	–	–
to 2 linin wheeles 10s: his wareing Aparell & Joyne Chest 93s	5	3	–
to 2 barrells of meat at 55s: a pair of tongs 2 tramells 14 s	3	9	–
to an old warming pan 3s: to 2 Chests 6s	–	9	–
to a table 6s a gallon glas botle 2s	–	8	–
to 2 fine Earthen Dishes and Chamerpott 4s	–	4	–
to 2 duzen ½ of napkins 45s one table Cloath 8s	2	13	–
to 3 Sheets 37s 6d to 2 Courser Sheets 20s: 3 pillow bears 6s	3	3	–
to 2 Shirts ten Shillings about 6 pound Cours yarne 5s	–	15	–
to an old Chest 3s: to aboute ten bushells of wheat & Indian Corn	2	8	–
to oast unthrest at 40s aboute 8 load of hay 8 £	10	–	–
to garner 5s a sedcut and tray –2–6	–	7	6
to a pillion and Cloath 8s Some yarne 5s a bushell Salt 2s	–	15	–
to a peec of old brasse 2s and all ye lumber In ye hous	–	17	–

to on new Sheet 10s one Auger Chisell gouge 3s)	-	13	-
to 2 pistells 1 £ to one paire of Shiers -2s= 6d	1	2	6
to tincker tooles	-	2	-
	492	-17	-3
the totall is acording to money) besides Lands and Houseing and Debts is) is	99	-00	=00

Aprized by us

Edward Howell
Obadiah Rogers
Willm Hakellton
John Howell Junr

A true Coppy of ye Origanall p John Howell Junr Clark

This Indenture indented made the nine and twenty eth Day of november in the year of our Lord one thousand Six hundred eighty and three and In ye five and thirtyeth yeare of ye Raigne of our Sovereigne Lord Charles ye Second of England Scottland &c king D:fender of ye faith &c. Between wenequaheag Indian Sacham and proprietor of Conetticutt on ye one part and William Nicolls now of ye the Citty of New York Gent - of ye other parte Wittnesseth that for and In Consideration of a Certaine Sum of money in hand paid by the Said willm Nicolls to ye Said wenequaheag the Receipt whereof he Doth hereby Acknowledge and there from for Ever acquit and Discharge the Said william Nicolls his Executors and Admin istrators: hath granted bargained and sould and by thes pre =sents Doth hereby grant bargaine & sell unto ye said william Nicolls his heirs and Assignes for ever all that neck tract piece or pcell of Land Sittuate Lying and being on ye South Side of LongIsland bounded on ye East by a Certaine River called Conetticutt on ye South by ye Sound: one ye west by a Certaine River Called Contasquattahab and on ye north by a Right Lyne from ye head of ye Said River Called Conetticutt to ye head of the before menconed River called Contasquatah To have and To hold the said neck tract peice or percell of Land butted and bounded as aforsaid with all and Singuler the Appurtenances unto ye said William Nicolls his heirs and Assignes unto ye only proper use and behoofe of him ye Said william Nicolls his heirs and Assignes for Ever. and the said wenequaheag for himselfe and his heires doth Covenant and grant to and with the Said william Nicolls his heirs and Assignes that hee

the

the Siad Wenequaheag and his heirs the Said neck of
Land will warrant and it to ye Said william nicolls his heirs and
Assignes for Ever Defend firmly by these pressents: and the Said
william Nicolls Doth Covenant and grant to and with the Said
wenequaheag that hee ye Said wenquaheag and his heire Shall
and May plant Hunt reside fowle and fish in any part of ye
Said Land not fenced and Improoved by the Said William Nicolls -
his heirs & Assignes at all times hereafter freely and without
any molestation In Wittnesse whereof the partyes to -
these presents have Enterchangably Sett to yr hands and Seals the
Day and year Above written

Sealed and Delivered in ye
presence of us — the mark of wenaquaheagh
Thomas Townsend
Swenony his mark — Will Nicolls
John wicks Constable of oyster bay
munguagh his mark Sachem of rokawaye

Nathaniell Colles
William Creed
William White

This within written Deed of Sale was
Acknowledged by William Creed and
William White before me that it was
Signed Sealed and Delivered in ther[e]
presence May the 22th: 1684: Sworne
before me
Elias Doughty Justice of ye peace

A true Coppy of ye Origanall Entered this 28th Day of
May 1684 p John Howell Junr § Clarke

In the Name of God Amen I Georg Harress
of Southampton in the East Rideing of Yorksheire on
LongIsland yeoman Being In perfect Strength of Memory
Blessed be Almighty god for it Though weak In body &
not knowing the Apointed Time of Change Doe make
this my Last Will and Testament In maner and forme following
Imprimis I give and freely Bequeath my [words crossed out]
[words crossed out] Soule to god my Creator &
Redeemer who at first gave it to me and my body After Decent
buriall to ye Earth from whence it was at first taken and
for my worldly Estate as is hereafter menconed -
Imprimis I give and bequeth my hous and home Lott

Lott and all my Land in Cow neck and all the Land I have
or Ever hereafter Shall have belonging unto my Said
House and home Lott within that tract of Land Comonly Called
and knowne by the north Sea Lyne and my land that fell
to mee by Lott and meadow In the Late Devistion Comonly
Called Hogneck Devistion: To: my Eldest Sonne Georg -
Harress and to his heirs and Assignes for Ever Provided yt
Iff he Departe this Life without Issue then it Shall fall
unto my Second Sonne Henrey Harress and to his heires
for Ever Alsoe I Give unto him my Said Son George haris
A fifty pounds Comonage withall After Increase of Land./

2dly I Give and bequeath unto my Son Henry Harriss and to his
heirs and Assignes for Ever all that my thirty Acres of Land at
Meacox and all that my Late Devistion of Land that fell to
To mee by Lott In ye Skuttle hole Devition and my three
Eights of a A hundred pound Commonage with all After Encreas
of Lands./

3dly my will is that notwithstanding my Above given grants of
my Lands and meadows to my Sons That my be=Loved wife
Mary Harriss Shall have and Enjoy all my house and orchard
and barne and meadoe and all other my Areable Lands Dur
=ing her widowhood and After if Shee Shall mary: untill that
my Sonne George - Shall be of ye age of one and twenty years
but In Case Shee never marry Againe then to Enjoy my
House and orchard Dureing her naturall Life and After to
Returne it to my Said Son George and his heirs -

4ly: I give and bequeath unto my Daughter Mary Harress to
be paid her by my Executrix within one month next After
her mariage twenty pounds of my Estate -

5ly: I give and bequeath unto my Daughter Ellizabeth -
Harress to be paid her by my Executrix within one month
next After her mariage ten Pounds of my Estate ./

6ly I give and bequeath unto my Daughter Jane Harriss
five pounds to be paid her by my Executrix at her Day
of Mariage out of my Estate./

Lastly I by this my Last will and Testament make
my beloved wife Mary Harress Sole Executrix of this my
will to have and Enjoy all other of my Estate whatsoever
that is not heretofore Disposed of and to pay all ye abovesaid
Legacyes and my Request and will is that my beloved bro
thers in Law Johnathan Rainer and John Jessup be the
over=Seers of this my Last Will and Testament In wittnes
whereof and for the further Confirmation here

of I

=of: I have hereunto Sett my hand and Seale In Southampton this
6th Day of December Anoquo Domo: 1683

Signed & Sealed in ye
Presence of   GH
Chistopher Lupton
John Laughton §

The Aforsaid will was presented to this Courte by John Jessup Requesting the Proofe thereof and according Ad ministration granted: whereupon the thereunto Subscribed were Depose to the trueth of the Same: whereupon the Courte Doe admit allow and Aprove of the Said Relict Sole Executrix to ye Said will and order her power to Administer acordingly and thes Doe alsoe allow and Aprove of and Confir =m the Said John Jessup and Jonathan Rainer as Supervisors and over Seers of the Said will according to ye minde and will of the Testator therein Specified the Inventory of the Said Decedants Estate is as followeth

Southampton Aprill ye 22 1684 An Estemate and An Aprizment of the Estate of George Harress Deceased../

	£		
Item 2 horse 4£ a peece 2 mares at 4£	12	-	-
Item 1 hors kinde two years old 30s) 4 oxen 20£	21	10	-
Item 5 Cows 17£ 10s: 1 Cow 3£:10s: 2 Steers 5£	26	-	-
Item 2 of 2 yers old 3£=15s: 1 Small Colt 30s	5	5	-
Item 3 yearlings at 50s: 6 pigs 30s: Cart plow Chaine Clevis 70s)	7	10	-
Item 2 yokes: 1 fork: 1 horse Chaine 13s one Small grindstone 3s	-	16	-
Item 1 bedtick 3£ two beds and furneture 16£:10s	19	10	-
Item 1 bed and blankets 5£: 8 bushells of wheate 2£=8s	7	8	-
Item 5 wheels old and new 20s to 6 poringers 9s	1	9	-
Item 4 bushells of oats 10s) 7 Small pewter Dishes 35s	2	5	-
Item 2 pewter pots 6s) 1 driping pan and bason 5s: Earthenware 6s)	-	17	-
Item 1 warming pan 20s 2 brass kettles 3 potts 1 Skillet all at	8	5	-
Item his wareing Cloaths 6£ 3 paire Sheets 5£: 24 napkins: 6 pellows) 1 Sheet 3 table Cloaths) 3 old Chest 25s: 2 guns one old Sword 3£)	18	5	-
Item Sadle pillions bridles 3£: 2 axes 2 hoes 20s	4	-	-
Item a grid Iron pott hookes Tramill and Smoothing Iron at	1	10	-
Item a barell of meat £2:10s frying pan 6s) 200 naile 2s: wooden bouls 20s)	3	19	-
Item 6 Sacks: old & new 20s) 1 Chayres 8s: 1 Small table 10s: to 20£ of yarne 3£	4	18	-
Item 4 Chayres 8s: to Small Chests 3s to parte of a barrell of Sope 1£)	1	11	-
to old barells pailes Tubs Churne and bellows & other Lumber at	2	-	-
	139	-18	-0
Itt is to be under Stood thatt this Aprizment) vallued as money is on third Less which is)	93	=05	=4

this Aprizment taken by uss

obadiah Rogers
his
John \ Jessup
mark

A true Coppy John Howell Clarke

Att The Afforesaid Courte was presented the Inventory of william Segrave of Southhold Late Deceased by his widow and Rellict widow Sagrave with a petion to be Admited to Ad minister gratis that is to Say without Charge of Letters of Admin istration which the Courte Doe order that Shee is and Shall bee Admitted as Administratix to the Said Estate to possess and Enjoy it for ye Comfortable Subsistance of her [crossed out words] Selfe and Chilldren: and to have power Soe to Doe from ye Court with the Charge the Inventory is as followeth

An Inventory of the Estate of william Segrave Deceased at Southold August ye 29th 1683

		£	s	d
Imprimis	three old beds one bouldster three pillows	4	-	-
itt	five Blankets two old blankets	2	-	-
itt	five Sheets two halfe Sheets	3	-	-
itt	five pillowbeers one pear of Curtaines	-	15	-
Itt	1 table Cloath one Duzen of Napkins	1	10	-
Itt	three bags 10s: all his wereing Cloaths 6£	6	10	-
Itt	one match Lock muskett one Repire	1	10	-
Ittem	2 Chests 6 boxes 2£: Six books 1£ powder bullet & match	3	5	-
Ittem	one pewter bason two poringers 1 cup 1 pott	-	16	-
Item	tin and Earthen ware	-	6	-
Itt	3 Iron pott one brass kettle one Skillet	3	-	-
Itt	one frying pan one axe: two pair of potthooks: tongs	-	16	-
Itt	2 Small tables and other Lumber at	2	10	-
Ittem	2 besteds	1	-	-
Ittem	foure glass bottles	-	3	-
		31	=01	=0

p us Stephen bayly Constable
Thomas Mapes Junr
Jonathan Horten

A true Coppy of ye origanall
p John Howell Jun § Clarke

At a Courte of Sessions held at Southold october ye 21: 1684 was presented the will and Inventory of william Halliok which was proved and the wittnes Sworne In Courte to ye trueth of ye Same which will is as followeth - - -

Southold ffebruary the 10: 1682

In ye name of god Amen To all Christiane Peple greeting Know yea that I william Halliok ^ of this Towne being through gods blessing of Sound memory and In good health of body doe Con stitute ordaine and declare these presents to bee my Last will and Testament In maner and form as followeth.

I Comitt my Soule In to ye hands of Jesus Christ my

gracious

gracious Redeemer and then my body being dead to ye earth
by decent buryall In ye assured Hope of its Ressurection at ye Last day
as for my worldly Estate my will is to give and hereby I Doe giv[e]
unto my beloved wife Margarett hallyok: all that my third Lott in
In ye towne platt next to Tookers Land with ye meadow Called
Booths meadow withall ye Comonage and Apurtenances thereunto
belonging to have and Enjoy to her use & benefitt Dureing her
Naturall Life and noe Longer only Shee is to give my Sonne
William Liberty to Sett up an house In Some Convenient place -
and what other benefitt of Said Land Shee Shall think fitt: Also:
I give her the third parte of all ye Yearly produce and profitt
of the Land now Improved in my Lott at accobauge: where
I now Dwell on both Sides ye land or way that Devides itt:
which parte Shee Shall have without any Charge of Improvement
whatsoever with full power to Dwell and reside in my Dwelling
house there at any time or all times as Shee Shall please without any let
as Shee Shall please: which third parte and house I give her only
Dureing her widowhood and noe Longer allso I give her foure
Milch Cowes as Shee Shall Choose to bee her property to keepe or
Allinate as Shee will and also I give her all payers of working Cattle
that Shall be in my possession at my death together with all Cartes
Carte wheeles plowes plow Chaines and all other Apurtenances belong
ing to Cartes And plowes to be hers and at her Dispose dureing her
widowhood: alsoe I Leave with her all my housold goods
of all Sorts for her use Dureing her widowhood also and when She
pleaseth to devid them Equally to my five Daughters according to
her Discrestion: alsoe all ye Rest of my Cattle horses and Swine
I Leave with her for her use and benefit Dureing widowhood
and when Shee pleases to Devide them Equally as Shee Can to my
Three Sons (viz) thomas peter and willm and it is my will yt
these Devitions of ye housold goods to my daughters and of ye Cattle
horses and Swine to my Sons be made In ye time of her
widow hood 3d I give to my Son Thomas Hallyok all ye land
Except ye Swamp lott on ye Western Side of ye land or way by
my dwelling house which land or way as it now runeth Shall
Soe for Ever divid ye land now In Tillage and Shall allway
remaine In Comon between ye said two percells but my will is
yt ye west of this my lott at accobauke to ye South end and to ye nor[th]
End thereof Shall bee Equally divided between him my Son
Thomas and my Son peter according to ye full halfe of ye hole
breadth thereof all which western Side of Said Lott I give
ye abovesd to my Son Thomas Except what is Excepted to have
and to hould: posess and Enjoy Dureing his naturall Life witha[ll]
Issues and profitts Shall there Arise except my wifes third
and what I Shall Hereafter order him to pay out of
the premises and at ye death of my Said Son Thomas I Doe giv[e]
all ye premises In this article Contained unto ye Lawfull heires
of the body of Said Thomas Dureing ye naturall life of Such
his heires and Soe my will is that it Shall decend from heire
to heire forever without any power of Sale or any other

or any other Allination whatsoever furthermore in
maner Aforsd I give unto him my Son Thomas and his Suc
essire Heire one halfe parte of of my three pices of medow which
are sittuate as followeth the one of them Layeth on ye East Side of
booths meadow it being by me Exchanged with Capt John youngs the
other peice Lyeth between Cases meadow and mr wells Meadow which
peice I bought of Samll king and the third peice Lyeth on ye west Side
of deep Creek being a 2d Lott halfe of Each of these peices of meado
I give unto my Said Son Thomas as I give the western Sid of my Lott
and In ye same tenure to his heirs for Ever to be devided in Equall
Share between him and my Son peter halliok all ways provided and Ex
cepted any thing in this my will notwithstanding: that if my Said
Son Thomas or my Son peter halliok or my Son william halliok or any
Suceeding heire of his or there bodyes whether Son or daughter whom
I doe hereby Constitute my heire: to Any part of my Land
given or to be given to any of my now named Sons and to Such as
I Constitute to Suceed them Shall Apostate from ye protestant doctrine
and faith of ye Church of England as it is there now by Law establ
=ished and if hee or they or any of them or any heire to my land
whom I ordaine to Succeed him or them or any heire that Shall
Succeed forever: Shall att any time hereafter take upon him
or them or any of them any profession of Such Doctrine &
faith whereby they or any of them: Shall be Drawne away from
Moved upon ye publick worship of god preached In this place
and warranted by holly Scripture Suteable to ye protestant Doctrine
and faith abovesd Soe that hee or they Shall or any of them Shall willfully
and on sett purpose Contemne and neglect ye publick worship of
god and farther it is my positive will that if hee ye Said Thomas or
any of my other Sons: or any Succesor Heir hereafter him or them or Either
of them Shall espouse and Contract mariage with any Quaker or to ye
Son or daughter of any Quaker as they are now Called then it is my
possitive will and I doe hereby wholly fully and Absoelutly disowne
and doe disinherit the Said thomas peter and willm and doe depriv
him and them and any of them and any that may Succeed him
them and any of them if they Shall Soe Apostate and Soe mary
utterly Casting Every of them out of my out of my land and
depriving Every of them of any Claime benefet and Advantage
of this my will and testament and in Such Case of Such Apostacy
or mariage I doe hereby will give and bequeath Such part of
my lands Soe forfeited by Such wicked practices unto ye next
Lawfull heire that Shall Stedfastly profess and owne ye
the Doctrine and faith first=above Specified and to ye heir
that Shall Succeed him in ye f[]rm tenure as I now give my land
to my present Sons Soe that this forfeture Shall Cutt of ye
Land from ye heir of ye bodys of Such Apostacy and mariag
4ly: I give unto my Son peter halliok all ye land on ye East
Side of ye land or way by my dwelling house at accobauk
and the Swamp Lott according to ye pvition abovesd in
the 3d article between my son Thomas and him I give

give unto him my Said Son peter to have hold possess and En
joy Dureing his naturall Life with ye Issue and profitts
that Shall there Arise except His mothers third and at his
death I give it to them tha Shall Suceed him In ye Same manr
as in ye third Article it is given to them Shall Succeed my Son
Thomas withall ye Conditions Expression reservations provisoes
deprivations and forfeture then copied in ye third Article of this
my will and in no other way and maner what soever

5ly: I give unto my Son Willm Haliok at his mothers Decease all yt
my third lott In ye Towne plott which third lott Lyeth next
to tookers land with ye meadow Called booths meadow and a per
cell of meadow being to ye East Side of Quash neck with all ye Com
monage and Apurtenances there unto belonging to have &
to hold to him ye ye Said willm haliok dureing his naturall Liffe
and at his Death I give it to them that Shall Suceed him
In ye Same manor as in ye third Article as is given to them
that Shall Suceed my Son Thomas withall ye Condition Exceptions
revertions reservations deprivations and forfeitures menconed
in ye Said third Article of this my will and In no other
way and maner whatsoever

Item I give unto my Son peter Halliok the other halfe of ye three
peices of meadow menconed In ye third Article whereof ye
former halfe is in Said third Article given unto my Son
Thomas to be devided between Thomas and peter as Equally
as may be In ye Same tenure as he hath the Esterne Side
of ye lott at accobouke and no other wise

6ly: My will is that ye first yeare After my wives Decease my Son Thomas
and Peter Shall Each of them pay or Cause to bee payd unto my daught[er]
Mary the Sum of five pounds In Curant pay of this place and
Each year followeing they Shall pay Each of them five pound to Each
of my other Daughters according there age that is to Say the Seco
nd yeare after my wives Decease to martha five pounds a peice ye
third year they Shall each of them pay five pounds apeice -to Sarah
the fourth year After my wives death: each of my Said Sons Shall
pay five pounds [crossed out] a peice to Elizabeth and the fifth
yeare they Shall pay each of them five pounds To Abygaile my
youngest daughter all ye these payments to be In Currant
pay of this place.

Lastly my will is that my beloved wife Margaret Halliok bee
and hereby I Doe apoint her the Sole Executrix of this my
last will and testament and I doe desire my two neighbours
James Reeves and Calleb Horton to be Assistants to my Execu
trix with there best Advice and Councell about Such matters as
Shee Shall think meet to Advise with them alsoe my will is
that all my debts and funerall Charges be payd by my Executor
out of Such Stock of Cattle horse and Swine as I leave with
her before that Shee devides them to my three Sons (vizt)
thomas peter and william alsoe my will is that my Son John
Halliok whom as an obstinate apostate I Doe Reject and de
prive of all other my Estate yet I Doe Hereby give unto him
his heires and Assignes forever my Second

Second Lott at ye wadeing Creeke with the Apurten
nances thereunto belonging which is all that hee
is Ever to have of my Estate and In Confirmation that
these presents are my Last and Irrivocable will I
have this tenth of february In ye 34 year of ye Rain
of our Sovereigne Lord king Charles ye Second Sett her
unto my hand and Seale

William Halliok
H
his mark

Signed & Sealed In ye presence
of us wittneses
Stephen bayley Thomas mapes Junr)
Joshua Horton Jonathan Horton)
Abram Corey

These four wittnes Sworn
In Courte of Session to ye
trueth of ye abovesd will &
testament that they See Sd
Halliok Sign and Seale this
as his Last will and Testament

Atest John Howell Clark

An Inventory of William Halliok: Aforsd deceased of
his Estate who deceased September 28 1684

	£		
Imprimis Lands and meadow and houses			
bed and beding	30	-	-
pewter brass and Iron at forty pound	40	-	-
wooden and Earthen ware	9	-	-
Sheets and table linen	6	-	-
wareing Cloaths	11	10	-
Horses Cattle and Swine at	80	7	-
all Implements of husbandry	12	-	-
	188:	17:	0

This inventory taken by us ye Sevententh
of october 1684

James Reeves
Thomas mapes Jur

the Abovesd Aprizement
is as money

An Inventory And Aprizement of ye Estate of Thomas Jessup of Southampton County of Suffolk in the province of new yorke on LongIsland deceased taken and Aprized by us Edward Howell obadiah Rogers and John Howell Junr this 17th day of September Anoquo domo: 1684

Item a dwelling House and home Lott with one halfe of all his fathers Land and Comonage within ye bounds of Southampton Excepting the whome Lott at towne and Land Adjoyning now in the perticuler possession of his brother John

to 2 mares and one horse 7£ and 3 young horsekind at 3£)	10	-	-
to 5 oxen & ½ 20£: to 10 Cowes 22£ 1:3 yearold 2 Cattle 2 year old 5£	47	-	-
to 7:2 year old 22£ to 2 Calves 20s: 12 Sheep 3 Swine 5£10	28	10	-
to Whale Crafte warps and Irons & c:2£: 2 guns 40s Iron pott 12s	4	12	-
to Indian Corne upon ye ground 70s oats 12s: wheat to thresh 40s	6	2	-
to hay 8£: to a sett of Iron hoops for wheels 12s	8	12	-
to powder 4s to a bed and furneture 10£	10	4	-
to Another bed bedsted blanket sheets and Rug boulster pillos	7	10	-
to his wareing Aparell 13£ Sword & belt 20s: a Chest 10s	14	10	-
to a bible and Small books 10s: a Looking glass 2s:6d: 3 Siccles 3s	-	15	6
to 5£ yarne 5s a Chamer pott 4s to Shirts 10s:6 porringers 12s	1	11	-
to 2 basons 6s: 6 Spoones 3s a warmingpan 10s a pr bellows 6s)	1	5	-
to a Chest 8s an Iron pott 10s tramell & pott hooks 3s) 2 tongs 2s	1	3	-
to a box Iron 4s6d a hansaw and 2 axes 6s wooden bottles 4s an ax 2s	-	16	-
to 3 glass bottles 1s:6d a ½ pint pott 18d: 2 panes of old glass 3s	-	6	-
to a boate 400 foot of board 16s a table Cloth 8s	1	4	-
to 5 Sieths and takle 17s to 13 yards of duffles 52s	3	9	-
to 20£ of old Iron 6s books 5s two Sieves 3s	-	14	-
to 2 Sadles 24s 2 broad hows 7s 3£ feathers 30s to Saks 4s	3	5	-
to aboute 6 gallons of Rum 18s ten wooden bowles 10s	1	8	-
to aboute a firkin of Sope 8s a Scillit 7s an Iron pitt 5s	1	-	-
to an Iron kettle 45s a brass kettle 25s to Cheese 25s	4	15	-
to 3 basons 8s to old pewter 6s a Syling bowle 1s	-	15	-
to a negro Slave 24£ Lumber 5s	24	5	-
	182:	17:	

To ye halfe of Six Acres of winter whet newly Sowed)

Edward Howell

taken and Aprised by us as money

Obadiah Rogers

John Howell Junr

In the name of god Amen I Thomas Burnet of Sout
hampton in ye East Rideing of yorksheire on LongIsland Hus
band man being Sicke of body but through ye mercy of god in
perfect Strength of memory blessed be his name for it & not
knowing the day of my Death doe make this my Last will
and Testament In maner and forme following

Imprs I give and bequeath my Soule to Christ my redeemer who
by his blood hath purchased the same/

2ly I Give my body to ye Earth from whence it was at first taken
After decent buryall to be made by my Executrix and for my
worldly Estate I give as is hereafter mentioned I give unto

3dly my Six Children John Joell Lott Hester Merriam Precilla
each of them five shillings A peice to be paid to them by my

4ly Executrix I give unto my son Aaron Burnett my house and
home Lott After my wifes Decease and my three Acres
In ye ten Acres Lotts and at my Deceas I Give unto him my
Said Son my ten Acres Lying at Meacoks Adjoyning to ye
Land of mr Jonah ffordham and all my ox=pasture devistion
and two heifers and two Steers to be Delivered to him by my
Executrix 5ly I give unto my two sons Mordecay and Dan
Burnet all my Land att a place Called Cormorants point to
be Equally Devided between them When they shall Ataine
to ye Age of one and twenty years only they Shall Sumer
six Cowes for my wife Dureing her Life 6ly: I give unto
my Son Matthias After my Said wives Decease my Cloas
In ye great plaines in halseyes neck 7ly I give unto
my Daughter Lois at her Day of Mariage or att ye age of
Eighteen which shall first happen the Sum of ten pounds
to be paid unto her by my executrix Lastly I by this
my Last will and testament make my Loveing wife
Mary Burnet Sole Executrix of this my Last will and
Testament and to have all ye Residue of my Estate that
is not here Disposed and to pay all my Debts and
Legacyes herein mentioned In wittness whereof I
have here unto Sett my hand and Seale this 16th day of
March Ano: Dom 1679/80 Thomas T Burnet
Signed Sealed and Delivered his mark
In ye presence
John ffoster
John Laughton §

A true Coppy p Jno Howll Clark
December ye 2d 1684

June ye 20 1749 Jeremiah Stratton gives In
his eare mark to be a crop on each eare and
a ell the uper Side of the right eare

[At a Court of Sessions] held at Southold upon the 21 say of 8tober 1684 was [presented] the Inventory of John benet of Setauket Alias Brookhaven Late Deceased as followeth

The Inventory of John benet Deceased the 23 of Augst 1684 taken by one of the Comissionrs John tooker and John thompson Constable

	£	s	d
A horse and Mare and Colt	8	–	–
one Cow and Calfe 3£ a Sow a 3 young Shotes & 5 pigs 30s	4	10	–
a feather bed & boulster & 2 pillows) with a Chafe bed 3 Coverleds & 3 blankets)	4	13	4
Curtaines and vallaines and a bedsted: 10 pare of Sheets 6 pillowbeers and 5 boulster drawers	15	16	–
three Sutes of wereing Cloaths	3	16	4
6 Shirts 40s wast coat 26s=8d 2 hats 12s	3	18	8
1 pott 1 kittle one betell goth houckes	–	18	4
3 pewter dishes one bason 2£=13s=4d 1 tankard 4 poringer 2 Duz Spoons	3	5	–
2 tin potts 1 pewter pott 3 tin pans 4s: 3 Earthen platers 2 candlestiks	–	7	6
1 white Jug a white porringer a little pott	–	1	8
6 plates 6 trenchars wood 1s 6 glass bottles 2s8d	–	3	8
1 table Cloath aduzen napkins 26s8d a Case looking glass 16d	1	8	–
2 barrels and an anker & halfe anker and runlett	–	7	8
2 Chaires 2 Stooles 2 tables 2 pailes	–	17	2
3 basskets a buter tub a linin wheele	–	9	–
a taylors Sheers and goose a Sadle bridle and pillion	–	16	–
5 bushll of winter wheat a bushell ½ of Indian Corn	1	3	–
½ an acres of flax 2 bushells ½ of moult 1 Acre of wheat	1	3	8
1 acre and ½ of Indian Corne 6£ of tallow 6 bages	1	7	–
2 axes 2 hatchets a Cradle a wheelbarrow a hat brush	–	11	4
2 paire of new shoose 3 paire of Stockens	1	–	8
6 yards of homspun Cloath 20s 30£ of cotten & linn yarn 1£	2	–	2
2 yds ½ of black Stufe 21s:8d a yd ½ of gray Sarg 5s	1	6	8
2 Cushons one bible & 4 books	–	6	–
2/3 of a barrall of pork 30s a homespun ticking for bed & boult	2	–	8
other Lumber about ye house	–	6	8
halfe abushell of Salt	–	1	8
3 Chests	–	16	–
the whole Sume at money price is	61	=0	=10

Drawne up by order of Courte by us under written

Andrew Miller
John tooker

Sworne in Courte Atest John Howell Clark

the Aforesaid Inventory was presented to the Courte by the John Tooker with a piticon from the widow of Said benet name ly mary benet to Administer upon Said Estate which by ye Court is granted Shee giveing in Security acording to Law Said tooker hath given to ye Clark Security accordingly:. –

At the Aforsd Courte was a piticon [ ]
Georg Owen that she the Said Martha [Owen] Widow and Relict to georg owen of Brookhaven deceased migh Adminster upon his Estate the Courte haveing Considered the Same doe Admit the Said Martha and Georg owen as Joynt Executors to all in tents and purposes upon the Estate of the Said Georg Owen Deceased they giving Security according to Law:. Security is given in to ye Clark the Inventory is as followeth.

A Inventory of ye Estate of Even owen Deceased ye 25 day of August 1684 dying Intestate

Item:	a house and home lott of aboute 10 Acres	14	-	-
	Alsoe 20 Acres the towne gave him	5	-	-
	One Cow and Calfe	4	-	-
	one Sow and five piges	1	4	-
	one feather bed and 2 feather boulsters	5	10	-
	1 flockbed 2 pillows two blankets	2	15	-
	2 rugs 2 paire of Sheets	4	10	-
	a wainscit Chest 2 Coats 1 pair of breeches	3	5	-
	2 Shirts on pair of Shoose 2 pr of Stockens	1	13	-
	1 old wascoat a Stufe Cloake a hatt	2	10	-
	2 Iron potts a bras kettle one Scillet	3	10	-
	6 pewter platters 3 pewter potts	2	6	-
	1 Chamber pott three porengers	-	6	-
	a broad Ax and ads and a handsaw foure Chizells	1	10	-
	one Iron hook a paire tongs and fire Shovell	-	16	-
	a Joynter 2 fore plaines and a hand plaine	-	6	-
	a Croas plaine a rabiting plaine one gouge	-	4	-
	three Augers a hamer	-	9	-
	a Small table with other Small lumber	-	15	-
	a paire of Curtaines and vallaines	1	16	-
		53	=5	=

this Estate was vallued by us whose names are under written we being apointed by Justice woodhull

Samuell Akerly

a true Copy p John Howell Clarke — John Thomas

At the Aforsd Courte was presented the Inventory of David Howell who Deceased on the 2d day of May 1684: with a pition by the widow of Sd David Deceased vizst Mary - Howell Requesting this Courte to Administer upon the Estate of her Deceased husband: which was Likwis grant ed Shee giveing in Security as the Law directs
The Inventory is as follow: taken by the Subscribed this 7 day of May 1684:

to one house and 23 Acres of Land	-	-	-

	£	s	d
to [tape]fers of 3 yearold	9	10	–
to 1 heifer [tape]: to 3 Steers 4 yearold 12£	13	–	–
to 1 Steer of 2 yearold 30s 2 yearlings 40s	3	10	–
to 2 mares and a twoyearold horse	6	–	–
to one riding horse	3	10	–
to 9 Small Swine	5	–	–
to 2 Sheep and a narrow ax	–	14	–
to a Sadle and bridle ½ worn	–	10	–
to a Small Spit and an old frying pan	–	8	–
to a good Iron tramell a box Iron and heeters	–	12	–
to a linin wheel ditto wollen	–	10	–
to a Small fouling peice rapaire and belt	1	4	–
to an old Cradle 4 old Chaires	–	8	–
to an old Chest a feather bed pillow and boulster) a Rug Curtains and vallaines)	6	–	–
anther feather bed and boulster Coverlid & pillows	4	–	–
2 bedsteds 3 blankets a Cubord and 2 bibles	3	10	–
to 5 pare of Sheets and a pare of Cards	5	–	–
to 6 pillow bears one Small table Cloath	1	15	–
to 5 table napkins 3 Cotton Shirts 5 yards linin	3	10	–
to a Caster hat ½ worne	–	15	–
to a Sarg Suit and 3 pr of Stokens a pair Sheets	3	10	–
to 7 pewter platers [ ]	2	–	–
to 3 old Small pewter basons	–	6	–
to 3 old poringers a cup Sauser an old pewter plater	–	7	–
to ½ Duzen Spoons a Salt Seller a Small looking glass	–	4	6
to a brass ten gallon kettle 30s 2 Iron potts	2	10	–
to a pint Scillet ½ Duzen of bowle & trays	–	7	6
to an old pint pott and Saucer ½ a barrell of beef	–	13	–
to a firken of sope five old Cask a runlet of lamp oyle	–	16	–
to a Churn a buter tub a old Cheese fatts	–	8	–
to 3 wooden dishes a Sileing boule a bras Candlestick	–	3	6
to 1 old paile 3 trenchers one old meale Seive	–	1	6
to an old kettle a Small table a quart botle a old qrt pot	–	8	–
to a Chamerpot and hamer and ashare of boat & craft	2	2	–
totall is –	83	=02	=0

ye totall is 83=2–0
his Debts is 22=9–6
60=12=6

Edward Howell
obadiah Rogers
John Howell Junr §

Articles of Agreement mad and Con[tape] between Mary Jessup widow and Relict to Thomas Jessup of Southampton deceased of the one parte and John Jessup Junr of ye Said Towne on the other parte as followeth: first that the Said Mary Jessup Administratrix ^ to ye Estate of her Deceased Husband Doth Mutually Agree to and with the Said John Jessup Junr that Shee will Ressigne unto him the Said John Jessup all her Right title and In trest that Shee hath or Ever had unto all and Every parte of her Said Deceased Husbands Lands tenements buildings fences or any privilledge of Comon Interest within the Said Town or Else where any way Apertaining to the Said Lands building meadow and Comonage whatsoever: unto him the Said John Jessup Junr his heirs Executors and Administrators to have and to hold for Ever Quietly to Enjoy and possesse the Same and Every parte thereof without any Lett hindrance or molestation of Mee my heires Executors Administrators and Assignes Lay ing any maner of title or Claime unto ye Same or to any pte thereof In my name or by my meanes & procurement 2dly the Said John Jessup Junr Doth for him Selfe his heires Ex =ecutors Administrators and Assignes doth herby these presents Allinate yeild up and Ressigne all his Right title and Interest that hee hath or Ever here after might have unto Any parte whatsoever of the Estate of his Disceased brother that is the moveable Estate as Cattle Horses household stuff utensells and all his moveable Substance whatsoever unto ye Said Mary Jessup her heires Executors and Administrators for Ever all and Every parte thereof wheresoever to be found freely and peacably to Enjoy and possesse without any the Least molestation of mee the Said John Jessup my heirs Executors Administrators or Assignes or any other person wt Soever Claiming any Rights in my name thereunto and wee doe hereby Discharge Each other according to ye tenure of these presents In witnes whereof both partys have here unto Sett there hands and Seales In Southampton the 20th day of March 1684/5

Signed Sealed and Delivered
In the presence of us
John Laughton
Samuell Johnes
John Howell Junr

her
Mary Jess x
mark
John Jessup Junr

the Above written Covenant is Acknowledged before me by the partys Concerened to be there act and Deed this 20th day of March 1684/5

John Howell Junr

A true Coppy John Howell Clarke

The following agreements were made and Concluded
upon before the Right Hoble ye governr at new yorke the
forth Day of october 1665 between the Inhabetants of the Towne
of Easthampton In the East Rideing of yorkshire upon Long
Island and the Sunck Squaw of mentaukett Daughter of ye
Sachem wyandance Deceased./
That that ye bounds of Easthampton to ye East Shall be to ye
fort pond the north fence from the Pond to ye Sea Shall
be kept by the Towne the South fence to ye Sea by the Indians
Sufficient against Trespass of Cattle
all the Rest to ye East end of the Island Shall belong to ye
1st Muntaukett Suncksquaw Daughter of ye Sacham wyandance
and her heires and the Indians belonging thereunto
The Said Suncksquaw of Muntaukett Daughter of ye Said
Sacham wyandance and her Indians for themselves and their
heires Engage that they will not Sell Lett allinate or dispose
of the Said Lands directly or Indirectly to any other person or
persons but Such as belong to ye Towne of Easthampton
2 That the Said Sunck Squaw and her Indians doe for them
and there heyres for Ever give full and free Liberty to the
Towne of Easthampton for the feed of there Cattle or Cutt
ing of grass In or upon any peice of her Aforesaid Land
provided that ye Said Towne Shall not at any time put there
Cattle Into her foresaid Lands untill Indian Corne be -
Cutt and Secured by the Said Indians: and that ye Cattle
Shall be Driven off the Said Lands upon notice given
that the Said Indians are to plant there Corne./
3 That if any time the Cattle of the Towne doe pre
Judice to the Indians by Default of the Towne fence the
Towne Shall give Satiss=faction and not otherwise: and if
the Indians or there Doggs doe Damage to the Cattle
the Indians Shall give Satisfaction, Such as Can Rea=
Sonably be Required
Memorandum that the grass only for food and Mow
=ing is Intended and understood to be granted and not
the Inheretance of the Said Lands

It is further agreed that [ ] Indians nor
there heyres Shall at any Time before the month
of March without Consent of the Towne Sett fire
to the grasse /
That in Consideratione of the Said grant from
the Said Sunck Squaw and Indians to ye Towne
of East hampton: the Said Towne doth for them
and there heyres Engage to pay yearly fourty Shill
ings to the Said Sunck Squaw and Indians there -
heires or Assignes to be paid In the Towne of East
=hampton where this agreement of both partys is
to be Acknowledged and Confirmed yearly the first
payment is to begin from ye Date hereof & So
from year to year which payment is acknowledged
to be Received before Mee

Richard Nicolls

Entered into the Records
In the office at new york by
me

Matthias Nicolls Secre:

This agreement following agreed & Concluded December 1st
Anno Dom: 1670 and In ye 22 year of our Sovereigne
Lord Charles the Second King of great Brittaine france
& Ireland Defendr of ye faith &c

Bee it knowne to all men by these presents that I
Ponnite Sachim of mentakut (Alias mousup) pehchouwan
mauhsianan Smith mah=tam=pait Obadiah and Checkanoo In
Counseller missaquate askammauge waissouwan
the name and with the Consent of paukquatowne ^ Anusin and
the Rest of our Associats the true and Lawfull propietors of a portion
or percell of Land Called montaukut beyond a Certaine pond Called
the fort pond Eastward whereas mr John Mulford mr Thomas
James minister and Jeremiah Conkling Inhabetants of Easthamp
ton in New yorksheire on the East Rideing were bounde In a bond
of a hundred pounds to the Commissioners of the Right honorable
frances Lovelace governor: In our behalfe wee haveing
bound over and mortgaged all our Lands for there Security
In Case of our non payment a Certaine Sum of money

(viz)

(viz) 400 [bushells] of Indian Corne wee haveing forfeited our
Land to ye fore[said] persons: at and upon the Advice of ye worship
full william Wells of Southold one of ye foresaid Comissionrs -
that wee Should Come to A Speedy Compossition with our foresd
freinds wee aforemenconed After Serious Consideration and de
=bate: have agreed and Concluded and by these presents Doe Deliv
=ver up bargaine for and Enfeofe a Certain percell of Land to ye
foresaid John Mulford Thomas James and Jeremiah Conkling
as it is thus Limmited and bounded by us the Aforesd partyes: 1:
Muchebehsuck a place by the fort pond being a vallye South-
ward from the fort hill to the beach Shahchippitchuge being on
the north Side the Said Land midway between the great pond
and fort pond Soe on a straight Lyne to Chebiakinnauksuk
from thence to a Swampe where the hedge stakes Stood Called
Machougitchuge and Soe through the Swampe to the great
pond then Streight from the hay Stacks to the great pond
Soe along by the great pond to a place Called Maminkquiaug
being on the furthest Side the reeds growing on the Southend
of the great pond Eastward and Soe along to the Sea Side South
ward to a place Called Cappautshapaugausuk Soe Streight
from thence to the South Sea together withall ye privil
ledges Emolluments apurtenances or profitts may any way
arise Issue from the Said Lands thus bounded as Aforesd
and wee doe Deliver up all our title of the Same to ye Af
foresd persons there heires Executors and Assignes to have
and to hold the Same for Ever without any Lett or
Molestation from us the foresaid Indians or our Succes
=ors or any In our behalfe Saveing the privilledges of ye
beach and whales Cast up thereon which is allready the
propriety of Thomas James and Jeremiah Conkling to
them there heires and Assignes for Ever: bee it known
Alsoe that wee the Aforsaid Indians have given -
possession of the Aforesaid Land to the foresaid John
Mulford Thomas James & Jeremiah Conkling to bee de
vided by them three and Disposed of as they three -
Shall Agree & Shall from time to time & all times Justif[y]
them In ther possession of the Said Land and if Ever here
After the fore menconed John Mulford Thomas James
and Jer= Conkling or there Sucessors Shall Soe Cause
to fence in the Said Land the Indians are to fence
fence in or bear the Charg of one half and they

and they the other halfe: In Ratifi[ ] & Confir=
mation of the premisses wee Sett our hande and
Seales /

poquatowne his mark and Seale

Subscribed Sealed & Delivered
in presence of us

Chokanoos mark A

Sunk Squaw mark

Benjamin Conkling
phillip Allcock

wuchikitaubit
his
mousup & seale
mark

memorandum that ye Indians are
to have the finns & tayles from time
to time for Ever (only) of all ye
whales Cast up at montauk or
other great fish as they have at
Easthampton

pecheawon mark
masianan mark
matompait mark
obadiahs mark

December ye 10 1670 this above written
Agreement was owned & Consented to by both
partyes in the presence of mee John Mulford
Justice of the peace

february the 8th 1670/1 wee three (viz) John Mulford Thomas
James Jeremiah Conkling Doe Assigne over and Deli
ver up to the Towne of Easthampton this former deed
expressed : and all the Intrest we have In it our Intrest
In the whales only Excepted as witnes our hands

John Mulford
Thomas James
Jer= Conkling

In the presence
of us
John youngs
John Howell

A true Coppy p John Howell Clark

---

this Agreement made between Samuell parsons
John Hopping and Enock fithian Select men of the
towne of Easthampton for thenmselves and there Aso
Siates of the Inhabetants of the Said towne the true
proprieters and purchasers of ye Lands belonging Either
to the towne of Easrthampton So far as Napeak Eastward
or at meantoukut Eastward of napeak the one party: -
Aquaas Sacham of mentauket and Sasakatake Sacham to
gether with the Advise and Consent of managubongon
alis Gentleman Chief Counseller wasowan Iyumpous
dick indian Checkanoo and awapetowne Auquaniet and

ned obadiah and k[as]kemaug together with the Rest
of the Indians [bel]onging to montauket the other party
as followeth: be it knowne that whereas there hath
been Severall Agreements made by the predecessors anssestors of
us the Aforsd Sachems with the Englishmen the true
and Lawfull perchasers and proprieters of the Land they now
possess together with there Associats: and these Said Agreements
have been Confirmed by the Governer at new york october 1665
and there being Some Conditions In the former Agreements
which we See Just Cause to alter by mutuall Consent of both
partyes as in Speciall the keeping up a fence upon both ends of
the pond Called fort pond also a Restraint of all Cattle to be
put Eastward of that Said pond untill After Indian Corne harvist
Doe therefore upon due Consideration finde it Convenient
farther to Indent and Agree with the English Aforsd and
By these presents wee the Aforsd Sachams and our Counsellers
and with the Consent of the Rest of the Indians doe firmly
and fully Confirm all former Agreements made by our Anses[tors]
and to Stand In as full force as thouh no Such alteration
had Even made and wee doe binde our Selves persons and
Estates together with our heirs and Successers after us for -
Ever to the Aforesd English men and there Associats
never to Sell Lett out or Lease out or give or grant or by any
other means ^ or way to Dispose of the Land Lying Eastward of ye
pond Called fort pond or any part of it or percell there
of or thereunto belonging Either directly or Indirectly
to any person or persons whomsoever without the Con
sent of the Aforsaid purchasers and proprieters of the
Land Aforesaid that our Assossiats with the abovesaid
Selectmen which have not Exempted themselves from thier
Agreement to them there heirs and Successors for Ever
also we the Said Sacham In the behalfe of our Selves &
Indians belonging to us doe owne and Acknowledg the
Aforesd purchasers of easthampton and there Associats -
there Intrest in the herbeadge and grasse for Cattle
both winter and Sumer betweene the said fort pond
and the great pond and beyond the great pond After Indi
=an Corne harvest as hath been formerly agreed
by our Ancestors and doe by these presents -

Confirme the Same fully to them to have and To Hold the Aforesd grass and herbeadg them there heirs and Successors for Ever upon which Consideration Aforesd we the Aforesd Inhabetants of Easthampton In be halfe of our Selves and our Associates binde our Selves and our Associats together with our persons and Estates to give to the Sacham and Indians of montaket and his Successors from time to time for Ever four - pounds In good pay Every year for Ever alsoe the persons Aforsd and there Associats and Successors After them to Sett up and maintaine from time to time for Ever a good Sufficient fence from the Southend of the great pond at montauket to a Sea bank at ye South Sea as the English and Indians have already agreed the Said Sacham and Indians upon there owne Cost Secureing the northend of the Aforesd pond-and In Ratification and Confirmation of the promesses wee do mutually Sett our hands and Seale this thirtieth of Sept 1684

the words: in the origanall (and Indians) was
John Enterlined before Signeing

wittness Joh Demon		The mark of	Q	Aquosh Sacham
John Lees	Samuell parsons	The mark of	T	Sasackataco Sacham
	Stephen Hand	The mark of	O	monacobongonocous
	John Hopping	The mark of	Q	wasawon
	Enoch ffithian	The mark of	G	Awabeton
		The mark of	9	Caine
		The mark of	S	Iyampaus Alis nat
		The mark of	1	Cowanunk allis dick
		The mark of	^	Checkanoo
		The mark of	J	obadiah
		The mark of	U	kunkamaug
		The mark of	ʖ	Quaquahide
		The mark of	ʃ	Toj allis Ben
		The mark of	ʔ	ungowan

Southampton July the 10th 1685)
There Apeared before mee the two Sachames of meantaucket with Some other of the Said Indians (viz) Achonck Sasackataco and Checkanoo and obadiah In the be halfe of the Rest and owned and acknowledged that ye above written agreement was there act and deed before me
John Howell

A true Coppy p John Howell Junior § Clark

Ri[chard Ni]colls Esqr Governor & Generall under
his Royall Highness James Duke of Yorke and Albany &c
of all his Territorys In America To all to whome these presents
Shall Come Sendeth Greeteing (Whereas there is a certaine
Towne in the East Rideing of Yorkshire upon LongIsland
Scituate Lying and being in the Easternmost part of the
said Island commonly called and knowne by the name of East
=hampton now in the Tenure or occupacon of severall
freeholders and Inhabitants who haveing heretofore made
Lawfull Purchase of the Lands thereunto belonging have
Likwise manured and Improved A Considerable parte thereof
And Settled a Competent Number of familyes there upon
Now for a Confirmation unto the Said freeholders and
Inhabetants in there Enjoyment and Possession of the
premises Know Yea That by vertue of the Comission and
Authority unto me given by his Royall Highnesse I have
Ratified Confirmed and Granted and by these prsents
Doe Ratifye Confirme and grant unto Mr John Mulford
Justice of the peace Mr Thomas Baker Thomas Chatfeild
Jeremiah Conkling Stephen Hedges Thomas Osburne
Senior and John Osborne as Patentees for and in the
behalfe of themselves and there Associates the free=
holders and Inhabetants of the Said Towne theire -
Heires Successors and Assignes all that tract of Land which
already hath beene or that hereafter Shall bee Purchased
for and on the behalfe of the Said Towne whether from
the Natives Indian proprietors or others within the
Bounds and Limitts hereafter Sett forth and Exprest -
(vizt) that is to Say there west bounds begining from
the East Limitts of the bounds of Southampton as they
are now Layd out and Stak:t according to Agreement &
Consent Soe to Stretch East to a Certaine Pond Comonlly
Called the fort pond which Lyes within the old Bounds of the
Lands belonging to the montauk Indians and from -
thence to goe on still East to the utmost extent of the
Island; on the north they are Bounded by the Bay
and on the South by the Sea or maine ocean all

which

which Said Tract of Land with[ ] Limits
before mentioned and all or any Plantation thereupon from hence forth are to belong and Apertaine to the Said Towne and to be within the Jurisdiction thereof; Together with all Havens Harbors Creekes Quarryes woodlands Meadows Pastures Marshes waters Lakes Rivers fishing Hauking Hunting and fouleing and all other Profitts Comodityes Emolluments and hereditaments to the Said tract of land and Premisses within the Limits and Bounds Afore Menti =oned described belonging or in any wise Apertaining - To have and To hold all and Singuler the Said Land Hereditaments and Premisses with there and Every of there Appurtenances and of Every part and percell thereof to ye Said patentees and there Associates theire heire Successors and - Assignes to the proper use and Behoofe of the Said patentees and there Associates theire Heyres Successors and Assignes ffor Ever: Moreover I doe hereby Ratifie Confirme and Grant unto the Said Pattentees and theire Associates there Heyres Successors And Assignes all the privilledges - Belonging to a Towne within this Goverment & That the place of theire psent Habetacon Shall Continue and Retaine the Name of East=hampton By which name and Stile it Shall be Distinguished and Knowne In all Bargaines and Sales Deeds Records and writings they the said patentees & there Associates theire heyres Successors and assignes Rendering and paying Such Dutyes and Acknow =ledgments as now are or hereafter Shall be Constituted and Establisht by the Laws of this Govermt under the obe =dience of his Royall Highness his heires and Successors Giv =en under my hand and Seale at fort James In newyork The 13th Day of March In ye 19th year of his majestyes Raigne Annoq Domini 1666

Recorded by order of the governor | Richard Nicolls
the Day and year above written

Matthias Nicolls Secr:

A true Coppy p John Howell Junr § Clark

Th[ ] [ ]d [ ]fieth an agreement between Wyan
dance of [Monta]uket Cheife Sacham of Long Island &
Thomas James Minister of EastHampton and Lyon -
Gardner John Mulford Robert bond Thomas Baker Jno
Hand and the Rest of there Associates the purchasers
and proprietors of the Towne of EastHampton as followeth
That upon Consideration that the Inhabetants of Easthampton
Aforesd doe Sett up and Maintaine a good Sufficient fence
from the South Side of this There Aforesd Towne to the head
of the Harbour Called the three mile harbor that is to Say from
Sea to Sea for the keeping off of horses from goeing
Eastward In the Sumer Dureing the Indians Corne is
upon the ground the Aforesaid Sacham Doth firmly bind
and Engage him Selfe his heyre and Successors to Lett &
Dispose of to these Inhabitants of Easthampton there -
Heyres and Successors all that hearbedge that is the grass
and feed for Cattle upon all his the Said Sachames Land now
in possesseon Eastward of Napeake to the End of ye Island
Eastward for Ever to have and freely to Enjoy the Same
without Mollestation and if it prove hereafter that this fence
aforesd doth not prove Sufficient to turne the horses and Soe -
Prevent Damage of the Corne yn the Aforesd English
men Shall pay the Aforsd Sacham his heyres & Successors
from time to time Every year fourty Shillings in
good pay for Ever and if at any time hereafter the Sa
cham or his Successors See Cause to allinate the Said Land at
mentauket: that it Shall not be Lett Sould or allynated to
any person or persons but to ye Inhabetants of Easthampton
Aforsd allso this is agreed upon that ye English are not
to turne any Cattle or horses upon any parte of ye land
Lyeth Eastward of a pond Called fort pond untill After
Indian Harvest and then they Shall have free Liber
ty to turne in what Creatures they See Cause and to
fetch them off from thence when planting time
is Come In Ratification and Confirmation of the pre
misses I Sett to my hand and Seale this 10th of Aprill one -
thousand Six hundred & fifty five

A true Coppy p Jno Howll Clarke

witnes Charles barnes
Jeremiah vales J mark)
John W Woolys
mark

it is ordered by both
partyes mr thomas James
to have the keeping
of this agreement

wiandance his
his mark
sasakaka
mark
(paquatowne his his
mark mark

At a Courte of Sessions held at Southold upon the 20: 21
and 22 days of october 1685 was presented the will and Inven
tory of william Edwards of Easthampton Deceased and the trueth
and Reallity thereof proved by the Testemoney of the two wittneses
thereunto Subscribed and the Said Ann Edwards Adjudged and Admited
to be the Lawfull Executrix to the Said will which is as followeth

In the Name of God Amen I William Edwards of
Easthampton In the East Riding of Yorkshire on LongIsland being
In perfect Strength of memory bllessed bee almighty god for it & not
Knowing the Day of my Death doe make and ordaine this my
Last will and testament as followeth first I give and freely bequeath
my Soule to god my Creator who first gave it to me and my body
After Decent buriall to the Earth from whence it was at first taken
and for my worldly Estate I Bequeath as hereunder written
ffirst I Give unto my Son John Edwards halfe of my aparrell
and that Little Lott Lying by hoock pond Thomas Osborne Junr
East and his own Land west to him and to his heires forEver
alsoe I give him one Cow to be Delivered to him one month
2dly After my Decease: I give unto my Son Thomas Edwards the
other halfe of my Aperrell Alsoe I give unto him that Lott
of Land that Lyeth between John Miller and William Miller -
and that Land Lying by the two mile hollow in the plaines
thomas osborne Junr Lying west and Thomas osborne Senr
east Also one Acre of meadow at napeack mr Mulford South
and thomas osborne Jur west and a third of the Privilledges of
my Lott to him and to his heires for Ever:
3dly: I give unto William Edwards Sonn to Thomas Edwards my house
and homstall with five Acres In the plaines Nathanll bishop
Lying west and Willm barnes Lying East and that Lott on ye old
Eastern Plaine Richard Brooks Lying west and Samll parsons
East and that neck of meadow at napeage with a Streight Lyne
mr Mulford on the uper End homward and one third part
of my Privilledges to my Said Home Lott to him and to
his heires to have and to hold for Ever and one Lott of mea
dow at accobonack Robert Dayton on ye one Side and Left
Wheeler on the other Side
4thly: I give unto Josiah Edwards Son to John Edwards that Lott I
gave to my Daughter Sarah with all the Said percells of
Land both meadow and up Land with halfe the Privelledgs
that belong unto that Lott the Land being In debate between
nathaniiell Domony and my Selfe at present and if I
Recover it not from him then my will is that william

Edwards Sonn to Thomas Edwards Shall pay unto him the Said Josiah Edwards
forty pounds In good Merchantable pay within Seven years after my Decease
5ly I give unto william Edwards Son to John Edwards and to Ephraim Edwards
Son to Thomas Edwards my Lott in plaine the out Side Lott Richard -
Stratten Lying west: and that Lott in the woods mr baker Lying East
and mr Mulford west Equally to be devided betweene them both & if
Either of them Dye without Child or Issue of there body Lawfully begotten
then the Surviver to Enjoy the others halfe as well as his owne -
To him and to his heires to have nad to hold as there owne for ever
with the rest of my meadow at napeage: I alsoe give unto the Said
Ephraim Edwards one third part of the privelledges of my Lott
6ly I give unto my Daughter Elizabeth baker one Cow to be Delivered to
her within one month After my Decease
8ly I give unto my Daughter An Squire one percell of meadow at ackobo
nack by the homack John wheeler on the one side and Robert Dayton
on the other Side one halfe the privilledges that belongeth to that
Lott Somtimes Called birdsalls Lott but haveing no Child or Issue from
her body then to returne mee or two my heires or order and I
give unto her one Cow to be delivered to her within one month After
9: my Decease: I give unto all my grand Children twenty Shilling a peece
to Every one of them to be paid one year After my Decease
10ly: I give unto my Children John Edwards Thomas Edwards Ann
Squire and those five Children of my Daughter Elizabeth namely
=ly Richard and thomas Isaac and benjamin and Elizabeth Straten
halfe my moveable goods to be Equally Devided Amongst them
at the marriage or death of my beloved wife An Edward which Shall
Lastly: first happen: Lastly I by this my will and Testamt make my beloved
wife An Edwards Sole Executrix of this my Last will to pay all -
Legacies and Receive all debts and to have and to hold all ye -
Residue and Remainder of my Estate that is not here above -
Disposed of and doe give unto her my Said beloved wife my abovesaid
House and Land given unto William Edwards Son of thomas edwards
Dureing her widowhood or naturall Life and After her Decease then to
bee unto him the said william Edwards and his heires for Ever
memarandum whereas It is given halfe my moveable In the
tenth Article to John Edwards tho. Edwards and Ann Squire and
the five children of my Daughter Elizabeth Baker it is to be under
Stood that those five Children Shall have an Equall parte with
there uncles and Ante amongst them five and wheras its Said
that if my beloved wife Should Either marry or dye then
halfe my Estate Should bee to the abovesaid Children and the
House and land to my grand Son

to my grand son william Edwards [ ] it is
to be understood that if Shee Shall marry Shee Shall keep the house and Land notwithstanding Dureing her naturall Life and ye halfe of my moveables then to be Delivered As abovsd
In wittnes wherof I have hereunto Set my hand and fixed my Seale In Southampton this first Day of february Annoq Dom 1680/81

Signed Sealed in the presence of us:
Sarah Laughton
John Laughton §

William Edwards

A true Coppy p
John Howell Junr Cl

Inventory of the Estate of william Edwards Late of East hampton Deceased taken this 19th day of Augt 1685

		£		
Imprs	the whole stock of horse Kind being vallued at	12	-	-
	4 oxen 5 Cowes 7 three olds 4:2 yearold 5 yrlings	40	15	-
	to Small Swine vallued at	3	-	-
	3 feather beds with pillows and bouldsters	6	-	-
	a rug Coverled a pr of blankets a pr of Curtaines all old	3	-	-
	7 pare of homespon & one pr of hollond Sheets at:	6	5	-
	his wereing Aparell valued at	9	10	-
	4 yards of Dufles 1£) 20 yard homspon Cloath 30s)	2	10	-
	a Larg bras kettle 2 Small kettle 2 Scillets a warming)			
	pan a bras morter and a Candlestick at)	4	5	-
	3 Large Iron potts 1 large kettle a Small kittle)			
	2 Small Iron potts all vallued at	3	-	-
	to pewter platters 4 Small pewter platters	3	-	-
	2 Larg basons 6 Small basons	-	14	-
	12 poringer 6 plates 4 Chamer pots a flagon & old pewter	2	10	-
	Cart wheeles plow Chaynes & other things for waynage	2	10	-
	a barrell and halfe of rum 90s) ½ abarrll of wine 40s	6	10	-
	2 barrell of nayles & other things Lately from boston	10	-	-
	Chayres bedsted tables and Chest vallued at	3	10	-
	Pewter trays tubs payles and other lomber	2	10	-
	a negro boy and woman vallued at	36	-	-
		157	=9	-0

the Above Inventory taken the day Aforsd
by us: Josiah hubert:
Robert Dayton

At the [Aforesd Courte] was presented the Inventory of John youngs Deceased and [ ] John youngs Dying Intestate the Courte upon her peticon Doe Admitt her to Administer upon the Said Estate namely mary youngs: Shee giveing In Security as the Law Directs: which Securyty Shee the Said Mary youngs hath given In to ye Clark of the Sd Courte; by her Suretyes: mr Thomas maps and mr Thomas youngs: the Inventory is as followeth.

Southold ye 16 of october 1685

Suffolk - Inventory of the goods and Chattles of mr John youngs being Deceased taken upon the perticuler Request of the widow and Relict of the Said Jno Youngs by us the Subscribed & Soe vallued

	£	s	d
Imprs 8 oxen at money price 26£: to 12 Cowes 24£) 3 Cattle 3 yearold 6£)	56	-	-
6 yearling 6£) 6 Calves 3£ 2 horses and mare 8£	17	-	-
57 Sheep 27£ 2s) 27 yearold Swine 20£) 15 piggs young and old 6£	53	-	-
Implements for Husbandry & other tooles vallued all at	9	5	-
a bedsted bed beding and one pr of Sheets	6	-	-
A bed boulster Coverled blanket a pr of Sheets for a trundle bed	2	-	-
a Cubord 10s) 2 pr Sheets 2 table Cloaths & 12 napkins 3£	3	10	-
a Table a Settle & a Chayre 6s a Sword a gun & a pr of Stillyards 35s)	2	1	-
A warming pan 7s) a linin wheele tongus & Cradle 5s	-	12	-
a geneva bible and other books 20s	1	-	-
In the Chamber: a bed boulster Coverled 3 blankets 1 pr Sheet & bedsted	6	-	-
an old Chest 2 pound powder tobacco 6s) 1 old trunk a blanket 8s	-	14	-
1 box 1 tubb & a box 4s) 1 Case & bottles 1 Saddle 16s) 1 blanket & pillow 4s)	1	4	-
In the kitching 4 brass kettles 3 bras Scillets 3£) 3 Iron potts 30s	4	10	-
7 pewter platters and 6 plates 45s) 2 basons 6 poringers 1 flagon 16s	3	1	-
1 drink=g Cup 1 apple roster 2 Candle sticks & a Choping knife	-	4	-
2 heaters 1 Spitt 1 tin Dripping pann 10s	-	10	-
4 pailes tubs barrells & other wooden ware at 20s	1	-	-
In the meale room a pr of wooll Cards 3 Seives 2 dearskins	-	8	-
In ye garret over the kitchen a bed boulster blanket 1 pr Sheets	1	10	-
2 tearces of Salt 20s: 7 bushells Indian Corne	1	14	-
5 raw deerSkins 10s: in the Leantoo: 1 tin kittle one Collender 2 Small Iron kittles	1	5	-
one frying pan 1 Saddle 8s	-	8	-
In the Entry wareing Cloaths 3£ In ye barne sumer & winter wheat 50 bush:lls 8£:15s)	11	15	-
Indian Corne 100 bushells 7£:10s Spanish money 13£10s	21	-	-
Totall is -	185	18	=0

Errors Excepted by us

Thomas more
Thomas mapes Junr
James Reeves

Att the Aforesaid Courte of Ssessions held Southold october the 20th 1685: was presented the will and Inventory of nathanll Bishop of Easthampton Deceased: and the reallyty thereof proved by one of the wittneses thereunto Subscribed the other being out of the government and doe Admitt of ye Said widow to be Executrix thereunto and doe allow and Confirme the Said Capt Josiah Hubert and Samuell Mulford as over Seers & Supervisers of the Said will according to ye mind and will of the Testator therein Specified the will is as followeth

In the Name of God Amen I Nathanll Bishop of East =hampton now being in my Right minde and understanding doe make this my Last will and testamt I give my body to ye Dust and my Soule to god that gave it & my Estate as followeth

1 I doe give unto my Son daniel all my Lands and meadows Lying and being in Easthampton Except Six Acres and A halfe on ye Indian well plaines which I doe give unto my Son Nathanell it is to be understood that Danll is not to possess the Lands wholly Dureing the Life time of my wife or Soe Long as Shee Remaines a widdow which time Shee is to be maintained by Daniell or Else have the house and soe much of the Lands as is needfull for her use but After her Decease or time of widow =hood then Daniell is to possess all the Lands as I give him above

Nathaniell bishop willed one halfe of his Comonage at home and at mentack to his Son Daniell the other halfe to his Son nathaniell which he Declared Should have been In his will
Atest Arter Creasey John wikwere

2ly: I doe give unto my Son Daniell 2 oxen readyworked and All my horses and mares young and old 3dly I doe give the forth parte of all my Cattle and Sheep unto my Son daniell besides the oxen and horse kinde: 4ly I doe give unto my Son Nathaniell one fourth parte of my Cattle and Sheep - Except two oxen and Horsekind: 5ly I doe give unto my Daughter Mary the one fourth parte of my Cattle and Sheep 6ly I doe give unto my wife the one fourth parte of my Cattle & Sheep Dureing her Life time or widow hood but After her Decease then I desire they should be Returned unto James hands Children which are my grand Children Lastly I doe give unto my wife all my movables in the house and make her Executrix and if Either of my Sons or daughter dye without heires then I will that what I give them be Equally de vided Amongst them that Survive Except Lands which Shall be my Sons Either Daniells or nathaniells if Either dye with out Issue: I desire that Capt Josiah Hubert and Samuell Mulford be over Seers of this my Last will and Testamt given under my hand & Seale this fift of may 1685:

Atest: John Wikware
Arthur Creasey

his
Nathaniell NB Bishop
marke

Inventory of the Estate of nathaniell Bishop Deceased
Taken and Aprized this 23 day of June 1685 by us whose
names are Subscribed

Imprs	a horse a mare a two yearold and a Could vallued att	3	-	-
	32 Sheep 20 Lambs :10£:10s:) 3 oxen 8 Cowes 27£) 6:3 yearold 9£	46	10	-
	7:2 yearold 8£:0s: 7 yrlings 5£:10s:) 8 Calves 2£	15	10	-
	8 Swine 50s: Iron pots & brass kittles 5£ a bed & beding 6£	11	-	-
	28 pound of Cotten wool 21s: his wareing Aparrell 6£	7	1	-
	5 dear Skins 7s) Carte wheels plow Irons & other things 4£	4	7	-
	a grindston and a percell of old Tooles	1	6	-
	a Sadle and a gun	1	3	-
	2 Chests with other Lumber	1	10	-
	a man negro	20	-	-
	Totall is -	113	:17	:0

John Wheeler

At the Aforesd Courte was presented the Inventory of the Estate
of Thomas Smith Decsed Intestate of Brookhaven: with a peticon
foe his widow namely Johanah Smith to Administer thereon,
who was Admited to Administer on ye Said Estate Shee giveing
Security according to law. the Inventory is as followeth:/

September the 6 day 1685:
The Estate of Thomas Smith was prized by us whose names
are under written

	£	s	d
2 oxen 7£ 4 Cowes 9£:) 2:3 yearolds 3£) 1:2yearold 1£)	20	-	-
1 yrling 16s) 2 Calves 12s) 1 hors 3£) 7 Swine 7£) 10 Sheep 70s)	14	18	-
6 Shoats 48s: Sum Carpenters tooles 26s: plow tackling 30s	5	4	-
housall goods and wereing Cloaths	8	2	-
	48	16	=0

his
by us thomas B Biggs
mark
John Thomas

At the Aforesd Court held at Southold october ye 20th 1685 was by mary
norten presented the Inventory of the Estate of Nat norten
Deceas and Shee Admited to Administer on ye Same giveing
Security according to Law the Inventory as followeth

Brookhaven)
in Comitt: Suffolk) An Inventory of the Estate of Nathaniell Norten Deceased August ye 14th 1685

		£		
Imprs	1 mare 50s) 2 oxen 6£) 5 Cowes 12£10s) 1 bull 3 yrold 2£)	23	-	-
Item	1 heifer 2 yearold 26s: 2 yrling Steer 26s	2	12	-
	5 Calves 30s: 1 yearling bull 13s) 9 Sheep 54s	4	17	-
	Eleven Swine 7£:10s) plow & Carte tackling 3£:6s	10	16	-
	Household goods Carpenters tooles & wereing Cloathes	20	-	-
		61	-05	=0

This accot taken and by the perticulers
vallued & apprized by
Thomas Helme
John Thomas

Know all men by these presents that whereas Ellis Cook of Southampton Deceased Did by his Last will an testa ment Make the widow Martha Cook Relict to ye Said Ellis Cook Deceas Executrix of the Said will: In and by which the Said Martha Cook is obliged to pay as a Legacy Contained and menconed in ye said will unto her Son John Cook Either the Houseing and Land at mecox or the Houseing and accomadations at ye Towne: now know yea that I martha Cook Executrix to the Said Elis Cook his will and testament doe hereby Assigne and makeover unto the Said John Cook all the Houseing and accomodations at the Towne: menconed and Contained in ye Said will as acord ing to ye mind and will of the testator therein Specified which the said John Cook Doth accordingly Except: This agreement was Concluded on by both partyes and by mutuall Consent - Comitted to Record this Sixth Day of November 1685 memorandum that the above Said widow Martha Cook and John Cook did both Come unto mee this 29th Day of May 1690 and did then both Mutually agree to make null and voyd the above Said assignment and that the above Said John Cook doth wholly Resigne and Disclaime all Rights Claims or Intrest In or unto the Said accomodations above menconed

Test John Howell Clark

Aprill the 29 16[48]

These present writing testefieth an agreement between the worship full Theophilus Eaten Esquire governr of the Colloney new haven and the worshipfull Edward Hopkins Esquire governer of the Col lony Coneticot and there Assossiats on the one party and pagaticus Sachem of manhansack wiandance sacham of mentakut momo weta Sacham of Corchaug nowedano Sacham of Shinecok and there Assosiats the other party the Said Sachams haveing Sould unto the Aforsd mr Eaton and mr Hopkins with there Ascociats all the Land Lying from the bounds of the Inhabetants of Southampton unto ye East Side of napeak next unto mentaket High Land with the whole breadth from Sea to Sea not Entrenching upon any in Length or breadth which the Inhabatants of Southampton have and doe possesse as they by Lawfull Right Shall make apeare) for and In Consideration of twenty Coats twenty four hows twenty four hatchets twenty four knives twenty four Looking glasses one hundred muxes allread Received by us the forenamed Sachams for our Selves and Associats and in Consideration there of we doe give up to the Said purchasers all our write and Intrest in the Said Land to them and theire heires for Ever Also doe bind our Selves to Secure there wright from any Claim of any other whether Indians or other nations whatsoever that doe or may here after Challeng Intrest therein Also: we the Said Sachams have Covenanted to have liberty freely to - fish in any or all the Creeks and ponds and hunt upon and downe in the woods without mollestation they giveing to the En =glish inhabetants no Just offence or Injury to there goods and Cattells, Likewise they are to have the finns and tailes of all Such whales as Shall be Cast up to there proper Right and Desire they may be freindly dealt with in the other part alsoe they Reserve Liberty to fish in all Conveni ent places for Shells to make wampam also if the Indians Hunting of any dear they should Chase them into the water and the English should kill them the English Shall have the body and the Sacham the Skin and Intestimony of our well performance hereof we have Set to our hands the Day and year first above written

witnes to this Richard odell
Thomas Stanton Robert bond
Job Sayre : Checkanoo his
mark x there Interpreter:

a true Coppy p Jno Howell Clark

Sacham of
the mark of paggatauut manhansuk
the mark of wiandanc
mentocket Sacham
the mark of momowetah Cor=
Chock Sacham: the mark of
nowedonna Shinicok Sacham

Whereas by Direction from the th[e Worshipfu]ll Theophilus
Eaten and mr Edward Hopkins A purchase was made by the tho:
Stanton and others of a part of the Eastern part of Long=
Island of the Indian Sachems the true proprietors thereof
In the name of Theofilus Eaton Esquire aforesd and my
Selfe with our Associats as by the Said Agreement Dated
the 29th of Aprill 1648 may more fully Apear which Said pur=
chase was paid by me Edward Hopkins and Amounted to the
Some of thirty pounds four Shilling 8d as may apear by a not
of perticulers under the hand of thomas Stanton to whom ye
said Sum was paid now Delivered to Robert bond of East
hampton this writeing wittnesseth that I have Received the
foremenconed Sum of thirty pounds four Shillings Eight pence
of the Inhabetants of East Hampton and have Delivered unto
them the writeing of the Said purchase and all the Intrest
that thereby was purchased In witnes whereof I have here
unto Subscribed the 16 day of Aprill 1651

I say received thirty pounds
four Shillings Eight pence
p me Edward Hopkins

Be it knowne unto all men by these presents that I the
Sunk Squa of mantakett wife of wife of wiandance of Late
years Deceased and also I wionkombone Son of the Aforesd
Deceased party Sacham of Long Island togather with pockatown
Cheife Counseller and the Rest of our trusty Councellers
and Associats Send greeteing know yea that whereas there
was a full and firm Indentiure Made between mr Thomas
Baker mr Robert bond mr Thomas James mr Lyon Gardner
Mr John Mulford John Hand Benjamin price together with
there Associats the Inhabetants of Easthampton upon long
Island the one party and I Sunk Squa and also mee wionk=
konbone with the full Consent of my Councellers and Servants
as also of my two gardians Left by my Deceased father
(vizst) mr Lyon garner of Easthampton and mr David garner
of the Ile of wight the other party In the year of our Lord
one thousand Six hundred Sixty upon the Sixth Day of August
whereby wee did fully and firmly Sell unto the Said party
our neck of Land Called mentakut from Sea to Sea from
the utmost End of that neck East ward Called wampinomit

to our utmost bound [ ] Called Napeak withall privilledges and - Apurtenances belonging to the Same upon Condition there and then Specified In that foresaid Indenture and a Counter bond bareing the Same Date Signed and Sealed to us by the foresaid partyes Inhabe tants of Easthampton by vertue of which Counter bond wee had free Liberty granted if wee See Cause to Sitt Downe againe upon the Said Land this being the full purpose of us the Sunksqua and of wienkombowen Sacham together with ours Associates in Convenient time to Sitt downe to Live at the Said Mentakut Know yea also that whereas of Late years there - having been Sore distress and Callamityes befallen us by Reason of the Cruell possition and viollence of our most deadly enimie ninicraft Sacham of narregansett whose Cruelty hath proceeded soe far as to take away the Lives of many of our dear freinds and Relations Soe that wee were forced to fly from the Said mentakett for Shelter to our beloved freinds and neibours of Easthampton whom wee findeing to be freindly in our Distres and whom wee must Ever owne and acknowledge as Instruments under god for the preserva -of our Lives and the Lives of our wives and Children to this Day and of that Land of meantokett from the hands of our enimyes and Since our Coming Amongst them they Relieveing of us in our Extremityes from time to time and now at Last wee finde the Said Inhabetants of Easthampton (our Deliverers) Cordiall and faithfull in there former Covenants Leaveing us freely to our owne Liberty to goe or Stay. being Ready to perform all Conditions of the foresaid Agreement after Serious Debate and Delibera- tion in Consideration of that Love which we have and doe bear - unto these our trusty and beloved freinds of Easthampton upon our owne free and vollentary motion have given and granted and by these presents doe give and grant and Confirm unto those our frinds the Inhabetants of Easthampton Excepting Such as have Exem pted themselves from the former Agreement and Shall from this our grant) all that peice or neck of Land belonging to Mentak kut Land westward to a fresh pond in a beach on this Side westward to that place where the old Indian fort Stood: on the other Side East ward to the new fort that is yet Standing the name of the pond being quaqununtowunk on the north and Scunkhunganik on the South together with all privelledges and Apurtenances belonging unto the Aforesd Land from South to north To have and to hold the Same as free Comonage to be ordered and disposed of for the benefitt of the Aforesd Inhabetants of Easthamp ton themselves there heirs Administrators Executors and

assignes

Assignes for Ever to possess the Same freely and quietly
without any matter of Challeng Claime or Demand of
us the Said Sunksqua and wiankombone Sacham or our
assosiats or of any other person or persons whatsoever
for us or in our names or for our Cause means or procure
=ment and without any money or other thing therefore
to be yeilded paid Done onely for the Said Land to us or
our heires for Ever and Shall Justifye the possession of this
forsaid Land by these Said Inhabetants of Easthampton against
any Shall question there propriety in ye Same know yea
also that this is not only the deed of mee the Sunksqua
and wiankombone Sacham but also the act and deed of all our
Assossiats and Subjects who have had formerly any propri
=ety in the foresaid Land they haveing manefested there Con
Sent freely by a voat not one Contradicting the Same as also
with the Consent of mr Lyon Gardner and mr David -
Garner whom the Deceased father Left as over Seers and
and gardians of the foresaid wiankombone Sacham know
yea alsoe that for the Securing of the Easterne part of -
montaukut Land which the Indians are to Live upon that
the Inhabetants of foresd Easthampton Shall from time to time
keep up a Sufficient fence upon the north Side of the foresaid
pond and the Indians are to Secure the South Side of the
foresaid pond from all Cattle During the time there
Corne is upon the ground and then Easthampton Cattle
Shall have Liberty Eastward according to former Agreement
and that the Indians of montaukut Shall have Liberty if
they See Cause to Set there houses upon montauket Land
westward of the Said pond and to have fire wood from time
to time on the foresaid Land know alsoe that what ever
Conos or deer Shall come on Shore on ye north Side of any part
of mentauket Land Easthampton Inhabetants Shall not
Hinder the Sacham of them and whereas the deceased
Sacham In his Life freely gave to mr Lyon garner
and mr Thomas James what whales Should at any time be
Cast upon montauket Land is also Confirmed by mee -
Sunksqua and wiankanbome Sacham Since and the Rest of
or Associats which not being minded when former
Agreement was made I Sunksqua and I wiunkonbone Sa
cham together with our Assciats do freely give to ye Said
Lyon garner and Thomas James to be Equally
Devided between them the first whale Shall be

Cast

Cast upon Montauket Land to them and there heires or Assigns for Ever wee give the one halfe of all Such whales as Shall be Cast upon montaket Land and the other halfe to be Devided by ye Inhabetants of Easthampton for Ever know yea alsoe that as ye sd Inhabetants of Easthampton Stand Engaged to us for pay for that Land Eastward of the foresaid pond Soe wee alsoe stand Engaged nether directly nor Indirectly to give Lett or Sell any part of that land without Con Sent of Easthampton know yea also that if at any time hereafter if Either thorow Sickness or warr or any other meanes it Shall - Come to pass that the Indians belonging to montauket be taken Away Soe that it Shall not be Safe for them to Continue there that then those that Survive Shall have Liberty to Come to Eastham pton for Shelter and be there provided of Land and to have the former Agreement fullfilled and to remaine as firme and Sure as tho there never had been any such act or deed as here is Specified and that dureing the time of the Indians abode at montauket they Shall be carfull of Doeing any wrong to ye - English Either by there owne parsons or dogs or any other way Whatsoever In wittness of the premises wee doe here Sett to our hands dated at Easthampton february the 11 Anno 1661

Sealed Signed and Delivered
In presence of us

Edward Codner	the Sunk Squa A her mark
William miller	wiankambone Sacham his mark
	pokatownes mark
	powhy his mark
	misaquat his mark
these two mr garner and	mokkatus his mark ?
his Son fully Confirming	Ackonu A his mark
the premises being gardians	Sianah his U mark
to the above Said Sacham	Soukinoush his mark
Lyon garner	Ackeanit his mark
David Garner	those in the name and Consent
	of ye rest of the Indians of mentaket

A true Coppy p John Howell Clarke §

At the Aforesaid Court of Sessions holden at Southold on ye 20th day of october 1685 was presented the Inventory of John Mappam of Southampton Deceased who dyed Intestate and the widow Mary Mapam & Relict to the Said John Mappam upon her request is Admited Administrat tor to the Said Estate giveing Security according to Law -

the Inventory is as followeth /

An Inventory of the Estate of John Mappam of Southampton Deceased on the 24th of September 1685

	£	s	d
Item one dwelling house and barne and home) Lott with the Rest of the accomaditions)			
Item 2 horses 6£: 2 oxen 7£) 6 Cowes 12£	25	-	-
Item 2 Steers of 2 yearold and 2 of 3 yearsold	7	-	-
to 2 heifers 2 yearold 50s 2 yearlings 24s	3	14	-
3 Calves 21s Swine at 4£: a fether bed & beding 4£	9	1	-
to another feather bed at 4£ to pewter at 45s	6	5	-
Som tin ware 3s) 4 Earthen platers and Some wooden platers 5s)	-	8	-
to 4 Iron pott 34s 2 Iron kettles 10s & a Spade 2s three brass) kettles and a pan 4£:10s 16 Sheep 4£: 4 axes 10s))	11	10	-
to a Chamer pott 2s paile bowle trays and Seives	-	17	6
to 2 pot hangers 10s to Cart and plow tackling 30s	2	-	-
to a Coopers broad ax four blanketts a rug and Coverled 52s	2	16	-
to a duzen of napkins 3 table Cloaths 6 Sheets 6 pillo beers 30 yd homespun	7	-	-
to 2 old Chests and an old trunk 20s his wareing Aparrill 3£	4	-	-
to about 15 bushells of wheate to thresh 50s Indian 30s	4	-	-
to an old match Lok gun and Sword and a warming pan	-	18	-
to 9 platter 2 basons 2 Cups of pewter	2	1	6
to a Chafe bed at ten Shilling & all ye Lumber in ye House 20s	1	10	-
to books and taylors Sheers	-	5	-
	88	:00	=6

taken and Aprized by us) obadiah Rogers
according to money) John Howell Junr §

A true Coppy of the origanall
p John Howell Junr § Clarke

At the Aforsesaid Court of Sessions holden At Southold on ye 20 day of - october 1685 was presented the Inventory of william Hakelton of Southampton Deceased with a peticon for ye widow Sarah Hakelton to Administer upon the Said Estate whoe is by the Courte Admited to Administratrix thereunto giveing Security according to Law: which Shee hath accordingly given in to ye Clarke: the Inventory is as foloweth

An Inventory of the Estate vizst ye goods Land and Chatells of william Hakelton Deceased upon the 6th day of September 1685 taken and Aprized this 23d Instant by us Subscribed

Item one Dwelling house and home Lot			
Item one Load of oats in the Straw and 2 Load of hay	2	4	-
to one table 8s to a Large Chest 15s) 7 Charyes 14s) a Cubord 16s	2	13	-
to an Iron pott an Iron kettle a payle and a bottle	1	7	-
to a Sett of Curtaines 30s) 5 yards Linin Cloath 7s6	1	17	6
to Some other Small things in the Chest	-	7	-
to 2 bedsteads 8s to 2 bedsteads more 8s	-	16	-
to his wareing Aparrell	5	-	-
to 7 Sheets at 43s a duzen of Napkin 9s	2	12	-
to pewter at 45s=6d a trunk at 12s	2	17	6
to another trunk at Six Shillings three feather beds and)			
Ruggs blankets and pillows at 12£:15s)	13	1	-
his workeingeer and Lasts at 25s=6d	1	5	6
to one horse and Sadle	5	-	-
to 2 good Cowes 5£) 2 Small hogs 20s	6	-	-
to one gun 20s a paire of tongs and peele 6s	1	6	-
to a bell mettle Scillet and Iron pott 11s	-	11	-
	46	=17	-0

taken and Aprized by us — Edward Howell
John Howell Junr §

A true Coppy p John Howell Clarke §

At the Aforesd Courte of Sessions holden at Southold upon ye 20th day of october 1685 was presented the Inventory of Joseph Marshall of Southampton by the widow Elizabeth Marshall who Desires to Administer upon ye Said Estate whereupon Shee is Admited Sole Administratrix to ye Said Estate Leaveing a peticon upon file and giveing Security as the Law Directs the Inventory is as followeth

An Inventory of the Estate of Joseph Marshall Deceased taken and Aprized upon this 2d day of September 1685 vizst) -

Edward Howell

Edward Howell John Jessup and John Howell Junr

Item		£	s	d
Item one dwelling House and Shop and aboute	)			
five Acres of Land at home	)			
to one horse 30s) 2 Cowes 1 yearling & 1 Calfe 5£		6	10	–
to 13 Swine and pigs at 4£=10s		4	10	–
to a thousand and halfe of Staves with Som heading	)	1	5	–
to a percell of hoops with Some new Cask and	)			
Some Stuff that is wrought		2	15	–
a grindeston 10s) 3 broad axes 14s) 2 hansaws 6s		1	10	–
to 6 old drawing knives & 2 heading knives		–	10	–
to 2 Crussetts 3s:) 4 Adses and 3 adses 12s		–	15	–
to 12 Joynter Irons 8s) a Crose Stock & 3 nimble Stocks	)			
and two broken long boarers 5s	)	–	13	–
to 7£ of Cotton wooll 7s to 7£ of flax 3s:6		–	10	6
to a bed and beding at 70s to his wareing Aparell 40s		5	10	–
a bushell Indian Corne 2s a Chest at 4s		–	6	–
a bed and furneture 4£=15s		4	15	–
to a Chest at 3s a table and a Chest of drawers 30s		1	13	–
to a fether bed bedsted & beding with Curtaines Silk fringed		6	10	–
to a warming pan 6s a Chest 5s a dozen napkins 12s		1	3	–
to 2 paire of Sheets one holland ye other homespun		1	14	–
to a table Cloath 2s a Cubard at 18s		1	–	–
to a trundle bedsted and beding with a feather bed		2	15	–
to Som Jakanaps plate 2 brass Candle Stik &c		–	5	–
to a trunk and books 10s a Linin wheele 3s:6		–	13	6
to five bowles and 2 Seives 6s 2 paire of Small Stilyards 15s		1	1	–
to pewter at 28s) 4 Small Iron pots & kittles 26s		2	14	–
to Small bras Scillets 5s to pailes 2s		–	7	–
to musket 18s a Joynters Stocks and trushoops 5s		1	3	–
to ye Lumber In ye hous with ye Chayres 20s		1	–	–
		50	=18	=0

Aprized by us according to money) Edward Howell
) John Jesup Junr
John Howell Junr §

The Last will and testament of John Corey february ye 1 1684 5
as followeth I give unto my Son John my brass kettle and
bellemetle Skillet bed ruge and bowlster the great -
bible Chest and what was In it and Cloke one halfe of a debt
of twelve pounds and halfe my weaveing Takell
I give to my son Jacob the price of halfe my Land In ye -
oyster pond uper=neck to be paid to him by my Son Abram
too Calves halfe my Sheep wearing Cloaths and halfe my
weaveing takell halfe my husbandry tooles with half my
Lumber and fourteen Acres Land to his Son
I give my son Abram my Lott of Land at ye oyster ponds -
uper neck: next to Thomas moors he paying halfe ye price
to his brother Jacob: halfe my Sheep halfe a debt of twelve -
pounds in his owne hands halfe my husbandrey tooles with half
my Lumber: my Son Abraham to Receive and pay all my
Debts which are but very Small he is to pay his brother
Isaac five Shillings which I give him: and to Satisfie
my freind John Tuthill for what trouble hee is at aboute
my will I give to my Daughter hanah my Lott by ye
mill and her Daughter hanah an Iron pot and one heifer
I give my Daughter Abigaile an Iron pott and one Iron
kittle my blankets and pillows a Chest and what is in it

The Aforesd will was presented to ye Courte of
Sessions holden at Southold upon the 20th day of
october 1685: by John tuthill as the will and
testament of John Corey Deceased which hee
Declared was as above written:
and then and there apeared thomas maps Senr
and Samuell wines who were Sworne in
Courte that the Said John Corey Deceased bid
them take notice that he had Left his
Instructions to Concerne his will with ye Sd
John Tuthill: The will being thus proved the
Said Abraham Corey is Admited Executor ther
unto:

A true Coppy p John Howell Clarke -

At the Aforesd Court of Sessions was presented the Inventory
of the Estate of Thomas Reeves of Southampton decea
sed Intestate with a pitition by the widdow Rebecha Reeves

Rebacha Reeves to Administer upon her Deceased Husbands Estate which is granted to the Said Rebacha to Administer upon the Said Estate giveing in Security as the Law Directs but not without Charge as Shee Requested: the Inventory is as followeth:

An Inventory of the Estate of Thomas Reeves Deceased August the 28 1685 taken and Aprized by us this 2d Day of September 1685

	£	s	d
Imprs to a Dwelling house and Smithe Shop)			
to aboute 40 Acres of Land At home 14 Acres)			
of Land at ye head of the Creek and a fifty)			
of Land at hogneck with a fifty of Comonage)			
to one horse 2 mares a yearling & Colt	6	10	-
to a paire of oxen 6£ to 5 Cowes 10£:) 2 Cowes 3 yearold 70s)	19	10	-
to 4 Cattle one yearold 70s) 5 Calves 40s) in Swine 12£	17	10	-
to 24 Sheep 6£ a horse Carte & takle 20s	7	-	-
to a paire of hopple 3s) two paire of Smiths bellows 4£	4	3	-
to an Anvill at 8£ another ditto 28s	9	8	-
to a great beakhorne 20s another Smaller 15s	1	15	-
to 2 vices at 4£ to ye Irons and grindstone 2s	4	2	-
to 2 howes 7s to Share moulds & Iron 37s: 6d	2	4	6
to 2 Sledges 14s to a pare of tongs 33s:	2	7	-
to 3 Small hamers 6s Some Small tooles 4s	-	10	-
to Coles Chizels a file 2s: a naile toole a punch for an)			
ax hand 2s:6 more old tooles 4s)	-	8	6
to 2 tuo Iron 3s:6: files 6s	-	9	6
to 3 old great files 5£:6	-	5	6
to a nob yoak with Irons 2s four Iron potts 50s	2	12	-
to Iron kettles 50s a Small pott 5s two pott)			
hangers 6s an Iron Scillet 3s paire of tongs 18d)	3	5	6
to a box Iron defective 2s: a warming pan 4s	-	6	-
to a bedsted bed and beding 5£	5	-	-
a trundle bed and beding 50s) 2 Coverleds 20s	3	10	-
to his wareing Apparrell at 40s	2	-	-
to 3 Chest old without Locks	-	10	-
to a Churne 3s a gun by information 12s	-	15	-
to a bedsted at 3s:6: milk vessells 6s	-	9	6
to Spoons trenchers and dishes 5s	-	5	-
to pewter pots and basons 6s) to porringers and pint pot 18d	-	7	6
to 3 pailes 5s) 2 Seives 4s 2 bras kittles 12s) a gallon bottle & ½ bushell 2s	1	3	-
to 2 pare of Sheets 16s to 20 yards of homespon 40s	2	16	-

to about four Acres of Corne upon ye ground	3	–	–
to about 15 bushels of wheat in the Stack	2	5	–
to an old bed tick with a few feathers in it	–	10	–
to 3 old wheeles 9s an old trunk 5s	–	14	–
Some woolen yarne and hops	–	10	–
flax at 5s the Lumber in the house and Chayres 15s	1	–	–
to Cheese at 20s	1	–	–
	97	–18	=6

The Above Inventory is Aprized by us according to money

Edward Howell
John Jessup Junr Consb
John Howell Junr

A true Coppy p John Howell Clarke §

At the Aforesaid Courte of Sessions holden At Southold the 20th Day of october 1685 was presented the will and Inventory of Samuell Mills of Soth Hampton Deceased the first Day of Aprill 1685 and the will was prov ed by the oath of Isaac Cory and John Laughton both Sworne In Court to the Reallyty thereof and the Said Mary Mills widow to ye Said Decedant is Admited Executrix to ye will according to the minde and will of the testator there in Specified the will is as followeth /

In the name of god Amen I Samuell Mills of Southampton In the East Rideing of yorkeshire upon LongIsland Husbandman being very Sick but in my perfect minde doe make this my – Last will and testament In maner and forme following I bequeath my Soule to god and my body to Christian buriall &c /
I give and be queath unto mary my wife my Land Lying and being at mecoks Adjoyning to ye Land of John foster I doe bequeath my Land at Stratford Lying at Oronoge unto my Son Richard Mills if he Live to the Age of twenty one years and to my wife Mary I bequeath one third parte of the Said Land at oronoge Dureing her Life time but at her Decease it Shall Come to my Son Richard Mills but if my Son Richard Shall Deceas before he Comes of age then I doe bequeath my Land at oronogue to my wife Mary and to her hiers Executors Administrators and assignes for Ever: I doe depute Joseph More and John Lupton to be the overseers of this my will
I doe make my wife mary wholl Administrator of my

My Estate as witnes my hand [and Seale] this first day of
Aprill Anno: Dom 1685

test:) Samuell Mills
Isaac Cory
Joseph more
A true Coppy p John Howell Clarke §

An Inventory of the Estate of Samuell Mills Deceased
Aprill the first taken by us the Subscribed Aprill the
11th 1685

Item an a Comadations of Land at Stratford			
to twenty Acres of Land at mecokes Adjoyning)			
to John foster his Land)			
to one horse and one Cow	5	10	–
to ten Swine whereof Five are Small and 5 Sheep	4	10	–
to 2 drinking potts 4s to one Iron pot of 3 gallons 6s	–	10	–
to a little brass kittle of aboute a gallon	–	3	–
to 2 Earthen things 2 pewter poringers	–	4	–
to 3 pailes one buter tub 4 woooden dishes	–	8	–
to 2 wooden platers and a boule & 2 Cream pots	–	5	–
to one tub one home Spon bed ticking filled with wooll	1	10	–
to one Coverled 2 blankets	–	18	–
to one Chest	–	4	–
to 2 pillow 6s 2 Stubing hows one broad how 8s	–	14	–
to one Shaveing knife and one good gun 20s: 2 meat barrell 5s	1	5	–
to halfe a barrell of meat 10s: a woolen wheele 4s	–	14	–
to Six pound of flax 4s to one Sadle & bridle 12s	–	16	–
to one pilion 6s to 2 old hatts 2 old Coats and wastcote 14s)	1	–	–
2 pare of old trowsers one Shirt 2 neckcloaths a barbars bason	–	10	–
	19	:01	=0

taken by us Edward Howell
John Howell Junr §

The Estate of John finch prised by us one feather bed & boulster	1	8	–
to one gun 20s an old Iron pot 1s: an old Square hancacheife 6d	1	1	6
two old trays 6d: one paire of tobacco tong 3d and on old pewter plat 6d)	–	1	3
an old Coat and peece Ditto: 2 pr old Stockins & old hatt and blue Shirt)			
and two peices of old blankets and an old Shot pouch is)	–	4	–
and 2 old Chayres 4s	–	4	–
In all is	2	=18	-9

Sworn this 17th Day of 8ber By us: Richard white
1685 before me Epenetus Platte : walter noaks

This Indenture made the Second day of March In the
Second Yeare of the Raigne of our Sovereigne Lord King James
the Second and In the year of our Lord one thousand Six hundred
Eighty and five Between John Thompson of Brookhaven
on Long Island
In the County of Suffolk ^ of the one parte and John Palmer
of the Citty of new york Gent: of the other part Whereas
the Right Honourable Richard Nicolls, Esqr Lift
and governour genarall of this province of newyorke -
and dependancyes under then his Royall Highness James
Duke of york and Alboney now his most Sacrad Majesty
Aforesd did by his Certaine pattent or writeing bear
ing date the Seventh day of March in ye year of our Lord
one thousand Six hundred Sixty and Six Give grant Rati
fie and Confirme unto Capt John Tooker Daniell Lane
Henry perring Richard Wodhull and John Geners for
and In the behalfe of the Inhabetants and free -
houlders of the Said Towne of Brookhaven and there
Associats and the heires and Assignes of them and
Every of them all that Tract or percell of Land and
Meadow within the Limitts and bounds In the Said
pattent set downe and Expressed to have and To
hold the Said Tract or percell of Land meadow and
premises unto the Said Capt John Tooker Daniell
Lane Richard woodhull Henry perring and John
Genner He and In the behalfe of the Said Inhabe
tants and freeholders of Brookhaven and there -
Associates there heirs and Assignes for Ever as by ye
Said pattent or writeing now Remaing on Record
In the Secretaries office Ralation being thereunto had
May more fully and at Larg Appeare And Whereas
the Said John Thompson by vertue of a grant from
the freeholders and Inhabetants Afforesaid Stands
now possessed of one home Lott of Land Sittuat Lying
and being within the Said Towne over against the
Meeting hous bounded To ye East and South east by the Land
of Anthony Thompson and Jacob Longbottom to ye
west with the Land of John Tooker Containing five
Acres or there abouts with the Rights privilledges and
Appurtenances thereunto belonging and Appert[ ]
ing and Whereas the Said John Thompson Stands [ ]
wise possest of the Severall and Respective Tract[ ]
percells of Land herein After menconed In R[ ]

of the Aforsaid Home Lott That [is to Sa]y five Acres of upland
or there aboutes Sittuate Lying and being on the little neck
Twenty Acres of upland Sittuate Lying and being to the East
ward of the Lotts on the Right hand of the path goeing to the
old mans: Sixty Acres of upland Sittuat Lying and being at
the Drownd meadow bounded to the South with ye Land of
John Roe to the East with the Comon Land of Mount -
Missery to the north with the High way that goes to the
Said Mount Missery and to the west with the Said Drownd
Meadow together with the Meadow Land thereunto be
longing Adjoyning and Apertaining ffifteen Acres of
up Land on the South together with the Meadow Land there
unto Adjoying Apertaining and belonging as alsoe his Share
part and proportion of meado at Mattamummax bounded
to the East with the Meadow of William Thompson to ye
north with the upland West by the meadow of Thomas
Biggs and South by the bay or Sound and Thirty Acres of
upland Sittuat Lying and being within the new fence
of the ould feild as by the Severall and Respective Entryes
In the Towne books may more fully Like wis and at Larg
Appeare Now this Indenture Wittnesseth that the
Said John Thompson for and In Consideration of the
Sum of one hundred pounds Law full money of this pro
=vince to him the Said John Thompson In hand at
and before the Enfeofeing and Delivery of these presents
by the Abovesaid John Palmer well and truly paid -
the Receipt whereof hee the Said John Thompson
doth hereby acknowledge and owne himselfe to be there with
fully Satisfied Contented and paid and thereof and of Every
parte and percell thereof doth Clearly Acquit Exonerat
and discharge the Said John Palmer his heires Executors
and Administrators for Ever by these presents Hath
given Granted bargained Sould allinated Enffeoffed Re
=leased and Confirmed and by these presents doth fully
and Absolutly give grant bargain Sell Allinate Enfeof
Release and Confirme unto the Said John Pallmer
his heires and Assignes for Ever all that before recited
home Lott of Land as alsoe all and Singuler the Afor
mentioned tract and tracts percell and percells of Land and
meadow Sittuate Lying and being as Afforesaid together with all
and Singuler the Messuages houses tenements barnes Stables
orchards gardens pastures feedings and Commons trees woods
under woods fenceings buildings brooks Rivers Creeks harbours
hunting houking fishing fowleing Rights Libertyes privilledges
acom

Accommadations Allottments Immunityes benefits & Advantages
whatsoever to the Said home Lott of Land and all and Every
the Said tract and tracts percell and percells of Land meadows
and premises or any part thereof belong or In any wise Aper
taing or which at any time heretofore did belong and Apertain
or which have been or hereafter Shall bee Accepted reputed
taken knowne had used Enjoyed occupied as part percell or -
member thereof: on the Reversion and Reversions Remain
der and Remainders of all and Singuler the premises beforemen
tioned and alsoe all the Estate Right title Intrest: possession Claime
property pretentions and Demand of him the Said John Thompson
in or to the Said home Lott tract or tracts peice or peices
percell or percells of Land meadow and premises or any part or
percell thereof Except and always reserved all such tract & tracts
percell and percells of Land and meadow to the Said home Lott be
Longing which by the Said John Thompson have been at any
time allinated before the twenty Eight day of october In the
year of our Lord one thousand Six hundred Seventy & Eight To
have and To hold all and Singuler the Said tracte and -
tracts percell & percells of Land & meadow and all and Singuler
the Above granted or mentioned to be granted premisses with
there and Every of there Rights members and Apurtenances -
Except before Excepted unto the Said John Palmer his heirs
And Assignes for Ever to and for the only proper use benefit
and behoofe of him the Said John Pallmer his Said Heirs and -
Assignes for Ever And the said John Thompson for himself
his heires Executors and Administrators doth Covenant promise
and grant to and with the Said John Palmer his heirs
and Assignes by these presents in maner and form following
that is to Say that hee the Said John Thompson the Said tract
and tracts peice and peices of Land meadow and premises un
to the Said John Palmer and his heirs to the only proper
use and behoofe of him the said John Palmer his heirs &
Assignes for Ever against him ye Said John thompson his -
heirs and Assignes and all and Every other person or person
whatsoever Claiming by from or under him them or any
of them or by there or any of there means act Consent
title Intrest privity or procurement Shall and will warrant
and for Ever defend by these prsents and furthermore that
the Said John thompson his heirs and Assignes and all
and Every other person or persons whatsoever any Estate
haveing or Lawfully Claimeing of into: or out of the
premises or any part thereof by from or under ym
or any of them Shall and will dureing the Space of

of Seaven years now Next Ensueing upon the Reasonable Re
quest and at the Cost and Charges in the Law of the Said -
John Palmer his heires and Assignes make doe and Execute
or Cause or procure to be made done or Executed unto the
Said John Palmer his heirs and Assignes for Ever all Such
further and Reasonable act and acts thing and things Convayances
and Assurances In the Law whatsoever for the further
and better Assureing Sure makeing Strengthening and Con=
firming unto the Said John Pallmer his heirs and Assignes
for Ever as Afforesaid the sd tract and tracts percell and
percells of Land meadow and premises hereby granted
or mentioned to be granted as by the said John Palmer
his heires or Assignes or his or there Councell Learned
in the Law Shall be Reasonably devised advised and Required
In witnes whereof the Said partys to these presents
have Enter Changably put there hands and Seales the
Day and year first above written /

Sealed and Delivered
in the presence of
Samuel Eburne
John Tuder

John Thompson

Memorandum that upon the Second day of March in
In the Second yeare of the Raine of king James the
Second and In ye year of our Lord one thousand Six hun
dred Eighty and five Apeared before mee Mathias Nicolls
one of the Judges of the province of new yourk the -
within named John Thompson and Acknowledged
the within written Instrument to be his act & deed

M. Niccolls

Memarandum that full and peacable possession and Seizin was
given and delivered by the within named John Thompson of &
all and Singuler the within bargained premises unto
Samull Eburne of the towne of Brookhaven by vertue of the Letter
of atturney to this present Indenture Anexed for and In the name
and to the use of the within named John Palmer his heirs and Assigns
according to the true intent and meaning of the Said Indenture &
Letter of Atturney the Eight day of March in the year of our lord
one thousand Six hundred Eighty and five in ye presence of us
whose names are subscribed

his mark
Jacob X Longbotom

John Tooker

his
Richard R Floyd
mark

To all Xpiane people to whom this present writeing
Shall Come John Palmer of the Citty of newyork Gent Sends
Greeting Know Yee that that ye Said John Palmer for div
=vers:good Causes and Considerations him hereunto Moveing hath
mad Constituted and In his Place putt Samuell Eburne of the
towne of Brookhaven within the County of Suffolk on Long
Island gent: his true and Lawfull Atturney to Enter into
and upon the Lands tenements and hereditaments mencon
ed In an Indenture bearing date even with these presents
and hereunto anexed and mentioned to bee made between
John Thompson of Brookhaven of the one part and the Said
John Palmer of the other parte purporting a ffeoffment
of ths Sd Lands tenements and hereditaments to him the Sd
John Palmer his heires and Assignes for Ever and to take
possession and Seisin thereof for him and to his use from ye
Aforesaid John Thompson or his Atturney in that behalfe
to take receive and keep according to the tenure forme
and Effect of the Said Indenture Ratifieing and by these
presents confirming all and whatsoever his Said Aturney
Shall doe or Cause to be done in the premises as fully and
Efectually as hee the Said John Pamer Could doe if he were
personaally present In wittness whereof the Said John
palmer hath hereunto Sett his hand and Seale this
Second Day of March in the Second year of the Raigne of
King James the Second and In the year of our Lord one
thousand Six hundred Eighty and five /

Sealed and Delivered John Palmer
in the presence of us
M. Nicolls
John Tuder §

A true Coppy of the Afforsaid Indenture the acknow
ledgement the Delivery and Seisin with the Letter of
Aturney: taken out of the orignall: and Enterd as be
fore written on this 11th Day of March 1685 6

p John Howell Clark §

Know all men by these presents that I John Houltem
of Brookhaven in the County of Suffolk upon Long Island
In the province of newyork Cordwinder have for vallu
able Causes and Considarations me thereunto moveing
and a Considerable Sum of money already Received to my
full Content and Satisfaction have given granted barg
gained and Sould and doe by these presents give grant
bargaine and Sell alien and make over unto mr Samull
Eburne of the abovesaid Towne and County a Certaine
percell and tract of Land that ye Towne gave mee
Sittuat and Lying between Arther futhys and John Tookers
Tayler aboute Eight Acres more or Less as it was Layd
out I Say that I John Houltem doe for my Selfe my
heires Executors Administrators and Assignes doth absolutly
Sell allien and make over the Above Said trackt of
Land unto the abovesaid Samuell Eburne to him his heirs
Executors Administrators & assignes To have and To hold
for Ever with all timber trees or what soever priviledges or
Immunityes doe belong to the within ye abovesd Land and
further I the Sd John Houltem will warrant this my Sale to Stand
good and firme in Law from any person or persons whatsoe
=ever of Clayming any Right title or Intrest from by or
under mee but it Shall be for ye use and behoofe of the
Abovesd mr Samuell Eburne his heires and Assignes for ever
without any lett disturbance or molestation whatsoever and
further I Shall if need Require give a more former deed or
bill of Sale hereafter and to the true and through Conferm
ation of all the above Said Premises I doe hereunto Set
my hand and fix my Seale this 17th Day of february 1685

Signed Sealed and Delivered
In the presence of us — John Houltem

John Tucker

John Tooker

Richard floyd his R mark

her
Sarah Houltam ⟨ mark

A true Copy march ye 11th 1685 6
p John Howell Clarke §

Know all men by these presents that I John Tucker tayler
of Brookhaven in the County of Suffolk upon Long Island in ye
Province of Newyork doth for valluable Causes and Considaration
mee there unto moveing and for a Considerable Sum of money
already Received and to Receive to my full Content and satisfac
tion have given granted bargained and Sold and doe by these -
presents give grant bargaine and Sell allien and make over unto mr
Samuell Eburne of the above Said Towne Towne and County all my
Right title and Intrest of a percell of Land given me by the -
Towne Lying and Sittuate between John holtems Land given
by the Towne and that which was apointed for a minister Lott
I Say I John Tucker doth for my Selfe my heires Executors
Administrators and Assignes doth absolutly Sell allien and make
over the above Said trackt of Land or any Adistion I purchased
by the Side of it as by the bounds will Apeare unto the above Said
mr Samuell Eburn to him his heires Executors administrators &
Assignes To have and To hold for Ever withall timber
trees or whatsoever privilledges or Imunitys doe belong to ye with
=in the abovesaid Land and further I the Said John Tucker
will warrant this my Sale to Stand good and firm in Law agast
any persone or persons whatsoever Claiming any parte or
percell of the above Said Land from by or under mee but if
it Shall bee for the use and behoofe of the above Said mr Samll
Eburne his heirs and Assignes for Ever without any lett mo
=llestation or Incumbrance and further I doe Engage if need
Require to give a more Ample and former deed or bill
of Sale hereafter and to ye true and through Confirmati
=on of all the abovesaid premises I doe hereunto Sett my
hand and fix to my Seale this thirteenth day of february
1685 6

Signed Sealed and Delivered John Tucker
In the presence of us -

Arthur ffuthy
John Tooker

A true Coppy p John Howell Clarke §

In the name of God Amen I James Herrik of
Southampton in the County of Suffolk upon Long Island in
the province of new york in america: yeoman beings through
Gods mercy at present in perfect health and Sound Memory
and being Sencible of the frailty of Human Nature the cer
tainty of death & the uncertainty of the time Doe make and
ordaine this my Last will and testament vizst

Imprs I bequeath my Soule unto God who gave it: to be pre
sented before his throne of Mercy Cleansed and Redemed
by the blood and merrits of my blessed Lord and Saviour the
Lord Jesus Christe: and my body (after Decent bury=all) to
the Dust there to Remaine untill the Day of Ressurection

2ly/- I Give & bequeath unto my Well-beloved wife Martha -
Herrik Dureing her Naturall Life all my house and Home
Lott Sittuate and Lying in the Towne of Southampton
Aforesd and my five Acres of Land Lying and being
in Halseys neck on the great plaines and my Close or
Acre of Land Lying by the water Mill Swamp and my Land
at flying pointe and my Two Acres of Land at the Plaine
gate and my fifteen Acres of Land at the west End of my
Wood Close at wickapouge and my meadow at Assopes neck
all which house Lotts and pcells of Land and meadow After
her Decease to be unto my three Sons as followeth. -

3ly I give and bequeath unto my well beloved son Thomas Herrik
all my Said House and barne with one full Acre of Land in
the home Lott Running the whole breadth at the Street
to the Land given to my Son William and My five Acres
of Land at halseys neck Aforsd and that Acre of Land at ye
mill Swamp to him the Said Thomas his heirs and Assigns
for Ever to be Delivered to him After the Deceas of my Sd wife
alsoe I give unto my Said Son Thomas halfe a fifty pound Com
=monage one feather bed and furneture with the Sum of ten
pounds in pay to be Delivered him when he is at the
Age of twenty one years - - - - - - - - - - -

4ly: After my wifes Deceas I give and bequeath unto my well
beloved Son William Herrik and to his heires and Assignes
for Ever all the Remainder of my home Lott and my
two Acres of land at ye plaine gate and the one halfe of my
twenty Acre Lott at hog neck

5ly After my wifes Deceas I give and bequeath unto my well
beloved Sone James Hirrik his heires and Assignes for
Ever all my fifteen Acres of Land at ye westernmost

End of

End of my Close at wicapauge and my meadow at Assops neck
and the other halfe of my twenty Acre Lott at Hogneck and a fifty
pound Comonage alsoe one fether bed and furneture

6ly It is my will and Desire that if my Son william please to Re
=Signe and give unto my Son James all that fifteen Acres of
Land which I gave him Lying Eastward to Henry Ludlam
his Acomadations then I give unto my Said Son William in Leiw
thereof all my Land at flying poynt other wise I give the
Land at flying point unto my Son James and to his heires and Assignes
for Ever - - - - - - - - -

7ly I give and bequeath unto my Daughter Mary Howell or to hers one
Cow to be Delivered to her by my Executrix within one Moneth -
next after my Decease - - -

8ly I give and bequeath unto my Daughter Sarah Petty the Sum
of twenty Shillings to be paid within one Month After my decease

9ly I give and bequeath unto my daughter Martha Herrik the
Sum of twenty pounds and one feather bed and furneture to be
paid and Delivered to her at her Day of Mariage - - -

10ly I doe make & Apoint my dear and well beloved Wife Martha
Herrik to be Sole Executrix of this my Last will and testament
to have and Receive all and Singuler my Estate and to pay
all Just Debts and Leagacys hereby given and to dispose of
the Remainder or Residue as Shee Shall See Cause only to and
Amonge the Children of us the Said James and Martha Herrik

11ly I doe hereby Recall disanull and Make voyd all former and
other wills and testaments and doe Apoint and ordaine -
these presents to be my Last will and testament In Witt
ness whereof I the Said James Herrik have hereunto
Sett my hand and Seale in Southampton aforesd the 12th day
of August 1685 annoqu R Rs Jac: 2d nunc angliae & p

Signed and Sealed as his
act and deed in presence
of us

after Enterlyning of (after her Decease)
(eastwards / all her / and blotting out
of Adjoyning and fifteen Acres twice

John C Moubray James Herrik
Andrew Gibbs § A true Copy p John Howell Clark §

At a Courte of Sessions held In Southampton for the County
of Suffolk upon the 16th day of March 1685/6 was presented
the Abovesd will in order to probate thereof and the Said
John Moubray was then Sworne In Courte that he See the Said
James Herrik Signe Seale and Declare this to be his Last
will and Testament

may ye 15 1686 andrew gibb made oth before mr Platt
at Huntington: that he See ye Said James Herrik Signe ye Same

At a Courte of Sessions Held at Southampton upon the 16 17 & 18
Days of March 1685/6 was presented the will and Inventory of John
pasons of Easthampton which is as followeth

I John Parsons now Liveing in the Towne of Easthampton upon
LongIsland in ye County of Suffolke: from the Consideration of the
Mutabillity & fraylty of my Life and being weake in body yet
through Mercy haveing my perfect reason and understanding I doe
make this my last will and Testament in manner and form folowing
First I Give unto my Eldest Son Samuell Parsons all this my hous
and home Lott Containg aboute Eight acres and a quarter more
or Less also I doe Give unto this my foresd Son all yt peice of Land on ye
Easterne Side of the Hook pond Containing aboute nine acres more
or Lesse and I doe give unto my Son Aforesaid all that peice of meadow
that doth belong to me at ye northwest & alsoe I doe give unto him two
Acres more Lying upon the Easterne plaine and bounded by Richard
Brooks on the one Side and John Kirle on ye other Side alsoe I doe Give
unto this my Son Samuell one third parte of ye Comonage that -
doth belong unto mee both about the Towne and at montaukat
alsoe I Doe give unto this my Son two oxen and Foure Cowes and one
horse and a barran Mare and one young Mare of three yearold/
2ly Also I Doe give unto my Son John Parsons nine acres of Land
that Lyeth on the Easterne Plaine westward of the Indian well
and bounded on the west by mr Schallenger and alsoe I doe give unto
this my Son John Six Acres of Land more or less that Lyeth on
the Easterne plaine Eastward of the two mile hollow and bounded by
John Millers Land west and alsoe aboute one acre & a halfe more or
Less I give unto my foresaid Son John that Lyeth Eastward of ye
two mile hollow and bounded on the East Side of it by Enoch ffithian
alsoe I doe Give unto my Son John one peice of meadow in accobon=
=nack neck and bounded by Thomas Chatfeild on ye one Side and Richard
Stratten on the other Side
Also I doe Give unto my Son Robert Parsons all that parcell
of Land that doth belong to mee upon the norwest woodland
plaine and bounded (I take it) by goodman Garlick on the on Side
and John Miller on the other Side and I doe alsoe give unto my
Son Robert all that my meadow at napeak and I doe give unto
those my two Sons Last above mentioned the other two third parts of all
my Comonage that doth belong to mee about the Towne and at
Montaukut to be equally parted between them and what horse
I give unto my other two Sons Last above menconed
flesh Remaineth as not being above menconed ^ to be parted Equaly
between them: And alsoe my will is that all my Cattle without
doors of what kind Soever & that is not above menconed and also
all my goods within doors I doe Give unto Every one of my Sons &
Daughters to be Equally devided between them and farther my
will is that my well beloved wife be by Every one of my Sons
Carefully provided for according to there abillityes while Shee
she Remaineth in a single State and Continueth here
only

only when my Eldest Son doth Come to age to Receive what I have given him then hee is to take Care for my deer wife & to provid for her according as god Shall Enable him and alsoe my will is that my Eldest Son Shall After my Decease take possession of my house and Land and Carry on with the Rest of my Sons the family occasions and bussiness together and I doe desire my deere brother Samuell parsons to be a gardian to take Care of all my Chill dren for directing and farthering of them what he Can for there good: To all and every of the Afore menconed premises as being my Last will and testament I have hereunto Set my hand this fift of march 1685/6

wittnes the mark C of John parsons
thomas talmage
the mark R:D of Robert Dayton

the Said Thomas Talmage and Robert Dayton Apeared in ye Courte aforesaid and were there Sworne that they See ye Said John parsons Signe and publish this Instrument to be his act and and deed: and the Courte Confirmed the Said will according to the mind of the testator /

A true Coppy of ye will aforesd & folowing Inventory test John Howell Clarke §

The inventary of the Estate of John Parsons Lately deceased March the 15th 1685/6

	£	s	d
It 2 oxen 5£: 5 Cowes 6£10s) 7:3 yearolds 7£14s	19	4	-
item 4:2 yearolds 3£:4s) 6 yearlings 3£12s) 8 Calves 3£:4	10	-	-
It 3 Mares 2£15s: 1 hors 30s one 2 yearold mare 10s)	4	15	-
it 3 yearling Hors kind 20s) 32 Sheep & lambs 4£10s	5	10	-
it 2 Swine 20s) 3 old wooll beds 20s	2	-	-
it 7 pr Sheets of home Spun 2£10s) 8 old blankets 25s	3	15	-
It 3 Coverlids 30s) 4 pillows & 2 boulsters 1£15s	3	5	-
It 6 pillow Coates 9s) for brass ware 3£14s) 7 Ironpots 1 Ironkittle 3£:10s	7	13	-
It in pewter 37s) for wainage 30s) for axes hows tramils & Sieths 18s)	4	5	-
It a fire Shovell tongs and Lamp 2s6d	-	2	6
it 1 bell mettle Scellet morter 2 guns 2 Swords	1	15	-
It a Small Case of bottles 9s) tin & Earthen ware 4s	-	13	-
It in graine 2£0s in Cloathing 3£10s in other Lumber 25s	6	15	-
	69	=12	-6:

Robert Dayton)
Benjamin Conklin) The Said Robert Dayton was Sworne In Courte
Jermiah Conklin) to the trueth of the Aforesd Inventory:

At The Aforesaid Courte of Sessions holden at Sout
=hampton upon the 16th &c days of March 1685/6 was presented
the Inventory of John Brookes of Easthampton deceased with
a peticon of Hanah Brooks widow to ye Said John Brooks to Ad
minister upon the Said Estate: which is granted by the Court
unto the Said Hanh to Administer giveing in Security as
the Law Directs: ye Inventory is as followeth

Inventory of the Moveable Estate of John Brookes deceased
as it was taken by us under written this 29th february 1685/6

Imprs	1 Mare halfe a mare and halfe 2 Coults aprised as money	£4	-	-
	four Cowes vallued in money 8£) 3three yearold Cattle at 4£10s	12	10	-
	1 foure yearold Steer at 45s) 2 twoyearolds vallued at 2£	4	5	-
	4 yearlings at 3£) 11 Sheep at 6s p peice is £3:6s	6	6	-
	2 Swine vallued at 12s) one Iron pott & Small brass Scellet 6s	-	18	-
	a pewter platter and a pint pott 6s) old beding & his wareing Cloaths 50s)	2	16	-
	a muskett 6s a chaine 6s) 2 Chests & a bedsted 10s	1	2	-
	two old spinning wheels	-	3	-
	a percell of tubs bukets and old Lumber	1	-	-
		33	-0	-0

The Above Inventory amounting
to the Sum of thirty three pounds in
money was taken and Aprized the
day abovesaid by us

Jerimiah Conklin
Robert Dayton

A true Coppy p John Howell Clark §

To all Christian People to whome these presents
Shall Come Richard Brooks of Easthampton on Long Island
in the Collony of newyork Sendeth greeting Know Yea that
Whereas I have formerly made a Convayance or deed of gift
unto my Son John Brookes of a certaine pcell of Land Lying at
wainscutt in the bounds of Easthampton Containing aboute -
twenty Seven Acres be it more or Less bounded with the Land of
Joseph Straten to the westward the Towne high way to the Eastward
the South Sea beach to the Southward and the towne Comons
northward with all edifices fences privilledges and Apurten
nances thereunto belonging: as alsoe two Acres of medo

at the northwest Creek to the Southward of the meadow of
mr John Mulford together with an halfe Share of the Land and
privilledges at montauk and halfe my privilledges of the town
Comons: which aforesd Deed of gift was not fully Compleated accord
ing to Law the providence of god haveing Soe prevented as to take
my Said Son out of this Life before the full Confirmation of the -
Aforesd deed of gifte as the Law Requires: I doe therefore hereby
fully freely & absolutly give grant and Confirme unto my grand
Child John Brooks: Son and heire to my Aforesaid Son John Brooks
all and singuler the Aforesaid privilledges and Apurtenances
To have and To hold all and Singuler ye above Lands
Apurtenances & privilledges to him my Said grand Child John Brooks
and his heirs for Ever and I doe hereby warrant this my gift
unto him the Said John Brooks and his heirs for Ever against
all and all maner of person or persons whatsoever that Shall Lay
Claime theretoo or any pt or pcell of the Afore Demised premises
Either by from or under mee or my heyres Executors Admin
istrators or Assignes: Soe as the Said John Brooks may at ye age
of twenty one yeares possess and Quietly Enjoy the premises: provid
ed allways that this deed nor any thing therein Contained Shall Extend
or be Construed to Impead or any ways hinder hanah the widow
or Relict of my Aforesaid Son John Brooks from ye peacable &
Quiet possession and Improvement of all the Aforesaid Demised
premises Soe Long or untill the years are Expired of my Said -
grand Child John brooks his minority or none age that is
to the age of twenty one years provided also that this deed nor
any thing therein Contained Shall be Construed to ye hindrance
of my Son Samuell brooks and his heires from being heire
In Reversion unto all the above Demised premises In -
Case my Said grand Child Jhon Brooks Shall Departe this -
Life before he Comes of age or without Issue: and for the -
Sure Confirmation of all and Every the above Said premises I
the Said Richard Brooks doe hereunto Sett my hand and
affix my Seale this 8th Day of March Anno: Dom 1685 86

Signed Sealed and Delivered in
the presence of
Josiah Hubert
Bazeliall osborne

Richard Brooks

the trueth of the above written deed of gift was -
acknowledged by the abovesaid Richard Brooks
March the tenth 1685 86 before me
John Topping Justice
A true Coppy p John Howell Clarke

Inventory of the Moveable Estate of [ ] Squire deceased
as it was taken this 4th Day of March 1685=6 by us whose names
Are subscribed

		£	s	d
Imprimis	a Lott of Land about 8 acres 3 Acres Meadow			
	1 Cow vallued at 40s a yearling horse 22s:6	3	2	6
	a horse 50s a Carsey Sute 40s	4	10	–
	6 yards and ½ of white ossen brigs	–	4	10
	an old Carsey Sute 10s an old black dublett	–	11	–
	a remnant of Red Cotten 1s.3d) 3 yards of harfords 2s6d	–	3	9
	an old Sarge Sute 5s a tin Lanthornes 2s	–	7	–
	a bed with Some feathers 3s	–	3	–
	some very old Linin 18d) an old Sheet pillow & pillow beer 6s)	–	7	6
	a paire of beetle Rings 2 old axes & a how	–	4	6
	an Iron pott & hooks 5s about halfe bushell of Salt 1s	–	6	–
	a Small paper book 6d: 2 pailes 2s:6d	–	3	–
	a percell of very old Cloaths	–	3	–
	a blue Rugg and very old Speckled Coverled	–	4	6
	an old Sadle	–	5	6
	a percell of Indian Corne	–	7	–
	old bags & Some feathers	–	1	–
	a peice of old Rope ten pence	–	–	10
	old Lumber vizst an old Stump how a glass bottle) and old basket 3 old Siethes &c)	–	3	–
	Thomas osborne	11	=7	11

Robert dayton
Jerimyah Conklin

[In the original document, this page was left blank]

To all Christian People to whome [these presents] Shall Come I Thomas Baker of Easthampton In the County of Suffolk in the province of new york Sendeth greeting Know yea that I the Said Thomas Baker as for and In Consideration of the naturall Affection which I have and beare unto my well beloved Son and heire Thomas Baker Junr as also for Diverss other good Causes and Considerations me at this present Especially hereunto Moveing Have Given and by these presents Doe Give grant and Confirme unto my Said Son Thomas Baker at my de cease my whole Estate Lying and being within the bounds of Easthampton or Else where (upon this terme of Consider ation following first that my wife Also Shall have Dure ing her Life The one halfe of all my houseing Lands meadow and Comonag & alsoe the one halfe of all my movable Estate whatsoever Dureing her Life and at her Decease Shee Shall have free Liberty to dispose of twenty pounds of my movable Estate to my Children and grand Children as Shee Shall See Cause and 2dly that my Said Son Thomas at my Decease Shall pay out of my moveable Estate to Each of my three Children namly Nathaniell Baker Hanah Leek and - Abigaile Tutill ten pounds a peice to be Disposed to my grand Children as they Shall See Cause: all the Rest of my Estate I doe by these presents freely and absolutely give unto my Said Son at my Decease namely all my houseing Lands meadows pastures Comonage and Comons withall the profitts privilledges Comodityes and advantages whatsoever doth In any wise thereunto belong together withall and and Singuler my goods Chattells utensills withall other my moveable and Imoveable Substance whatsoever that is accepted used or reputed as any parte or percell of my - Estate withall the Remainders and Reversons that - Shall or may here after thereunto belong or In any - wise Apertaine Excepting only what is before Excepted - that my wife allice to have the one halfe of all for her Life and then to Returne to him my Said Son Thomas baker all the above menconed premises as above Expressed I give unto him my Said Son and heire Thomas baker and to the male heires of his body Lawfully begotten to have and to hold for Ever and for Default of Such Issue to the female heires of his body Lawfully be gotten; and for default of any such Issue then Surviveing at my Said Son Thomas his Deceas my houseing and Land to be

be unto my Son Nathaniell Baker and to the heires of his
body Lawfully begotten for Ever and my Stock and goods with
all my moveable Estate to be Devided Amongst my Daughters
to my Daughter Ann now wife to my Said Son thomas to
have the one third part of all my moveable Estate what Soe
ever Quietly to possess the Same for Ever together with the -
Liberty of my houseing to Dwell in Dureing her widow hood and
the other two thirds of my moveable Estate I give unto my Dau
ghter hanah and Abigaile Aforesaid: to be Equally Devided between
them but if Either hanah or Abigaile be not then Survive
ing then her Respective proportion Soe Deceased to bee unto
her Children and for the further Confirmation of this my
Deed of gift never to be Revoked I have hereunto
Sett my hand and fixed my Seale In Southampton this -
twenty Eight Day of may Anno Dom 1686

it is to be understood that the
twenty pounds to be Disposed
of by my wife and the thirty
pounds to be paid to my three
Children above menconed Shall be
vallued in Contrey pay -

Thomas Baker

Signed Sealed and Delivered
in presenc of
Ephraim Howell
John Howell Junr §

Thomas Baker of East
hampton apeared before me
this 28th of may 1686 and
acknowledged the above
written Deed to be his -
owne act:
John Howell Justice

A true Coppy of the origionall this 29th Day of
May 1686 p John Howell Junr Clark §

Know all men by these presents that I David Smith
Son and heir unto Roger Smith formerly of Easthampton
Deceased have Received of John Hopping the Husband of
my mother Rebacha who was the widdow or Relict of my
Aforesaid father Roger Smith the full and Just Sum of
thirty five pounds which I doe hereby avow to be full
payment and Satisfaction for all my Right title and Claime
of Intrest unto the Estate of my Aforesaid father Roger
Smith and I doe hereby for my Selfe my heirs Executors
Administrator and Assignes: fully freely and absolutly -
acquit and for Ever discharge the Aforesaid John Hopping
his heires and assignes and all other person or persons what
Soever that are any ways Concerned in the Aforesaid

Estate

Estate from all and all maner of Clame of Right title
or Intrest in the Estate or any part or percell
of the Same Either by my Selfe or any other by
from or under mee as wittnes my hand & Seale Set
to this 28th day of May in the Second year of the Reign
of his Majesty King James the Second Anno Dom 1686
Signed Sealed and Delivered the mark of
In the presence of David) Smith
Josiah Hubert
Stephen Hand

Know all men by these presents that I peter whithere
of Brookhaven in the County of Suffolk upon Long Island in the
Province of newyork yeoman doe for valluable Causes & Consideratins
me thereunto moveing and a Considerable Sun of money all ready
in hand Received to my full Satisfaction and Content have given -
Granted bargained and Sould and doe by these presents give grant
bargaine and Sell allien and make over unto mr Samuell Eburne of
the above Saide Towne and County a four Acre Lott in the old feild -
more or Less as it was Layd out Lying and bounded by Thomas -
Smith on the west and Bejamin Smith on ye east buting upon ye
high way South and butting upon John Munces northward and yt Lot
which was formerly Joseph Davis the weavers lott I Say that I peter
Whitehere doth for my Selfe my heires Executors Administrators and
Assignes doe absolutely and firmly Sell allien and make over the
abovesd four Acre Lott as Above bounded unto Samuell Eburne to him
and his heires Executors Administrators & assignes To have and to
hold for Ever with all privilledges or Imunitys doe belong to ye
above Said foure Acre lott without any Lett trouble or mollestation
whatsoever and further the Said peter Whithere my heires
and Assignes doe warrant this my Sale to Stand good and firm
in Law from any person or persons whatsoever Claiming
any right title or Intrest from by or under mee but yt the above
Said Land Shall be for the proper use and behoofe of the above
Said Samuell Eburne his heires and assignes for Ever and further
I the Said peter whitehere will give amore Ample or -
firmer deed or bill of Sale hereafter if need Require
and to the true and through Confirmation of all the a
bove Said premises I doe hereunto Sett my hand and
fix to my Seale this 20 day of March 1685 6
Signed Sealed & delivered his
in the presence of us peter W whitehere
Arthur futhy mark (rachell + whitehere
John Tooker Junr Recog: Coram me 26 March
1686 J: Palmer

A true Coppy p John Howell Junr § Clarke

Know all men by these presents that I Joseph Davis of Brook haven in the County of Suffolk upon Long Island in ye province of newyork weaver doe for valluable Causes and Considerations me thereunto moveing and a Considerable Some of money allready in hand Received to my full Content and Satisfaction have given granted bargained and Sould and doe by these presents give grant bargaine and Sell allien and make over unto mr Samuell - Eburne of the abovesaid Towne and Sheer a three Acre Lott in the old feild which I did Exchang formerly with Thomas - Thorp the 8th of Decembr 1683 as by Record In the Towne old book it doth apear Lying and being betweene peter whiteheres Lott westerly and John heards Lott Easterly and now In the - possession of Richard floyd runing from the high way Southeast downe to ye beach northerly I Say that I Joseph Daves doth for my Selfe my heirs Executors Administrators and Assignes doe absolutly Sell allien and make over the above Said three Acre Lott more or Less bounded as abovesd unto mr Samuell - Eburne to him his heires Executors Administrators and Assignes To have and To hold for Ever with whatsoever privilledges or Imunitys doe belong to ye abovesaid Land with out any Lett trouble or Mollestation whatsoever and further I the Said Joseph Davis my heires and Assignes doe warrant that my Sale to Stand good and firme in Law from any person or persons whatsoever Claimeing any Right title or Intrest from by or under me but that the abovesaid Land Shall be for the proper use and behoofe of the above Said Samuell Eburne and to his heires and assignes for Ever and further I the said Joseph Davis will give a more Ample and firm =mer deed or bill of Sale hereafter if need Requires: and to the true and thorough Confirmation of all the abovesd prem misses I doe here unto Set my hand and fix my Seale this 17th Day of march 1685

Signed Sealed and Delivered
in the presenc of us
John Tucker
John Tooker

his
Joseph I Davis
mark
her
Elizabeth E davis
mark

A true Coppy p John Howell Clark

Know all men by these presents that I Abram
Dayton of Brookhaven in the County of Suffolk upon
LongIsland in the province of new york yeoman
doe for valluable Causes and Considerations me ther
unto moveing and a Considerable Some of money
allready in hand Received to my full Satisfaction &
Content have given granted bargained and Sould and
doe by these presents give grant bargaine and sell
allien and make over unto mr Samuuell Eburne
of the abovesd Towne and County all my Intire
Right and title of a purchase of Land Lying and
being between the great Swamp Southerly and the
beach northerly and peter whitehere Easterly and but
=ing upon william Jane westerly I Say that I Abram
dayton doe for my Selfe my heires Executors Admin
istrators and Assignes doth absolutly Sell allien and make
over the above Said trackt of Land that was formerly
Samuell akerlys as it is buted and bounded in ye old feild
unto ye abovesaid Samuell Eburne to him his heires
Executors Administrators and Assignes To have and
to hold for Ever withall the timbers trees or wtsoever
privilledges doe belong to ye abovesd pcell of Land -
without Any Lett hindrance or Mollestation what
Soever but that it Shall be for the proper use and
behoofe of the abovesaid Samuell Eburne and his
heires for Ever and further I the Said Abram Dayton
doe warrant this my Sale to Stand good and firm
In Law from any pson or persons Claiming any
Right title or Intrest from by or under me and
further I doe Ingage to give a more firm and Ample
bill of Sale or deed hereafter if need Require and
to the true and through Confermation of all the
above Said premises I doe hereunto Sett my -
hand and fix to my Seale this Second day of Aprill
on thousand Six hundred Eighty and Six: and in the
Second year of his Majestyes Reigne James the 2d
King of England Scotland france and Ireland
Defendr of the faith &c: his

Signed Sealed and Delivered Abram A Dayton
Peter Chock mark
John Thompson Mary + dayton
John Tooker:

A true Coppy p John Howell Clarke

Know All men by these presents that I Thomas Ward of Brookhaven in the County of Suffolk upon Long Island in the province of new york yeoman for valluable Causes and Considerations me thereunto Moveing and a Considerable Some of money all ready Received to my Content and full Satisfaction have given granted bargained and Sould and doe by these presents give grant bargaine and Sell allien and make over unto mr Samuell Eburne of the above Said Towne and County a five Acre Lott Lying and being in the Little neck nathaniell norten Lying Northerly and Samuell Smith Southerly and Thomas Biggs westerly I Say that I Thomas Ward doe for my Selfe my heires Executors Admistrars and Assignes doe firmly and Absolutly Sell Alien and make over the Abovesaid five Acre Lott more or Less as it was Layd out: unto mr Samuell Eburne to him his heires Executors Adminrs and Assignes To have and To hold for Ever withall the privilledges that doe belong to ye above Said Land without any Lett hindrance or Mollestation what Soever but that it Shall be for the proper use and behoofe of the above Said Samuell Eburne his heires and Assignes for Ever and further I the Said Thomas Ward doe warrant this My Sale to Stand good and firm In Law from any person or persons what Soever Claiming any Right title or Intrest from by or under mee and further if need Require I will give a more firm deed or bill of Sale here after and to ye true and through Confirmation of all the above Said premises I doe hereunto Sett my hand and fix to my Seale this 23 of March 1685 6

Signed Sealed and Delivered	mark
In the presence of	Thomas w Ward
John Thomas	his
his	Martha ward + her
obed S Seward	mark
mark:	Acknowledged by ye above
John Tooker his	named Thomas Ward this 26th of
Jacob Longbotham X	March 1686 J: Palmer
mark	

A true Coppy p John Howell Clark §

This Indenture made the fifth day of Aprill in ye Second year of the Reigne of our Sovereigne Lord James The Second by the grace of god of England Scottland france and Ireland king defendr of the faith &c and In ye year of our Lord Christ one thousand Six hundred Eighty and Six between Richard Smith of Smith towne Senior In The County of Suffolk upon Long Island In the province of new york in America gentleman: of

the one parte and Samuell Eburne of Brookhaven in
the Same County of the other part Wittnesseth that the Said
Richard Smith for divers good Causes and Considerations
him thereunto moveing and more Especially for and in
Consideration of Sundry good and provistion to the vallue of
ninety pounds Currant pay of this County to him in
hand payd and delivered befor the Ensealeing of these
presents by the ye Said Samuell Eburne rhe Receipt wher
of he doe here by acknowledg and Confess himselfe to bee
therewith fully Satisfied and Contented and there of & of -
Ever percell and part there of doth by these present acquit
and Discharge the Said Samuell Eburne his heires Executors
and Administrars for Ever: Hath Given granted bargained
and Sould and doth by these presents freely Clearly and -
absoluty give grant bargaine and Sell allien assigne
and Sell over unto ye Said Samuell Eburne all his Entire
Right title and Intrest in all Lands and meadows within
the bounds of the said Towneship of Brookhaven that is to
Say a home Lott Containeing five Acres more or less Ly
ing between that Land which was formerly Samuell -
Terrills northerly and the Land of widow fancy
Southerly butting upon the high way westerly as also
another five Acre Lott in new towne being ye lott
number Seven Lying between Zachary Haukins and
John Tooker and Alsoe another five Acre Lott in
newtown being the lott number twenty foure Lying be
tween the Land of John Row and John Jenners and
alsoe a Six Acre lott in the old feild Lying between John
Tooker and that Land which was formerly Thomas -
Wards and alsoe a four Acre Lott at ye uper End of the
old feild Lying between John Tooker and Thomas Smiths
Lotts and alsoe a five Acre Lott in the old feild in a place
Comonly Called Cranes neck being the Lott number twenty
four Adjoyning to ye Land now in the ocupation of -
Zachery Haukins butted and bounded by the Records of
Brookhaven Aforesd and alsoe five Acres in the
Little neck butting upon the harbour Easterly the wood
Land westerly the Indian Land northerly and John
Jenners Land Southerly and alsoe fifty Acres at a place
Comonly Called the old mans being the Lott number twenty
Seven butting upon the north Sea and Eastward of ye path
goeing downe upon the beach: westwardly upon one
Side of the Comon and the Seward End of it upon another
parte of the Common and alsoe a Share of meadow at
the South in the new purchase being the Share num
ber

number five Lying next to John Thomas Senior and
alsoe a Share of meadow in the old purchase being the Share
number twelve between John Thompson and Samuell dayton
with a fifteen Acre Lott of up land belonging to it and alsoe
a Share of meadow at ye old mans and alsoe another -
Share of meadow at ye old feild beach Lying between peter -
whiteheres and John Tookers and also twenty Acres of land
more when and where the Said Samuell Eburne Shall Chuse :
and apointe it to be Layd out To have and To hold all
the Said tracts Lotts Shares and percells of Lands and med
dows together withall the privilledges and Apurtenances
Comonages and Enlargements to the Same belonging
or In any wise Apertaineing to him the Said Samuell
Eburne his heirs or Assignes there Sole and proper use and be
hoofe for Ever and the Said Richard Smith doth hereby
Covenant and promis to and with the Said Samuell Eburne
that he ye Said Richard Smith is the true Lawfull and Sole
owner and proprietor of the above granted Lotts Shares
and percells of Lands and meadows: and all other the -
above bargained premises and that he hath in him Selfe
full power good Right and Law full Authority to Sell &
dispose of the Same and of Every pt and percell thereof
and that ye Said Samuell Eburne his heires or Assignes -
may now and at all times hereafter Quietly and peacably
Occupy possess and Enjoy the Said Severall Lotts Shares and
percells of lands and meadows and all other the above grant
ed premises free and Clear freely and Clearly Acquitted
Exonarated and Discharged of and from all former and
other gifts grants bargaines Sales Mortgages Rents taxes
dowers Intailes or any Any other titles or in Combran
=ces whatsoever had made or Comited at any time:
or times heretofore with warranty of the Said Tracte
and tracts of lands and meadows and all other ye above
granted premises agst all persons whatsoever Claime
ing by from or under him the Said Richard Smith
his heires or Assignes or Either of them and ye Said Richd
Smith doth further Covenant and promis that he ye
Said Richard Smith his heires or Assignes will Signe
Seale and Deliver unto ye Said Samuell Eburne his
heires or Assignes any other or firmer Deeds Con
vayances for the above bargained premises the Said
Samuell Eburne his heirs or Assignes Shall be Ad
vised to by his or there Councell lerned in ye
Law In wittnes whereof the above Said partys to

to these presents have Sett there hands and Seals
the Day and year first above written /

Signed Sealed and Delivered
In the presence of
John Tooker
Petter Chock
James Siddall:

Richard Smith
Sarah Smith mark
3

The within menconed tracts and percell of
were Delivered by Richard Smith unto Samuell Eburn
on the twenty first day of Aprill in ye year of our
Lord Christ one thousand Six hundred Eighty and Six
In the presenc of

John Tompson
peter W Whitehear
his mark

A true Coppy p John Howell Clark

Know all men by these presents that I william Jane of Brookhaven in the County of Suffolke upon Long Island in the province of new york Cooper doe for valluable Causes and Consideration me thereunto Moveing and a Considerable Some of moneys already received to my Satisfaction and Content doe give grant bargaine and Sell alien and and made over unto Samuell Eburne of the above Said County and province an accomadations of Land medow and Commonage the partes and percells hereafter - Expresed that is to Say a fifteen Acre Lott fronting upon the Highway Eastward of floyds Swamp and Soe run ing from the highway runing northward as also a five Acre Lott in the old feild Lying on the South East Side of the Swamp butting upon the fresh pond the Swamp on the one Side and mr bruster the other Side as allsoe a five Acre Lott in the Little neck Lying the Souther Side of that Lott which was Arther Smiths and a five Acre Lott in ye little neck which was formerly Joseph Davis Lying by the lott of mr brusters as allsoe halfe of a five Acre Lott that was devided between John Muncy and the Said William Jane as also twenty Acres that is to be taken up by the Last towne grant where it Can be Conveniently found as alsoe fourteen Acre at the old mans of the Easter Side of that Land which was formrly william Janes as also fifty Acres Lott number 9 buting towards the Indian feild at ye oldmans as alsoe a Share of meadow at the new purchas at ye South number 23 and ashare in the old purchase number 6 as alsoe a Share of upland and meadow at the South that

I

I bought of Robert gouldsbury number 8 Lying in the old -
Purchase I Say that I William Jane doe for my Selfe my heires
Executors Administrars and Assignes Sell Alien and make over
unto ye above Said Samuell Eburne his heirs Executors Administrs
and Assignes To have and to hold for Ever with all timbers
trees parts and percell of lands and meadows with Comonage for
a whole Allotment with all privilledges Apurtenances Imuni
=tyes or whatsoever doe or Shall belong to ye above Said parts
and percells of Land and further I the Said william Jane -
my heires and Assignes doe warrant this my Sale to Stand good
and firme in Law from any pson or psons whatsoever from
by or under mee or any others but that it Shall be for the -
proper use and behoofe of the above Said Samuell Eburne his heirs
and Assignes for Ever and further if need Require I Shall give
a more Ample and former deed bill of Sale hereafter if de
Sireded and to the true and through Confirmation of all the above
Said premises I doe hereunto Sett my hand and Seale the Second
year of his Majestyes Raine James the Second king of Eng
=land Scottland france and Ireland defender of the faith and
the Eleventh day of June in the year of our Lord god one thous
Sand Six hundred Eighty Six

his
William W I Jane
mark
An Jane A her mark

Signed Sealed and Delivered
In the presence of us
John S Smiths mark
John Tooker

A true Coppy p John Howell Junr § Clarke

Know all men by these presents that I John Thomas
of Brookhaven in the County of Suffolk upon LongIsland
in the province of new york planter do for valluable
Causes and Considerations me thereunto moveing and
a Considerable Some of money allready Received to
my full Content and Satisfaction have given granted
bargained and Sould and doe by these presents give grant
bargaine and Sell unto Samuell Eburne of the above Said
Towne and County all my Right tittle and Intrest of a
twenty Acre Lott Lying and being by the Side of the
parsonage Lott and butting to the Cleft westerly and
upon the Comon Easterly and by the Side of the old feild
fence northerly as alsoe I have Sould twelve Acres
more where it is to be found in the Comons I Say yt
I John Thomas my heires Executors Administrator and
Assignes doth absolutly Sell allien and mak over the above
said twenty Acres already Layd out and twelve acres
to Lay out unto Samuell Eburne to him his heires
Executors Administrars and assignes To have and

to

To hold for Ever withall timbers trees or what
Soever privilledges Imunityes doe or Shall belong to
the abovesd trackts of land without any lett incom
brance or Mollestation whatsoever but that it Shall
be for the proper use and behoofe of the above
Said Samuell Eburn and hieres for Ever and fur
ther I the Said John Thomas doe warrant this my
Sale to Stand good and firme in Law from any
person or persons Claiming any Right title or
Intrest from by or under mee or any others: and
further if need Require I Shall give a more -
Ample and fermer deed or bill of Sale if de
sired hereafter and to the true and throught
Confirmation of all the above Said premises
I doe hereunto Sett to my hand and Seale this
this 14th day of June in the Second yeare of our
Soveraine James the Second king of England Scott
land france and Ireland and In the year of our
Lord god 1686

Signed Sealed and delivered — John Thomas
In the presenc of us — her
John Tucker — Elizabeth E Thomas
John Tooker — mark

Know all men by these presents that I John
Smith of Brooke haven In the County of Suffolk up
=on Long Island In the provence of new york weav
ver doe for valluable Causes and Consideration me there
unto moveing and a Considerable Sum of money already
received in hand to my full Satisfaction and Content
have given granted bargained and Sould and doe by these
presents give grant bargaine and Sell allien and make
over unto mr Samuell Eburne Liveing in the abovesd
Towne and County a five Acre Lott of Land Lying and
being in a place Comonly Called new towne numbe 1
and Lying by the Side of that was formerly Zachery
Houkins: I Say that I John Smith doth for my Selfe
my heres Executors Adminrs and assignes doth absolutly
Sell allien and mak over the above Said five Acre Lott of
Land more or Less as it was Layd out unto him the above
Said Samuell Eburne his heires Executors Administrators
and assignes To have and to hold for Ever withall

the

the timber trees whatsoever privilledged doe belong
to the above Lott of Land without any Lett Disturbance
hindrance or mollestation whatsoever but that it Shall be
for the proper use and behoofe of ye above Said Samuell
Eburne and his heires and Assignes for Ever and further
I the Said John Smith will warrant this my Sale to
Stand good and firme in Law from any person or per
Sons Claiming any right title or Intrest from by or under
mee and further if need Required I will give more
Ample and firmer deed or bill of Sale hereafter if
desired and to ye true and through Confirmation of
all the abovesaid premises I doe hereunto Sett my
hand and fixto my Seale this Eleventh Day of June
1686

his
Signed Sealed and Delivered John Smith I
In the presence of us her mark
William Jane W his Rebacha + Smith
John Tooker mark mark

The Last Will and Testament of me John Stratten
Senr of Easthampton in Suffolk County upon Long Island in
America being it this present through gods mercy of
perfect mind and understanding I Give my Soule to god
who gave it and bequeath my body to ye dust from whence
it Came and my Estate as followeth
1st first I give to my beloved wife Sarah the South End of my
house wholly from bottom to ye Topp of it Dureing her
Life and halfe my home Lott and addition to it Dureing
her life and I give to her Dureing her Life halfe my Closse
Lying at the Side of ye pond Called Hook pond also my will
is Shee shall have for her use dureing her Life my peice
of meadow I formerly bought of Georg Miller Senr Lying
at ye northwest also my will is my wife Dureing her Life
Shall have the use of all my goods Lying within doors and
after all that to be disposed of according as I apointe in
this my will
2dly My will is my Eldest Son John Stratten Shall have my hous
I Live in and barne (viz) one halfe of my dwelling house
being the north End of it Dureing his mothers Life and -
After mine and her Decease the whole Shall be his
and his heires for Ever alsoe I give to him halfe my home
Lott and the Adition to it Dureing his mothers Life and After
mine and her decease the whole Lott and Adition to it Shall
be his and his heires for Ever: also I give to my Son Jno and his
heires halfe my Closse Lying by hook pond that parte next
Jerimiah Millers Lott alsoe I give to him and his heires
thirteen Acres of Land lying at Wainscott (viz) Six Acres of land
to Adjoyne to ye Seven acres I formerly gave him this to
Come downe to ye beach also I give unto ~~my Son John~~ the
nine acres he hath already fenced in Eastward alsoe I give
unto this my Son John my woodland Lott lying by william
Mulfords lott Eastward and mr Mulford westward being
ten Acres or there aboutes alsoe I give unto my Son John
and his heires besides the meadow he hath possion of: all
my meadow at napeak and at akkabonak alsoe I give unto
him halfe my Lott of meadow I had of Jerrimy Conkline
Lying at ye Northwest alsoe I give to this my Son John
Comonage Soe much as Comes to a Share of a thirteen acre
Lott both at ye Towne and at montaukut be it further known
my will is that After my deceas my Son John Shall take
possession of halfe my house and Lott at home as Afor
Said-upon this Condition hee deliver up the hous hee

now

now Lives in and the home Lott and Adittion to it to ye possesion
of his brother Cornelius Stratten as I Shall further apoint

3dly I give to my 2d Son Joseph fifty Acres of Land more or Less Lying
at wainscot viz) all my Land there undisposed of to my Son John
as aforsd also I give unto him two percells of meadow one Lying at ye
northwest the one by the west Creek next Capt Talmages ~~undevided~~
meadow the other percell Lying with Capt Talmages undevidid this
Land Aforsd I give to him and his heires for Ever

4ly I give to my 3d Son Stephen thirty one Acres of Land Lying in ye
woods bounded upon the South by Robert Daytons Lott upon ye west
by william Mulfords lott and the high way north: To him and his
heires for Ever alsoe I give Six Acres of Land more Eastward
Lying upon the plaine neer the Indiane well alsoe I give
unto him and his heires Six Acres and a halfe Land Lying upon
the Easterne plaine by goodman bishops Lott: upon the East: also I
give this my Son Stephen that percell of meadow is mine Lying
at ye Little northwest by Samuell parsons meadow alsoe I give
to him halfe my meadow at ye great norwest Lying by Samll
Mulfords meadow

5ly I give to my 4th Son Cornelius Stratten the house, home Lott
and Adittions my Son John now Lives upon to him and the
heires of his body to take possession of it at his Marriage
or After my decease alsoe I give unto him After mine and
and my wives decease halfe my Cloase Lying at ye hoock pond north
alsoe I give to him my Son Cornelious and his heires for Ever my
ten Acre Cloase lying Eastward now fenced in Lying by Stephen
Hedges lott Alsoe I give unto him Six Acres of Land I bought
formerly of Jerimy Meecham Lying by mr mulfords Lott East: also
one Acre of Land Lying South of hook pond by tho: osbornes Lott
west alsoe I give him three Acres and halfe more Lying
upon the mill plaines also I Give him a percell of meadow at
little norwest bounded by Stephen Hedges upon the South
alsoe halfe a peice of medow at ye great norwest Lying by
Samll Mulford South: also another percell of meadow Lying
upon the East side of ye norwest the part being his brother Johns
as aforesd alsoe a percell of meadow after my wifes decease
which I bought of Georg miller /

6ly I give to my grandchild Joseph hand my three Acres and halfe
and Sixteen pole of Land Lying north of Samuell parsons
Cloase also foure Acres of Land Lying by Tho: bees Lott hee
not to have this Land Aforesaid untill he Comes of age: neit
=her Shall hee allinate or dispose of it without ye Ad
vice and Consent of his father Stephen hand and his
uncles John and Stephen alsoe I give him twenty pound

out

out of my Estate to be paid him by my Executors one year
after mine and wives decease in good Currant pay and price
he not to dispose of it without Advice and Consent of aforesd of
his father and my two Sons

7ly I give to my Daughter abigaile wife of Henry norris ten
pounds out of my Estate to be paid by my Executors After mine
& wives decease in good pay and price Currant within one
year as aforesd

8ly I give to my Daughter Rebeka Busnell twenty pounds after mine
and wifes decease to be paid her at price currant in good pay within a
year by my Executors

9ly I give to my daughter Ruth white my negro girle Called hager
and five pounds besides out of my Estate to be paid as aforsd
to my other daughters

10ly- I give to my Son Joseph Stratten ten pounds out of my Estate
to be paid as aforesaid to my Daughters

11: I give to my grandchild Steven Hand five pounds
to be paid by my Executors in maner aforesaid

five pounds
12: I give to my grandchild Stephen hedges ^ to be paid in maner as aforesd

13 I give to my Son John all Debts and Leagacyes paid: a duble
portion of my moveable goods both within doors and without
after his mothers decease

14 I give to my two younger Sons Stephen and Cornelious all debts
and Legacyes paid the remaines of my moveable goods
after there mothers decease to be Equally devided between
them and the Remaines of my Comonage I will to bee disposed
of to my three Sons Joseph Stephen and Cornelius both that at
the Towne and montauket

15:- Also my will is if any of my Sons Aforesd Should Deceas without
any heires of there body Lawfully begotten the Land bequeathed
aforesaid to any of them Shall goe to my other Sons Shall Surviv or
there heires to be Devided in equall Shares amongst them
due Consideration being allowed for what Charges hath been
Layd out by any one of them upon the Lands aforesaid

16: my will is my three Sonns John Stephen and Cornelious to
gether with there mother Soe Long as Shee Lives be Executors
of this my will and testament Lastly I desire Stephen Hedges
and Stephen Hand to be overseers of this my will with due
Consideratione to be paid them by my Executors for what pains
and Charge they my be at Concerning it and In Confirma
=tion of this my will and Testament I Set to my hand & Seale
this 30th day of august Anno Domoni 1684

Signed Sealled in presence of us John Straten
Thomas James
Stephen hand the said Stephen hand was Sworne

In Courte of Sessions held in Southampton the 16: &c day of March 1685 6 that he see the testator Signe this Instruement as his Last will and testament Alsoe mr Thomas James one of the wittnesses Subscribed to this will within written made oath before me that hee See the Said John Stratten Signe & Seale this instrument as his Last will and Testament

John Howell Justice

At the Aforesaid Courte of Sessions holden at Southampton upon the 16 &c days was presented the aforsd will of John Stratten Deceased of Easthampton together with an Invento ry of his Estate: whic is as followeth

March the 12:1685 6: the Imatary of John Strattens Estate
& 2 Small bassons and 2 old potts

9 pewter platters: 2 quart pots the rest of ye things being old	2	8	-
2 brass kettles one of them old	5	-	-
3 Candle Sticks 2 of them old	-	4	6
2 pairs of fire tongs and a grid Iron	-	7	-
1 bras Ladle and a Choping knife	-	4	-
1 old driping pan 1 old kan	-	2	-
1 tub 1 Churn 1 wheele	-	13	-
7 old Chayres two table and form	1	5	-
beding blankets and Sheets	7	14	-
2 negro and a Childe	50	-	-
7 potts Cettles and Scelletts	3	5	-
Cart and plow takleing being all old	3	10	-
1 grindestone 12s: boules keelers and pailes 11s	1	3	-
3 howes 2 tramils 12s: 1 old wheele 2s a musket 7s	1	1	-
9 Cowes 18£: 2 oxen 6£:10s	24	10	-
2 Steers 6£: 6 more Small Cattle 10£ 8s	16	8	-
6 more young Cattle 7:10s	7	10	-
6 Calves 4£: 1 mare one horse 1 yearling horse 6£)	10	-	-
36 Sheep 8£10: 7 Small Swine 40s	10	10	-
By Stephen Hand and) Stephen Hedges) the totall	145	14	6

These Subscribed Sworne in Courte of Sessions to the trueth of the Aforesd Inventory test John Howell Clark

a true Coppy

Att a Councill held at fort James In newyorke
July the 29th 1686

Present

The Governor: &c:

Robert Cady John Parsons Jacob Dayton John feild Samuell Sherry Olliver Norris William Hamilton Daniell Kieft Simon Hilyer John Richardson makeing there Complaints that the Towne of Easthampton will Lay them out no Land as they were ordered In Councell to Doe and it - Appeareing that ye Said Inhabetants have for more then the Space of foure years payed all dutys in the Aforesaid Towne and are become Associates in the Same Ordered that Capt Joshiah Hubert High Sherrif of the County of Suffolk See that a Surveyer Lay out to Each person of the Afore - Menconed Inhabetants Thirty Acres of Arable Land within the bounds of Easthampton that is not yett fenced or Inclosed and Apropriated by any person they paying the Charges which the Said Sherrif and - Surveyer Shall bee at In the performe ance of the Same and giveing Security not Dispose or Sell any of the Said Land untill it Shall be - Improved by them. -

By Order in Councell &c

A true Coppy p John Howell Clark -

J. Sprage Secr:

To mr Peter Benson of Easthampton -

By vertue of an order from ye Governor in Councill Re quireing me thereunto these are to order and Impower you to Lay out and Measure unto Robert Cady John parsons Jacob dayton John feild Samuell Sherry Simon hilyer - and John Richardson and oliver norris: Each person

of

of them [thirty Acres] of Arable Land within the bounds of Easthampton that is not yett fenced or Inclosed and Apropriated and for your Soe doeing this Shall be your Sufficient warrant given under my hand this 11th Day of Augst 1686

p Josiah Hubert Sherrif

By Order of Capt Josiah Hubert High Sherrif of ye County of Suffolk I have Layd out unto Simon Hilyer Thirty Acres of Arable Land to the southwest of Alewife Brook bound ed from a Large white oake by the beach the Sea or harbour to the westward 80 poles: Eastsoutherly Soe a Long there to ye northward 60 poles and then Eastsoutherly 80 poles – bounded with the Land of John parsons weaver to ye north ward as atest my hand this 12th Day of August 1686

Peter Benson

By Order of Capt Josiah Hubert High Sherrif of the County of Suffolk I have laid out unto John Parsons weaver thirty Acres of Arable land Southwest of Alewife Brook from Cratched black oake Next the Sea or harbour to ye westward and Soe along Eastsouthe[rly] by Eighty poles and then Sixty poles to ye Land of Simon Hilyer and bounded Eighty poles on his Land to ye Southwards untill it Comes to ye Sea againe as atest my hand this 12th of August 1686

Peter Benson

A true Coppy p John Howell Clarke

By order of Capt Josiah Hubert High Sherrif of ye County of Suffolk I have Laid out unto Robert Cady Thirty Acres of Arable Land: Bounded with ye – meadow of John Miller at Duck Creek and three Mile harbour on three Sides and to ye East wth a Lyne Run from a Corner of ye Said meadow to ye – Southward near the highway to another Corner of the Said millers Meadow to ye northward: August the 13th 1686 atest my hand

Peter Benson

A true Coppy August ye 21 1686 p Jno Howell Clarke

By Order of Capt Josiah Hubert High Sherrif of
the County of Suffolk I have Layd out unto Samll Sherrill
Thirty Acres of Arable Land bounded with ye high
that Leads to the Southward John Richardsons Land Lying
to the westward the Lyne between them Runs north
and then bounded along by the Said highway 80 poles to ye Eastward then 60 poles
Sixty poles ^ upon a Lyne northerly Augst ye 14th 1686
Atest my hand

Peter Benson

A true Coppy p John Howell Clar

By Order of Capt Josiah Hubert High Sherrif of
the County of Suffolk I have Layd out unto John feild
thirty Acres of Arable Land bounded by ye harbour against
Alewife Brooks to ye west ward and then Easterly
Sixty three Rods Southerly 96:Rods and westerly to
the harbour againe twenty Eight Rods August
the 12 1686 Atest my hand

Peter Benson

A true Coppy p John Howell Cla:

By Order of Capt Josiah Hubert High Sherrif of the
County of Suffolk I have Laid out unto Jacob Dayton
thirty Acres of arable Land bounded with the three
Harbour to the Eastward below the Spring banks a Lyne
from a Red oak west Southwest fifty pole the bounds a
Cratched Stake a Long the harbour Northward one hundred
poles bounded with a Crooked oake then up west Southwest
twenty poles to a Small walnot markt tree August ye 13: 1686

Atest my hand Peter Benson

A true Coppy p John Howell Clark

By Order of Capt Josiah Hubert High Sherrif of ye County of Sufulk
I have Laid out unto John Richardson Thirty Acres of Arable Land
bounded against ye highway that Leads to Indian well to the
Southward from a white oak Eastward along the high way Eighty
pole and then up Northerly Sixty poles at Each End August ye 14:1686

Atest my hand

Peter Benson

A true Coppy p John Howell Clark

By Order of Capt Josiah Hubert High Sherrif of the County of Suffolk I have laid out unto Oliver Norris thirty Acres of Arable Land Laying at a place Comonly knowne by ye name of fire place neck at accobonack the neck Containg - twenty two Acres and Eight acres more next the Said neck bounded from a Large white oak tree to ye East ward along Shore westward forty poles to a black oak and then upright from ye Sea: to the Southward Thirty two poles and alsoe from ye Said white oak a Long the Side of a little meadow Right up from ye Sea - thirty two poles to a Cratched Stake August 11th 1686

Atest my hand peter Benson

A true Coppy p John Howell Clark §

At a Courte of Sessions held at Southold october ye 19: 1686 the will and testament of mr John toping proved:

In the name of God amen I John Toping being Sick of body but of perfect memory doe make this my Last will and testament and first I give and bequeath my Soule to god and my body to ye Earth my Goods I bestow as followeth first I give my wife Deborah Eighty pounds the one halfe out of my Stock the other halfe out of the houshold Stuffe with my house and Lott and one third of my land at fairfeild plowing land - meadow and pasture Land Dureing her widow hood: I give unto my Son Josiah all the Land at fairfeild (Excepting Six Acres which must must bee Laid out to ye water:) with four Acres In the new Close: I give unto my Son John all the Land at Smiths with the Remainder of the new Closae: I give to my Son zerobabell Six Acres at fairfeild with my house and Lott after his Mothers Decease or mariage I give unto my Daught ters fifty pounds a peece with what they have had already I give unto my Son Ephraim twenty pounds and Doe order my Sons Josiah and John to pay as followeth namly Josiah forty pounds and John twenty pounds I further give unto my Sons and Zerobabel all my Lands at Quake and at hog neck I give unto my Son Josiah one fifty and John my other - fifty I give my Cloathing to my Son John Except

ing

Excepting my Cloack which give to my Son Josiah: more
over I Doe apoint my Loveing freind mr perigrine
Stanbrow and my Loveing brother Elnathan Topping
over Seers of this my will I Doe make my Sons Josiah
and John my whole and Sole Executors of this my
Last will and Testement Southampton may the 28th:1686

Signed Sealed and Delivered
In the presence of us
John Anings
Elnathan Topping
James Hand

John Topping

the Afor Said will was presented
to the Courte aforesaid and proved
by the testimony of two of the
Subscribed wittneses vizst: Elna: toping
and James hand being both Sworne
In Courte that See the Said John toping
Signe Seale and heard him Declare
the Same to be his Last will and testamet
and the Executors Admited according to ye testator
Test John Howell Clerk §

An Inventory of the Estate of mr John Topping of Southampton
Late Deceased taken and aprized by us the Subscribed perigrine -
Stanbrow John osborne John Howell Junr and william Herrik
being Sworne thereunto by Major Howell

Item	11 Cowes 44£: 6 heifers 17£: 2 Steers 8£	69	-	-
	19 Swine great and Small	13	-	-
	26 Sheep 10£ all the books 3£	13	-	-
	A paire of Andirons	-	18	-
	a feather bed (below:) the blankets and Sheets)			
	boulster 2 pillows and pillow drawers)	9	10	-
	the bedsted	-	16	-
	a Joyne Chest 45s) 3 table Cloaths 7 napkins 34s	3	19	-
	all the Chayres in the house	1	5	-
	five Cushions and one ell of Cushion Stuff	1	5	-
	to one table in the Chamber	-	8	-
	to a feather bed in the little chamber 1 pillow)			
	two pillow beers two Sheets 1 quilt)			
	a Small flock bed under the feather bed the)			
	Curtaines and Coverled bedsted and Courd all at)	11	10	-
	a flock bed a blanket Coverled and flock pillows)			
	with three remnants of homspon 6 yards 29s)	2	9	-
	to 3 new Sheets 3£ 3 more Sheets 45s	5	5	-

		£	s	d
Item	13 napkins 32s:6d a diaper table Cloath 20s	2	12	6
	3 pillow beers 10s 8 Spoons 8s: 12 trenchars 2s	1	-	-
	2 Chests 14s 3 pound of Sheeps wooll 3s	-	17	-
	a feather bed boulster 2 Sheets a good old rug and Coverled	7	10	-
	To a Joyne 16s the great table 20s	1	16	-
	2 oxen 12£) 8 Steers 36£) 8 Cows & bull with 2 Sucking Calves 33£)	77	-	-
	2 Small Steers and a heifer 8£) 2 yearlings 55s	10	15	-
	16 Calves 16£ 2 bulls and a heifer 2 yearold 6£	22	-	-
	Cattle in the woods given In two red Steer 4 yrold & 2 yrold and one three yearold	9	-	-
	one old horse 5£ to 51£ of pewter 3s p £ 7£:10s	12	10	-
	To a tanker a flagon 9s a pwter Candle Stick 2 Salt Sellers a little poringer 8s a Dripingpan 4s	1	1	-
	To 16£ of old pewter 24s) 2 tramills and a Spit 20s	2	4	-
	1 gun 30s) 3 Iron potts one great one 2 Little ones 65s	4	15	-
	two brass kittles & little bras Scellet all old 35s	1	15	-
	a bell metle Scellet 6s tong & pot hooks 8s	-	14	-
	ten trenchers 3 pailes 2 boules 4 dishes: 2 Spoons 6 Sileing boule	-	7	-
	a great tub 6s a frying pan 2s:6	-	8	6
	8 milk bowles 23s one keeler 4s ye Churne & 2 tubs 7s	1	14	-
	1 paile & the halfe bushell 5s Chees fatt 18d	-	6	6
	the Cheese press 5s 3 linin wheele 20s	1	5	-
	a woolen wheele 6s 7 old barrells 14s	1	-	-
	a box Iron & heaters 7s another Iron 2s	-	9	-
	2 axes a hatchet and an ads	1	-	-
	waynage at 4£:5s: a grindston 12s	4	17	-
	aboute 40 bushells of Indian Corne 5£ about 15 bush:lls wheat 75s)	8	15	-
	a Churne and a buter tub 5s a pr Stillyards 12s	-	17	-
	to 557½£ of Cheese 6 p pound	13	18	-
	to 36 pound of Chees at 4d p £	-	12	-
	a firkin of butter 60£	1	10	-
	Sum tot	326	=2	-6

Aprized according to Country)
pay the Day Aforesd by us)

Perigrine Stanbrow
John osborne
John Howell Junr §
William Herrik

The Last will and Testement of me John Mulford
Senr of Easthampton upon Long Island Eastward in
America being of perfect understanding is as followeth /
first I give my Soule to god that who gave it and me my body
to the Dust &c and my Estate as followeth /
all my debts being discharged

1 First I give to my beloved wife freezwed foure good
milch Cowes if she Survive after my Decease alsoe foure
Acres of Land Dureing her Life which Land is to be Laid
her out from the Adition of the home Lotts at the End
next the Towne two out of my owne home Lott and two
out of that I bought of Thomas Thompson but if Shee
Shall Leave this towne this four Acres of Land Shall Returne
to my two Sons Samuell and John they allowing her a vallu
able Consideration for it by the year Dureing her Life: also
I give to this my wife dureing her Life halfe my home
Lott if Shee Continue In this Towne otherwise my Son -
John Shall have it for valluable Consideration Dureing
her Life alsoe two Acres of Land upon the Easterne plaine
out of both my Sons Land there to plant on Dureing her Life
and after to Returne to my two Sonns: alsoe my two Sons I
will Shall Each of them provide for my wife yearly a load
of hay Soe Long as Shee Liveth if Shee need it also I give to
her Six good Sheep to dispose of as Shee Sees Cause and to
have the use of the north parte or End of my house and the
Leantoo to it Dureing her Life but if Shall Leave this town
then my Son John Shall have it wholly to himselfe

Secondly I give to my Eldest Son Samuell my home Lott I bought
of Thomas Tompson with the Adition to it Save that 2 acres
I give to my wife for Life: at her Decease he Shall have ye
whole alsoe I give to this my Son Eight Acres of Land Lying
west of the Little pond and my Two Acres of Land Lying by
Hoock pond alsoe my peice of plaine Land upon the Eastern
plaine Reaching to ye beach Southward alsoe I give him
a fourth parte of my Devition of Land in the woods north
of the Indi: well alsoe three Quarters of that Devition of
Land belongs to thomas Tompsons Lott I bought Lying In
the Woods Eastward alsoe I give him Six Acres of Land Lying
Eastward of the Little pond bounded on the west by Stephen Heges
Lott also I give him one half of my Land Eastward of the
Indian well upon the plaine alsoe I give him halfe my
meadow at napeage parte of the foure Acres and parte of
one Acre Lying by it Selfe alsoe I give the Salt marsh
meadow is mine Lying at Accobonnak next by the Sea Side
alsoe that Lyeth upon the East Side of the afore Said meadow

which

which I bought of Thomas Tompson also a peice of meadow at ye
Northwest my owne allottment there Lying upon the west
Side of the harboure norwest from ye Towne alsoe I give to this
my Son Samuell three Quarters of the Comonage belonging to
the Lott I bought of thomas Thompson both at ye Towne and -
montauket alsoe I give to hester ten Shillings and to
the three Children five Shillings a peice
the home Lott
3dl thirdly I give to my Son John ^ I Live upon and the Adition
to it Save the one halfe my wife Shall have for Life and at her -
decease the whole to be his (my wife to have halfe the home Lott
for her use Dureing her Life and no more: and two Acres of the
Adition of aforesaid: alsoe I give my Son John all ye houseing is
upon my Lott aforesaid only my wife to have as aforsaid Dureing
her Life: alsoe I give him my Closae westward of ye Towne Called
the girdled trees to be wholly his also I give him my woodland
Lott I bought of Thomas Thompson Eastward by ye Lott was mr James
Lott Southward alsoe a fourth parte of my Lott in the woods Lying north
ward from the Ind: well also I give him three Quarters of my
Last Devition of Land Lying Eastward in the woods alsoe I give
to my Son John halfe my Land upon the Easterne plaine be -
yond the Indian well alsoe I give to him my three percells of
medow Lying in the great meadow at accobonak alsoe one
halfe of my meadow at napeake to be Devided as aforesaid
also I give to him all my meadow upon the East Side of the
harbour at the northwest alsoe I give to this my Son John
three quarters of my Commonage belongs to my allotment
both at the Towne and montauket alsoe I give to this my
Son John my whole Stock of Cattle I Shall Leave at my Decease
he paying out of it what Leagacyes I here bequeath in this
my will alsoe I give to him my Negro Servant Called dando
and my Indian maid Called Dilligence only my wife Shall
have the help of her when Shee needs Soe Long as Shee Lives also
I give unto my Son John (besides what goods are his owne
already) halfe my household goods within doors and all my
moveable goods without doors as Carts plowes Chaynes and -
other tackling to them
4ly Fourthly I give to my Daughter Hanah wife of Benjamin -
Conkline Ten Acres of Land Lying North from ye Indian well
and five Acres near the Towne Eastward alsoe a peice of me
dow at ye north west Lying next the Swamp which I bought
of Thomas Tompson also I give her a peice of meadow is -
mine Lying at ye harbour Eastward by the hamuck next mr
Bakers meadow alsoe I give to her ten Shillings and to Each
of this my Daughters Children four Shillings a peice being 20s
In all to be paid by my Son John After my decease
5 fiftly I give to my youngest Daughter Mary wife of Jerimy
Miller twenty Acres of Land Lying northward from the Ind
dian well also Six Acres of Land upon the west plaine next
Robert Daytons Lott East also a peice of meadow I bought of tho:

I bought of Thomas Thompson East of the Spring at akobon
=nuk alsoe halfe the household goods is properly mine with
in doors after my Decease alsoe I give to her ten Shillings
and to her two Children five Shillings Each of them to be paid
by my Son John After my decease

6 I give to my brother william Mulford all my wearing Cloaths
I Shall Leave only my Cloake my Son John to have alsoe-
I give three pounds to the Church of this towne to be-
paid by my Son John and to be disposed by them as they-
See Cause Lastly I Constitute by this my will my Son John Sole
Executor of this my will and doe desire mr Thomas James
and my brother william Mulford to be over Seers for due
performance with full Satisfaction for there paines aboute it

Subscribed and sealed) December 4th 1683 as Confirmed
in presence of us) by my hand and Seale his
Thomas James John Mulford I M
Richard Brooks mark
Kather: James

A true Copy p John Howell Clark §

the Aforesaid will of mr John Mulford was presented to this
Courte of Sessions now Sitting In Southold this ninteenth of octo
=ber 1686 where the Said will was proved by the oath of two of
the Subscribed wittneses namly mr Thomas James and Richard
Brooks who were both Sworne In Courte that they See the testater
Signe and Seale the afore written of his Last will and testament

Test John Howell Clark §

The Inventory of the moveable Estate of the Said John
Mulford was Likewise presented to this Courte and is
here Entered as followeth : /

An Inventory of the Estate of goods of mr John Mulford
Lately Deceased according as they were prized by us Jerimiah
Conklin Senr and Leift John Wheeler the 22 of September 1686

	£	s	d
Imprimis 8 pewter platers 3 plates & a)			
Bason weight 39£ 3/4 at 15d p £)	2	3	-
a Large pewter Candle Stick	-	6	-
1 cup a pewter pott 4s) 2 old brass kettles 40£ 20s	1	4	-
2 brass kettles more 32s: 1 Large brass Scellet 5s	1	17	-
2 old Scellets 2s) 2 old Iron potts 12s:6d	-	14	6
15 old worne Sheets 88s) 5 pr of pillowbeers worne 9s)	4	17	-
3 paire of Course pillowbeers worne	-	6	-
1 Diapar table Cloath 12 diapar Napkins	1	6	-
1 Course table Cloath more 3s) 4 Course napkins old 6s)	-	9	-
11 old Course towells 5s beding at 7£	7	5	-

A table and Six Joyne Stooles	1	10	-
3 old Chests 10s) 5 old Chayres 8s	-	18	-
8 old books 9s:6d	-	9	6
an old table and wooden ware and other Lumber	1	10	-
a Spit tongs and grid Iron	-	7	-
	25	=2	-0

Easthampton September the 24 1686)
John wheeler
Jerimyah Conklin

At the Aforesaid Courte of Sessions was presented the Inventory of James Herrik of Southampton Late Deceased which was accord ing proved and ordered to be Entered the Last will and testament being proved at the Courte before as apaers by these Records In folio 200: and the Inventory is as followeth /

An Inventory of the moveable Estate of John Herrik of Southampton taken and Aprized according to money by us the Subscribed Edward Howell John Jessup and John Howell Junr being all Sworne thereunto by Major John Howell october the 14th 1686

Item one old feather bed boulster and Rug	3	-	-
1 feather bed boulster rug and pillow and bedsted	5	-	-
a looking Glass 5s a Chest 4s	-	9	-
a Couch a Cord a wheele	-	18	6
a Chest at 6s a table & ye fourme 10s	-	16	-
9 pillow beer 2s:6 p ps	1	2	6
12 napkins 15s 2 table Cloaths 8s:6	1	3	6
5 Sheets 50s 5 Sheets more 38s	4	8	-
4 oxen 12£ Carte & wheels with takleing &c 42s	14	2	-
his wareing Aparrell at	1	10	-
Cattle abroad given in 4 Calves 20s: 3 Cattle 3yerold 90s)	5	10	-
2 yearlings twenty Shillings 1 beast 4 yearold 35s	1	15	-
6 Swine 72s) 4 Swine aboute halfe a yearold 20s	4	12	-
6 Sheep 30s one very old hors 10s	2	-	-
6 Cowes 11£ one more at 12s	11	12	-
one old peice of a Rug and a blanket	-	5	-
a bed bedstead Rug boulster & Sheets	3	10	-
aboute 3 bushells of Corne 4s:6 a Chest and table 8s:6)	-	13	-
a little table Carpet an old Lanthorne	-	6	6
a table at 7s) 5 platers and a little one 18s	1	5	-
7 platers 10s 3 Candlesticks ½ pt pott porringers & Cup 7s)	-	17	-

halfe a duzen of Spoones 2 Saucpans 4s	–	4	–
2 Iron potts and a kettle 40s	2	–	–
an old brass pott and a Scillet 7s a brass ketle 35s	2	2	–
2 old Chamber potts a bason 7s a frying pan 2s	–	9	–
the Churne payles & bowles 6s Andirons 15s	1	1	–
2 tramills 3s–6 a pare of Stillyards 6s	–	9	6
Sieths and takleing 6s:6d plow Irons 6s	–	12	6
Indian Corne 9s 3 narrow axes beetle rings 9s	–	18	–
the broad ax and some other tooles and hows	–	10	–
a matuk and fire tongs 5s three pewter potts 6s	–	11	–
the Chayres and all the Lumber In ye house	1	–	–
	74	:12	:0

Edward Howell
John Jessup
Jno Howell Jur

The Demands of the widow Haynes
That Shee may have the thirds of all & Every part of the Moveable Estate of her Deceased Husband Cleer of all Charg: and her Daughters ten pounds presantly Delivered and the third parte of the wheat now upon the ground and that Shee may have free Liberty of ye house till June next and that Shee may have Soe much meadow for this year as Shee Shall or may Mow three Loads of hay to keep her Cattle the next Winter: and whereupon the Said widow Johanah Haynes doth Relinquish all her right and title to the Land for Ever and the House after her Said time of June next in wittnes that this is – there finall Agreement between them we have – hereunto Sett our hands this 23d of November Anno Dom: 1687

In presents of
John Howell
Jos: Hubert

his
Benjamin X haynes
mark
Samuell Clark
her
Johanah Haynes C
mark

A true Coppy p John Howell Clark §

Be it Knowne to all men by these prsents that I Richard Smith of Nessequage neare Seatauke in New Yorkeshire on LongIsland in America doe acknowledge to have Sold and delivered to Andrew Miller of the adjacent Island called the Isle of Wight alias Man= chonack I say I have sold and doe hereby make over allien and Sell unto him the Sd Andrew all my lands allottments and Acco modacons lying and being within the bounds of the Said Seatauke Vizt by Estimacon a Six acre lott and a ffoure acre lott both in the Old ffield, a two acre lott in the little neck, a home lott in the Towne plott for him to choose where as if I myselfe were to choose for my Selfe, with the pcell or pcells of land laid out to me or to be laid out unto me, in the pcell of Land called New Towne in the bounds of the said Seatauke with all my right Title and Interest unto any Sort of lands and meadows both upland Marsh ground within the bounds of the said plan= tacon with all the fencing appurtenances emoluments profitts Easments and Comonag and enlargemt that at present any way doth or hereafter may belong unto my said accomodacons I say I sell and Make over the same as aforesaid unto him the sd Andrew his Heyres Executors administrators and Assignes To Have and To Hold as their owne proper right and Estate for ever from me my heyres Executors and administrators- or any claiming right or interest thereunto or any part there of in my name And further I hereby assure him to Satisfie all or any tax rate or Debt whatsoever due upon any the accom modacon demised and Sold as aforesd to this psent time all - which is for valuable Consideracon received Wittness my hand and Seale Septemb 21 - 1670

Wittness Richard Stratton Richard Smyth
Henry Peirson

Know all whom it may Concerne that the above named Andrew Miller together with his wife have both Signified to me by a writting under there hands and wittnesed by - Richard Hulse and his wife that they the Said Andrew and his wife have agreed with Richard Smith to make voyd the above written deed of Sale: and the Land to re turne to him the Said Smith againe:

test John Howell Clark August ye 2d 1687

To all Christian People To whome this presents Shall Com
Peter Benson of the Towne of Easthampton in the County of Sufolk
upon LongIsland Sendeth greeting know yea that for good Causes
mee thereunto moveing & more Especially for & In Consideration
and Considerations ^ of a valluable Sum to me In hand payd by -
Richard Straten of Easthampton aforesd to mee In hand payd
wherewith I doe acknowledge My Selfe to bee fully Sat
tis=fied and from the Same and Every parte therof doe
hereby acquitt and Discharge the Said Richard Stratten and his
heires: have given granted bargained and Sould and do
hereby fully freely and absolutely give grant bargaine &
Sell allinate Infeoffe and Confirme unto the
Said Richard Stratten one percell of Land In Easthampton
aforesaid Containing Six Acres be it more or Less as it was
Measured by the Towne of East hampton aforsaid unto willm
Edwards Deceased and Lyeth on or Neare a place Called
Lilley Hill bounded with the highway that Leads to acco
bonack to the northward and with the Land of Jerimy
Conklin to the Eastward: with the Land of Samuell -
persons to the Southward and with the Land of Edmond
Shaw to the westward To: have and To hold the afor
Said percell of Land withall the woods underwoods privillidgs
and Apurtenances thereunto belonging or any wayes Aper
taineing to him the Said Richard Stratten his heires and
Assignes for Ever as thereowne proper Right and Estate
and I the Said peter Benson doe avouch that before
and at the Ensealing of these presents I was the prop
=per and Rightfull owner of the afore bargained premises
and doe for my Selfe my heires Executors and Assignes
Ingage to warrant and Defend the Said Richard Stratten In
his title to the aforesd Land against all and all maner
of persons that Shall Lay Claime to ye Same or any pte
or percell thereof Either by from or under mee or by
from or under my Executors Administratrs or Assignes In
testimony whereof I have Sett to my hand and affixed
my Seale this thirteenth day of october In the Second
year of the Reigne of King James the Second Annoq
Dom: 1686

Signed Sealed and Delivered
In the presents of
Josiah Hubert
John Chatfield

Peter Benson

October the 13: 1686 this Day peter
Benson apeared before mee and -
Acknowledged the above written
Insruments to be his act and deed
John Howell Justice

A true Coppy p John Howell Clark § december ye 21: 1686

Know all men by these prsents that William Colman of
Southold In the County of Suffolk in ye province of Newyork on -
LongIsland yeoman for Divers good Causes and Considerations me
hereunto moveing as alsoe for the Sum of nine pounds of good
and Currant Boston money of new England already by me In hand
Received as full Satisfaction for the Same Doe allinate Bargaine
make over and Sell and by these presents Have Allinated bar
gained made over and from me and mine for Ever hereafter
formerly Sould unto Benjamin Conkling of Easthampton and
to his heires and assignes for Ever all that my Lott or accoma=
dations of Land I formerly bought of one Richard Clark Late of ye
Said Southold Sittuate Lying and being in the bounds of the Said
Southold Except one Lott that Lyeth next to mattituk and ye
meadow belonging unto the Said first Lott I bought of him ye
Said Richard Clarke Sittuate Lying and being at ye Sid of accobag
River all other the Said Lott of Land meadows privilledges
Apurtences benifits and Comodityes whatsoever is or In-
any ways doth belong unto the Said Lott or acomadations be
Long or Appertaine I doe hereby acknowledge to have for mee my
Selfe heires Executors and Administrrs for Ever hereafter
owne and declare to have Sould unto him ye Said Benja
Conklin his heirs and Assignes for Ever hereafter To
have and To hold possess occupy and Enjoy as his or
there owne free Land In fee Simple for Ever without
any the Least Lett hindrance mollestation or disturbance
of me the Said william Coleman my heirs Executors
Administrators or Assignes or any other person or persons
whatsoever by from or under mee Claimeing or Lay
ing any maner of title or Clayme unto ye Same or any
pt or percell of it only Except before what is here
in Excepted alsoe I bind my Self heires and Executors
at any time or times hereafter whensoever I Shall be
thereunto Required to Signe Seale and Deliver any
farther or better deed or bill of Sale as hee the Said
Benjamin Conkling his heires and Executors Shall
by there Learned Councell in the Law gett drawn
and bring unto mee to Signe Seale and Deliver In
wittnes whereof I have here unto Sett my hand
and Seale this 18th Day of March Anno: Domin
1686/7

his
William 0 Coleman
mark

Signed Sealed and Delivered
In presence of
Andrew Gib
John Laughton

William Coleman apeared ye
Day abovesd before me and owned
this to be his act and deed before
mee Isaac Arnold

A true Copy p John Howell Clarke

The Last Will and Testament of mee William Mulford
Inhabetant of Easthampton In the East Rideing of
newyorksheire upon LongIsland being throw the grace
of god In perfect mind and understanding first I
give my Soule to god that gave it and my body to ye
Dust from whence it Came and my Estate as follow
eth: 1st I give to my beloved wife Sarah my house
halfe my home lott and half the Adition to it Dur
ing her Life alsoe the one halfe of all my Land Either
East or westwards upon the plaine Dureing her Life also
I give to her Dureing her Life the use of my meadow
Land all but what is After Excepted to my Chilldren
After here Expressed together with a third parte of my
Comonage both here and at montauket alsoe I give to
My wife aforesd all my Movable goods both within or
without doors only my will is Soe long as Shee Shall
Continue a widdow Shee Shall have the Absolute dispose
of these my goods for her use and the benifit of my
younger Children but if Shee Shall Joyne her Selfe in
Mariage then these moveable goods: vizst, Cattle and
household Stuff to be Secured for my younger Children
untill they be Come at age and then to bee Equally -
Devided Amongst them 2dly I give to my Eldest Son
Thomas one halfe of my home Lott and Adition -
he to take this his halfe at the uper End In the
Adittion onely hee Shall have Liberty for one Acre
out of the home Lott if hee please and After my wives
Decease I give him my house and the other halfe of
my Lott at home and the Adition to it and half
my land In the plaines whether East or west and ye
other halfe after the Decease of Sarah my wife alsoe
I give him the third parte of my meaddow and Com
monage and the other third parte after the Decease of
my wife only with this provisso that if my Sonn -
Thomas aforesd dye before Mariage or before he hath
any heires of his body this Land and house Shall bee to
my other two Sons william and benjamin if he
Leave a wife then all Saveing one third parte Shall
be theres that is william and benjamins thirdly I -
give to my Son william my twenty five Acres and -
halfe of Land Lying to the northwest of this towne
if hee Live till he Come at age alsoe I give him

my

my peice of meadow Lying upon the greate norwest but if hee
Dy before he Comes to age or have any heirs of his body or have A
wife this Land above Said Shall decend to my Son benjamin after my
wives Decease alsoe the third parte of my Comonage both here &
at montauket I give to my Son William but if he Dye without heires
4ly of his body then to be my Son benjamins 4ly I give to my two -
Eldest Daughters Sarah and Rachall that are maryed Each of
them twenty Shillings: I will my wife Sarah to be my Executrix
and Stephen Hedges and Samuell Mulford to be overseers of this
my will the premises Confirmed by my hand and Seale
february the 26: 1678 9

Signed and Sealed before us William Mulford
Tho: James his M mark
John Mulford Senr

Bee it knowne that this will as it is written upon the
other Side of this paper is the Last will and Testament of
me will Mulford Senr of Easthampton and to Stand In
full force notwith Standing what other will or wills I have
Signed to Since the writting thereof only this to bee
knowne my Son Thomas hath already Received of me the -
Acre of Land Specified In my will aforesaid which is the
parte of that halfe of Land he is to have after my De
cease: vizst the home Lott and Adition to it also whereas
it is not menconed to my Son benjamin as haveing any
parte of my Land aforesaid it is my will hee Shall have that
Land is mine Lying upon the Indian well plaine Eastward
of the towne alsoe if any Land be Layd oute to my Allott
ment here In the towne woods anywhere I give it -
Also to my Son Benjamin if he Live till he Come to age
alsoe with proviso if he See Cause to Sell this Land -
Aforesd his Elder brother to have the Refusall of it also
I give to my Son benjamin what Intrest I have in a peice
of Land Latly purchased by John osborne of the Indians at
montauket this is my Last will and Testament as wittnes
my hand and Seale november the 26: 1684

Signed and Sealed In presence his
of us Tho: James William X mulford
John Mulford Junr mark

vera Copia p Jno Howell Clark

At A Court of Sessions held for ye County of Suffolk at Southam
=pton upon the 15th of March 1686 7 was presented
the aforesd will of willm mulford and proved acording
to Law and the widow Admited Executrix thereunto -

Easthampton february 10th 1686 7
An ventory of the estate of william Mulford Deceased

one Iron pott	–	8	–
three pewter dishes	–	6	–
Severall wooden bowles	–	5	–
two payles 2s one Iron kettle 10s	–	12	–
one Iron Scellet 18d two brass kettles 30s	1	11	6
2 beds and blankets	1	–	–
1 Small Chest and box	–	5	–
one woollen wheele 3s one table 6s	–	6	–
2 Chayres 18d: one Sett of Cart wheele hoops 6s	–	7	6
on plow Share and Coulter 5s	–	5	–
2 Chaynes yokes and Staples 10s: one old horse 25s)	1	15	–
2 Cowes 3£ three oxen 7£10s: 2 two yr olds 2£	12	10	–
4 yearlings one pound ten	1	10	–
20 Sheep and Lambs	3	10	–
3 Swine	–	15	–
	25:	09:	0

At a Courte of Sessions held for ye County of Suffulk at Southampton March ye 15 &c days 1686 7 was presented the Inventory of John Corey of Huntington with a peticon for the widow to Administer and to Settle the Land to ye Children. whereupon this Courte doe Admitt her to Administer Shee giveing Security as the Law Directs but upon de fault of Such Security (as yett none Can be had) Shee may Improve the whole Estate for the good of the Children and mr Epenetus platt is by the Courte Desired and ordered to have Inspection Into her manage ment thereof to See that it be done according to Law and for whate words hee the Said John Cory was heard to Say upon his Death bed aboute his Land is here re Corded after the Inventory in page 249 which Inventory is as followeth –

The Estate of the Late Deceased John Cory of the towne of Huntington in the County of Suffolk Aprized by us whose names are under written March 7th 1686

Item: 1 horse very old at	1	10	–

	£	s	d
Item 3 Cowes 7=10 one twoyearold heiffer 26s 8d	8	16	8
3 young Swine 25s: Eight Sheep 28s	2	13	-
to beds and bedsteads witha) belonging thereunto)	8	5	-
to pewter 16s	-	16	-
2 Iron potts & a kettle with hook & bayls	2	7	6
3 Brass Kettles & bellmettle Scellet	2	10	-
a Chayre tramell tongues gridirn 2 hooks & tongs	1	3	-
to old tools a gun and a Sword	2	17	6
a payre of Stillyards	-	10	-
a Smoothing Iron Candlestick & other Small things	-	5	-
due to ye Estate by bill for a horse Sould	3	13	4
2 Chests and 2 boxes	1	-	-
to wearing Cloaths	3	2	6
to books	1	-	-
to old Cask an old Sadle bridle warping barrs	1	-	-
to Some other thing that were forgott at	-	14	-

to a house and Lott about 8 Acres ye home Lott the totall is 43 =3 -6
bareing the Denomination of a 150£ Allottmt
with forty four Acres of meadow and Some
Land at at Southold

Sworne before me (Thomas wicks Isaac Platt
Epenetus platt (John wicks James Smith

See more in folio 249

A true Coppy p John Howell Clark §

At the aforesaid Courte held at Southampton March the 15. 16. & 17 Days 1686 7 was presented the will of mr John Jenings to have the Same proved: which being accord dingly done the widdow being Admited to Execute the Said will is here Recorded as followeth

In the name of God Amen I John Jenings of South hampton In the County of Suffolk on LongIsland Being in perfect Strength of memory blessed be almighty god for it though weake In body and not knowing the Day of my death doe make and ordaine this my Last will & Testament In maner and forme following first I - give and freely bequeath my Soule to god my Creator and Redeemer whoe at first gave it to mee and

my

And my Body After Decent bur[iall in the] Earth
from whence it was at first taken and for my worldly Est
=ate as is hereafter Inserted Item I give and bequeath
unto my Eldest Sonn John Jenings that Land that doth
belong to mee on the East Side of the Creek at north
Sea Adjacent to ye Land of John Davise and the Cloase
at Cow neck=gate with the Land Ajoyning to at Lately -
Layd out to mee Item I give and bequeath to my Son -
Willm Jenings the Lott I bought of Thomas Shaw Joyne
ing to the Land my house Stands on Item I give and
bequeath to my Son Samll Jenings my house and home
Lott withall the houseing thereon to be possessed by him
when he Shall be twenty one years of age:/
and the Rest of my Lands meadows and Comonages
my will is that it be Equally Devided betwixt my
three Sons John willm and Samll and In Like -
maner all my Millitary Armes and in Case any of
my Said Sons dye without Issue that Estate Shall be Equaly Devided
to my Surviveing Sons Item I give and bequeath to my
beloved wife Anne: full and free Possession of my
house and home Lott withall Improvements there
=on till my Son Samuell Shall Come to ye age of one and
twenty years if Shee Shall Live a widow but In Case my
Said Son Should dye before the Sd time and my wife Should
Marry againe then when ny Son William Shall Come
of Age and whoesoever Shee Shall bring Into ye Said
House Shall make the house and all other building when
they leave them as they were at there first Entring
upon them Item I give unto my Daughter Ann=Jane
ten Shillings to be paid to her by my Excutors Ite I
give unto my Daughter Johanah Haynes ten Shill
ings to be paid by my Executrix Item I give and bee
queath unto my Daughter Sarah Jenings a feather bed
and boulster with furneture thereunto and Soe -
much more out of my Estate as Shall make up the bed
and furneture to be twenty five pounds Lastly by
this my Last will and testament make my wife
Executrix of this my Said will to pay out all my Said
Lagacys and to have and Receive all debts due to
mee and to pay all Just Debts that I am Endebted
and to Enjoy and dispose of all the Rest of my Estate

that I [ ] herein given and disposed of as Shall-
Seeme best unto her In wittnes whereof I have hereunto
Sett my hand and fixed my Seale In Southampton abovesd
This 6th Day of November Anno Rgg Regis Jacobas
2d Nunc Angliae &c Prima ett Annoqe Dom 1685
Signed Sealed In his
presenc of John + Jenings
Isaac Howell mark
John Laughton § A true Coppy p Jno Howell Clark

Inventory the Estate of the Moveables of mr John -
Jenings Deceased Aprized by Samuell Clark Benjamin
Haynes and Charles Sturmey January ye 21 1686

	£		
To 4 beds and beding	17	5	-
to 6 payre of Sheets 4 table Cloaths & 6 towells	2	11	-
to 2 Carpetts and 8 Cushings & one yard of holand	1	4	-
to platers flagons & other Small pewter	5	3	-
to Iron potts brass ketles & other Ironware) and two Small Silver Cups)	5	11	-
to three Small guns and one Rapiar & belt	3	-	-
to 2 Andirons & other Small Ironware & 1 ladle	1	7	6
to 2 payre of Stillyards	-	16	-
three tables a table Leafe and one fourme	1	8	-
to 2 Chests and Chayres	1	10	-
1 barrell of beefe 12 bushells wheate & 2 Indian	3	10	-
to bottles Earthen ware & tin tunill	-	11	-
3 bibles 2 Sadles and Sum Loose fethers	2	-	-
2 axes 1 how & other Lumber	2	-	-
to 7 Small Swine	1	10	-
to 1 horse one mare	4	10	-
to 5 Cows and other Small Cattle	23	4	-
	77	:00	=6

as wittnes our hands
Samuell Clarke No: Sea
Benjamin Haynes
Charles Sturmey A true Coppy p John Howell Cla:

At ye aforesaid Courte was presented the Last will and Testa
ment of Bazelliell osborne of Easthampton which was yn
proved by the oath of benjamin Conklin and John greenfeild
too of the wittnes Subscribed to ye Said will that they heard
the tastator Declare as after written and Joseph osborn
Jonathan

Jonathan osborne and Capt Josiah Hubert In the
behalfe of his Daughter Elizabeth and Admitted
Joynt Executors to this following will

Wee whose names are hereunto Subscribed doe testifie yt
upon the 11th day of february 1686 7 at ye house of Joseph
osborne: Bazeliell osborne Lying there Sick though
very Ratianall (well in his understanding: he did de=
Clare to us and bid us take Notice of it of His Last will
That hee then gave unto his brother Johnathan the
great byble that was his fathers and to his wife Eliz
=ebeth the fether bed he had of his mother with all
its furneture and to The Two Sons of mr Arther Howell
ye Share of Montauk Land which he formerly bought of
his Said brother In Law Arther Howell and also unto his
neece Martha Howell a yearling Mare Colt that now
Runs with his mare at at muntauck and for all ye
Rest of his Estate whatsoever after his Debts paid
he gave it In Equall parts unto his wife Elizebeth
osborne and to his brother Joseph osborne and his
brother Jonathan osborne to be Equally Devided be
tween them and to be to them and Each of them
and Each of there heires and Assignes for Ever as
Atest our hand the Day above Said

Benjamin Conckling
A true Coppy p John Howell Clark § John Greenfeild
John Enorrs

In the name of god Amen I Christopher
Lupton of north Sea belonging to Southampton
In the County of Suffolk In the province of Newyork
In America Husbandman through the goodness
of ~~god~~ Almighty god being in perfect Strength of
memory though at present weak In body and not know
ing the time of my apointed Change doe make and or
daine this my Last will and testament as followeth first
I give and freely bequeath my Soule to god my Creator
and Redeemer who at first gave it to mee and
my body after decent buriall to the Earth from whence
it was at first taken and for my Estate as is hereafter
Inserted first I give and bequeath unto my Son

John

John Lupton and to his heires for Ever all ye Land hee now hath In his owne possession and within one month next - After my Decease I will that my Executors pay unto him a Cow: Secondly I give and bequeath unto my Son Thomas Lupton and to his heires for Ever all that my Lands & meadow At ye place Comonly Called and knowne by the Bridge in Cow neck and all ye Rest of my medow In ye Said Cow neck and my water Mill and the three Acres of Land on ye Eastside of the millpond thirdly I give and bequeath unto my Son Christopher Lupton and to his heirs and Assignes for Ever halfe of a meadow at a place Comonly Called the Island and my Little Claypitt Cloase and the west Side of ye great Clay pitt Cloase as it is this Day parted by a fence also my Six Acres of upland Lying on the west Side of Cowneck forthly I give and bequeath unto my Son Joseph Lupton and to his heirs and Assignes for Ever all that my Devition of Land Layd out unto mee at a place Comonly Called and Knowne by the name of ye long pond: and My Devition of of Land In hogneck and ten pounds to be paid him with in one month next After my Deceas fifthly I give and bequeath unto my Son benjamin Lupton and to his heires and Assignes for Ever all that my East parte of the greate Claypitt Cloase and my Six Acres of Land at ye Entring on Cow neck and the other half of my meadow on the Iland my house and home Lott and my Land that is fenced In at Seponack Sixtly I give and bequeath unto my Said Son Joseph Lupton my meadow at accobauge and my meadow at great Noyake: and my privilledges for the place Called ye Little neck to be Equally between my two Sons - Christopher Lupton and benjamin Lupton and my fifty pound Comonage to be Equally Amongst my Abovesd five Sons: Seventhly I give and bequeath unto my Daughter Lidia wood to be paid her After my decease a Cow 8ly I give and bequeath unto my daughter Mary Clark five Shillings to be paid her by my Executors as for my two youngest Daughters deborah Lupton and abigaile Lupton I will that my beloved wife

wife Shall give unto Each of them when they Either
Marry or Shall Come of age which Shall first happen
out of my Estate what Seemeth good unto her: 9thly my will
is notwithstanding all the abovesd gifts and grants of Land
to my Said five Sons: Except to my Son John and my Son Thomas
they are not to have it Into there owne possession Dureing
my beloved wives Life unless Shee Shall give it unto them
tenthly I give and bequeath unto my dearly beloved wife
Lidiah Lupton all my houshold goods Cattle and Chattells wt
Soever I have not heretofore in this my will given
and bequeathed to be at owne free will and disposseing
Lastly I by this my Last will and Testament make my
Beloved wife Liddiah Lupton and my beloved Son Thomas
Lupton Joynt Executors of this my Said Will In wittnes
whereof I have hereunto Sett my hand and Seale this
first Day of october In the Second year of the Raine of
our Soveraine Lord James ye Second &c And Annoqe
Dom 1686

his
Christopher C Lupton
mark

Signed Sealed and Delivered
In the presence of
John Rose
John Laughton §

the Aforesd will was presented
to the Courte of Sessions held at
Southampton March ye 15th 1686 7
where the Said John Laughton
was Sworne to ye trueth of this
will that he See the Same Signed
by the testator as his Last will and
Testament

mr John Rose apeared
before Mee and made
oath that he did See the
Subscriber Leave this
as his Last will March
the 17: 1686: Epenetus platt)
Just -

A true Coppy p John Howell Clark §

Southampton March the 3: 1686 7

An Inventory and Aprizement taken of the Estate
of the Late Deceased Cristopher Lupton at ye Request
of his widow Lidia Lupton by us John Jager -
Charles Sturmey and obadiah Rogers is as followeth

Item:	5 oxen and Steer 18£	18	-	-
	3 Cows at	-	8	-
It	4 Cattle of two years old at	6	-	-
	3 Small Cattle	1	10	-
	1 horse at	2	-	-

1 horse 3 yearsold runing In ye woods	1	10	-
1 Sheep at 5s 5 poor Swine 50s	2	15	-
2 yokes and 2 Small Chaynes & Clevis & pin	1	-	-
1 old Carte and a plow both at	2	-	-
1 Course bed tick 13s: to 8 payre of Sheets 4£	4	13	-
1 bed & Coverled and a blanket	4	-	-
1: old Chest 8s ten milk boules & tallow & lumber 20s)	1	8	-
to beefe and pork for ye house	2	10	-
to 2 brass kettles 40s: to 4 Iron potts 45s	4	5	-
to 2 Spining wheels	-	6	-
to 40 bushell of wheat	8	-	-
to one adse three Aagurs one Saw beetle 2 wedgs) and Drawing knife)	-	19	-
2 old books 2 narrow Chizells 4 old hooks	-	5	-
2 falling axes 2 hows old Cask & lumber	1	-	-
1 Small tramell 5s: one table 1 Small table 15s	1	-	-
to 2 beds and furneture to them	8	10	-
to 2 Chests at	-	15	-
to one payre of Small Stillyards 6s to 2 pans 14s	1	-	-
to 8 Small pewter dishes: 3 plates 1 bason 2 poringrs	1	10	-
2 potts one Candle Stick Earthen ~~ware~~) dishes 3 bowles)	-	7	-
to one dripping pan 1 tunill 3s) 1 Lomeem	-	3	-
to tubs Chayres Stooles & ye remaids of all Lumber	1	-	-
to his wareing Cloaths	3	-	-
John Jagger obediah Rogers Charles Sturmey	69	-14	-0

A true Coppy p John Howell Clark §

In the name of God Amen I Jermiah wood of hem
=psted In new yorksheire In ye North Rideing on Long
Island being In perfect understanding & memory throw the great
mercy of god make this my last will and Testament

Imprs I bequeath my Soule to Jesus Christ my mercyfull Redeemer
and my body to a decent buriall and the wordly Estate
that god of his goodnes hath made mee possessor off I give
and bequeath as followeth to my Son Jerimiah wood I
give and bequeath my house and home Lott which hee
Lives In: In hempsted Towne and all my Eight devitions
of Land upon the plaines and in the hollows belonging
to them: alsoe my wood land Lott on the north side of ye

the plaine and halfe my Long planting feild at marracock
and the third parte of my fifteen Acre Lott of meadow: and
halfe my Salt Lott of meadow beyond ye Iland att marracock

Item To my Son Jonas wood I give and bequeath my house ~~Lott~~ at -
Marracock and all my household goods and other goods In ye
house Excepting only my bed which I Lye upon my Selfe with
all furneture belonging to it which bed and furneture I give
to my Daughter phebee but to my Son Jonas I give all my
tooles and Instruments of Husbandry as Carte plow and takle
=ing &c Alsoe a home bevell Lott at the towne and all my
planting land at marracock Except what is in ye feild before -
of meadow also I give him my meadow Lot
menconed and a third parte of my fifteen Acre Lot ^ at ye Spring
near the house and halfe my Salt meadow lott beyond the
Iland:

Item To my grand Child Joseph williams I doe give
and bequeath my East bevell Lott at ye north Side of
the plaine and all ye hollows belonging to me without
the devitions

Item To my Son Joseph wood I doe give and bequeath on third
parte of the Long meadow lott at merracockneck alsoe
I doe give to my grandchild william thirstone a mare
and Colt: my debts and funeral Expenses being Discharged
I give and bequeath all my Estate In horse Cattle Sheep
and Swine to be Equally Devided between my Six Children
Jerimiah Joseph Jonas Elizabeth Mary and phebee
Elizabeth being deceased her parte to decend to her Children
that this is my Last will and testament is witnesed by my
Subscribeing this third of June In ye year of our Lord
1684 before Subscribing I doe will that my Daughter
Marys Children Shall have there parte as Elizabeths

Signed Sealed In ye presence
of us - - -

his
Jeremiah S wood
mark

Isaac platt
Epenetus platt

It is my desire that John Tredwell and
Joseph Smith would be my over Seeres
to See this my will performed

At a Courte of Sessions held for the County of Suffolk at ye towne
of Southampton upon the 15th Day of march 1686 7 was the afore
Said will presented In order to ye probates thereof where
Mr Epenetus platt apeared and made oath that he see the
testator within menconed Jeremy wood Signe and Seale the
within written will as his Last will and testament and the
Courte doe order that ye other wittnes may be Sworne before
mr platt or Some other of his majestyes Justices of the peace
Aprill the 12th: 1687 Isaac platt apeared before mee and made
oath that the within menconed testator did Signe and leave this
as his Last will: Epenetus Platt) A true Coppy p Jno: Howell Clark

Aprill the 5th 1687
Being at John Corys house a little before his Death and Speak
ing to him aboute the Settleing his Estate He Called out to know
who was In the house and then Said my Eldest boy Shall
not have one foot of Land In Huntington it being my Law
full purchase: what my father gave mee that I give to him and
I Doe not Remember that I heard him Speak anything -
furder of that mater and this was a few days before his death
and when he was very weake in body yet in perfect un
derstanding Soe far as I was able to Judge

Eliphalett Johnes

Aprill the the 5th 1687 Sworne before mee

Epenetus Platt

A true Coppy Aprill ye 21 1687 p John Howell Clark §

This Indenture made the eight & twentieth day of November in the
first yeare of the Reigne of our Soveraigne Lord James the Second by the grace of
God of England Scotland ffrance and Ireland King defender of the ffaith &c: and in the
Yeare of our Lord God One Thousand Six hundred eighty & five Between Goodyer
Bombrast (als:) Wawassaquohague Robin (als:) Catchawahtow Indians of Brookehaven
in the County of Suffolk upon LongIsland of the one part & Andrew Gibb of the same
place Merchant of the other part Wittnesseth that the sd Goodyer Wawaassaquo=
hague & Catchawahtowe Indians for diverse causes & Good consideracons them &
each of Them Thereunto moving & more especially for & in Consideracon of the
Sume of ffive & ffourty pounds currant money of this Country to them the sd
Goodyer Wawassaquohague & Catchawahtowe Indians in hand paid by the sd
Andrew Gibb the receipt whereof The sd Goodyer Wawassaquohague & Catchawah
towe Indians doth hereby acknowledge & themselves & every of them to be therewth
fully Satisfied & Contented & thereof & of every part & parcell doth freely & clearly
Acquitt & discharge the sd Andrew Gibb his Heyres Executors & Administrators for
ever by these presents Hath given granted bargained & Sold & doe by these prsents
freely clearly & absolutly give grant bargaine & Sell unto the Sd Andrew Gibb
all theire ffarme or tract of land lying & Scituate upon Menassoucke a litle
Neck within the Towneshype of Brookehaven aforesd adjoyning to the ffive
Acre Lott belonging to Richard Smith Southerly & to the Land in the occupacon
of John & Samll Muncy Westerly being butted & bounded as by the Records
of Brookehaven abovesd & Containing Seaventy Acres more or less To
Have and to hold the aforesd tract of land together with all priveleges
& appurtenances to the same belonging of in anywise appertaining to him the
Sd Andrew Gibb his heyres or Assignes to his the sd Andrew Gibb his heyres
or Assignes their sole & proper use & behoofe for ever And the sd Goodyer
Wawassaquohague & Catchawahtowe Indians doth hereby Covenant &
promise to & with the sd Andrew Gibb that they the sd Goodyer & Wawassaquo=
hague & Catchawahtowe Indians are the sole & lawfull proprietors
of aforesd tract of land & all other the above bargained prmisses & have in
themselves full power good right & lawfull authority to sell & dispose of
the same & of every part & parcell thereof & the sd Andrew Gibb his heyres or
Assignes the Sd tract of land & all other the sd bargained premises shall &may
now & at all times hereafter peaceably & quietly occupy possess & enjoy
ffree & cleare & freely & clearly exonerated acquitted & discharged of & from
all former & other gifts grants bargaines sales mortgages rents dowers
Entailes or other titles or encumbrances whatsoever had made or

Comitted

Comitted at any time or times heretofore with [ ] tract of land & all other the above granted prmisses against all persons whatsoever claimimg the same by from or under them the sd Goodyer Wawassaquohague Catchawah towe Indians their heyres or assignes or either of them as also to deliver unto the sd Andrew Gibb his heyres or Assignes any other or firmer Deed or Convey= ance for the prmisses as the sd Andrew Gibb his heyres or Assignes shall be ad= vised by his or their Councell learned in the law In Wittness wherof the abovesd parties to these presents have put their hands & Seales the day & yeare first above written

his	his	his
Catchawah X towe	Wawassa quohague Indn	Goodyer Indn
marke	marke	marke

Sealed & Delivered in the prsence of
Edward King
Charles Lodowikus

A true Coppy of the origanall
September the third 1687
p John Howell Clark §

Thomas Dongan Captaine generall Governor in Cheife & Vice Admirall in & over the province of New Yorke & territoryes depending thereon in America under his Majesty James the Second by the grace of God King of England Scotland ffrance & Ireland Defender of the ffaith &c: To all to whome these prsents shall come Sendeth Greet= ing Whereas Andrew Gibb of Brookehaven Gentlemn by my lycence Consent & apro bacon hath purchased to him the sd Andrew Gibb his heyres & Assignes for ever of And from the Indian natives a Certaine tract piece or parcell of land Comonly called the Indian ground Scituate & being on a certaine place called or knowne by the name of Minassouke or the litle neck in the Towne of Brookehaven aforesd in the County of Suffolk on LongIsland bounded Eastward by the harbour Southerly by the five Acre lott late in the tenour or occupacon of Richard Smith of Smithtowne Westerly by the land now or late in the tenure or occupacon of John Muncy & Samuell Muncy & Northerly by the Harbour aforesd Now Know Yee that by Vertue of my Comicon & authority under his most Sacred Majesty & power in me being & residing in Consideracon of the quittRent herein after reserved & for diverse other good & lawfull Consideracons me thereunto especially moving I have given granted Released & Confirmed and by these prsents doe give grant release and Con= firme unto the sd Andrew Gibb his heyres & Assignes for ever all the before recited tract piece or parcell of land & prmisses with Their & every of Their appurtenances together with all & singular Woods Underwoods waters rivers Streames ponds meadowes Marshes fish= ing hawking hunting & fouleing & all other liberties priveleg es & hereditaments & appurtenances to the sd piece or parcell of land & pmisses belonging or in anywise appertaining To Have and to hold the sd tract peice or parcell of land & prmisses with all & Singular the appurtenances unto the sd Andrew Gibb his - heyres & assignes for ever to the only proper use benefitt and behoofe of him the sd Andrew Gibb his heyres & Assignes for ever To be holden of his most Sacred Majesty his heyres & Successors in free & comon Soccage according to the tenure of east Green wich in the County of Kent in his Majestys Kingdome of

England [yeilding rendring] & paying therefore yearly & every year
on the five & twentieth day of March unto his most Sacred Majesty his heyres
& Successors for ever or to such officer or officers as from time to time shall
be empowered to receive the same one bushell of good winter wheat at
the Citty of New Yorke in Liew & Stead of all Services dutyes & demands
whatsoever Provided allwayes & it is the true intent & meaning
of these prsents that this prsent grant nor any thing therein contained
shall not extend nor be Construed to extend to the enwriteing or destroy
ing any other persones right or title to the prmisses anythin here
in contained to the Contrary thereof in anywise notwithstanding
In testimony of the prmisses I have caused these prsents to be entred
& Recorded in the Secretaryes Office and the Seale of this his Majestys
province to be hereunto affixed the Seaven & twentieth day of De=
cember in the Second yeare of his Sd Ma:ties reigne & In the yeare of
our Lord one thousand six hundred and eighty six

Thomas Dongan

By his Excell:cys Comand Isaac Swinton

May it please yor Excell:cy

The Attorney generall hath perused this Patent and
finds nothing contained therein prejudicall to his
Majesties Interest

Exaed Xber 24th 1686 James Graham

At a Councell held at ffort James December 27th: 1686

Psent his Excellcy
Majr Anthony Brookholls
Majr ffred: fflipsen
Mr John Sprague
Majr Geo: Baxter

this patent was approved of

Is Swinton S Conc

Recorded in the Secretaryes office for the Province of
New Yorke in Lib: No: 2 begune in Anno 1686

Is Swinton D Secry

A true Coppy of the origanall September ye 3d 1687

p John Howell Clark §

This Indenture made the Eigh[ ] May in ye third
year of the Raigne of our Sovereigne Lord James the the Second
by the grace of god of England Scotland ffrance and Ireland king
Defender of the faith &c: and In the year of our Lord god one thou
=sand Six Hundred Eighty Seaven Beetween Catchegan Sachem
Pamequage Cayesen Wills Quoring Piepe Nousouce Pumshan
John Mahue Pisecataouse packham Nanamihair Petunke
Amputinue and Ambamacke Indians Propriators of a tract
of Land Lying and being on Minossoucke or Little neck within ye
Towne of brookhaven aforesaid Comonly Called and knowne by ye
name of the Indiane ground of the one parte: and Andrew Gib
of Brookhaven aforesd Marchant of the other Parte Wittnesseth
that whereas Goodyer Wawassaquohague and Catchawatowe
Indians parte of the propriaters of the abovesd tract of Land
Did on ye Eight and twentieth Day of november In ye first
year of our Sovereigne Lord ye King abovesd and in ye year of
our Lord God one thousand Six hundred Eighty five grant bargain
and Sell unto the Said Andrew Gibb all the aforesd Tract of Land
To have and to hold the aforesd Tract of Land together with
all privilledges and Apurtenances to the Same belonging or In any
wise Apertaining to him the Said Andrew Gibb his heires and
Assignes to his the Said Andrew Gibb his heires and Assignes
their Sole and proper use and behoofe for Ever and the Said
Goodyer Wawassaquohage and Catchawahtow Indians did ther
by alsoe Covenant and promise to and with the Said Andrew
Gibb to warrant the Said Tract of Land and premisses unto ye
Said Gibb his heires or Assignes from all persons Claymeing
the Same as by the Said Deed Sealed with the Seales of the Said
Indianes Relacon thereunto being had Doth and may more
At Large Appeare and Whereas his Excell:cy Thomas Don
=gon Capt Generall governr In Cheife and vice Admirall
In and over the province of Newyork and Territorys Depend
ing thereon In America under his Sacred Majesty aforesd
Did by vertue of the power and Authority to him given by
his Said Sacred Majestye on the Seven and twentyeth Day of
December In the Second year of the Raigne of our Said Sover
reigne Lord the king by a Certaine Deed or patent Sealed with
the Seale of the province give grant Release and Confirme
unto the sd Andrew Gibb his heyres & assignes for ever all the sd
tract peice or parcell of land & prmisses with their & every of
their appurtenances together with all & singular Woods under
woods Waters Rivers streames ponds meadows marshes fishing
hawking hunting & ffowleling & all other libertyes & priveleges

Hereditam[ents & appurten]ances to the sd peice or parcell of land
& prmisses belonging or in anywise appertaining To have and
to hold the sd tract peice or parcell of land & prmisses with all and
Singular the appurtenances unto the sd Andrew Gibb his heyres and
Assignes for ever to the only proper use benefitt & behoofe of him
the sd Andrew Gibb his heyres & assignes forever To be holden
of his most Sacred Majesty his heyres & Successors in free & comon
Soccage according to the Tenure of east greenwich in the county
of kent in his Majestys Kingdome of England Yeilding Rendring
and paying therefore yearly & every yeare on the five & twen
tieth day of March unto his most Sacred Majesty his heyres and
Successors for ever or To such Officer or Officers as from time to -
time shall be empowered to receive the same one bushell of good
at the Citty of New Yorke
winter wheate ^ in liew & Stead of all Services dutyes & demands
whatsoever as by the sd Patent Recorded in the Secretaryes Office
at New Yorke doth & may more at large appeare Now this Inden
ture further Wittnesseth that the sd Catchegan Sachem Pame
quage, Cayesen, Will, Quoring, Piep, Nawsouce, Pumshan John=,
Mahue, Pisecataouse, Packham Nanamihaire Nauwetousimm
Petunke Ampatinue & Ambamacke Indians for diverse good
causes & consideracons Them & each of Them thereunto moving
& more especally for & in Consideracon of the sume of five and
twenty pounds currant money of This province to Them in hand
paid by Goodyer &c: Indians for Accompt of the sd Andrew Gibb
theyr receipt whereof they doe hereby acknowledge & themselves
& each of them to be therewith fully satisfyed paid & contented
& Thereof & of every part & parcell thereof doth by These prsents
acquitt & discharge the sd Andrew Gibb his heyres executors
Administrators & Assignes for ever hath given granted Releas
ed & Confirmed & doe by These prsents give grant Release &
Confirme unto the sd Andrew Gibb his heyres & Assignes for
ever all The before recited tract peice or parcell of land together
with all the priveleges & appurtenances thereunto belonging
or in anywise appertaining To have and to hold the sd
tract peice or parcell of land & prmisses with all & singular the
appurtenances unto the sd Andrew Gibb his heyres & Assignes for
ever to The only proper use benefitt & behoofe of the sd
Andrew Gibb his heyres & Assignes for ever And the sd Cache
gan pamequage, Cayesen, Will, Quoring, Piep, Nawsauce
Pamshan John Mahue, Pisecataouse Packham Nanami
=haire Nauwetousimm Petunke Ampatinue & Ambamacke

for

for themselves their heyres Successors [& Assignes & eac]h of them
their heyres Successors & Assignes & each of them doth hereby
Covenant & promise to & with the sd Andrew Gibb his heyres &
Assignes & each of them that he the sd Andrew Gibb his -
heyres & Assignes shall & maynow & att all time & times
hereafter for ever quietly & peacably occupy possess
& enjoy the sd tract peice or parcell of land & prmisses
as his or their free Estate of inheritance in fee simple
free & cleare & freely & clearly exonerated acquitted &
discharged of & from all former & other gifts grants bar=
gaines sales Mortagages Rents Dowers Taxes entailes or
other titles or encumbrances whatsoever had made or
Comitted at any time or times heretofore In Wittness
whereof The sd partyes have hereunto sett their hands &
Seales at Brookehaven the day & yeare first abovewritten

his Pamequage) marke — his Cayeten X marke — his Cachegan { Sachem marke

his Quoring v marke — his Piep B marke — his Jeremy 0 Indn marke

his Pumshan + marke — his John ℽ Mahue marke — his Nawsauce 0 marke

Sealed & Delivered in prsence: of the sd Indians
being each of them Sober & noe wise overtaken with
drinke John Tucker Hanah X Tooker her marke
Tom T ffrancis Interpreter

A true Coppy of the origanall
Sept=ber ye 3d 1687 p John Howell Clark

This Indenture made the Second day of Aprill Anno: Dom: -
1687 & in The Third yeare ^ of the reigne of our Soveraigne Lord James the Second
by the grace of God of England Scotland ffrance & Ireland King De=
fendr of the faith &c: Between Obed Sayward of Brookehaven
In the County of Suffolk on LongIsland in the province of NewYorke
planter of the one part & Samuell Eburne of the sd Towne & County
Clerke of The other part Witnesseth that the sd Obed Sayward for
& in Consideracon of five pounds currant & lawfull money of New
Yorke to him the sd Obed Sayward in hand paid & delivered by the
sd Samuell Eburne before The ensealing & delivery of these
prsents the receipt whereof he doth hereby acknowledge &

himself Therewith to be fully Satisfyed & contented & thereof & of
every part & parcell thereof doth by These prsents acquitt & discharge
the sd Samuell Eburne his heyres Executors & Administrators: for ever
hath given granted bargained Sold released enfeofed & Confirmed
& by These prsents doth give grant bargaine Sell release En=
feofe & Confirme freely clearly & absolutly unto the sd Samuell
Eburne a Certaine ten Acre lott (be these more or less) of
upland of which allotment the sd Obed Sayward stands possessed
by Vertue of a towne devicõn Scituate lying & being in a
Comon that is between the westermost part of The Towne of
Brookehaven & the west meadows bounded East & west by the
Comon North & South between two highwayes leading to the
aforesd West Meadowes To Have and to hold the aforesd ten
Acre lott of Upland together with all & Singular the improvemts
privileges appurtenances & members thereof to the use & be
hoofe of The sd Samuell Eburne his heyres & assignes for ever
To have hold occupy possess & enjoy as his or their owne Estate of
Inheritance in fee Simple free & cleare & freely & clearly Acquit
ed exonerated & discharged of & from all former & other gifts
grants bargaines Sales Mortgages Dowers Rents taxes imposicons
titles or incumbrances whatsoever had made or comitted by the
sd Obed Sayward at any time or times before the ensealing &
delivery of These prsents And the sd Obed Sayward doth hereby Covent
promise grant to & with the sd Samuell Eburne his heyres & Assign
es to deliver quiett & peacable possession of the before granted
prmisses or lott of Upland & to warant & defend the sd tract of
land beforemenconed against any persone or persones what
soever laying claime thereunto moreover if it be needfull or
required to make & deliver any better assurance Deed or Con=
veyance in Confirmacon of the sd prmisses In Wittness
whereof the sd Obed Sayward with the Consent of his wife
doe hereunto Sett his hand & Seale the day & yeare above
written

his
Obed ~ Sayward
marke

Signed Sealed & Delivered
in the presence of
Andrew Gibb
Symon Lane

A true Copy September
the 3d 1687
p John Howell Clark

This Indenture made the Eighth Day of Aprill
In the third year of the Raigne of our Sovereigne Lord
James the Second by the grace of god of England Scotland
ffrance and Ireland King Defender of the faith &c and in
the year of our Lord god one Thousand Six hundred Eighty
and seaven Beetween John Smith and Rebacha his wife
of Brookhaven In the County of Suffolk upon Long Island
weaver of the one parte and Samuell Eburne of the Sam
Towne and County Clerke of the other pate Wittnesseth
whereas Richard Niccolls Esqr: governour generall under
his then Royall Highnes James Duke of york & Albany &c
now his Sacred Majesty over the province of new yorke
and Territorys In America did on the day of
in the year of the Raygnes of our Late Sovereigne
Lord Charles the Second Late King of England &c and in
the year of our Lord god one thousand Six hundred
Sixty Six give grant Release and Confirm unto Capt John
Tooker mr Daniell Lane Richard woodhull Henry pering
and John Jenners as patentees for and in behalfe of themselvs
and there Ascociates the freeholders and Inhabetants of
Brookhaven aforesd all that tract of Land Sittuate and
Lying upon LongIsland afforesd bounded by the red Creek
or wadeing River Eastward the SouthSea or main ocean
Southward the Sea or Sound northward and the Lyne
Run between the Said Inhabetants of Brookhaven and mr
Smiths Land of nesequage westward together with all -
Meadows Marshes Creeks harbours and privilledges & apur
tenances to the Said Track of Land belonging or in wise
appertaining To have and To hold the said Tract of
Land and all other the granted premises to ye Said John
Tucker Daniell Lane Richard Wodhull Henry perring
and John Jener and there Ascociates & there heyres
for Ever to the proper use and behoofe of ye Said John
Toocker Danyell Lane Richard wodhull Henry pering
John Jenner and there Associates there heyres and Ass
signes as by a Certaine patent Sealed with the Seale of the
Said Richard Nicolls Esqur governr Aforesd Remaining
upon Record In the Secretarys office at new york Doth
and may more at Large Appeare and whereas william
Sallyar Late of Brookhaven aforesd one of the Associates
aforesd Stood In his owne Right possessed of a Certaine
Share or Allottment of meadow ground Scittuate and Ly
ing upon a neck Comonly Called and Knowne by the
name of ninacrascrans neck at the South Side of
Long

LongIsland within the Limits and bounds before Expressed
bounded as by the records of Said Brookhaven did on the
day of in the year of the Reigne
of our Said Late Sovereignne Lord Charles the Second: Sell &
grant unto thomas Smith and the Said John Smith all the
Said Share of meadow ground To have and To hold
all the Said peice or Share of meadow ground together
withall privilledges & Apurtenances belonginging or in
Any wise Appertaning to the Said Thomas Smith and John
Smith there heyres and Assignes to the onely use of the
Said Thomas Smith and John Smith there heyres and As
Signes for Ever as by the Said Records of the Said Towne of
Brookhaven Doth and may more At Large Appear and -
whereas Andrew gibb and Thomas Genner by order
of the Said Inhabetants of Brookhaven aforesd upon apli
cation made unto his Excellancy Thomas Dungon Capt
gen:ll Governer In Chief [crossed out]
under his Sacrad Majestye James the Second aforesd
to Confirme the Said trackt of Land and premises by
patent under the Seale of the province and whereas
the Said Thomas dongan Capt generall and Governr as
afforesd did on the Seaven and twentyeth Day of December
Last past in the Second year of our Said Sovereignes
Lord James the Second by vertue of his Comicon and the
power and Authority to him granted by his Sacred Majesty
aforesd give grant Releas & Confirm unto John Palmer
Esqr Richard wodhull Samuell Eburn andrew gibb thom[as]
Jenner William Satterly and Thomas Helme Trustees for
the freeholders & Comonalllity of the Said Towne of Brook
=haven all the beforemenconed tract of Land and pre
mises To ave and to hold ye Said tract of Land and
premisses to ye Said John Palmer Richard wodhull
Samuell Eburne Adrew gibb Thomas Jenner william
Satterly & thomas helme Trustees as aforesd there -
and Sucessors
heyres there Asignes to ye only use and behoofe of y[e]
present freeholders & Inhabetants of the Said broo[k]
=haven there heyrs and Assignes for Ever according to
there Severall Devistions & Allottments and to noe
other use or uses whatsoever and whereas the Said John
Smith and Rebecca his wif by vertue of the aforerecited
Rights Stands possessed of one moitye or equall halfe -
part of all the aforesd peice Share of Allottment
of

of meadow ground Now This Indenure ffurther
Wittnesseth that the Said John Smith and Rebecca his
wife for Sundry good Cause & Considerations them and Each of
them thereunto moveing and more Espeacially for and in
Consideration of the Sum of Eight pounds Ten Shillings Cur
=rant and Lawfull money of newyork to them ye Said Jno
and Rebecca Smith in hand paid & Delivered by the Said
Samuell Eburne, before the Ensealeing and Delivery of
these presents the Receipt whereof they doe hereby
acknowledge & themselves & Each of them to be therewith
fuklly Satisfied Contented and payd & thereof and of Every
parte and percell thereof Doth by these presents acquitt &
Discharge the Said Samuell Eburne his heyres Executors and
Administrators for Ever: Hath given granted bargained Sold
Released Enfeofed and Confirmed & doth by these presents free
ly Clearly & absolutly give grante bargaine & Sell Release
Enfeof and Confirm unto the Said Samuell Eburne all the
aforesaid Moity or full half parte of all the aforesd Share
allottment or peice of meadow ground together with=all
ye previlledges and Apurtenances to ye Said Moity or half
of the Said Share of meadow belonging or In anywise aper
=taining or that may belong or appertaine at any tim or -
times hereafter To have and To hold all and Singuler
the Sd moytye or halfe parte of all ye Said Share of meadow
ground and all other the Said granted premisses to him ye
Said Samuell Eburne his heyres and Assignes to ye Sole
and proper use & behoofe of the Said Samuell Eburne his
heyres and Assignes for Ever To have hold ocupie and
Enjoy as his and there owne Estate of Inheretance in
fee Simple and the Said John and Rebecca Smith for
and In behalfe of themselves there heyres Executors
Administrators and Assignes and Each of them there
heyrs Executors and administratrs and Each
of them doth hereby Covenant and promise to and with ye
Said Samuell Eburne his heyrs Executors Administrators
or Assignes or either of them for Ever the Said Moity
or halfe parte of the Said Share or Lott of meadow ground
to the Said Samuell Eburne his heyrs Executrs Adminisrs
and Assignes against all persons whatsoever Shall and will
warrant and Defend as alsoe That the Said John and Re
becca Smith there heyres Executors and Administratrs
or Either of them or any other persons Clayming the
Same

Same by from or under the Said John and Rebecca Smith there heyrs Executrs Administrars and Assignes or Either of them Shall and will at any time or times hereafter for Ever upon re quest and Aplication Made unto them by the Said Samull Eburne his heyres Executrs Administrators or Assignes any other or firmer Deed or Conveyance or Assurance for the Said Moitye or halfe parte of the Said Share of meadow & and premisses as the Said Samuell Eberne his heyres Executrs Administrars or Assignes Shall be Advised and procure to be made by his or there Councell Learned In ye Law Seale and Deliver In wittnes whereof The Said partyes have hereunto Set theire hands and fixed there Seales at brookhaven the Day and year first above - written

his
John I Smith
mark her
Rebecca Smith X
mark

Sealed and Delivered In the presence of

Gusta: Kingsland
Andrew Gibb

A true Coppy of the origanall Septemberye 5th 1687 p John Howell Clark §

This Indenture made the three and Twentyeth day of Aprill in the third year of the Raigne of our Sovereigne Lord James the Second by the grace of god of England Scottland ffrance and Ireland King Defender of ye faith &c and In ye year of our Lord god one thousand Six hundred Eighty and Seaven between Obed Seward and bethiah his wife of Brookhaven In ye County of Suffolk upon LongIsland yeoman of the one parte and Samuell - Eburne of the Same towne and County: Clarke of ye other parte Wittnesseth whereas Richard Nicolls Esqur governr generall under his then Royall highnes James Duke of york & albaney &c now his Sacred Majesty over the province of new york & territoryes in amer ica did on the Day of in the Year of the Raigne of our Late Sovereigne Lord Charles the Second Late King of England &c and In ye Year of our Lord god one thousand Six hundred Sixty and Six give grant Release and Confirme unto Capt John Tooker mr Daniell Lane Richard wodhull Henry perring and John Jenner as patentees for and on behalfe of them Selves and there Associates the freeholders and Inhabetants of brookhaven aforesd all that tract of Land Sittuate and Lying upon LongIsland aforesd bounded by the Red Creek or wadeing River Eastward the South Sea or maine ocean Southward the Sea or Sound northward and the Lyne Run between the Said Inhabetants of brook haven and mr Smiths Land of nessequage westward together withall meadows Marshes Creek harbours and privelledges and Appur

ten

Appurtenances to the Said tract of Land belonging or In any wise
Appertaining to have and To hold the Said tract of Land amd all
other the granted premises to the Said John Tooker Daniell Lane
Richard wodhull Henry perring and John Jener & there Associates & there
heyres for Ever to the proper use and behoofe of the Said John Tooker
Daniell Lane Richard wodhull Henry perring John Jenner and ther
Associates there heires and Assignes as by a certaine patent Sealed with
the Seale of the Said Richard Nicolls Esqur governr as aforesd Remaining
upon Record In the Secretarys office at newyork doth and may
More at Large appeare And whereas Thomas Dongan Capt genll
and governr In Cheife under his Sacred Majestye James the Second
Aforesd & upon aplication made unto him by Andrew gibb & Thomas
Genner by order of the Sd Inhabetants of brookhaven aforesd to Confirm
the Said tract of Land and premises by patent under the Seal of this
province did on the Seaven and twentyeth Day of December Last past
In the Second year of our Said Sovereigne Lord James the Second -
by vertue of his Comicon and the power and Authority to him
granted by his Sacred Majestye aforesd give grant Releas and Confirme
unto John palmer Esquire Richard wodhull Samuell Eburne
Andrew gibb thomas Jenners William Satterly and Thomas Helme
trustees for the free houlders and Comonallyty of the Said towne
of Brookhaven all the Aforemenconed Tract of Land & premisses
To have and To hold the Said tract of Land and premises to
the Said John Palmer Richard wodhull Samuell Eburne Andrew
Gibb Thomas Jenner william Saterly and Thomas Helme trustees
as aforesd there heyres and Successors and There Assignes to ye only
use and behoofe of the present freeholders and Inhabetants of
The Said Brookhaven there heyres and Assignes for Ever accord
ing to theire Severall Devistions and Allottments and to noe
other use or uses whatsoever and whereas the said obed
Seward and Bethiah his wife by vertue of the afore Recited
Rights Stands possessed of one full Share allottment or peice of
meadow ground Sittuate Lying and being at a neck or place Comon
ly Called and knowne by the name of Snake neck at ye South Side
of LongIsland within the Towne Shipp of Brookhaven aforesaid
and bounded by the upland in the tenure and occupacon of ye
Said Samll Eburne Northerly the meadow ground In the occupa
tion of Richard wodhall Easterly the South bay Southerly and
the meadow In the tenure of the Said Richard wodhull west
=erly Now this Indenture ffurther wittnesseth that
the Said obed Seward and bethiah his wife for Sundry good -
Causes and Considerations them and Each of them thereunto
Moveing and more Especially for and In Consideration of ye
Sum of fifteen pounds Currant and Lawfull money of new
york to them the Said obed and bethiah Seyward in -

hand payd

In hand payd and Delivered by the Sayd Samuell Eburne before
The Ensealeing and Delivery of these presents the Receipt
whereof they doe hereby acknowledge and themselves and Each
of them to bee therewith fully Satisfied Contented and paid and
thereof and of Every parte and percell thereof doth by these
presents acquitt and Discharge the Said Samuell Eburne his
heyres Executors and Administrators for Ever hath given grant
ed bargained and Sould Released Enfeofed and Confirmed & doe by
these presents freely Cleerly and absolutely give grant
bargaine and Sell Release Enfeofe and Confirme unto
the Said Samuell Eburne all the aforesd Tract Share allotmt
or peice of meadow ground together withall the privilledges
and Apurtenances to the Said Share of meadow belonging
or In any wise Appertaining or that may belong or Apertaine
at any time or times hereafter To have and To -
hold all and Singuler the Said tract of meadow ground and
other the Said granted premises to him ye Said Samuell Eburne
his heyres and Assignes to ye Sole and proper use & behoofe
of the Said Samuell Eburne his heires and Assignes for ever
to have hold occupie possesse and Enjoy as his or theire
owne Estate of Inheritance in fee Simple free & Cleer
and freely and Cleerly acquitted Exonarated and discharged
of and from all former & other gifts grants bargaines Sales
Mortgages Dowers Rents taxes Impossitions or other titles or
Incumbrances whatsoever had mad or Comited by the Said
at any time or times before the Ensealeing and Delivery of ye prsents & ye Said obed & behiah
obed & bethiah Sayward ^ for and In behalfe of themselves
theire heyres Executors &Adminrs or Assignes and Each of them
their heyres Executors and Administratrs and Each of
them Doth hereby Covenant and promise to and with ye
Said Samuell Eburne his heyres Executors Administratrs
and Assignes [crossed out] or Either of
them for Ever the Said Share of meadow ground to ye Said
Samuell Eburne his heyres Executors Administratrs and
Assignes against all persons whatsoever Clayming by from
or under them the Said Obed & Bethiah Seyward their
heyres Executors Administrators or Assignes or Either
of them Shall and will Warrant and Defend as alsoe that
the Said Obed and bethiah Sayward there heyres Executrs
Administrators or Assigne or Either of them or any -
other person or persons whatsoever Clayming the Same
by from or under them the Said Obed and Bethiah -
Sayward there heyres Executors Administrators or Assi[gnes]

Assignes or Either of them Shall and will at all or any time
or times hereafter for Ever upon Request and Aplication
made unto them or Either of them by the Said Samuell Eburn
his heires Executors Administrators or Assignes any other or
firmer Deed or Conveyance or Assurance for the Said tract
Share or percell of meadow ground and premisses as the Sd
Samull Eburne his heires Executors Administrators or Assigns
or either of them Shall be Advised and procure to be made
by his or theire Councell Learned In the Law Seale and de
=liver: In wittnes whereof the Said partyes have here=
unto Sett their Hands and fixed theire Seales at Brook=
=haven the Day and year first above written

Sealed and Delivered
In presence of
Richard Wodhull
Andrew Gibb

his
Obed ^ Seyward
mark
A true Coppy p John Howell
Clark Septber ye 7: 1687

This Indenture made the Seventh day
of June in the third yeare of the Reigne of our Sovereign
Lord James ye Second by ye grace of god of England
&c King Defender of the faith &c Annoqe Dom 1687
Between John Wood and Georg wood of Brookhaven in
the County of Suffolk on Long Island In ye province of
Newyork of the one parte and Samuell Eburne of ye
Said Towne and County of the other parte wittneseth
that the Said John and Georg wood for and In Con=
Sideration of a valluable Sum of money in hand re
and delivery
ceived at or before the Ensealeing of these presents
the Receit whereof they doe here by acknowledg
and him ye Said Samuell Eburne Acquitt and -
fully discharge of Every parte and percell therof
Have given granted bargained Alliened Enfeof
ed Sould and Confirmed and by these presents
doe give grant bargaine alien Enfeof Sell and
Confirme a Certaine three Acre Lott Sittuat Lying
and being In the old feild near the fresh pond being by
number the Eight bounded by the Land in the tenure of Richard
Clark on the one Side and the Land of John and Samuell
muncy on the other Side on the East Side of the fresh
pond unto the Said Samuell Eburne his heyres Execu
=tors and Administrators for Ever To have and To -
Hold the Said Land withall its members and Apur
tenances

Appurtenances unto the only use & behoofe of the Said Samll Eburne and his heyres for Ever and the Said John & Georg wood doe hereby Covenant promiss & grant to and with ye Said Samuell to warrant and Defend the Right Title & Intrest of ye Said Land against any that Shall Lay Clayme thereto and that they Shall & will deliver quiet & peacable possession thereof free from Any former Grants bargaines Sales Mortgages Joynt ters Rates or other In Combrances whatsoever More= =over to Seale and Deliver any further Assurance deed or Conveyance Concerning the premisses if need Require - In Confirmation where of the partyes aforemenconed John Wood & Georg Wood doe hereunto Set their hands & Seales the Day and year above written

his
Sealed Signed & Delivered John I Wood
mark
his
In Presence of George I Wood
mark
Thomas Helme Mary wood her mark M
Mary Helms / A true Coppy p John Howell Clark

This Indenture made the Seventh Day of June in the third yeare of his Majestyes Ragne James the Second of England &c King Defender of the faith &c Annoq Dom: 1687 Between Samll Dayton of Brookhaven in the County of Suffolk on Long Island in ye province of New= york of the on parte and Samuell Eburne of ye Said towne and County of ye other part Wittneseth that the Said Samuell Dayton ^ for and In Consideration of a valluable Sum of mon =ney In hand Received at or before the Ensealing of these presents [crossed out words] the Receipt - whereof he Doth acknowledge and him ye Said Samuell Eburne of Every part and percell thereof acquit & discharge by these presents hath Given granted bargained Sould Aliened Enfeofed and Confirmed and by these presents Doth give grant bargaine Sell Enfeofe and Confirme unto ye Said Samuell Eburne his heyres Executors and Administrators a Certaine Allotment of meadow Situat Lying and being in ye old purchas on ye South Sid of this towneship - knowne by the number 13 haveing the Allott ment Layd out for mr Richard Smith Senr

on the East Side and the Allotment of Henry Rogers
on ye west to have and To hold the Said meadow
with the upland Adjacent to it on ye South Side of the
Highway together withall its members and Apurtenances
and all and Singuler the privilledges belonging or In
any wise Apertaining to the within bargained premises
to the Said Samuell Eburne and his heires for Ever to
his and there proper use and behoofe and the Said -
Samuell Dayton doth hereby Covenant promis and -
grant to and with ye Said Samuell Eburne to warrant
and Defend the within recited premisses from any Claym
of any person or persons preteing any Right therein
and to give Quiet and peacable possession thereof
free from any former Sales bargaines Morgages
Joynters Rates or other Incumbrances whatsoever
Moreover the Sd Samuell Dayton Shall and will Signe
Seale and deliver unto the Said Samuell Eburne
Any further Assurance Deed or Conveyance at ye
Reasonable Request of the Said Samuell Eburne In
Confirmation of ye premisses In wittnes whereof
the Said Samuell Dayton doth Set to his hand and
Seale the day and year above written

Signed Sealed and delivered / Samuell Dayton
In presence of
Thomas Helme
Mary Helme
A true Coppy p John Howell Clark §

This Indenture made the twentyeth Day of June
Anno dom: 1687 and in the third year of the Raigne
of our Sovereigne Lord James ye 2d by the grace
of god of England &c King Defender of the faith &c
Between Richard Clark of Brookhaven in ye County
of Suffolk on LongIsland in the province of new
yorke of the one parte and Samuell Eburne of ye
Said Towne and County of the other parte Wittneseth
that the Said Richard Clarke for and In Considera
tion of a valluable Sum of money allready receiv
=ed In full Satisfaction the receipt whereof hee
doth hereby acknowledge and him ye Said Samuell

Samuell Eburne from Every parte and percell there
of accquitt and discharge hath given granted Aliened
Enfeofed and Sould and by these presents doth give
grant Alien Enfeofe Sell and Confirme unto ye Said
Samuell Eburne his heyres and Successors for / -
Ever a Certaine Allotment of Land Sittuat Lying
and being In Cranes neck by Computation five -
Acres as it was Layd out bounded Eastward by ye
Land of peter whiteheire westward by the beach
northward by the Land of Samuell Eburne and Southward
by the Land that was given to maintaine the water fence
as Likewis a certaine Allotment Sittute Lying and being
Near to the fresh Pond In ye old feild being or Re=
puted to bee four Acres as it was Layd out bounded
by the Land of thomas Biggs and the Comon Land on ye
East by the Land of Andrew Miller on ye west by ye
highway near the fresh pond on ye north and the
Land of Jacob Longbothom on ye South To have
and To hold the Land aforesd withall and Singuler
the Improvements privllegdges members thereof
and Appurtenances to ye use and behoofe of the Said Samll
Eburne his heyres and Successors for Ever without
any Lett hindrance or Mollestation from ye Said
Richard Clerke or by his meanes or procurement and
the Said Richard Clark Doth hereby Covenant promise
and grant to deliver unto ye Said Samuell
Quiet and peacable possession of the Said Land and
to discharg the Same from any In Combrance what
Soever and Shall warrant the title of the premises
against any that Shall Lay any Clayme thereunto
moreover if it Shall be needfull the Said Richard
Shall Signe Seale and deliver unto ye Said Samll Eburne
any further deed or Conveyance for the Ratifieing and
Confirmg the premises In wittnes whereof Richard Clark
with the Consent of Margret his wife have hereunto
Sett his hand and Seale the Day and year above mencon
ed

his
Signed Sealed and D Richard R Clark
In presence of mark
Thomas Helme
his
Georg J Wood
mark

Suffolk:) This Indenture mad this 25th Day of July 1687
wittneseth that wee wyandance and Sasakatacco
Sachames of montauket with the Consent of the
Mentauk Indianes for Divers good Causes and us
thereunto moveing and More Especially a valluable Sum
of money In hand Received to the vallue of one hund
dred pounds doe allinate bargaine and Sell and by these
presents Have allinated bargained and Sould and made
over all our tract of Land at montauket bounded by part
of the fort pond and fort pond bay west the English Land
South by a Lyne Run from the fort pond to ye great pond
and Soe from the South End of the great pond over to the South
Sea: and to the utmost extent of the Island from Sea to Sea
bounded by the maine ocean on the South and by the bay or
Sound on the north Side all which wee have Sould unto Leift
John wheeler Samuell Mulford tomas osborne Stephen -
Hand Stephen Hedges Samuell persons: John Mulford trustees
of the free houlders and Comonallity of the Towne of East
hampton and benjamin osborne Implyed by the Trustees to
them in the behalfe and for the use of themselves and the
propriators namly John Hands widow John Stratten thomas
Talmage Thomas osborne John Mulford Samuell Mulford
Thomas Baker Thomas Mulford widow Elizabeth baker
two Allotments Samuell fithian Samuell Brooks Joshua
garlick Richard Shaw Jacob Scellenger John Miller Senr
Nath: Bishops Lott William barnes Samuell persons the
Lot which was Birdsalls John Edwards william Edwards
Leift John wheeler Capt Josiah Hobart Robert Dayton thomas
Chatfeild Jerimiah Conklin mr Thomas James that Lot which
was Georg Millers that Lot which was Jerimiah Meechams
Lot Stephen hedges Benjamin Osborne that which was thomas
osbornes Lot John Hopping Thomas diaments Lot Stephen
Hand John osborne to them there heyres and Assignes &
to Every of them there Respective heyres and Assignes
and Administrators all and Every of the Demised premises
To have and To hold to Enjoy and possess to them
and there heires for Ever withall privillidges and Appurten
nances thereunto belonging without the Least Lett hindra
=ance or Mollestation by from us our heires or Assignes
or any In our names and wee doe by these presents give them
further and better Security as any Learned Councell in
the Law Shall think meete for there Security and -
Saftye they being at the Charge of writing and for the
true performance hereof wee have hereunto

hereunto Sett our hands and fixed our Seales the
Day and year first above written

Atest
John Meredith
Thomas Harress

the words: (our heires or assignes) Enter
lined was done befor ye acknowledgemt hereof

wyandance his mark
Sasakatacco S his mark
obadiah his mark
Checkanoo A his mark
peepee allias nat his mark
penoso ? his mark
ungonet uo his mark
Auabetem X his mark
Awampequod C his mark
Shine his mark
wodhood I hanniballs mark
witnes M his mark
Magoe matomas his mark
ned allias Matamaus his P mark
Sadams his mark
wichabooy his mark
Suchanockow his X mark
gentleman his mark U:
Mashandus his M mark

August the third one thousand Six hundred Eighty and Seven the Said Indians hereunto Subscribed namly wyandance Sasataka Checkanoo obadiah Shine Shine: Am= moox Sungy woscedumsh to pocowean: mamatamash Sukianackow these in ye name and for the behalf of all the Indians of Montauket Apeared before mee this day and Acknowledged that they and Every of them have from themselves there heyres and Assignes Sould and made over the Said Lands and privilledges as above Expressed unto the Said trustees of the towne of Easthampton according to the tennure of this Deed:

John Howell Justice

A true Coppy p John Howell Clark

Memorandum that Samuell persons Junr and Benjamin Conkling are accounted propriators and there names Should have been Entred above Amongst those that the purchase was made for but were omitted Atest Samuell Mulford

A true Coppy p John Howell Clarke

This Indenture made the tenth Day of August
in the year of our Lord one thousand Six hundred Eighty and
Six Between Thomas Edwards of Easthampton in the
East Rideing of yorksheir on LongIsland on ye one pte
and Abraham Schallanx of the Said Towne of East=
hampton on ye other parte Wittnesseth that ye Said
Thomas Edwards for and In Consideration of the Sum
of ten pounds to him payd by the Said Abram Schallenx
whereof ye Said thomas Edwards doth hereby acknow
ledge himselfe to bee fully Satisfied and doth hereby
Acquitt and discharge the Said Abram Schallenx his
heires Executors and Administrs for Ever By these
presents hath given granted bargained and Sould &
Confirmed unto ye Said Abraham Schellenx the
one Moitye or halfe parte of that his halfe Share
of Land at montauket which was given unto
him by his Late Deceased father william Edwards
the which his Said father purchased of nathanell
ffoster and which was granted to him by the Sd
Towne of Easthampton to have and To hold
the Said halfe parte of the Said halfe Share of
Land withall and Singuler its benefitts privill
ledges Advantages and Aputenances thereunto be
longing whatsoever unto ye Said Abram Schall
=lenx his heires and Assignes [crossed out]
[crossed out] to the only proper use of the Said
Abram Shallenx and to his heyres and Assigns
for Ever without any Lett hindrance or Mollesta
=tion of me the Said thomas Edwards my heyres Exe
cutors Administrators or Assignes or any of them or
Any other person persons whatsoever by from
or under me pretending or Clayming any maner
of pretence Clayme or title to any parte or pcell
of the Said halfe parte of the premises but that the Sd
Abram Schallenger his heyres and Assignes Shall &
may from time to time and at all times hereaf
=ter peacably and Quietly have hold use possess and
Enjoy the Said halfe parte of the Said halfe Share of
Land for Ever provided alsoe and it is hereby to bee
understood that if in process of time the above

mentioned halfe Share of Land of which the one halfe is
hereby Sould and Confirmed to the Sd Abram Schellenx
Shall bee Augmented unto a whole Share that then
by vertue of these presents I acknowledg and Confirme
unto the Said Abram Schellenx the one halfe of -
Such whole Share for as much as the one halfe of all
my Right and Intrest in the Said Land at montauk
ket is here Intended as wittnes my hand and Seale ye
day and yeare above written.//

Thomas Edwards

Signed Sealed and Delivered)
In ye presence of us
John Roberts
Richard Steers

this indenture of bargaine and
Sale was done and made with
my free and vollentary Consent
as wittness my hand her
Abygayle A Edwards
mark

September ye 13th 1687 then Apeared before mee
Thomas Edwards and the Consent of Abigaile his
wife owneing the above bill of Sale To be his &
her act and deed

John Howell Justice

A true Copy p John Howell Clarke

Be it knowne by these prsents that I Thomas
James minister of Easthampton upon ye Est Rideing
of newyorksheire upon LongIsland In America
doe by these prsents Sell bargaine Allinate and make
feofement to Abraham Schallenger Cooper of ye
Towne aforesd for a valluable Consideration by mee
the aforesd Thomas James already Received: A Cer
tayne tract or percell of Land Lying In ye woods East
ward of the towne aforesd Containing fifty two Acres
of Land be it more or Less withall ye Apurtenan
=ses belonging to ye Same: the Land aforesd being that
bounded upon the East Lying by Jerimy Conkling of ye
Same Length with his and upon the west Lyne Lying
by the Remainder of Thomas James his Land upon
the South bounded by the highway goes towards Na=
peak and upon the north bounded by the highway

Comonly

Comonly Called Amagansuck way and have given
the Aforesd Abram free and Legall possession of the Land
aforesd to have and To hold the said Land him his
heyres Executors Administrators or Assignes for Ever
without any Lett or Mollestation from mee the aforesaid
Thomas James or any In my behalfe for Ever
and for the Ratification and Confirmation of ye -
premises I doe Sett to my hand and Seale this
12th Day of June Anno Dom: 1683:

Signed Sealed and Delivered
In ye presence of
Jerimiah Conklin
Nathaniell Baker

Thomas James

Mr Thomas James acknowledged
the above deed to be his act and
Deed to which hee hath Set his
hand and Seale before mee
In Easthampton this 18th day
of may 1685:

Isaac Arnold Justice

A true Coppy p Jno: Howell Clark

In the nam of God Amen I Christopher ffoster of South
Hampton In the County of Suffolk on LongIsland in the province
of newyork being in my perfect Strength of memory bless
ed be Almighty god for it though at present weake of body
and Not knowing the time of my apointed Change do make
and ordaine this my last will and testament in maner &
forme following ffirst I give and bequeath my Soule to God my
Creator and Redeemer and my body after decant buriall
to ye Earth from whence it was at first taken and for my worldly
Estate as is hearafter Inserted first I give and bequeath unto
my Son Nathaniell ffoster two Cows and ten Sheep if they are
to be found After my decease if not the Sheep then in Som[e]
good pay after the rate of Eight Shillings p Sheep
2dly I give unto my Son John ffoster my four Acres of Land in
halseys neck 3dly I give unto my Son benjamin ffoster
my Acre of Land I Exchanged with Capt Howell Lying East
ward of Joseph ffosters Land In the little Playnes and Six load of
good dung out of my yard 4thly I give unto my grandson Christo=
pher ffoster Son of Joseph ffoster when hee Shall Ataine to the age of
one and twenty years my divident att Scuttle hole // 5th:ly I
give unto my grand Son Joseph Sayre when he Cometh of age
my divident at hogneck being a fifty £ divident - - -

6:ly I give unto Jerimiah ffoster Son of Joseph ffoster my two
Acres of Land and a halfe I had of mr Edward Howell Lying and
being In ye midle of Halseys neck: 7thly I give unto my daughter
Hanah Sayre A ewe Sheep and one third parte of all my Moveable
Houshold Stuff I Leave 8thly I give unto my daughter Sarah Johns
A Ewe Sheep and one third parte of all my moveable houshold Stuff -
I Leave 9:thly I alsoe give unto my Son Nathaniell ffoster my
bed and furneture I Lye on Lastly I by this my Last will give and
bequeath unto my Son Joseph ffoster and to his heirs for Ever
all that my house and home lott and Land at the first neck &
all other of my Lands meadows and Commonages whatsoever I have
not heretofore given by this my Last will and testament and
doe hereby Constitute and Apointe him my Sole Executor -
of this my Last will and to have all the Rest of my Estate
both Reall and personall that is not heretofore by me given
and he to pay and performe all the abovesd
Leagacyes In wittnes whereof I have hereunto Sett my
hand and Seale In Southampton abovesd this 8th Day of -
Aprill Annoq Dom 1684

Christopher ffoster

Signed Sealed and delivered
In the presence of us
her
Mary M Howell: davids)
mark wife:
John Laughton §

Mary Howell whose mark & name
and wittnes to ye will above written
october ye 13 1687 apeared before
me and made oth that ye above writt[en]
will and Testament of Christopher
ffoster deceased was his owne act and
deed

John Howell

At a Courte of Sessions held at Southold october ye 18th 1687 was
presented the aforesd will of Christopher foster In order to the
probates thereof mr John Laughton was Sworne In Courte
that he See the Testator Signe and Seale and heard him de:
clare this to bee his Last will and testament and thereupon
the Said will is proved and the Executor Confirmed

A true Coppy p John Howell Clark §

here followeth ye Inventory of the Estate of the Said Chris
topher ffoster: In ye word following:

The Estemate of the Estate of the Late deceased
Christopher foster: by ffrances Sayre and Samuell
Johnes being Chosen to aprize the Same

one horse at Six pounds In pay	6	-	-

	£		
Item: 2 cows	8	–	–
It: 2 yearlings Cow kind	2	10	–
Ite: 2 Calves	1	10	–
It: 2 Sheep	–	16	–
It: 1 bible 10s	–	10	–
It: a bed and boulster a rug & one blanket) 1 paire of pillow beers 2 pr of Sheets and a–) Chamber pott all old)	6	11	–
In pay as ye Leagacyes are to be payd is	25:	17	–0
but in Lawfull money of this goverment) we doe vallue ye above Estemate att)	12	–18	–6

as witnes our hands this 24th of october
In Southampton ye year of our Lord 1687

ffrances Sayre
Samuell Johnes

A true Coppy p John Howell Clarke §

Know all men by these presents that I Thomas Osborne the Son of John osborne deceased: Live ing at Elizabeth towne In the province of East= new jersey doe binde my heirs Executor Admin istrators and Assignes In a bond of five hundred pounds Not to make any demand of any Land or Lands belonging to the Estate of the abovesd John osborne Deceased Nether Shall any of mine by vertue hereof Ever have power to make any demands of any Lands lying within the bounds of Easthampton and In Case that Either my Selfe my heires Administrators or Assignes Shall break this my agreement we Shall Sure ly forfeit the five hundred pounds above menconed and to the true and faithfull per= formance of the premises I Set to my hand and fix my Seale october ye 26: 1687

witnesed by James Hand
Thomas bencraft

Thomas osborne
Thomas osborne above writen

Apeared before me this 1 of november=1687 and acknowledged ye above written bond to be his act & deed

John Howell

Know all men by these presents that wee whose names
are under written (vist) Thomas osborne John osborne
Ephraim osborne doe for themselves and In behalfe of
those underAge doe binde our Selves by a Joynt agree
ment that if one or more of us Should dye and Leave
Noe heire neither Male nor female then the Estate yt
did belong to the deceased person or persons Shall be
Equally Devided Among those that Remaine alive and
Allthough thomas osborne the Eldest brother be Ex=
=Cluded by a Certaine bond yet wee his brethren to
whome hee is under obligation by the Said bond -
Doe vollentarly and freely give him Equall privill
lidge with us In all Such Estates and that this agree
ment may be due ly kept according to the true
Intent hereof wee all Joyntly Sett to our hands
this first of november 1687

wittnesed by us — Thomas osborne
James Hand — John osborne
Thomas bencraft — Ephraim osborne

The above written John osborne and Thomas -
Osborne apeared before mee this first of Novem
=ber 1687 and accknowledged the above written
to be there act and Deed

John Howell

A true Coppy p John Howell Clark §

September the 17th in the year of our Lord 1687

In the name of god Amen I Benjamin Haynes
of the North Sea belonging to Southampton In the -
County of Suffolk in new yorksheire being very weake
& not knowing the apointed time of my death doe make
this my Last will and testament as follows 1st I bee
queath my Soule to god that gave it me and after -
death my body to the Earth by decent buriall and for my
worldly Estate I give as follows I give unto my two Sons
namly Samuell Haynes and James Haynes all my Land Lying
and being one peice Lying against kellys pond and the other
against the Long pond and the Said Land to be Equally devid
=ed between the Said Samuell and James and Either of them
a Cow

a Cow and the Cows to be Delivered to them by ye discres
=tion of the overseers of this will and I give to My beloved wife
namly Johanah Haynes a thirds of my Land and meadow &
houseing and orchards dureing the time of her widow hood also
all Swamps or marshes within the North Sea Lyne: with the
thirds of my movable Estate which I give to her for Ever

3ly I give unto my daughter hanah Haynes my Cotton bed with all
furneture to it and two pewter platters and 2 poringers
and two Cows: and to my daughter Sarah Haynes I give
ten pounds:
and I give unto my Son benjamin Haynes my fifty pounds
Commonage withall my Land and meadow or Marshes or Swamps
or Marshes belonging to me Inye northSea Lyne withall apur
tenances or privilledges belonging to ye Same to him and his
heires for Ever and my young horse and all my tooles & tack
=ling but hee is to give Sam and James Some of them if
there be any lefte: and my warming pan I give to him Lastly
I make my wife Johanah haynes and my Son benjamin Haynes
Joynte Executors of this my Last will and testament
to see it faithfully performed in all things alsoe I
make John Davis of the northsea and my brother Samll
Clark over Seers of this my will to See it performed In all
perticulers as above menconed or as the Law dus Require
it to be done I wittnes hereof I have Sett to my hand and
fixt my Seale In the year of our Lord above written

In the presence of us
John Davis Thomas Shaw
Samuell Clark
Deborah Sturmy

Benja: Haynes

this 23th day of november 1687
Samuell Clarke thomas Shaw and de
borah Sturmy who are wittneses to
to the within will made oath that they
Saw the Said Benjamin Haynes Signe
Seale and deliver it as his act and
deed

John Howell
Josiah Hubert

Alsoe the Same day Came before us the widow Johanah
Haynes and at the Same time did renounce and wholly disclaym
Executorship to the within will and Said Shee would not
Stand to the will but to what the law will allow her:
as attest

John Howell
Josiah Hubert

A true Copy p John Howell Junr Clark §

An Inventory of the Estate of Benjamin Haynes Late Dece[as]
ed taken at Southampton this 28th Day of September 1687

		£	s	d
Imprimis 4 oxen 14£: 5 Cows 14£	£	28	-	-
3: 3 yearolds Heifers 6£:10s) 4: 2 yrolds 5£		11	10	-
3 Calves & A halfe 28s: 1 Steer 4yearold 45s		3	13	-
2 yearling Steers 30s) 3 horses & a mare 7£		8	10	-
8 Sheep 40s: 1 hog & 2 pigs 15s		2	15	-
aboute ten bushells of wheat Inye Straw		1	10	-
aboute ten bushells of Indian Corne		-	15	-
the hay In the barne and flax		6	-	-
an old Carte and plow and tackling		2	10	-
Joners and Carpenters tools wheele wrights tooles		4	-	-
4 old howe & 2 old Spades		-	9	-
2 tramells tongs and grid Iron		-	12	-
one musquet & amanition Sword		1	-	-
wareing Aparell 70s		3	10	-
1 brass kettle 2 frying pans 2 Iron kettles and Iron pot & bras Schellet and other Lumber In the Lean =too as tables barrells payles &c	)	3	5	-
tobacco In ye house and barne		1	-	-
a woollen wheel		-	3	6
1 fether bed 2 boulsters one rug & old blanket and one pillow & 2 blankets	)	6	-	-
one bed tick and feathers		3	-	-
10 pound Cotten wooll 7:6 ditto 10 Sheeps 7s:6		-	15	-
1 Chest 6s: a Side of Sole leather bags & Seives 12s		-	18	-
old barrells & other lumber In ye Chamber		-	10	-
a linin wheele 3s:6d: a warming pan 8s		-	11	6
a diaper table Cloath & ½ doz: Napkins		1	-	-
2 old Chests & a box		-	13	-
one paire of new Sheets & one paire of old Sheets and one old Sheets	)	2	-	-
a feather bed boulster Coverled blanket & pillows		6	5	-
a table & old Cheast Cradle & Standing Stoole		-	16	-
pewter on the uper Shelfe 19s:) 7 poringers 7s		1	6	-
foure pewter basons a gill pot & a quarte pot and a beer pot a Cup a halfe pinte pott: Saltseller and 4 glass bottles	)	-	14	-
2 old Sadles & bridles and old pilion & Cloath		-	15	-
Chayres and Stooles and other Lumber		-	4	-
		105	7	0

John S Jessup
his mark
obadiah Rogers
John Laughton

Whereas I Johanah Haynes by the Last will and testament of my Husband benjamin Haynes Deceased was to have the one third of his moveable Estate now know yea that I the Said Johanah Haynes doe hereby acknowledge to have Received of Benjamin Haynes Executor to his fathers Said Last will all and Every parte of what is any way due to me of my Said Husbands Estate together with ten pounds that by the Said will is bequeathed to my young Childe Sarah Haynes whereupon I doe hereby for Ever acquitt and discharge ye Said Benjamin Haynes his heyres Executors Administrators and Assignes of and from all and Every parte of my Said proportion of the Said Estate together with the Said ten pounds my Said Childes portion according to the Said will and our agreement thereupon made as wittnes my hand this 24th Day of novembr 1687

her
Johanah ⲕ Haynes
mark

wittnes Charles Sturmey
John Howell Junr

[In the original volume, the writing beneath this point on the page is upside-down. The] beginning of the entry is on Page 279]

by	2 ploughs Cart & Harrow & fowr Chains	8	-	-
by	axes wedges rings Shovels a Spade mattuk hows & Sieths	3	10	-
by	7 Sicles three yokes foure forkes	1	13	-
by	two old Swords and a pr of bandyleers & other things	1	10	-
by	Suger: warming pan: Close Stoole Some Soure wine ^	7	-	-
by	woolen yarn a basket of flax, baggs and old bedsteads	3	14	-
by	a grindston and pipstaves and sheeps woole	30	2	-
by	567 foote of board and backen	4	5	-
by	Six pr of Shoose and one old share & 9 hives of bees	11	5	-
by	a duzen of Spoones and trentchers	-	8	-
by	Horse Kinde	113	-	-
by	Swine	15	-	-
by	fifteen oxen and 9 yearling Catle	109	-	-
by	Eight 2 yearold Cattle and 7 foure yearolds	48	-	-
by	five three yearolds and two: two yearolds 12 Cowes	83	-	-
by	nine Caves & a bull	13	-	-
by	two hundred and Sixty Sheep	91	-	-
by	a Sarvant negerin	40	-	-
by	one negro boy	10	-	-
by	one English boy	10	-	-
by	one English boy more	10	-	-
by	book debts and rates	200	-	-
by	a Jak	2	-	-
	in all-	2349	:02	:00
	Debts and Charg being Subtracted the totall is	2052	:05	:00

Aprized by us whose names are hereunder written
All goods and Chattells and Estate whatsoever was aprized Excepte the phissek

John Howell
John Jessupp
John Howell Junr:
& mr Joseph Fordham Sworne in Courte to the trueth of this Inventory

A true Coppy p mee John Howell Jur

Southampton October the 26th: 1674

An Inventory of the Estate of Mr. Robert ffordham lately deceased as followeth:

	£	s	d
by houseing and land with the devistions appertaining there unto is Aprized at	1164	–	–
by pt of a Catch	30	–	–
by books	53	7	6
by Corne and hay	80	7	6
by a bed and furneyture	12	–	–
by 3 woole beds wth Sheets & blankits to them	11	–	–
by a feather bed & boulster pillow & Sheets	8	–	–
by a Coverled & a home made rug	3	10	–
by a pr of Sheets & five yds of home Spun Cloath	2	10	–
by 3 yds of home Spun Cloath & a pr of Sheets	1	12	–
by a Coverled & abed tick with two bits of the Same & carpet	5	5	–
by fourteen yds of home Spun and a peice of fustin ticking	4	6	–
by 2 peices and a remnant of linin	9	15	–
by Some Small remnants of Cloath & Stuff	2	6	–
by a trunke & Cuboard & a Set of old Curtaines	13	10	–
by 2 pr of Sheets & a Single Sheet	2	10	–
by 13 yds ½ of duffles	6	15	–
by five quoshens and a remnant of hom Spun Cloath	1	15	–
by Cheese Cobb Irons & tongs & fire shovell	12	17	–
by 2 leather Chayres & 2 Stools & fifteen yds of oxenbrigs	4	5	–
by Mr fordhams wearing Cloaths	6	–	–
by 5 Chests linin yarn & oat meal with other lumber	4	15	–
by hops and old leather Skins	3	10	–
by 9 leather Skins & an Indian bag & peas & a Still with lumber	3	15	–
by fethers and Candles and foure barrills of Salt	6	19	–
by Some other lumber & 2 pr of Sheets	2	15	–
by pewter 2 Cetles and 2 guns:	15	15	–
by 3 old Cetles and 2 Scellets & four Iron pots and 2 Iron Cetles	7	8	–
by 2 tramills four pr of pothooks Spit dripping pan Cob Irons	3	5	–
by a Scimer a pewter dish a peele & 2 barrils of pork	6	14	–
by 2 pails dishes Chees fats & a Cann	1	–	–
by a frying pan Churn and fan bras morter & pestle	1	6	–
by tallow & Suet a part of a hogshed of Sugar & lumber	2	–	–
by a Sadle five Shovells & Cream pots & trays wth other lumber	3	–	–
by a Cetle tunill tramill Smoothing Iron & tongs	1	17	–
by a lanthorne Stillyds and a Chest with Some Smal thing in it	2	–	–
by 2 Chests and a Jug	–	15	–
by gold and Silver money	13	14	–
by a Cuboard a box five Chayres and a table	2	–	–
by a looking glas 2 brushes bellows and hour glass	–	12	–
by 2 pr of hollon Sheets 5 table Cloaths) and pillow beers)	7	–	–
by plate	7	–	–
by Scals and weights and abotle	1	4	–

[In the original volume, the writing on this page is upside-down. The rest of this inventory is on the bottom of the opposite page.]

and one home lot of three Accres which Mr Robert fford
=ham Sometime bought of Mr Browne All which perticulers
Shall bee and remaine unto him the Sd Mr Jonah fordhame
his heires ans Asignes forever Sixthly That Leiftennt
Edward Howell and his wife Mary Shall have out of the
Said Estate of the Said Mr Robert fourdham fourty Accres of
land lying and being at meacocks afforsd unfenced or not
yet laid out twenty accres of land in the next devission wher
the Sd Mrs Elizabeth Fordham Shall apoint viz: in Land not fenced
in with a fifty pounds Comonage at present and what privilledges
Shall belong thereunto in all future devissions of land unfenc[ed]
Also the two: a lot ments of medow in Shinecock neck which be
=longs unto Mr Robert ffordham and also fourty pounds Estate out
of the living Stock as it riseth: the Sd pticulers and every pa[rt]
thereof to bee and remaine unto them the Sd Leiftennt Edward
Howell and mary his wife there heirs Executors administrators
And Assignes for ever: Seaventhly: That Mrs Elizabeth
ffordham Shall and will Sattisfye her daughter the Said Mrs
Hanah for what is due unto her of the Sd Estate: out of the Said
one third part belonging to her Eightly: if it Shall fall out
that the Sd John ffordham hereafter Shall prove Chargable
to them with whom he shall dwell that then his Charges
and necessary expence Shall be paid out of the Estate belong
=ing unto him as aforesaid: by the appointment of his bro:
=thers Mr Jonah ffordham and Leiftenant Edward howell wth
John Jessup or any two of them whoe are his guardians - -
9 Lastly That upon Mr Joseph ffordham and his mother Mrs
Elizabeth fordham or either of them makeing paymt to
Any pson or psons according to the intent of this agreemt
that then he or they that Soe receive there proportion or
proportions Shall give ample receipt to give Such acquitan[-]
as may fully discharge the Sd Mrs Elizabeth fordham and
Mr Joseph fordham from for ever they (whoe Soe receive) or
there Claming any more paymt or intrest in the Said Estate
of the Sd partyes herin agreeing as aforsaid heve hereto
Set their hand and Seals the day and year first above writen

Signed & Sealed: the mark of Elizabeth E ffordham
In psence of us
John Howell
John Youngs
Henry peirson

Joseph ffordham
Edward Howell
her
Mary m Howell
mark

A true Coppy p mee
John Howell Clark:

[In the original volume, the writing on this page is upside-down. The above agreement begins at the top of the opposite page]

These prsents wittnes an Agreement made this six and
Twentieth day of november Ano Dom one thousand Six
Hundred Seaventy foure Between Mr Joseph ffordham &
His mother Mrs Elizabeth ffordham of the one pt Mr Jonah
ffordham by his agent Leiftent Edward Howell him the Said Leiftent
Howell with his wife Mary; and for & respecting John fordham
and Mrs Hanah Clark the daughter of Mr Robert ffordham
deceased: which Said agreement is a totall and finall Conclussion
Between the Said pties: Concerning the Estate left by him the Sd Mr
Robert ffordham for themselves there heires Executers add=
ministrators & assignes for ever and the Said agreement is as
followeth: Imprs that the said Mr Joseph ffordham with his
Mother Mrs Elizabeth fordham Shall be lawfull possessors as
Executors of all the Said Estate belonging to him the Said Mr
Robert ffordham deceased: Secondly: that the Said Mrs
Elizabeth fordham Shall have and Enjoy to her Selfe and
and at her Sole dispose her one third part of the Said
Estate in the movable goods is they amount thereunto
as they are Apprissed or if they fall short then the Said third
pt to bee made up out of the rest of the Said Estate thirdly
That the Sd Mr Joseph fordham Shall have and Enjoy to
him & his heires for ever two hundred and fifty pounds
Allotment of lands which is now in his possession and part
of his fathars accomodations in this towne of Southampton ~ ~
together with the remainder of whatsoever Shall bee left
of the Estate after the Said one third thereof to his mother as
aforesaid is deducted with what else by this agreement is
to bee paid: ffourthly: That John fordham Shall have fourty
five accres of land which was his fathers and is lying at ~
mecocks with in the fence there now Standing with a home
lot in the towne plot adjoyning unto the Sd Mr Robert
ffordham his home accomodations Comomonly Called by the
name of Jonas H: his lot being three accres more or less
Allsoe hee the Said John Shall have Seaventye five pounds in currant pay
(as it Ariseth one thing with another without dore) out of the per=
Sonall Estate of him the Sd Robert fordham the Same to be to
him the Sd John ffordham and to his heires and Assignes for
5: ever fifthly that the Sd Mr Jonah ffordham Shall have one
Hundred pounds out of the living Stock (which is of his deceas
=ed fathers Estate) proportionably; the Same to be payd and
delivered to him on his order at demand in Southampton by
or before the first of may next ensuing. Alsoe the books
bequeathed to him by his father in his Life time also the
fifty Accres of land formerly laid out unto the Sd Mr Robert
fordham lying against the mill path between the towne and
the hollow Commonly Called little worth alsoe fifty pound ~ ~
Comonage in whatsoever devissions of lands (now not fenced in)
Shall be made in This Towne of Southampton for the future
also the Little pcell of land by Estemation three roods ly=
=ing in the Captaines neck between John woodruf and Ellis
Cook alsoe foure Acres and a halfe of land in the little plaines

[In the original volume, the writing on this page is upside-down. This agreement concludes on the opposite page.]

The Demands of the widow Haynes

That Shee may have the thirds of all and Every part
of the Moveable Estate of her Late Deceased Husband
Clear of all Charge and her Daughter ten pounds -
presently Delivered and the third parte of the wheat
now upon the ground and that Shee may have free
Liberty of the house untill next June: and
Soe Much meadow for this year as Shall or may mow
three Loads of hay to keep the Cattle next winter
and whereupon the Said widdow Johanah Haynes Doth
Relinquish all her Right and title to the Land for
Ever and the house after her Said time of June
next In wittness that this there finall agreement
between them wee have hereunto Sett our hands
this twenty third of November Anno Dom 1687

In presence of
John Howell
Jos: Hobart §

his
Benjamin X Haynes
mark
Samuell Clarke
her
Johanah C Haynes
mark

A true Coppy p John Howell Clarke §

This Indenture made the Twelfth Day of December in
the third year of the Reigne of our Sovereigne Lord James ye Second
by the grace of god King of England Scottland france and Ireland
Defendr of the faith &c and In the year of our Lord god one
thousand Six hundred Eighty and Seaven Between Abraham
Dayton and Mary dayton his wife of Brookhaven in the County
of Suffolk upon LongIsland In the province of newyork In ame
=rica Yeoman of the one parte and Andrew Gibb of the towne
and County Aforesd Esqr of ye other parte Wittneseth that the
Said Abram and Mary Dayton for divers good Causes
and valluable Considerations them and Each of them there
unto moveing and more Especially for and In Consideration
of the Sum of Six and twenty pounds Currant and Lawfull -
money of new york to them the Said Abram & mary Dayton
In hand payd by the Said Andrew Gibb the Receipt wherof they
Doe hereby acknowledge and themselves and Each of them to be
there with fully Satified Contented and payd and thereof and of
Every parte and percell thereof doth freely and Cleerly aquitt &
discharge the Said Andrew gibb his heyres Execut:rs Admrs & Assigns
for Ever: by these presents hath given granted bargained Sold
Released Confirmed and doe by these presents fully and Cleerly &
Absoelutly give grant bargaine and Sell Release and Confirm
unto the Said Andrew gibb his heyres and Assignes for Ever

all

all there two fifteen Acres Lotts of Land Lying and being
upon Georges Neck within the towneship of brookhaven afforesaid
being Number one and Number three and bounded as by the -
Records of Brookhaven May and doth appeare together withall the privill
=ledges thereunto belonging or In any wise Apertaineing To ha
=ve and To hold the Said two Lotts of Land & premises to him
the Said Andrew gibb his heyres and assignes for Ever to ye only pro
=per use benefitt and behoofe of him ye Said Andrew gibb his heyres
and Assignes for Ever and the Said Abram and Mary dayton doth
hereby Covenant and grant to and with the Said Andrew Gibb
that the Said Andrew Gibb his heyres and Assignes Shall and
may now and at all times hereafter for Ever quietly and
peacably have hold occupy possesse and Enjoy the abovesd two Lotts
of Land and all other the above bargained premises as his or
there owne free Estate of Inheretance in fee Simple
free and Clear and freely and Clearly acquitted Exonerated
and discharged off and from all former and other gifts grants
bargaines Sales mortgages Rents dowers taxes Impocissions
Entayles or other titles or Incombrances whatsoever had -
made or Comitted at any time or times hereto fore and ye
Said Abraham and Mary dayton doth hereby for and In be
halfe of themselves there heyres Executors Administrators
and Every
and Assignes and Each of them further Covenant to and with
& each of them the Said two Lotts of Land & all other the above granted prmises to ye Said Andrew
the Said Andrew gibb his heyres and Assignes ^ against all or
gib his heyres & Assignes
any person or persons Clayming the Same by from or under
them the Said Abram & mary dayton there heyres Executrs
Administrators and Assignes or Either of them or by ther[e]
or Either of there procurement Shall and will warrant and
Defend as alsoe to Seale and Deliver unto the Said Andrew
Gibb his heyres and Assignes any other or firmer deed or Con
vayance for the Said Lotts of Land and premises as the Said
Andrew Gibb his heyres and Assignes Shall be Advised and
procure to be drawne by his or there Councell Learned in
the Law In Wittness whereof the Said partyes have
hereunto Sett there hands & Seales the Day and year -
first above written

Signed Sealed and Delive — Abraham Dayton his A mark
In presence of
Samuell Eburne
John Moubray — Mary Dayton her ɑ mark

An Inventory and Aprizement of the Estate of Thomas Travally of Southampton Deceased taken and Aprized January ye 13th:1687 by the Aprizers Apointed namly John ffoster & Obadiah Sarle
as it was given In by the widow travally upon her oath the Day aforesd:

to one Thousand of Staves at ye End of the Shop	2	17	6
to 500½ & 20 peices of hewed heading & 100¼ of unhewed	2	10	-
to 1100 of Staves by the gate	2	5	-
to a Chest with Lock and key	-	10	-
to 2 Joynters one 6s ye other 4s) 2 Croasestacks & Irons 4s	-	14	-
2 howells 8s to 1 ax 12s: Compases & Crussett 18d: a frough 2s:6d	1	4	-
a Spoke Shave 3s an old ax 2s a round Shave 18d: another ditto 2s	-	8	6
the best heading knife 4s/ 2 old ditto 4s: a drawing knife 4s:6	-	12	6
2 old drawing knives 4s: another ditto 3s 2Adses 10s	-	17	-
a plaine Iron 18d a bullet mould 18d aSpike 6d	-	3	6
a padlock 1s a Jak plaine Stock 2s: truss hoops 10s	-	13	-
a handsaw 8s a brestwimble Stok 18d: a bongboarer 5s	-	14	6
to 5 payre of old trowsers & 2 wast Coats	1	10	-
to 2 black hatts one a Caster	2	-	-
2 Coats boath Lyned	2	5	-
to 3 payre of old Stockins and a payre of Shoes	-	5	-
a Sword and belt 10s: 3 glass bottles and a little kan 3s)	-	13	-
tinware a Candle Stick tunill 3 old potts all old	-	3	6
a Scellet and 2 Cups of Earthen	-	4	-
an old Spade and how 4s: a Sash Caps and neckcloaths 15s	-	19	-
a Sicle 18d a great Chayre 4s Small Stillyards 12s	-	17	6
to ½ a Crosscut Saw 5s	-	5	-
to the Shop 40s: a broken gun 15s	2	15	-
a grindstone 5s In Thomas Coopers hands 2£=10s	2	15	-

28 :3 :6

Three Courtes haveing passed and none peticons to Administer upon the aforesd Estate of Thomas Travally and the Creditors being wholly unpayd whereupon Samuell Cooper and John Howell Junr and In behalfe of his father together with mr John Campell did peticon the Courte of Sessions now held at Southold october ye 20th 1687 to Administer thereupon being 3 of the principle Creditters: first to pay ther owne debts and the Requessett Charges and then the rest of the Credrs Soe far as the State will reach and to give an accompt of the over pluss if any bee: and that the widow might be Sworne to give in a true Inventory: and Aprizers apointed which was accordingly granted to the peticonrs: test John Howell Clark

		£	s	d
Item	one tynn lamp	–	1	–
It:	one Smoothing Iron	–	4	–
It:	one brass Smoothing Iron	–	2	–
It:	one Iron Candlestick	–	1	–
It:	1 payre of tonges	–	2	–
It:	1 marking Iron	–	1	–
It:	1 Spade	–	2	–
It:	1 payre of taylers Sheeres	–	1	6
It:	1 wooden Shovell	–	1	–
It:	13 bowles and other wooden wares	–	15	–
It:	1 churne	–	5	–
It:	1 chaire	–	1	6
It:	for 2 knives	–	–	8
It:	for 1 ould great chest	–	4	–
It:	1 new chest	–	7	–
It:	for 1 old chest more	–	1	6
It:	one bible	–	5	–
It:	1 Sermon booke of Reinoulds his works	–	5	–
It:	for Some other Small books	–	4	–
It:	1 pr of bridle bitts, grassnayle, & 2 Iron bayles	–	2	–
It:	15 brass womens thimbles	–	1	6
It:	1 pr of fork tynes & a horne Combe	–	–	10
It:	for some whalebone	–	3	–
It:	one stone quart bottle wth vinegre	–	–	6
It:	for a pcell of old stockings	–	2	6
It:	for 2 alcumy Spoones	–	1	–
It:	for 1 pr of cards	–	2	–
It:	1 Coulter & a hand bill	–	6	6
It:	for 1 ould gun	–	1	–
It:	for 1 yellow blanket	–	14	–
It:	1 white blanket	–	10	–
It:	1 yellow little blanket wth Sare wtt: in it	–	6	–
It:	1 white blanket more	–	2	6
It:	for 3 pillowes	–	15	–
It:	one bagg fill'd wth chaffe	–	3	–
It:	for 1 pillow filled wth wool	–	4	–
It:	one fether bed marked w:th m: w	2	–	–
It:	for one wallet & a bushell of Salt	–	8	–
It:	for 1 black hatt	–	10	–
It:	one white hat	–	5	–
It:	for 3 streeked whome Spun Curtaines	1	6	–

The above written was apprized & valued accord=
=ing to order by authority by us under written

Thomas Talmage
Tho: Dyment
Jeremiah Conklyng
Benjamin Conklyng
John Parson

A true Coppy of ye Originall
with this onely erour, that ye
4th page in ye Originall is herein
entered in the place of ye 3 page
Recorded and Compsred p me
Henry Peirson //

[In the original volume, the writing on this page is upside-down. This estate begins on Page 288.]

	£	s	d
Item: 1 pewter wine quart pot	–	2	6
It: 1 old pewter platter	–	1	6
It: 2 linsy woolsey curtaines	–	10	–
It: 1 yellow rugg	4	–	–
It: 1 white Coverlet	–	14	–
It: 1 fether bed and bowlster	5	–	–
It: 1 white Blanket	–	10	–
It: 1 white blanket more	–	6	–
It: 1 little yellow Blanket	–	2	–
It: 1 payre of worsted Stockings	–	3	–
It: 12£ ½ of linen yarne	1	16	6
It: 3 greene aprons 2 of yem 12s 1 at 3s	–	15	–
It: for 17£ of flax	–	1	3
It: for 53 Cheeses	1	5	–
It: for 1 white apron with Strings	–	4	–
It: 1 more white apron w:thout Strings	–	7	–
It: 1 payre of Cotten gloves	–	2	6
It: for 12 £ of wooll	–	12	–
It: for 1 old Cloke & night wastcoat	–	3	–
It: for Small linen	2	7	–
It: for Scarf & neckcloths	–	15	–
It: good cotten & linen Sheet made into a bagg	1	–	–
It: 3 bush ½ of wheat	–	14	–
It: about 1 bush: of poore drossie wheat	–	2	–
It: 9 Shifts, wth a cloth they are bound up in	2	10	–
It: 1 bushell of Salt	–	3	–
It: 1 oulld Course	–	6	–
It: for 1 payre of Shoes	–	4	–
It: for 2 hand towells	–	1	–
It: for Some Suet	–	4	–
It: for 1 ould brush	–	–	6
It: 5£ of feathers	–	3	–
It: for 2 gallons of Mallasses & ye Anccor	–	5	–
It: for 1 Stirop 1 Iron boult & 1 hinge	–	2	–
It: 2 earthen pots wth hoggs far in yem	–	3	–
It: about 18£: of buter in 2 earthen potts	–	7	–
It: for 1 payre of old shoes	–	2	–
It: for English hay	4	–	–
It: sor Some Sope & ye vessell yt it is in	–	6	–
It: for 3 payre of knitting needles	–	1	–
It: 3s– in Silver & 1 m ½ of pins	–	6	–
It: for Some thrid and Silke	–	1	–
It: 1 linen bagg w:th 15£ of woolen yarne	2	–	–
It: one pewter ½ pinte bottle	–	1	–
It: 1 pewter dram cup	–	–	6
It: 1 old pewter basin	–	1	6
It: 1 tin tunell	–	1	–
It: 1 Dripping pan	–	2	–
Item			

[In the original volume, the writing on this page is upside down]

Item	2 yrds 3/4 of lockrum	-	5	-
It:	5 yrds of fine holland	3	-	-
It:	½ a yrd of Shaloone	-	2	6
It:	29 yrds of white tape	-	3	-
It:	5 yrds of linen made into a bagg	-	15	-
It:	one payre of Sheets	2	-	-
It:	one course Sheet	-	15	-
It:	2 yrds ½ whome Spun woollen	-	9	-
It:	4 yrds ¼ of whom Spun woollen	-	15	-
It:	1 payre of cotten & linen Sheets	2	-	-
It:	1 great Copper	8	-	-
It:	1 great brass kittell	6	-	-
It:	1 great furnace	6	-	-
It:	1 brass pan	2	-	-
It:	1 old brass kettle	-	5	-
It:	1 brass kettle about 4 gallons	1	8	-
It:	1 Small brass pan	-	15	-
It:	1 Small brakk kettle wth one are off	-	12	-
It:	1 brass Skillet 15s one warming pan 10s: 1 Small brass kettle 14s	1	19	-
It:	1 brass Skillet	-	6	-
It:	1 bell mettle kettle	-	6	-
It:	1 old Iron pott wth Severall holes in it	-	6	-
It:	1 Iron pott	-	11	-
It:	1 Small Iron pot	-	8	-
It:	1 more Small Iron pot	-	8	-
It:	1 Iron little pot	-	7	-
It:	1 Spit	-	1	6
It:	1 Little Iron kettle	-	5	-
It:	1 more Iron Small kettle	-	8	-
It:	1 more Iron Little kettle	-	6	-
It:	1 Iron hanger over the fire	-	5	-
It:	1 payre of pot hooks	-	1	-
It:	1 frying pan	-	4	-
It:	1 flaggon	-	5	-
It:	1 pewter pinte pot	-	3	-
It:	1 pewter Cup	-	2	6
It:	3 pewter pinte basins	-	7	6
It:	1 pewter platter	-	8	-
It:	1 more pewter plater	-	7	-
It:	2 poringers	-	3	4
It:	2 pewter platters	-	10	-
It:	1 pewter basin	-	7	-
It:	1 pewter Salt Seller	-	1	-
It:	1 pewter Saucer	-	-	6
It:	1 more pewter platter	-	7	-
It:	1 old poringer	-	-	6
It:	1 pewter Chamber pot	-	6	-

Item

[In the original volume, the writing on this page is upside down]

A true Inventory of the Estate of Mris: Alice Stanborough Deceased this 22th Day of December 1673: And apprized ye 26th of this Instant by those whoe are here under written: /

			£	s	d
Imprs:	the house and land both upland & meadow & ye Comonidg, wth all pvilidges thereunto - belonging	)	50	-	-
Item	two great Cowes		8	-	-
It:	1 black cow, & 1 short taild cow		7	-	-
It:	2 heifers		5	-	-
It:	all ye meat both pork beef & bacon		3	-	-
It:	one black Gowne		1	5	-
It:	one Searge gowne		1	5	-
It:	one kersey gowne		3	-	-
It:	1 Stuft peeticoat		-	12	-
It:	1 red kersy petticoat		1	15	-
It:	1 red half=thick petticoat		1	10	-
It:	1 broad=cloth petticoat		3	-	-
It:	1 gray kersey kersey wastcoat		1	-	-
It:	1 gray Searge Wastcoat		-	15	-
It:	1 Darke kersey wastcoat		-	16	-
It:	1 ould gray wastcoat		-	3	-
It:	1 blew whome=Spun petticoat		-	12	-
It:	1 Copers cullered petticoat		-	15	-
It:	1 ~~gray~~ white & gray under petticoat		-	10	-
It:	1 blew petticoat		-	8	-
It:	1 white petticoat		-	10	-
It:	5 ould under petticoats		-	16	-
It:	1 yrd 3/4 of red Searge		-	18	-
It:	3 yrds ½ of red woollen cloth		2	10	-
It:	1 yrd ½ of cloth rash		1	5	-
It:	1 yrd 3/4 of gray kersey		-	18	-
It:	3 yrds ¼ of liver cullered half thick		-	18	-
It:	5 yrds ½ of red Searge		2	4	-
It:	1 yrd 3/4 of thick kersey		-	17	-
It:	1 yrd 3/4 of kersey		-	17	-
It:	8 yrds of Sad cullered Searge		2	10	-
It:	6 yrds of blew peniston		1	10	-
It:	1 yrd 3/4 of Sad cullered kersey		-	17	-
It:	½ yrd of red Searge		-	3	-
It:	¼ yrd of yellow Cotten		-	1	-
It:	3/4 of white flanell		-	2	-
It:	4 yrds 3/4 of linen cloth		-	15	-
It:	3 yrds of Canvas		-	9	-

Item

[In the original volume, the writing on this page is upside down. The inventory which begins on this page concludes on Page 283.]

The Co:rt finde that John Wheeler Francis Sayre and Joshua Horton, (the psons covenanting as afore= =said) are the psons to whome of right ye Sd estate belongeth; of which Sd estate the land (by agreemt of ye Sd psons) is pt, and being valued at fifty pounds belongeth to him ye Sd John Wheeler as pt of his proportion: And the Cort Doth Order that the Sd pties Shall peaceably possess and enjoy the Sd Estate according to theire owne afforesaid - agreemt: disstribution and possession thereof for themselves and theire heyres for ever; They or Some of them putting in Security to ye Corts Sa= =tisfaction, to Save the Co:rt harmeless: And the Sd John Wheeler haveing rec:d a double pro= =portion of ye Sd Estate, Is to defray the one halfe of ye charges of ye Co:rt & fees: and the other two psons Namely ffrancis Sayre & Joshua Horton to pay the other halfe: onely at prsent ffrancis Sayre to pay & disscharge the last Said half, & Joshua to Satisfy him, for his pt thereof: the Sume they are to - pay is 20s towards ye publique wth ye fees - allowed by the law: /

At a Co:rt of ye Comissioners of the three Townes held by his Ma:ties Authority in Southampton: february ye 4: 1673.

Whereas the Sd Co:rt hath Ordered mee John Wheeler, My brother ffrancis Sayre and My brother Joshua Horton to possess and enjoy the land & goods of my Mother deceased (& dyed intestate) according to an agreement made Mutually by us about it: Know all men by theise prsents, That I John Wheeler of Easthampton Doe hereby binde my Self my heyres Executors and Administrators unto the Sd Co:rt in the Sume of two hundred poundes to Save harmeless the Sd Co:rt in there Said act or Order whereby wee come Lawfully to bee possessed of the Said Estate, witnes my hand the Day and yeare above written

In prsence of — John Wheeler
Henry Peirson
Zorobabell Phillips/

A true Coppy p me
Henry Peirson Cleark

[In the original volume, the writing on this page is upside-down.]

At a Co:rt held by his Ma:ties Authority in
Southampton by the Comissioners of ye three
Townes on ye East End of this Long Island.

Was presented unto the Co:rt the Inventory of ye esta[te]
of mris: Alice Stanborough of Easthampton whoe
dyed Intestate. Alsoe a firme agreement in
writeing, betweene her children, Manifesting
theire Mutuall consent in the devission or distri
=bution of the Sd Estate amongst themselves to
theire full and finall Satisfaction for ever
to prvent all molestation each of other about
amy pt of the Sd Estate or ye Said devision thereof
A true Coppy of which Sd agreement
is as followeth:

Whereas the Widdow Stanborough is lately
deceased And there is not will to bee found -
for the present Wee John Wheeler ffrances
Sears and Joshua Horton have devided the
goods left by her to our Satisfaction: ye goods
Devided between us, is Such as was prized
according to ye Inventory. And John Wheeler
is to pay Such debts as Shee owed, And Such
Debts as was due to her, hee is to have.
And if at any time hereafter ther bee a
Will found, yet Notwithsatnding wee Doe
engage our Selves our heyres and Assignes
each to other to Stand to the Devission - -
made between us: Alsoe wee doe ingage
never to Mollest each other, or any by, from
or in our names Shall Mollest each other. - -
And for the true pformance of our engagemt
to Each other, Wee have hereunto Sett our
handes at Easthampton this 9th of Janr:
1673. Memorandum, the goods above
mencioned is to bee understood to bee land
and goods left by the deceased and devided -
betweene us:

John Wheeler
Francis Sears
Joshua Horton

Signed Sealed in
the presence of us
Samuell Mulford
Enoch ffithian

the Co:rt

[In the original volume, the writing on this page is upside-down.]

This Indenture made the ninteenth day of May in the third year of the Reigne of our Sovereigne Lord James ye Second by the grace of god of England Scotland france and Ireland King defender of the faith &c and In ye yeare of our Lord God one thousand six hundred Eighty Seven Between Cachegon Sacham Pamequage Cayeton Pumshan Quoringe John Mahue will Peipe Massatuse Jerimy Goodier wawashaquahauge and Catchawahtow Indians propriators of all the unpurchased Lands upon the north Side of LongIsland within the towneship of Brookhaven of the one parte and Samuell Eburne of Brookhaven aforesd Clark of the other parte Wittnesseth that whereas ye Inhabetants of the Said towne of brookhaven did on the three and twentyeth of november in the first year of the Reigne of our Sovereigne lord and In the year of our Lord God one thousand Six hundred Eighty five Amongst other things freely and Cleerly give and grant unto the Said Samuell Eburne all that Island of meadow Lying and being between the little neck & old feild being the midlemost Island next to the wood Island To have and To hold all and Every the Said Island of meadow together withall the privilledges and Appurtenances to the Same belonging or In anywise Apertaining to him the Said Samuell Eburne his heyres Assignes there Sole and proper use and behoofe for Ever as by the Said grant Remaining upon the Records of the Said Towne of brookhaven doth and may more at Large apeare And whereas his Excellency Thomas dongan Capt generall governer In Cheife and vise Admirall in and over the province of new york and territorys thereon depending in America under his Sacred Majestye aforesd did on the Seven and twentieth day of december in the Second year of the Reigne of our Said Sovereigne Lord by vertue of the Comission and Authority from his most Sacred Majestye aforesd and the power In him Resideing amongst other things give grant release and Con firme unto the Said Samuell Eburne his heyres and Asignes three - Islands of meadow or beds of Creek thatch Sittuate In Seatallcott where of two Lying between the old feild beach and the little neck and the other beetween the old feild and little neck in all Containg thirty Acres or ther aboutes and another percell of meadow in the old mans harbour not Exceeding twenty Acres together withall the profitts benifitts Comoditys hereditaments and Apurtenances to the premises belonging or In any wise Apertaining to have and To hold the Said Islands and meadows and premises withall and Singuler the Apurtenances to the Said Samuell Eburne his heyres and Assignes for Ever To the only proper use and behoofe of the Said Samuell Eburne his heyres and Assignes for Ever to bee holden of his most Sacred majestye his heyres and Successors in free and Comon Soccage according to the ten nure of East greenwich In the Contrey of kent in his majes tyes kingdome of England as by a certaine deed or patent Sealed with the Seale of the province and recorded In the Secretarys office at newyork Relation being thereunto had doth and may more at Large apeer Now this Indenture further witt nesseth that the Said Catchegon pamequage Cayeton pumshan Quoring John Mahue will peip Massatuse Jerimy goodyer

Wawassaquahegue and Catchawtow Indians for divers good Causes & Considerations them and Each of them thereunto moveing and more Especially for and in Consideration of the Sum of fifteen pounds Curant
to them the Said Indians in hand paid by the Said Samuell Eburne
money of this province ^ the receipt whereof they doe hereby aknow ledge and them Selves and Each of them therewith to bee fully Satis fied Contented and payd and thereof and of Every parte and percell thereof doth by these presents accquitt and discharge the Said Samuell Eburne his heyres Executors Administrators and Assignes for ever have given grantted Released and Confirmed and doe by these presents doe give grant Release and Confirme unto the Said Samuell Eburn his heyres and Assignes all the before recited Islands and meado =dow and premisses together withall the privilledges and Appur tenances thereunto belonging or In any wise Apertaining to have and To hold the aforesd Islands and meadow and all the other the Sd premises to him the Said Samuell Eburne his heyres and Assignes for Ever to the only proper use benefit and behoofe of the Said Samuell Eburne his heyres and Assignes for Ever and the Sd Cachegon pamequage Cayetan pumshan Quoring John Mahue will peip Massatuse Jerimy goodyer - wawassaquahague and Catchewatow Indians for themselves there heyres Successors and Assignes and Each of them his heyres Successors and Assignes and Each of them doth here by Covenant and promis to and with the Said Samll Eburne his heyres and Assignes and Each of them that he the Said Samuell Eburne his heyres and Assignes Shall and may Choose the aforesd - twenty Acres of meadow at ye old mans in any parte or place of the unpurchased Islands of meadow there: and that the Said Islands and premises and Each of them are free & Cleer and freely and Cleerly aquitted Exonorated and discharg ed of and from all former and other gifts grants bargains Sales or other titles or In Combrances whatsoever had made or Comitted at any time or times heretofore In wittness where of the Said partyes have hereunto Sett there hands and Seals at brookhaven the day and year first above written

Sealed and delivered	Catchegon \ Seachem	John Mahue Y
In the presence	wawasquaheag B	peip B
of the Said Indians	Cayeton X	Jerimy J
being all Sober &	pumshan +	Sombombon
no wayes over=	Qoring O	Massatuse ~
taken with drink	Catchawatow	Goodier ^
John Tucker	Nawsouces O	
Andrew Gibb		
Tom T frances Interpreter		

A true Coppy p John Howell Clark §
January the 17 1687 8

At a Courte of Sessions held Southampton March ye
15 1686 7 1686 7 was presented the Inventory of Nat
=thaniell baker of East hampton whoe died Sudinly: In
testate: also the widow Elizabeth baker presented a
peticon to Administer upon her husbands Estate which was
accordingly granted: giveing in Security: which Shee hath
done: the Inventory is as followeth

Inventory of the Estate of nathaniell baker of -
East hampton Deceased as was taken and aprized by benja
min Conklin and Samuell fithien upon ther oaths the
13 day of March 1687 8

Imprs 2 oxen 7£) 5 Cows 34s pp: 8:10 22s pp	15	10	-
3 three yearolds at 30s pp: 4£:10:) 8 twoyearolds 8:16)	13	6	-
4 Calves or Yearlings 11s pp	2	4	-
2 horses 4£:5s) 27 Sheep 5s p head 6:15s	11	-	-
7 Swine 35s: 5 pigs 5s	2	-	-
2 mares and a two yearling horse in the woods	3	5	-
a Carte plow & waynage	3	10	-
Spade how and old hatchets	-	11	-
An Indian Captive Servant not prized)			
because his time not knowne)			
a Sarge Sute vallued at	1	14	-
a homspon Coate and a hat: vallued at	-	10	-
	53	=10	=0

p us Benjamin Conkling
Samuell fithian

At a Courte of Sessions held at Southold october the
20 1687: was presented An Inventory of the goods
of Nathaniell domony: with a piticon for his wife to
Administer: which was granted giveing Security: which
Capt Hubert hath taken and Returned to the office
the Inventory and Aprizment follows

An Inventory of the Estate of nathaniell
=Dommony of Easthampton Deceased as it was
taken this 18th Day of July 1687 by us Henry Ludlam
and Josiah Hubert: (turn over)

Imprs one old Cow and a thre yearold heifer and a threeyearold bull vallued	)	4	10	-
two Cattle 2yearold		2	-	-
a ½ a bull of fouryearold & 2 yearlings		2	10	-
one mare and a 2 yearling mare Coult		5	-	-
2 Sheep 10s: 3 Swine 20s		1	10	-
Carte wheeles & plow with Chaynes & yoaks		2	10	-
2 axes a how and a Spade		-	12	-
his wareing Aparrell		1	10	-
a feather bed & boulster with furneture with other blankets & homspon Covering	)	4	10	-
2 Large Iron pots & 1 kettle		2	5	-
a Small Iron pott & kettle 10s		-	10	-
3 Small brass kettles a Skellet & puter		1	10	-
4 pr of home Spun Sheets vallued at		2	-	-
1 musket vallued at		-	15	-
2 Chests with boules & bukets & tubs and other Lumber in the house	)	2	-	-
		33	=12	-0

This Inventory was taken the
Day abovesd by us

Josiah Hubert
Henry Ludlam

At a Courte of Sessions holden at Southold octo=ber the 21 1684 was presented the will of thomas prickman which was accordingly proved: but whereas he mad his wife Executor and Shee being now besides her under Standing and not Capable of Executing the Same this Courte doth order and apoint Stephen bayly thomas Mapes Senr & thomas maps Junr and Jonathan Horton to be Executors In trust to Said will of thomas prickman and are Impowered by this Courte to put out the Child to John tuthill untill Shee is Eighteen years old and to use the best discresion in referance to widow and Relict of the Said prickman who being voyd in Some measure of her reason and under Standing & in Capable of managing the afaire of an Executrix and further they are to take an acompt of the Estate and to Returne an Inventory thereof And aprizment to the next Court of Sessions to be held at Southampton in ordr to ye

Satisfation of

of the Crediters and Comfortable Subsistance of the widow and
Child and the Requisitt Charges to be Satisfied out of the Said Estate

the Last will and testament of the Said thomas prickma[n]

Suffolk Southold Sept ye 23: 1684

whereas I thomas prickman find myself very
weak in body not knowing how Soon it may pleas ye
Lord to remove me from this Earthly Stage from ye Land
of the Living I am willing to dispose of that Small estate
what god hath bestowed upon me as followeth

Imprs I doe first will and bequeath unto my well beloved Daughter
Deliverance prickman that percell of Land which I pur
Chased of John Swazey Senr which is all the Right that Said Swazey
had in Calves neck and one Cow now in my possession
and a Sow that is big with pig alsoe a flock bed and bed=
Steed three blanckets and a Coverled and two pewter
platters: and two quarts potts pewter: and one halfe
pinte pewter pott also: 2 pewter porringers and one
two Ear=ed Cup with my bible and all the Rest of my
books one Small trunk with two Chests one box one Iron
pott and one Iron kettle allsoe one paire of Sheets one boul
Ster and two feather pillows and between thirty &
forty pounds of feathers now in my owne possession all
and Every parte to be Delivered to her when Come
to ye age of Eighteen years or the day of mariage with
the full Increas of the Cow and the Sow: that is to Say
when keeping paid of Said Creatures which is to be
allowed out of the Encrease= but if Should please god to
take her away by death before Come of age or maried
then all to Returne to my beloved wife

Secondly I doe make my beloved wife my Sole Executrix of
all my debts due by book and all other visable Estate
Except what before bequeathed and my Said Execu
trix to pay all Just debts thus haveing disposed of my
Small Estate I bequeath my body to ye Earth and my
Soule to god: to ye Confirmation of this written
will and my Last testament I doe hereunto Sett
my hand and fix my Seale this 23d: of Septr in ye year
1684:

Signed Sealed In ye presence of us — Thomas his P mark prickman

Jonathan Horton)
Stephen bayley) both Sworne at the aforesd Court

the Inventory follows: Turn: over

An Inventory of the Estate of Thomas prickman
who deceased 28th day of September 1684

Imprs	6: blanketts one old Coverled 2 feather pillows one feather bed leather one flock bed	6	–	–
It	2 paire of Sheets & pewter her parte	1	5	–
It	brass and Iron	5	10	–
It	Earthen ware and glass bottles	–	14	–
It	tin ware	–	6	–
Itt	wooden bowle dishes trenchers and payles	1	10	–
Itt	Chests tables bedsteds fourmes and Chayres	3	–	–
Itt	one gun and belt 20s Itt: old Caske 20s	2	–	–
Itt	homspone Cloath and linin Cloath	4	–	–
Itt	Indian Leather and wareing Cloaths	4	19	–
Itt	Sheepskins and Rackons	–	8	–
Itt	29 gallans of Rum	5	–	–
Itt	one horse and one Swine & wampom	3	9	–
Itt	one Spade beetle Rings and wedges	–	11	–
	all as money	38	=12	=0

Deliverances part as the will derects

Imprs	one bed 3 blankets one boulster) 2 pillows one paire of Sheets a Cover)	3	–	–
Itt:	pewter 24s) 2 Chests 1 box) 1 little trunk 16s)	2	–	–
Itt	one Iron pott 1 Iron kettle	–	12	–
Itt	bookes: 20s: one Cow one Swine 3£	4	–	–
Itt	68 pound of feathers	3	–	–
	all as money	12	=12	=0

thomas mapes
Jonathan Horton
Thomas Mapes Junr
Stephen Bayley

APPENDIX

Liber A of Deeds

[Page 3] In the name of amen I Thomas Mapes Senr of Southold in the y^{e} County [of] Suffolk on LongIsland in the province of Newyork in America finding my Selfe very weak in body body but of perfect memory & sound minde am willing to Dispose of my Estate as followeth: first I bequeath my Soule to god y^{t} gave it and my body to y^{e} dust and deceantly buried &c:

first I give and bequeath to my beloved wife Sary my house and house lott in y^{e} towne withall the accomadations belonging to it in the old bounds of the towne (Except four Acres of upland Adjoyning to y^{e} Lane or high=way that goeth into the Cal[]=neck alsoe Except one Lott of the Last Devition of upland in y^{e} old bounds of Towne and one Lott of Comonage all which is Soe Excepted is to be given to my Son Thomas Mapes: Alsoe I give to my wife that meadow Called and knowne by the nam of the Little meadow at accobauge alsoe on percell of medow on the South Side the deep Creek at occobauge and two Shares of ye meadow on the South Side the great River at accobauge all and Every parte before Exprest: Except what is Excepted to my wife Dureing her naturall life and then to Returne to my youngest Son Jonathan Mapes alsoe I give to my wife all my household goods moveable goods Swine and Cattell of all Sorts Except what shall be here after disposed off by this my will but after my wife dye and not dispose of what goods and Cattells I have bequeathed to her as afores^{d} then after her decease my will is that ye Cattle is then left Shall be devided Amongst my Sons and what houshold goods is then Left Shall be devided Amongst my Daughters

2^{ly} I give and bequeath to my Eldest Son Thomas Mapes all y^{e} Land & y^{e} [ ] now In his possession at Carchauge that is to Say the Lott where his Dwelling house now Standeth witha second lott on y^{e} north side the high=way Excepting fifty Acres to be given to my daughter Sary also I give my Son Thomas Mapes that four Acres of Land Excepted in y^{e} first Article and one Lott of upland in the old bounds of the towne lying beyond y^{e} Inlett in the Last devission also on Lott of Comonage in the towne plott or old bounds and alsoe halfe that devistion of upland and meadow on the west Side of Mattituck=Creek with my meadow In the great meadows at Carchauge and also my Creekthatch Layd out in the Last devition in Carchaug bounds and a th[ ] Lott Share in the meadows on the South Side the great River at accobauge

Thirdly I give and bequeath to my Second Son william Mapes all the accomadations now In his possession that is to say the house and the house lott [ ] fifty Acres alsoe I give him my lott of upland on y^{e} north Side y^{e} high=way over against ye fort=neck the Land of thomas Thomas Tusteen on y^{e} East [ ] land of Jeremy veale on the west with my meadow on y^{e} north side [ ] deep=Creek and halfe my meadow at the Sawmill Creek In accobauge [ ]itions also a Second lott Share of meadow at y^{e} Southside y^{e} great River at Accobaug with one Eight parte of that lott of upland and [ ] on the west Side mattituck Creek also I give him one yoak of oxen [ ] William is to allow his mother a fixt parte of the produce of all [ ]proved Lands During her Life or widowhood./

[ ]rthly I give and bequeath to my Son Jabesh Mapes all my land at Nab[ ] or Matituck houses withall the meadow Adjoyning to it alsoe one Lott of Land on the northside the highway against the [ ] Carchauge [ ] Land of Christopher youngs on the west alsoe I [ ] my meadow at peconeck on the north Side ye great River [ ] Sawmill brook and a Second lott Share on the S[ ] Accobauge alsoe one Eight parte of my lott of m[ ] west Side of Mattituck Creek alsoe one yoak of

[The remainder of this will and the inventory are on pages which have not survived.]

[Page 4] An Inventory of ye Estate of Jerimy Vale who Deceased May the [-] 1687

Imp[rs] house barne and Lands	£
Itt: Neat kinde 12£ Itt Sheep 6£:10s horse kind 50s)	21 0 0
Item Swine 3 pound: 2 feather beds 2 boulster pillows 5£)	08 0 0
Itt: 5 blankets 2 old Coverlids 20s four Sheets & other linning 30s)	02 10 0
Item pewter and brass 2£: Itt: 1 Iron kettle & pot & hakes 20s	03 00 0
Itt bedsteads table Chayres and other Lumber	1 00 0
the totall is=	35 10 0

The Last will and Testament of me Thomas Chatfeild Sen[r] of Easthamp[ton] In Suffolk County of newyork Colloney being of perfect minde and understanding as followeth I give my Soule to god that gave it & my body to ye Dust and my estate as followeth

first I give to my Eldest Thomas my house and all my land at home the houseing stands upon, alsoe I give him my land upon the mill plaine being about ten or 11 Acres alsoe my devission of Land Lying Norwest from ye towne being abo[ut] thirty five Acres alsoe I give him all my meadow Land at ye norwest alsoe my will is that my Son thomas Shall provide due maintenance for his mother Soe Long as Shee Liveth if god take mee Away before her alsoe my will is this my Son Shall allow and give to his fowre Sisters of my daughters after his mothers decease ten pounds to Each of them In Comon pay or five pounds A peice In money also provided that this my Son Thomas Shall not at any time Charge my Son John his brother any thing for Any work or other wise he hath done towards the building of the house for his brother aforesaid - Also I give this my Son thomas the one halfe of the Comonage belongs to me both at the towne and montauket also about three Acres of the Last deviston Lying between Cap[t] talmage and m[r] bakers /

2[ly] I give to my Son John the house Eastward of the towne and all the Land or Allottment it Stands upon being Sixteen Acres of land more or Less also I give him all the Land belongs to ye Swamp without ye fence both upland and Meadow Reaching from the ditch Lying beyond Samuell Sherryes to ye Rear End of Enock fithians home Lott and Arther Creasseys home Lott together with a peice of land of mine Lyeth between Enock fithian and Arthur Cresseys home Lott also I give him a peice of Land aboute four Acres Lying at a place Called Lilly hill alsoe I give this my Son John a peice of Land Lying upon the Easterne playne lying between Cap[t] Talmage and Robert Dayton being nine Acres alsoe I give him A peice of Land Lying at ye two myle hollow lying between John kirle and Nathaniell Dominys lott: being ten Acres and a halfe also I give him ye peice of Land Layd out this Last devission Lying withinthe fence East ward being fifteen Acres also I give my Son John all my meadow at accobanak neck Lying between Jo[-] Parsons deceased and Jer: Conklins alsoe I give him all that peice of meadow Lying in the great meadow at accobanak Richard Shaw being on that Side of it next the hamuck: also I give him all my meadow at Napeak and half my Comonag both at ye Towne and montauket alsoe I give my Son John my plow and Cart yoke and Chaynes and all tackling belongs to my teame also one fether bed and the furneture belonging to it. /

3ly I give to my foure Daughters Anne wife of Josiah Stanbrough Elizabeth wife of Edward Joanes Sarah and Mary all my moveable goods both within [Page 5] Doors and without Save what I give afore to my Son John) to be Equally between these my daughters Aforesd /

4 - I Apointe my Son Thomas to be Executor of this my will and testement

5 - I desire John Mulford Jun[r] Benjamin Shaw and m[r] Thomas James to be overseers of this my will for the Due performance thereof to be Satisfied for what Just time they may Spend upon this account out of the Estate I Shall Leave and for the firm Confirmation of this my will and testament I Sett to my hand and Seale this twenty second of Ju[-] Anno Dom: 1686. / Thomas Chatfeild

Signed and Sealed in the presence of us.
Thomas James
Thomas Harress
Benjamin osborne

This will and testament was presented to this Courte of Sessions now sitting In Southold this 20th Day of october 1687 and the will proved by the Evedences Sworne In Courte name[ly] Thomas Harress and benjamin Osborne and the Said Thomas Chatfeild is Confirmed Executor

thereunto according to ye will of the testator here in Specified
A true Coppy p John Howell Clark §

An Inventory of the Estate Moveable of the Late Deceased Thomas Chatfeild of Easthampton

to 2 oxen 5£ 10s to five four yearold Steers 11£:5s	16 15 0
to 5 ditto 3 yearold 8£ to nine 2 yearold 10£:16s	18 16 0
to Six one yearolds at 4£:10 to Six Calves 1£:16s	06 06 0
to one bull 3 yearold 25s two three yearold heyfers 2£:15	04 00 0
to 6 Swine great & Small 2£:5: to Sheep & lambs 33) 6£:5	08 10 0
to bed ticking 42s:to 3 old feather pillows 7s:6: a remn[t] homspon Cloath 3 yards5s)	02 14 6
to 4 yards duffles 14s) 2 paire of Sheets and one pillow beer 21s	01 15 0
to 1 pillow 2s:6:) one old bed & boulster 35s) 1 rug & 2 Coverleds 2£	03 17 6
to ditto beds & boulster 1£:16s:6) old hanging 14s) 5 old brass kettles 5£ 17s	08 07 6
to brass morter & warming pan 8s: to 3 brass old Candlesticks 3s	00 11 0
to 2 Iron potts 12s to 2 Iron kettles 18s to 21£ of pewter 25s	02 15 0
to one quarte peweter pott and Cup 5s6 to Some old pewter 2s	00 7 6
to old Spitts & tramills 5s to 2 ox Chaines & one hors ditto 10s:6	00 15 6
to one old Spade & old tooles & old Iron 7s) to 40£ of whalebone 13s:4	01 04 0
to 4 old blankets 12s: one harrow 10s: one broken bible & 2 Small book 2s:6)	1 00 0
to 2 more old books 6s: to old axes & Iron wedges 4s: to Irons for plow & Carte 21s	1 11 0
to one old Small table 2s to old lumber within doors 21s:6d	1 3 6
to old plate 18s to boston money 5s to two peices of 8: 12s	1 15 0
Totall is	98 3 10

Surveyed and Aprized the
22[d] of this Instant october 1687 A true Coppy p John Howell Clark
by us heer Subscribed: -

An Inventory and Aprizement of the Estate zerobabell phillips of Southampton Late Deceas[d] In the County of Suffolk in the province of newyork: taken by us Jo[hn] Jessup John Howell Jun[r] and Samuell Johns who were Sworne therunto before Major Howell this tenth day of october 1687

Ittem: 2 oxen 7£:10: 2 Steers 4£:10 three Cows 6£:10) 3 heifers 4£	22 10 0
to one yearling bull & a yearling Steer 40s 3 horse: 7£ =10	09 10 0
5 Shotes 2£: and 8 Sheep 2£: a feather bed and furneytur: a boulster rug 2 Sheets a blanket and pillows and Curtaines 7=10	11 10 0
[Page 6]	
his wareing Apparrell Sword and belt 4£:15s old table Cloath & 6 old napkins 9s	5 4 0
Itt 2 old Course table Cloaths ½ duzen of Napkins 8s: three payre of Sheets: 4 of y^m old 35s	2 3 0
to a Small featherbed boulster old rugg & old Sheets with another p[r] of old Sheets & bedsted	3 0 0
a great Chayre and a Chest 8s to 4£ of wooll 2s:6 Indian Corne 2:12s:6	3 3 0
a Cubert and 2 Chests 2£: ten platters Sum of them old 25s: to pots basons flagon and other pewter	4 10 0
a great old brass kettle 35s a Spitt and old hows & warming pan & Churne 11s	2 6 0
to 2 tramills tongues gridIron & peele 11s: to 1 Iron kettle 15 & 3 Small Iron potts 18s	2 4 0
to 2 brass pans 28s 2 little brass Scellets: a little kettle 1=2	2 10 0
the negroes beding and bedsted 20s: 2 Chests 2 Seives a Cream pot 13s	1 13 0
2 bags 4s: an Iron kettle 9s Sadle pillion & Cho[-]h all old 10s	1 3 0
three tables &c: 30s and Chayrs ten Shillings to a Negro woman 20£	22 0 0
plow and Cart tackling and harrow &c	2 5 0
Sithes and grindston 2 old Axes & y^e Spade 15s the hay 50s a p[r] of andirons 12s	3 17 0
forks beetle and wedg, 1 old mattuk 5s: a Small brass morter and Lanthorne 6s:6	0 11 6
to 4 pillow beers 9s a wicker Chayre & Sicles 7s y^e lumber	

in y^e house 5s 1 1 0

98=18=0

the Afores[d] Inventory is taken and Aprized by us according to money the tenth Day of october 1687 Attest our hands John Jessup John Howell Jun[r] Samuell Johnes At a Courte of Session held at Southold october the 19th 1687 was by martha phillips Relict to ye Said zerobabell phillips the Aforesd Inventory presented with a peticon to Admister there upon without giveing bond for the Same which was accordingly granted to Letter of Administration to Adminis thereon according to Law:

Atrue Coppy p John Howell Clark §

In the Name of god Amen I John Teed of huntington on LongIsland being Sick of body but of perfect memory have made this my Last will and Testament In maner and form following first I bequeath my Soule to god my maker and Redeemer and My body to ye Earth from whence I was [-] Item I give and bequeath unto my Son John all that Land that Lyeth on ye Norwest Side of James Chichester Jun[r] when he hath accomplished ye age of one and twenty: Except two Acres of that Land which I Leave to my wife[ ] use and behoofe to dispose off Item I give and bequeath to my two Sons Benjamin and Joseph all that percell of Land at ye Cove and my parte of meadow on the west neck both Land and meadow to be equally devided between them when they accomplish the age of one and twenty years Item all the Rest of my Cattle goods Lands and meadows I give and bequeath to my Loveing wife goods and Cattells to be at her use and dispossall with thirds of my orchard home lott and Lands undevided with my meadow at the halfe neck but the other two parts of house orchard home lott Lands undevided I give unto my Son John after his mothers decease paying unto all my daughters that then are alive four pounds a peice: for Seeing the performance afore Specified I Leave to my Loveing wife which I make my Sole Executrix to See this my Last will and testament performed In wittnes whereof I have here unto Sett my hand this 25 of october in the 35th year of his Majestys Reigne and In the year of our lord 1683 John

Signed and published in the presence of John Teed

Sarah Sopper Joseph Bayley

[Page 7] At a Court of Sesion held at Southampton March 16 1683 4 the within being presented but not proved at this Courte for want of one of ye wittnese Subscribed but is by the Courte Referr[d] till the Justices Some time in [-] next Shall Come there for the profe thereof m[r] Joseph bayly and m[r] Joseph whit[ ] of the Said Towne to be Aprizers of Said Estate p ord[r] of Courte

Memorandum

That on the 6th Day of September 1687 Apeared Before us Cap[t] Joseph bailey and Sarah the wife of Henry Sooper wittneses to the within written will and Testament and made oath that they Saw John Teed Subscrib and publish the Same as his Last will and Testament and was Soe proved before us according to the Above order of Courte the Day and yeare afores[d]. /

At a Courte of Sessions held at Southold october ye the 18th: 1687 was Returned the Afores[d] will and Testament where the Said probates was Exepted and the widow Confirmed Executor. /

Test Is[a] Arnold §
[ ] Coram
Epenetus Platt

A true Coppy p John Howell Clark §

Easthampton May ye 24th: 1687 An Inventory of the Estate of John Osborne Deceased who dyed May ye 2[d] 1687.

Itt by pewter 12s by Iron and brass 30s	2 2 0
Itt by beding 5£ by Lumber in ye house 2£	7 0 0
These perticulers wer Aprized by us John Wheeler Samuell persons	
Itt by one ox 3£ by 2 Small oxen 5£ by nine Cows 17£	25 0 0
Itt by Seven three yearold 10£:10s by Eight 2 yearolds 8£	18 10 0
Itt by Seven yearlings 5£5s by an old horse 2£: a mare 2£	09 05 0
Itt by thirty five Sheep 8£:15s by Swine 1£:10	10 05 0
These above perticulers were prized by us Totall	72 02 0

John Wheeler Samuell persons
the Above Inventory was presented to ye Courte of Sessions holden at Southold the 18th 19: days of october 1687 with a peticon for the Relict of the Said John osborne namly Mariam osborne to Administer there upon which was granted to her giveing In Security according to Law which shee Hath accordingly done

A true Coppy p John Howell Cl[ark]

Articles of agreement made and had this Eight Day of february in fourth year of our Sovereigne Lord James the Second over England Scottland france and Ireland King $Defend^r$ of the faith &c and In y^e year of our Lord 1687/8 between Joshua Silvester Late of Shelter Iland now of Southold In the County of Suffolk on Long Island in the province of New york on y^e one parte and Isaac Arnold of the towne and County $afores^d$ one y^e other parte Wittnesseth as followeth

Imprimis that the Said Joshua Silvester Shall assigne Seale and Deliver unto the Said Isaac Arnold one firme deed of writing whereby he Shall Assigne
[Page 8] over unto him the Said Arnold all his now vissible Estate that is belonging unto the Said Joshua Sylvester and as it now Lyeth in Lands and meadows upon Shelter Island in the province of new york afforesaid and In debts and moneys Scattered In the hands of any person or persons who Soever to be Received by the Said Isaac Arnold and by him to be made use of for the Comfortable Maintenance and Suport of the Said Joshua Sylvester Dureing his Life as in Said Deed of writing and in the following Article Shall be more at Large Specyfied Declard and Restrained hereby Revoking Nulling and makeing voyd and Null all former Act and acts Will & Wills Deed of Gift or gifts Covayances and all other writeings Instruments what Soever and more Especially one writeing made In y^e Costody of Grissell the wife of James Loyd of Boston $March^t$ somtime In June past in the year of our Lord 16<u>87</u> which In Sicknes I passed without Consideration or Advice

Secondly That the Said Isaac Arnold Shall maintaine the Said Joshua Silvester as well In Sicknes as In health and In Such maner as he hath been formerly maintaind withall Sutable meat drink washing Lodging and houshold accomadations whatsoever according to ye age and Quallyty of Said Joshua Silvester and with Suitable Respect & usage that the Said Joshua Silvester Doe and will allow unto the Said Isaac Arnold (for his yearly Maintenance) from year to year and Every year that y^e Said Joshua Sylvester Shall Live the full and Just Sum of thirty pounds Currant money with y^e $March^{:ts}$ if god Shall Soe order that y^e Said Isaac Arnold Shall Departe this Life before the Said Joshua Silvester that the the Rest of the Said Joshua Silvesters Estate Not Soe Expended in his yearly maintenance as aforesd Shall Returne unto the Said Joshua Silvester for his further and future mantenance and what then there of hee Shall Dye Seized off Shall by the Last will and Testament or other wise be Equally Devided between the female Chilldren that Shall be then Liveing of his brother Capt Nathaniell Silvester Deceased and of Said Isaac Arnold Each one her Equal parte m^{rs} grissell Loyd Excepted: but if god Soe order it that the Said Joshua Silvester Shall Departe this Life before the Said Isaac Arnold: then what Estate Shall be and Remaine he [-] first order and give the Said Isaac Arnold out of it one pps of Plate of Six pounds vallue and if the Said Jshua Silvester Shall Dye possest of a negro be it man or woman then that ye Said Negro Shall goe unto Said Arnold as his proper Estate and to his use and disposall for Ever and then the Rest of of Such His Estate Shall bee Equally Devided as Aforesd Between the Daughters of his Said brother and Cousen Isaac Arnold Except grissill the wife of James Loyd who at his Death when Ever it Shall happen is to have one pps of Gold of twenty Shillings vallue: and the Daughters of Said Arnold in Equall parts as is before Expressed

Quarto and the Said Joshua Silvester Shall forthwith after the Ensealing of these Articles Shall make a firme and Irrevocable Letter of Atturney fully Impowering the Said Isaac Arnold In his name & Stead to Recover and Receive all his Said Estate from all persons in all places what Soever

Quinto that the Said Joshua Sylvester and Isaac Arnold Shall upon the Sealling of these Articles pass to Each other one firme obligation [-]
[Page 9] Bond for the vallue of five hundred pounds of Currant money of this province

for the well and true performance of all and of all these articles and of Ev[ery] parte and perticuler thereof faithfully and Inviolably to be Observed for E[ver]

Sexto and Lastly That the partys aboves[d] Doe mutually agree and Resolve th[ ] these Articles and all other writteings Assignements bonds and Conclussions bee all owned before Authority and Leagally acknowledged there: and alsoe to be Leagally and Authenticky Recorded as the Laws of this province [-] Require and derect In Confirmation of thse promises the partyes ab[ ]Sayd doe Mutually putt to ther hands and Seales the Day and year Afores[d] Joshua Sylvester
Signed Sealed and Delivered Is[a:] Arnold
In the presents of Simon Grover Thomas Longworth Samuell King Thomas Youngs

[Page 12] Know All men by these presents that Richard Brooks of East Hampton in the East Rideing of yorksheire on Long Island for and In Consideration of the Love and Affection that I bear unto my well beloved Son Samuell Brooks have freely given granted alined enfeofed and Confirmed and doe hereby fully freely and absolut[ly] give grant Allien Enfeofe and Confirme unto my Said Son Samuell Brooks my house and home Lott withall other Allottments both of up land and meadow that are already Layd out by the afforesaid towne or that Shall hereafter be Layd out to my afores[d] allotment also my halfe Share of Land and privilledges at montauk withall Libertys privilledges and Apurtenances to the premises or any parte or percell thereof To have and to hold the Afforesd Land & to him the Said Samuell Brooks and to his heyres for Ever [in] fee Simple: and I doe for my Selfe my heyre Executor Admin[-] or Assignes warrant and Confirme this my deed of gift against all & any person or persons which Shall Lay Claime to y[e] Same or any parte or percell thereof Either by from or under mee- the Said Rich[d] Brooks or my heyres Executors Adm[rs] or Assignes Excepting only from this Deed whatsoever Lands meadows or privilligde I have granted and given unto my Son John Brooks as p deed of gift bearing date y[e] tenth Instant february may apear and it is to be under Stood and Allways provided that this foresaid Land and all the above Demised premises Shall Remaine and be for the proper use of my Selfe and wife for our Necessary maintenance Soe Long as both or Either off us Shall Live and not Come In to the hands and possession of my Said Son Samuell b[-] untill after both our Deaths and for Sure & certaine performance of this my my deed I doe hereunto Set my hand and Affix my Seale this twelfe Day of february Anno Dom 1680 81
Richard Brooks
Signed Sealed and Delivered
[Page 13] and Delivered In the presence of Josaih Hubert Th Shaw
The trueth of the Above written deed of gift was acknowledged by the above Said Richard Brooks March the tenth 168[-] Before mee John Topping Justice
A true Coppy p John Howell Clark §

To all Christian people to whom these presents Shall Come Richard Brooks of Easthampton on Long Island Send Greeting Know yea that whereas I have formerly made a Convayance or deed of gift unto my Son John Brooks of a Certain percell of Land Lyeing at waynscut in y[e] bounds of Easthampton Containing about 27 Acres be it more or Less bounded with y[e] L[and] of Joseph Straten to the westward and the towne highway to y[e] Eastward [the] beatch to y[e] Southward and Towne Common to y[e] Northward withall Edifices fences privilledges and Appurtenances thereunto belonging also two Acres of meadow at y[e] Northwest Creek Southward of the meadow of m[r] John Mulford together with a halfe Share of Land and privilledges at montauket and halfe my privilledges of the towne Comons heare, which aforesaid Deed of gift was not fully Compleaded according to Law the provedence of god haveing Soe prevented as to take my Said Son out of this Life before the full Confirmation of the afores[d] Deed of gift as the Law Requ[ ] I doe therefore hereby fully freely and Absolutly give grant and Confirm unto my grand Childe John Brooks Son and and heyre to my afores[d] Son John Brooks all and Singuler the afores[d] Lands privilled and pre[ ] To have and To hold all and Singuler the above Lands privilledges Appurtenances and premiss to him and my Said grand Childe John Brooks and his heyres for Ever I Doe hereby warant This my write to him y[e] Said John brooks & his heyres for ever against all and all maner of person or persons that Shall Lay Clayme thereto or any parte or percell thereof by from or under mee or by from or under my Executors Admin^rs or Assignes Soe as the Said John Brooks may at the age of twenty one years possess and Quietly Enjoy the [ ] provided allways that this Deed nor any thing therein Contained Shall Extend or be Construed to Impead or any ways Hinder Hanah the widow or Relict of my aforesd Son John Brooks from the peacable and Quiet possession and Improvement of all the Afores^d Demised premises soe Long as until the years are Expired of my Said Grand Child John Brooks his minorrity or untill he Shall Come to ye age of twenty one years provided alsoe that this Deed nor any thing herein Contained Shall be Construed to ye hindrance of my Son Samuell Brooks and his heyres from being heyre In Reversion unto the above Demised premises In Case my Said grand Child John Brooks Shall dye in nonange or without Issue and for Sure Confirmation of all and Singuler the abovesaid premises I the Said Richard Brooks hereunto Sett my hand

be it knowne alsoe that In Consideration my Son Samuell brooks is [Page 14] Constrained to pay both for the patent (my proportion and other Charges with Respect to my Comonage both in the towne and montaukut: I the aforesaid Richard Brooks Doe grant give and bestow upon my Son Samuell afores^d my whole Comonage both at ye towne and montauket untill Such time as my grand child John brookes Shall Come to ye age of 21 yeares and that without Mollestation from any psons but when my Grandchild John aforesaid Shall Come to age then to have the free and full possession of the one halfe of all my Comonage as is afore expresed and for the full and firm Confirmation of all this writeing aboves^d I Set to my hand and fix my Seale this 26: of May Anno Dom: 1687 Richard RB Brooks
Signed & Sealed In ye presence of us his mark
Thomas Edwards Enock Fithian
A true Coppy p John Howell Clark §

November the 20th in the year of our Lord 1686 being the Last will & testament of the widow Susanah Clark Relict of Samuell Clark deceased: being very weak but haveing my understanding yet and not knowing my Change when it may be doe make this my Last will and testament as followes: 1st I bequeath my Soule to god that gave it mee and after death my body by decent bury[ ] to the Earth and for my worldly Estate which my Husband Left mee and what I have gotten Since I dispose on as followes first I give to my Son Thomas Shaw a Sheep and to my Son benjamin Haynes a Sheep and to my Daughter Mary Clark a Sheep and to my daughter Mary ffordham a Sheepe and to my Son william Mason a Sheep I give my Cuberd to my grand Child phebee Herrik I give unto my Daughter martha burrell my bed and boulster and an Iron kettle and brass kettle and Scellit and pot hanger and my Rugg and a Cow a Sherge gowne & my Rideing hood a pint pot and my flanill westcoate and for my linin I Leave it to my two daughters namly Sarah Clarke and Martha burrell to dispose on as they Soe Cause and for the Rest of my Cattell and Sheep or horse kinde or goods I Leave them with my Son Samuell Clark upon the account of my Liveing with him and of his trouble to bury me and for the Legacys that I was to pay on I have payd out already for I have Maryed two of my Chilldren Since my husbands death as namly Edmond Clark and Sarah Clark the which my husband took Care off and I have given them there portions out when they Marryed according as it was willed to them by ther father and this may Satisfie any if they be on Satisfied how I have disposed of that which my husband Left mee the things above menconed I Leave them in my Son Samuell Clarks hands to give them out as above menconed In wittnes whereof I have hereunto Set my hand and fixed my Seale this twentyeth of november 1686 her
Signed and Sealed in the presence off Sussanah Clark
John Davis Jonathan Davis John Davis Junr mark
this above written was Sworn before mee John Howell Justice
A true Coppy May the 8th 1688 p John Howell Clark §

[Page 15] At a Court of Sessions holden at Southampton March the 21:16[ ] was presented the Last Will and Testament of John Poast of Southampton Deceased and the Same was proved by the oath of two of [-] witneses Subscribed Namely John Laughton and Joseph post: and the widow Mary post Relict to the Said John post is Confirmed Executrix to the Said will: which is Entered as followeth

In the name of god amen I John poast of Southampton In the County of Suffolk in the province of New york on Long[Island] being in my perfect Memory though weak of body Doe make and ordaine this my Last Will and testament in maner and form following first I give and bequeath my Soule to god my Creator and Redeemer and my body after decent buryall to the Earth from whence it was at first taken: Imprimis I give and bequeath unto my Son John post my house and home Stall and all the Land that is mine Adjoyning to it and my Closae at the head of the [Creek] to him and to his heyres for Ever and my fifty pounds Comonage throughout all the bounds of Southampton: 2^{d}: I give unto my Son Jerimiah poast and to his heyres for Ever the house and home Lot of my fathers that hee hath given me and the Cloase that [ ] my fathers between the mill path and Cobs pound path 3dly I give and bequeath unto my Son Richard post and to his heyres for Ever all that my Cloase at the Long Springs and my Acre of Land Lying by it and my fifty pounds allotment of Land at mecocks: and for my hundred and fifty pounds allotment of Land in [ ]neck my will is that it Shall be Equally devided between my three aformenconed Sons as also all my Lands meadows westward of [ ] Conoo place to be Equally devided between the Said three Sons and also all Land in the great plaines belonging to Southampton to be Equally devided amongst my Said three Sons: 4^{th}ly: I give unto my five daughters Namly Mary post Sarah post dorithy post Martha post Deborah post five pounds a peice to be payd unto them at the days of Mariage or when they Shall ataine to the age of Eighteen years which Shall first happen: Lastly I make my beloved wife Mary post Sole Executrix of this my Last will and testament to have and dispose of all and Singuler all the Remainder of my Estate and doe order that my aforemenconed three Sons John Jerimiah and Richard Shall all and Every of them Live and dwell with there Mother till they Shall ataine the age of one and twenty years if Shee Shall Live So Long and that She Shall Live in my lest End of my house and to have the full Comand of it dureing her Life in witnes whereof I have hereunto Set my hand & Seale in Southampton this 9th day of december in the 3^{d} year of the Reigne of our Sovereigne Lord James the Sec[ond] over England Scotland france and Ireland king &c: Annoq Dom: 1687

his
Signed & Sealed in presence of — John IP poast
Joseph Post: John Piny John Laughton — mark

[Page 16] An Inventory of the Estate of John post Late of Southampton deceased taken this 16 day of March Anno Dom: 1687 8

$Impr^{s}$ 2 oxen 6£ 5 Cows 8£:15s) 1 four yearold Come 30s	16 5 0
4: 3yearolds Come 4£:10s) 1:2 yearold Come 15s) 1 yearling 10)	5 15 0
2 horses 5£ one Mare 30s: 27 Sheep 6£:15s) 5 Swine 37s:6d	15 2 6
4 beds and beding being old	10 10 0
pewter dishes & basons pots and Cups & bottles &c	2 10 0
3 brass kettles old and 2 Skellets	2 10 0
5 Iron pots & one Iron kettle	3 00 0
a Negerin	18 00 0
wareing Aparrell	2 15 0
a gun Sword and Halbert	2 00 0
Carpenters tooles	1 10 0
Cart plow and other Husbandry tooles	2 00 0
5 Chests one with Drawers	2 00 0
10 bushells wheat & 5 of Indian Corne	2 05 0
10 bushells of Oats	0 12 6
2 barrells of beef & one of pork	4 10 0

tubs Chayres tables & other Lumber	1 0 0
6 payre of Sheets & other Linin	6 5 0
a tramell tongs and fire Shovell	0 10 0
tin: Jackanaps plate & glass bottles	0 8 0
	99 8 0

Taken and Aprized the under Subscribed this 16 day of march 1687 8
Charles Sturmey thomas Cooper John Laughton

At the Aforesaid Courte holden At Southampton March y[e] 20th 1687 8 was presented the Last will and testament of Josiah Barthollomew of the Said Southampton deceased and the Same was proved by y[e] oaths of the wittneses Subscribed namly John Howell John Mobray and the Said henry willis Confirmed Executor to y[e] Said will and ordered to have Letters of Administration thereupon The will is Recorded as followeth

In the Name of God Amen: Josiah Barthallomew of Southampton in the County of Suffolk upon LongIsland in the province of newyork in America Carpenter being of Sound and perfect Sence and memory though weak of body and being Sencible of the mortallity of human Nature and the uncertainty of the time when it Shall please almighty god to
[Page 17] Take him to himselfe doth by these presents dispose of his worldly [-] as followeth Imp[rs] he doth bequeath his Imortall Soule to god who Gave it to be presented before his throne of grace and mercy Cleansed from all its Sin and Impurity by the above merritts of [ ] blessed Saviour the Lord Jesus Christ and his body to the Earth from whence it was taken decently to bee interred in h[ ] owne yard at Southampton afores[d] there to Remaine until the Day of Ressurection - - - -

2ly that all his Just debts which at the time of his deceas he Standeth Indebted to any person may bee Justly and honestly Satisfied withall Convenient Speed

3[ly] he doth will and order that John Jagow of Southampton Shall have the free use and possession of his house and y[ ] for one whole year after his decease Rent free

4[ly] hee doth give and bequeath unto Joseph Howell of the Said Southampton Cooper the Sum of twenty Shillings money as a Legacy to be paid him upon demand after his deceas by his Executor

5ly He doth give and bequeath unto John Elce two Sheep which are in the Costody of Cap[t] Joseph fordham to be delivered him after his decease

6[ly] He doth give and bequeath unto Patience Lloyd of new york his Lands Lying and Sittuate and Lying within the township of Southold To have and to hold to the Said patience Loyd her [heyres] and Assignes for Ever being for and in Consideration of a debt [-] which he oweth her

7thly: he doth give and bequeath unto Henry williss Near Hemps[stead] plaines in Queens County upon Long Island afores[d] all his House and Land at Southampton afores[d] to have and to hold To him the Henry Williss his heyres or Assignes for Ever to have possession thereof after the term of one year after [ ] decease and he doth further Constitute and apointe the Said Henry Willis to be his Sole executor to take all his goods and Chatte[lls] Into his Costody and pay his Just debts and Especially to demand and Receive of and from Edward White of oyster bay in Queens County afores[d] what he the Said Edward White oweth him or unjustly detaineth from him which is the Sum of five and thirty pounds boston money: and five pounds from Samuell Spicer and five pounds from John bound and five pounds w[ ] he Received from Samuell Andross besides his Cattle which he Received at Huntington and his accompt he oweth h[ ] as by Said accompt may apear

8ly he doth ordaine these pr[e]sents to be his Last will and testament and doth hereby make voyd all former and other wills testaments whatsoever in wittnes whereof the Said Josiah Barthallomew hath hereunto put his hand
[Page 18] and seale at Southampton the 3[rd] Day of June 1686 Anno R:R[s] Jac 2[d] nunc anglia &c 2[nd]

Sealed &c in the presence of
John Howell John Moubray

his
Josiah A Barthollomew
mark

A true Coppy p John Howell Clark §

An Inventory of the Estate of Josiah Barthallomew Late deceased as alsoe of his Estate In partnership with John Jagow taken and Aprize[d] by Edward Howell John Jessup and John Howell Jun[r] and first his perticuler Estate as followeth

Item: one Iron kettle of aboute four gallons and 1 pott ditto	1 5 0
one tenant Saw one Joyners plow: 3 croas plaines 2 rabitting plaines all with Irons	0 13 6
1 Rabit plain Stock a broad ax 4s: a feather bed 50s	2 14 0
a Coverled 5s: 3 Shirts 8s	0 13 0
a feather pillow three Sheets 1 Indian tray & platers	1 10 0
a water payle 7 pewter plates 1 pewter bason	0 14 0
2 pewter platters 1 a great one: 1 tin driping pan	0 10 0
a Small brass kettle a tin drinking pot 2 tin tunills	0 7 0
3 poringers a ½ pint pewter pot ditto bottle	0 5 0
2 pewter pots Each 2 quarts: a quart pot a pint pot	0 15 0
1 gill pot a ½ gill pot a wooden beer bowle	0 02 0
a great Earthen Jugg 1 Earthen pot a Candlestick	0 07 0
a Red Coverled 1 pillow 2 blanket 1 feather bed	4 06 0
2 payre of Breeches 1 payre of drawers one bowlster	1 00 0
1 Searg Coate and wast Coat one blanket a quill	0 17 0
a Matt one good Chest with Lock and key Containing three Shirts & 3 diaper Napkins & Sixteen Shillings in money whereof seven is boston Coyne & one book foxes works	1 10 0
a Small book fire Shovell 2 payre of old tongs	0 6 0
1 flesh fork a pot hanger a frying pan 2 Chayres	0 13 0
2 fourms 2 old tables 1 peck payle a whip Saw 1 Square	0 15 0
a handsaw a Chamer pot a little Skillet	0 7 0
1 Sheet 2 terses ½ 1 grindstone one mare and her Increas not found one narrow ax	0 15 0
a barrell a gridIron a Lathing hamar a payre of Stillyards	0 11 0
2 neckcloaths 1 muff one paire of Shoes	0 4 0
6 old augars a little Saw an old brass kettle	0 8 0
a Can a bowle an old Drawing knife	0 3 0
	21 11 0

follow the things of the Said Estate that are in partnership between the Said Josiah barthollomew and John Jagoe

to one firkin of butter 30s	01 10 0
one Silver bowle Dram Cup & Spoon: a pewter tankerd pot	04 10 0
[Page 19] 2 beer quart pots 3 Earthen pots 6 glass bottles	0 11
1 new Chest and fifteen Cheeses one Looking glass	2 0
3 Small Earthen porringers a water payle a great brass ketle	4 16
to five barrells of beefe and 3 barrells of pork	12 00
one hogshead with aboute Seven gallons of Rum in it	00 18
one barrell with five Cakes of tallow a Small Iron pot: 4 hides	3 06
ten new payles 1 mat nine boards on y[e] west garret	1 03
aboute thirty bushells of threshed Indian Corne: 12 ditto: in y[e] Ear	3 03
a new Chest [] Sieve 3 Rakoons 1 otter 1 fox a bag of feathers	2 01
1 Rake one horse abroad a halfe bushell	2 08
6 yards of Searg: 1¼ yard of blue linings: ½ white ditto	1 04
3 Barrells 5 Chayres	0 13
to 2 yds of blue Cotten	0 04
the whole parnership is	40 9 2

whereof the one halfe belongs to the Estate Josiah Barthollomew which is 20=4:7: the totall of Josiahs Estate is 41 15 7

[Page 22] An Inventory of the Estate of m^{r} John Annings of Southampton Deceased taken and Aprized by Job Sayre and John Howell Junr this 5th day of March 1687 8 as followeth

Item: 2 Cowes both Small at	3 10 0
Itt: 5 Sheep at	1 00 0
Itt: a young horse 20s a mare at 30s	2 10 0
[ ] bedsted feather bed and and beding	3 00 0
[Page 23] A peice of Sarge 4£ to 25 yards of Silk Druggets 3£:2:6	7 2 6
to a piece of Callico at 26s to 12½ yards ditto 18s:6d	2 4 6
to a peice of ossenbrigs 46s a pound of Silk 25s a bagg of buttens of two grose ditt 3½ grose 1£11:6 ditto 6 grose 18-	6 0 6
to a peice of Callico 26s to Six yards of Sarge 21s	2 7 0
to a remnant of Camlet of 12 yards	1 4 0
to a Small Remnant of black Crape & 2 of Callico	0 9 0
to manchester and tape 5s / 2 yards of bengales 6s	0 11 0
to a boute 7 yds of buckaram 9d p yd	0 5 3
to a Chest at 5s to a Chest and two Cards of buttens 9s	0 14 0
to a payre of old pistalls 2 guns a Sword all old	1 15 0
to his wareing apparrell	7 10 0
to bibles and other books at	1 12 0
to apothecary medicines with the boxes	2 00 0
to ½ duzen of pewter platters pots & other old pewter	1 00 0
to a brass kettle a pan and brass pot	1 15 0
to one Iron pott: frying pan 2 p^{rs} of tongs 2 tramills	1 02 0
to 2 wheels one linin ye other woolen	0 08 0
to a feather bed beding and bedsted at	6 00 0
to a box 3s feathers 5s	0 8 0
to 2 Joyne Chayres 5s: to oats 3s	0 8 0
to one paire of taylors Sheers 2 p^{r} of Sheep Sheers	0 4 0
to a woollen Come 3s an Earthen Jarr 1s	0 4 0
to 300 pound of bone 6d p pound	7 10 0
To tables Chayres and all the other Lumber in ye house	2 00 0
	63 14 0
to book debts Substantiall to the vallue of	30 00 0

taken as afores^{d} by us Job Sayre John Howell Junr §

A the Courte of Sessions holden at Southampton march ye 20th 1687 8 was presented the aforesaid Inventory with a peticon for John Moubray and m^{rs} Elizabeth Anning widow to ye Said John Annig deceased Joyntly to Administer upon Said Said Estate which was granted to them accordingly: giveing Security which they have performed Test John Howell Clark §

At the fores^{d} Courte of Sessions was presented by John Rayner the Last will and testament of the widow Mary Rayner Deceased: where the Said will was proved by the oath of the wittnesses thereunto Subscribed namely Hanah Howell and John Moubray: and the Executor Confirmed: but in
[Page 24] Regard the Said Josiah is absent the Letters of Administration in his behalfe is granted to his brother John Rayner to Execute the Same in the noneage and absenc of the Said Josiah: the will is as followeth:

In the Name of god Amen I Mary Rayner Relict of the Late Joseph Rayner of Southampton in the County of Suffolk and province of Newyork on LongIsland yeoman being in full and perfect Strength of memory at present though weak in body and not knowing the time of my Departure Doe Constitute and Apointe this to be my Last will and testament in manner as followeth

Imprimis I give my Soule and bequeath it to god that gave it and my body after Deceant buriall unto y^{e} Earth from whence it was taken

2$^{ly:}$ I give and bequeath to my Son Isaac Rayner two Sheep after my Decease to be Delivered by the Executor

3^{ly} I give unto Josiah Rayner my Son five oxen Six Cows and th[ir]teen young Cattell and all my Sheep besides Six that are to be Delivered to John and two to Isaac after my decease also I give unto my Said Son Josiah all my pouter brass and Iron potts o[ne] Iron pott and the Copper only Excepted

4$^{ly:}$ I give the foremenconed Copper and one Iron pot and the foremenconed Six Sheep to my Son John Rayner and one white Rugg and one feather bed which he hath already Received to him

5^{ly} I give and bequeath all the Reast of my beds and beding and all other moveables that Shall be then Extant or in being at my Decease I give unto my Son Josiah Rayner

6^{ly} I doe by vertue of these presents Constitute prefix and appointe my Son Josiah Rayner to be the Sole Executor of This my Last will and testament In wittnes whereof: I have hereunto Sett my hand and fixed my Seale at Southampton aboves^{d} this 21 Day of March Anno: 1686 7; Mary Rayner
Signed Sealed and Delivered her M mark
In the presence of us John Moubrey Hanah tusteen her mark Hanah Howell Ephraim Howells wife

[Page 25] An Inventor of the Estate of Richard Brook of Easthampton Deceased was presented to this Court now Sitting In the Said Southampton March ye 20: 1687 8 with a peticon from the widow that her Son Samuell brooks may have Lett[ers] of Administration to Administer upon Said Estate which is granted hee haveing given bond: Inventory follows

Inventory of the Estate of Richard Brooks Deceased

Imp^{rs} 2 Cows vallued at 4£ a 2 year heifer 1£ 10: a threeyear Steer 40s	7 10
a yearling Calfe 10s to 3 Sheep 15s halfe a mare and Coult 20s	2 05
an old bed blankets & Sheets 3£ an Iron pott Som pewter & brass 40s)	5 0
wareing Cloaths 20s: a percell of old Lumber in ye hous 15s	1 15
an old Chayne and plow Coulter	0 6
this inventory was taken the first day of March 1687 8	16 16

Robert dayton Jeremiah Conkling

[Page 29] Att a Courte of Sesions holden at Southold upon the 16 17 18 day of october 1688 was presented the Last will and testament of Capt Joseph fordham Late Deceased in order to have the Same proved and Executors Confirmed which will was accordingly proved by the oaths of m^{r} John Laughton and m^{rs} Mary Tayler who were two of the wittneses thereunto Subscribed and Sworne in Courte: the will is as followeth

In the Name of God Amen I Joseph fordham of Southampton In the County of Suffolk in the province of newyork on LongIsland Being in perfect Strength of Memory blessed be allmyghty god for it though at present weak of body doe make and ordaine this my Last Will and Testament in maner and form following first I give and freely bequeath my Soule to god who at first gave it to mee and my body after decent buriall to the Earth from whence it was at first taken and for my worldly Estate as hereafter followeth

first I Give and bequeath unto my Son Joseph fordham and to his heyres for Ever all that my Now dwelling House and all other Houseing together with all the Land thereunto Adjoyning Sittuat Lying and being in the towne of Southampton and my great Closae in the Captins Neck & [ ]ing Land and meadow In halseys neck and my Land in the Oxpasture and my Closae Comonly Called toilesome and my meadow at ye North Sea Lyne

Secondly I give and bequeath unto my Sonn Nathan fordham my house and Land Adjoyning to it Sittuat Lying and being at Mecox and the Choyce of my two Lots in hog neck and on third of my meadow at accobauge

Thirdly I give and bequeath unto my Son pelatiah fordham and to his heyres all that my Lott of Land Sittuate Lying and being at Sagaponack together with my Land at Huntington and the other Lott of Land in hog neck and one third parte of meadow

at accquabauge and a fifty pound Comonage [ ] out the bounds, alsoe I give unto my Said Son nathan fordham a f[ ] pound Commonage and to my Son Joseph fordham a hundred [ ] fifty pound Comonage further my will is that if Either of [ ] two younger Sons Nathan or pellatiah Shall Either dye before [ ]
[Page 30] Come of Age or without Issue that then his Land and Meadow and Comonage Shall bee to y[e] Surviver and if my Eldest Son Joseph Should dye without Issue then his Estate of Lands meadow and Commonage to be Equally devided between the two younger brethren

4[th]ly I give unto my Daughter Mary Whitehead with what Shee hath allready Received being the Sum of twenty two pounds Eighteen Shillings and nine pence the Sum of fifty pounds of good Currant money of this province

5th I give unto my daughter phebee Herrik with what Shee hath already Received being thirty Six pounds Six pounds Six Shillings the Sum of one hundred pounds of good Currant money of this province

Sixtly I give and bequeath unto my three youngest daughter Namly Hanah fordham Elizabeth fordham and Allathea fordham one hundred a peice to be payd to each of them at there day of marriage by my Executors in good Currant money of this province or other goods or pay Equivalent thereunto

Seventhly I give and bequeath to Charles fordham one hundred fifty pounds of good currant Contrey pay to bring him up and to fitt him for good trade to be pa[yd] by my Executors yearly or offtener as Ocassion Shall Require to pay Such Nurs or Nurses as hee Shall be with untill hee be bound out to a trade and if then there Shall not bee disbursed the Said Sum then the Remainer to be payd to him when hee Shall be out of his time by my Executors which Executors is to See him to bee Competently Learnt both to Read and writte

Eightly my will is that my beloved wife Mary fordham Shall have which End of my Dwelling House Shee pleaseth dureing her Naturall Life or Soe Long as Shee Remaineth a widow and two Hundred pounds of good Currant pay out of my Estate

Lastly that my Son Joseph keep and maintaine with Sumer in good pasture and winter with good hay at home for her two good milch Cowes

Lastly I by this make and ordaine my Said wife together with my Son Joseph fordham Joynt Executors of this my Last will and testament to pay all my Said Legacyes and alsoe to pay unto my two Sons Nathan fordham and pellatiah fordham one hundred pounds apeice as they Come of age out of my estate and to have and Receive all my debts and all other Estate of mine whatsoever alsoe my desire and Request is that my beloved freinds m[r] John Howell Jun[r] and m[r] Abram Howell be overseers of this my Last Will and testament to See all things herein performed according to my desire In wittnes whereof I have hereunto Sett my hand and Seale this 28th Day of August in the fourth year of the Reigne of our Sovereigne Lord James the Second over England Scottland france and Ireland king &c: and Anno Dom <u>1688</u> alsoe before Signing hereof it is my will that my other thirds of my meadow at accobauge be my Son Joseph fordhams and his heyres for Ever Joseph ffordham
Signed and Sealed in presence of John Howell Mary Tayler John Laughton §
A true Coppy of the origanall p Jn[o] Howell Cl[ ] §

[Page 31] An Inventory and Aprizement of the goods and Chattles and Movable Estate of Cap[t] Joseph ffordham of Southampton deceased September y[e] 7th 1688 taken And Aprized by us John Jessup m[r] Jonah fordham John Howell Jun[r] and Abraham Howell all Sworne there unto before Maj[r] Howell this 14th Day of September <u>1688</u>

Itt Sixteen oxen 52£ and 16 Cows 32£: Six Steers 18£ Six Steers & heifers at 12£ to 8 Calves 50s Six Rideing Horses 18£	134 10 0
It five Cattle 3yearold 7£-10s two Cattle oneyearold 50s	010 00 0
86 Sheep 21£10s about 40 Lambs 5£ 9 wild horses and mares 18£	044 10 0
3 twoyearold Horse kinde 3£ In Swine ten pounds 12s	013 12 0
2 old feather beds and one bedsted with furneture	009 00 0
a trundle bedsted and beding	005 00 0

a box and a Chest 7s & and a Cubard 20s a trunk 3s	001 10 0
a Chest and his wareing apparrell	014 00 0
6 Leather Chayres all old 20s a box & 2 tables 5s	001 05 0
a pair of pistoll and houldsters 30s	001 10 0
bibles and other books	003 13 0
a Leading Stafe 25s a Looking 10s	001 15 0
in the Clossett Scales glassbottle a Case and other Small things	001 10 0
3 augers Square and other tooles a broad ax	000 15 0
4 brass Cocks 7s Sillver platte 15£	015 7 0
an old Clock out of order 30s: 3 Sicles & a warming pan 8s	001 18 0
a Chafeing dish and three tramells fire Shovell and tongs	000 17 0
10 turky work Chayres old 4£) 3 Sheets 40s	006 00 0
table Cloaths napkins and pillow beers	003 10 0
five Sheets 3£: a paire ditto old 8s) 3 ditto new 22s	004 10 0
a good Chest of west India wood 18s a Chest 5s	001 03 0
a bedsted and feather bed and furneture at	007 00 0
to a Standing Candlestick a Lamp a little brass Candlestick	000 10 0
a Still 8s an old bed 10s a table 12s	001 10 0
to a percell of English goods Came Last from England	090 00 0
to a little Suger flower & pipes	000 16 0
to a duzen of pewter plates 16s) 7 platters 25s	002 01 0
a Small feather bed and blankets 30s a a hechell & Square table 16s	001 11 0
to old pewter at 55s to 5 great Iron potts ditto a little one 3£:10:	006 05 0
to brass kettles Stupan Scimer and Scillets	004 10 0
an old Jak grid Iron a Spit and pot hooks	000 12 0
14 bushells of Salt and frying pan	001 12 0
In the Chamber 2 trunks 18s 21 yards of Cotten 40s	002 18 0
a quilt 20s a remnant of karsey 8s 4 yards ditto 20s	002 08 0
to 6 duzen Sisers 20s a peice of kersey ten yard 50s	003 10 0
to a Remnant of kersey 63s to 13 yards of Cotten 22s	04 05 0
to a new bed bested and furneture	07 00 0
to ten yards of broad Cloath 4£ to 14 yards Swanskin 28s	05 08 0
to 8 bunches of thrid 14s to 8 tobaco boxes 5s:4d	00 19 4
to 5 duzen of horne Combs 20s: 6 duzen ditto Ivory 33s	02 13 0
to 21 yds of hollon 4s p yd: 4£:4s) 15½ yds Striped muslin 40s	06 04 0
to 7 paire of Small gloves 7s) 15 duzen of Coate buttons 7s	00 14 0
to 17 yds Stryped muslin 40s 3 yds Course dowlas 4s	02 04 0
to white ossenbrigs 5 yds ½ 4s: 62 yds of dowlas 6£ =4s	06 08 0
to 116 yds Ribon 5d p yd 2=18-4 to 89 yds Ditto 9d p yd 66s	06 04 4
[Page 32] to 210 yards of osenbrigs 10d p y^d	8 15 0
to 14 yds duffills 4s p y^d 56s to 8 quire of paper 4s	3 00 0
to 18½ yds due=Cape 9s p yd	8 06 0
to 47 yds of Lute String 6s p y^d	14 05 0
to ten yds of Silk Mohare 3£ 2 trunks ten Shillings	3 10 0
to 2 Rugs and 2 blankets	4 00 0
a gun 35s to a bed bedsted and Covering 3£ 10s	5 05 0
a feather bed boulster and Covering	4 10 0
to aboute 12 bushells of wheat 36s & 20 $bush^{lls}$ Indian Corne 25s	3 01 0
to a percell of feathers aboute 18 pound	0 15 0
to aboute 50 £ of flax 20s a Sieth and takleing 6s	1 06 0
to aboute 80 pound of Sheeps wooll 2£:13s:4d a bag of hops 5s) 100 Iron 25s)	4 3 4
a percell of Sicles and two Sieths 10s) 3 harping Irons all old 16s	1 6 0
to 3 old Rugs 3£ a Cradle 5s) 3 old guns without Locks 20s	4 5 0
to a plush Sadle: a bridle 30s a Carte hoops and boxes 35s	3 5 0
to 2 plows harrows and Chaynes and yokes	3 16 0
to 5 hows 4 mattuck 2 old axes Spade and Shovell	1 04 0
to 2000 foot of deelboard 3£-10s to part of a boat and Craft 40s	5 10 0

to one negro woman and a negro man 30£	30 00 0
to 2 mallotta Chilldren at ten pounds	10 00 0
to the hay wheat and oats in the barnes	28 00 0
to the Indian Corne upon ye ground	06 00 0
to a grindstone 6s Ceder boulls 3£	3 06 0
to milk vessells payles wheels and Lumber in ye hous	2 00 0
to parte of a Ship abroad being 1/8 not knowne ye vallu	
	601 16 3
to book debts out in good hands to ye vallue of in Cash	100 00 0

Jonah fordham John Jessup John Howell Junr Abraham Howell
A true Coppy p John Howell Cla §

At the Aforesd Courte of Sessions held at Southold upon the 16 &c day of october was presented the Inventory of the Estate of Isaac overton of Southold deceased with a peticon for the widow Sarah overton to have the Estate for the bringing up of the Chilldren but it is by this Courte granted to her to Administer upon Said Estate giveing in Security to Save this Courte harmeless which Shee hath accordingly done by her Suretys bond namly Stephen Bayley and Joseph mapes of Said towne: Inventory Coppy follows)

Sothold March y^e 27: 1688 An Inventory of y^e Estate of Isaac overton Deceased March y^e 25: 1687/8

$Impr^s$ house and Land	£ s d
neat Cattle 21£ 1 horse 35s Swine 20s	23 05 0
a feather bed & Covering and Curtaines bedsteds a Chafebed: 4 Sheets	7 00 0
2 old Iron potts 1 Small brass kettle	1 2 0
to pewter	0 12 0
[Page 33] His wareing Cloaths 5£ two Chests 8s to wheat and Indian Corne 3£)	8 08 0
gun and Sword	1 10 0
plow takleing hows and axes	1 15 0
Lumber and Necessarys in the house	1 10 0
	45 2 0

A true Coppy p Jno Howell Cla § John tucker Stephen Bayley

The Inventory of the Estate of Calleb dayton Deceased taken and Aprized by us John Howell Junr and Joseph peirson this 8th day of october 1688 prized according to money

to one Chest 7s 3 hatts 20s to one new Sarge Lynd Coate 45s	3 12 0
to an old broadcloath Coate 16s a new wastcoat of halfe thick 10s	1 06 0
to 1 paire of Sarg trowsers 5s an old Shirt 4s a black Caster hat 15s	0 19 0
a paire of worsted Stockins a p^r ditto Cotten a pair ditto wollen	0 07 0
a pair of halfe Sleeves 18d 2 muslin neckcloaths 7s	0 08 6
a pair of Linin Sleeves 2s to 1 neckcloath 8d an old norwester 5s)	0 07 8
2 white kercheifs hand: and one Speckled ditto	0 04 0
to one Inkhorne powderhorne and a Rule	0 01 3
to a writeing book 4s a duzen of pewter buttens 3d	0 04 3
to 2 Saspans and Candlestick tinn	0 02 0
to ½ duzen of pipes gun Sword belt and bandileires	2 08 0
a basket with Som threds a linin Cap	0 01 0
one old Chest 2s to 1 $Lac:^d$ neckcloath 18d 2 paire gloves 2s:6	0 06 0
a hors at 50s 2 harping Irons 14s: old linin trowsers Shirt & kercheif 4s	3 08 0
Due to Estate from Joseph fordham in pay 3£-10s-0 in mony	1 15 0
	15 14 2

A true Coppy p Jno Howell Clar § John Howell Joseph peirson aprizers &c -

[Page 34] At a Courte of Sessions held at Southampton upon the 22^d day of March 1687 8 was presented the Inventory of the Estate of Christopher Lupton deceased with a peticon for John Lupton his Eldest brother to Administer upon Said Estate which was granted to the peticon[r] giveing Securityes as the Law directs which hee the Said John hath accordingly performed and thereupon Administration granted to him the Said John Lupton the Inventory follows

An Inventory of the Estate of Christopher Lupton y[e] younger deceased and Aprizemen of all his moveable Estate taken and Aprized by Job Sayre and John Howell Jun[r] this 3[d] Day of March 1687 8 Aprized according to money

	£ s d
to a paire of oxen at	5 0 0
to 2 heifers of 2yearold and upward	2 0 0
to one horse	4 0 0
to one Sword and belt	1 0 0
to a Sadle and Sadle Cloath	0 18 0
to aparrell 2 Coates	1 05 0
to one new Coate at obadiah Rogerses	1 05 0
to 2 Shirts & apaire of Stokins and Shoes	1 05 0
to a Caster hett	0 08 0
Totall in money	17 1 0

A true Coppy p Jn[o] Howell Cla § p us Job Sayre John Howell Jun[r] §

Know all that this may Concerne that I Catherine ffancy form[erly] the wife of william fancy deceased have given granted and by these presents doe give and grant unto my daughter Rachells youngest Son whom She hath or Shall have by peter whiteheare of brookhaven all my mead[ow] at the place Comonly Called Conscience: to have and to hold for Ever af[ter] my decease and Also if I Shall have need whilst I Live I Reserve Liberty to Sell the meadow for my Reliefe and further the above[sd] Meadow is granted upon this Condition that peter whiteer In y[e] beh[alfe] of the youngest Child that Shall possess the meadow Shall pay unto will[iam] fancys heyres and Assignes five pounds In Cattell as two Indiferant men Shall prize them and also that the aboves[d] peter whitheer Shall pay unto Hannah Jennens five pounds to her or her Assignes In Cat[tell] as two Indiferant men Shall prize them provided alsoe that I have Reser[ved] the meadow dureing my Life peter whithear is to have the meadow whilst I Live he paying the Rent which is fifteen Shilling the year the above Said ten pounds to william and Hanah is to be payd within a years time after my decease and I doe further Injoyne peter whithear to give unto Robert gouldsbury a threeyearold heifer with a Calfe by her Side when the boy Shall bee Sixteen
[Page 35] years of age and to be kept by the Said peter whithear her and her Increase to y[e] halves till the boy be twenty one years of age at my decease if I have any Cattell Lest I give hanah Jenens one Cow and the Rest of my Cattell to peter whitehears youngest Children: the peece of Land which the Towne gave mee I give to peter whitheare after my decease To all and Singuler the aboves[d] premmises I have hereunto Sett my hand and fixed my Seale in brookhaven the 27th of october 1684
Signed In the presence of us wittneses Catherine fancy 3 her mark
Richard Smith Richard wodhull
this above written is Recorded In the towne book of Brookhaven in page 149 p me Jn[o] tooker Record[r]

the above written will of Catherine fancy was presented to y[e] Courte of Sessions held at Southampton upon the 22[d] of March 1687 8: where the Same was proved by the oaths of the Subscribed wittneses Richard Smith & Richard wodhull and the Said peter Confermed in the managem[t] thereof to Administer till the Childdren Come of age

[Page 40] A Courte of pleas holden at Southampton upon the 16 Day of Janu[ary] for the County of Suffolk In the province of newyork Anno: Dom 1688 [ ]

Was presented the Last will and testament of Thomas Halsey of Southampton Deceased: In order to y[e] proving of the Same with a peticon of the Executrix to Administer accordingly: which Said will was then & there proved by the Evedence thereunto Subscribed namly Benjamin ffoster and Ephraim foster: which will is here

Recorded in these word[] following to gether with the Inventory:

In the Name of God Amen I Thomas Halsey of Southampton In the County of Suffolk and province of Newyork upon LongIsland being weak in body but in full and perfect Strength of memory &c not knowing the time of my Departure doe Constitute and apoint this to be my Last will and testament In maner as followeth

Imp[rs] I Bequeath my Soule to god that gave it me and my body after Decent buriall to the Earth from whence it was taken and my worldly goods and possessions to be disposed in maner as followeth

2ly: I give unto Mary my Loving wife Dureing her Life my now dwelling House and all the houseing that standeth upon the Said Lott and the Lott it Selfe with the neck of Land Called Cobpound and my Close Called the Eagles ne[st] and one Acre and halfe of Land that was my father halseys Home Lott at Towne also I doe give unto my wife Mary Dureing the time of her widowhood the one halfe of my new house that I built at the towne namly The west Leantoo and halfe the north Leantoo and halfe the Sellar provided
[Page 41] that my Said wife doth Soe Cause to Live in the Said House in her owne person alsoe I doe make my wife Sole Executrix of this my Last will and Testament to dispose of my Estate and to pay all Dews and Legacys hereafter menconed &c

3[ly] I give to my Son Josiah Halsey after my wife marys Deceas twenty five Acres of my wood Close alsoe at my deceas I give to my Son Josiah Halsey my hundred and fifty of meadow in ogdens neck at quaquanant[uck] and a fifty of Comonage and my best Lott of meadow at accobaug - - -

4ly I Give unto my Son Isaac Halsey four Acres of the Home=lott at Towne y[t] was my fathers Halseys to begin on the North Side of the Lott and also the other halfe of the new House that Standeth upon the Said Lott and the other halfe of the Said House after the time is Expired that my wife is to have in [it] alsoe my Closse of Land in the Little plaine with a road Lying at the East End or Side thereof also the one halfe of my beach Lotts to Ly upon the South parte of the Said Lotts as alsoe the halfe of my Lott of Land at Scutle hole and the halfe of my Lott of Land that I bought of thomas Reeves and halfe of my meadow at ononk and Land thereunto belonging and the h[] of a fifty of meadow in Assups Stalkes with Isaac Halsey and the halfe of a fifty of meadow In Shork neck with Isaac Halsey and a fifty pound Comonage and two Cows to be payd him by my Executrix and the halfe of my meadow [ ] Shinecok I give to my Son Isaac Halsey

5[ly] I give to my son David Halsey my neck of Land Called the mill neck & my neck Called by the name of peters neck and my hundred of Land in hogneck that Lyeth with his uncle Isaac Halseys and one quarter parte of my Lott of Land at Scuttle hole with his brother Isaac and halfe my meadow at Shenecok with his brother Isaac and three Cows to be payd by my Executrix

6ly: I give to my Son Jonathan Halsey the home Lot at towne that I bought of m[r] wodhull and a third parte of the home Lott that was my fathers my w[ife] Enjoying one Acre and a halfe of the above[sd] Lott dureing her Life as is before menconed alsoe I doe give him my Closse Called troublesome: one gin Acre of Land in the Little plaines and the other halfe of my Land in the beach Lotts with his brother Isaac and halfe the Lott of Land that I bought of thomas Reeves and a quarter of my Land and meadow at wononck and a quarter parte of a fifty of meadow In Assups Stalks with his uncle Isaacs Halsey and a quarter parte of a fifty of meadow In Short neck twenty Acres of Land Adjoyning to my Land at Callis pond which I had of the towne In Exchange and a fifty of Comonage and foure Cows or cattle Equivollent & a fifty of meadow at fourth neck at quaqua.

7[ly] - I give unto my Son Jerimiah Halsey my three Lotts of Land that ly together at Callis pond and one quarter parte of my meadow and Land at wonunck and a quarter parte of assups Stalks a quarter parte of a fifty of meadow In Short neck and a fifty of Comonage and five Cows or Cattle Equivollen to be paid to him by my Executrix

8[ly] - I Give unto my Son Nathanell when he is at the age of twenty one years the twenty five Acres at my woodcloase to have it unto the time of my wifes Decease and

then to Returne to his brother Josiah as aboves^{d} alsoe I doe give to my Son Nathanell after my wifes Decease my dwelling house at Cobspound and all the other houseing and the Lott the house Standeth upon and the neck Called Cobs pound and the Close Called the Eagles neast and a quarte parte of my lott of Land at Scutle hole and my Lott of Land in hogneck and my Lott of meadow at Rapahamuck at accoba[uge] a fifty of Comonage and three Cows to be payd by my Executrix./ whereas I have given Legacys to all my Sons as is before Expressed my will and meaning is that Every part and percell of Land and meadow herein given to Each and Every of my Said Sons Shall be to y^{m} and to the heyres of there body Lawfully begotten or to Such of the Said heyre or heyres as he or they Shall Respectively apoint: but In Case any of my Said Sons Shall Dye Intestate without any Such heyres or heyres as afores^{d} that then Such meadows and Land as hee or they possessed then Naturall brethren of that brother or brothers Shall
[Page42] Have Equall Intrest In the Estate of the Intestat brother; and then Every Naturall sister of these brethren that Shall then Survive Shall Receive as a Legacy from those brethren that doe possess there Intestates Estate twelve pounds a peice In Cuntry pay and that not only once but Soe often as Such possess there deceased brethrens Estate twelve pounds apeice a time is to be pay by Surviveing brothers to there Surviving Sisters: nevertheles if any of my Sons Shall Leav a widow his or there Relict behinde them there Said wife to Enjoy one third of there husbands house and Lands Dureing her Life and After her discease to be Disposed off to the Naturall brethren fore menconed that is Resigned up to them as there owne proper Right

9^{ly} I doe give unto my Son Isaac Halsey fourty Six pounds to be payd In Cattle at ye Rate of Contry paye as they Shall be prized by men this he shall Receive of my Executrix if he Live to Returne from albany if not Shee may keep it in her owne hands and doe with it as Shee Sees Cause alsoe I doe will and apoint that if any of my Sons See Cause to Sell or Exchange any of the afores^{d} Lands or meadows that then the prod[ ] thereof Shall be disposed after the Same maner as the Same Individuall Lands or med[ows] Should have been if they had not been Sould or Exchanged

10^{ly} I give to my daughter Mary four Sheep my daughter Sarah More four Sheep: un[to] my daughter Hanah Howell a Cow unto my daughter Elizabeth Rescue and her heyres four Sheep: unto my daughter phebee Halsey when at ye age of Seventeen years five Cows or Cattle Equivollent unto my daughter abigaile Halsey when at ye age of Seventeen years four Cows or Cattle Equivolent: Southampton August 3^{d} Anno Reg Reg: Jacb 2^{d} nunc Anglia quarto: Annoque Domi <u>1688</u> Thomas Halsey
Signed Sealed and Delivered in presence of us
Benjamin foster Ephraim ffoster John Moubray

An Inventory and Aprizment of the Moveable Estate goods and Chattel[ls] of thomas Halsey of Southampton deceased taken and Aprized by Edward Howell Obadiah Roggers Job Sayre and John Howell Junr being Sworne there unto by by Maj^{r} Howell this 28th Day of December Anno Dom - <u>1688</u>

	£ s d
Imp^{rs} 2 horses 4£) 12 oxen 34£) 14 Cows 28£	66 0 0
ten 3yearolds 16£) 14 two yearold 14£) 6 yearlings 4£	36 00 00
13 Calves 6£:10s) 84 Sheep 21£) 23 Swine 5£:15s	33 05 00
100 bushells wheat in Straw 15£) hay and oats 24£	39 00 00
3 barrells of beef & 3 of pork 9£:12) about 40 bushell of Indian Corne 2£:10s	12 02 00
the wainage all old 3£12s) 4 axes 1 mattuk 3 hows 2 tramalls 32s	05 04 00
a Spitt a peel & tongs 10s a Spade & 2 Shovell 5s	00 15 0
a fether bed & Covereing 5£ a trundle bedsted & beding 45s	07 05 00
to 2 tables Chayres and Stooles 30s) a flagon 3 poringers 2 Cups 15s:6d	02 05 6
old pewter and tin ware 22s Earthen ware 5s	01 07 0
a gun & Sword 20s) bibles & other books 10s	01 10 0
a Chest & woollen wheele 6s) 38 pound of pewter 20d p pound 3£	03 06 0
2 great old brass kettles 3£:10s) 4 Iron pots Skillet & brass pott 40s	05 10 0
a pare of Stilyards 10s some old Carpenters tools 10s	01 00 0
Sieths & Sicles 15s a firkin of buter 20s	01 15 0

4 payles and a firkin of hogs fatt	01 00 0
a Churne and trays and bowles 15s	00 15 0
an Iron Morter Earthen ware a hetchell	00 10 0
a Cake of tallow a frying pan 6s:6d: to 3 Seivs and wooll 8s	00 14 6
halfe a barrell of Mallasses 15s: 2 beds and beding all old 2£ = 10s	03 05 0
to 3 bushell: of Mault and hiare Cloath	01 00 0
to Chees at 25s: to 2 Ridles 2s	01 7 0
[Page 43] to 2 feather beds and furneture 7£ a duzen of diaper napkins 18s	7 18 0
a hollen table Cloath 12s pillow beer and old table Cloath 7s	0 19 0
6 payre of Sheets 3£ = 10s old Carpet and Curtaines 8s	3 18 0
his wareing aparrell 5£) to barley in the Straw 20s	6 00 0
2 Chamber potts looking glass & box Iron	0 08 0
to ten pound of Cotten wooll	0 08 0
to 12 pound of flax	0 06 0
an Indian girle a Slave	0 05 0
the Lumber In the house	0 12 0
	248 15 0

Aprized by us according to money Edward Howell obadiah Roggers Job Sayre John Howell Jun[r] §

Whereas at a Courte of Sessions held at Southold on y[e] 20th Day of october 1685: Sarah hakelton the Relict of william Hakelton: was Admitted to be Administratrix to all the Estate good and Credits of the Said william Hakelton and m[r] John Campell of Southampton haveing maryed the Said Sarah and Soe hath Entermedled with y[e] Said Estate and the Said Sarah being alsoe Deceased the power of Administration is Extinc[t] the Said John Campbell therefore peticons this Courte now Sitting this 16th Day of January: 1688 that he may be Impowered to Cary on the Said Administration and to Recover the Debt Due to Said Estate and Satisfie the Cred[rs] which is accordingly granted hee giveing Security to perform the Same and Save this Court harmless:

whereas obadiah Rogers and Job Sayre warr formerly put In by this Courte to be Executors In trust to the Last will and testament of william Russell his wif[ ] be made his Executor is alsoe Deceased: and there upon the Said obadiah Rogers and Job Sayre have Administered upon Said Estate and the Said obadiah hath Rendered an account thereof to this Courte and then was Sworne to y[e] Said account which is Accepted and he to have his Quietusest

[Page 48] In the name of God Amen I John Laughton of Southampton in y[e] County of Suffolk in the province of NewYork on LongIsland in America Yeoman be very Sick in body but blessed be the Lord of perfect Strength of memory Doe mak and ordaine this my Last will and Testament as foloweth

first I give and bequeath my Soule to god and my body to the Earth from whence it was taken and for my Estate as followeth first I Give and bequeath to my beloved Nephew Josias Laughton my little gun

2[dly] I give and bequeath unto my beloved wife Sarah Laughton Dureing [her] Naturall Life my house and Land in Southampton with my little Island at Meacocks and my three Acres of Land In Halseys neck and Eleven Acres behind gersham Culvers and my Six Acres in the ox pasture and my Land at hog neck

3[d]ly I Give and bequeath unto my Nephew John Laughton At his Said Ants deceas all the aboves[d] Houses and Lands to him and to his heyres for Ever after his Said Ants decease To have and To hold as his & there owne free Land in fee Simple for Ever also I give unto him my great gun and Cutlas and the feather bed in the Little Chamber with two paire of Sheets and a blancket & Coverled and two Cows and my Mare that is on the beach and the Long table that is in the house after his Ants deceas and my Case of Instruments

Lastly I by these make my Said beloved Wife Sarah Laughton the Sole Executrix

of this my Last will and testament to ha[ve] and Receive all the Rest of my Estate whatsoever that is not here before given away and to Receive and to pay all my Debts In witnes whereof and for the more sure makeing hereof I have hereunto Set my hand & Seale In Southampton aboves^{d} this first day of January Annoq: Dom: 1688 9
Signed and Sealed by the Subscriber John Laughton §
and acknowledged to be his Last will and testament in y^{e}
presence of us
John piny
John Bishop

at A Courte of Sessions: alias pleas held at Southold Aprill the 16: 1689 was presented the abovesaid will and Testament of John Laughton and proved by the oath of on of the witneses namly John piny: and the other ordered to be Sworn at Southampton before Maj^{r}: Howell or Some other Justice of the peace and the Said Sarah Laughton widdow [of] the Testator is Confirmed Executor to the Said will
Test John Howell Clar §

Southampton Aprill the 8 1689 An Inventory of the Estate of John Laughton deceased as it was the aprized by us ye Subscribed

To 5 Cowes at 42s Shillings p head 2 yearling 15s p head	12 00 0
to 10 Sheep at 5s p head 1 horse at 4£	6 10 0
to 2 mares at 50s p head and one yearling at 10s p head	5 10 0
[to 5] Swine at 4s p head and two little tables at 5s p table	1 10 0
[to -] feather beds two boulsters 2 pillows	6 00 0
[Page 49] To 1 ditto and one pillow at 30s and 2 paire Curtaines 30s	3 0 0
To 3 Coverlids & 5 blankets 3£ & 9 paire of Sheets: 6 old 3 new: 10s p p^{r}	4 10 0
To 4 paire of New ditto 3£: to 5 napkins 4 pillow beers 2 table Cloaths	0 15 0
To a Larg trunk one Case and desk 15s to a meale trough & a Chest 5s	1 00 0
To a Chest at 6s: a long table 10s: two Larg platers 10s to 4 ditto 10s	1 16 0
To 10 porringers 5 plates 2 Saltselers 3 basons one plater	0 14 0
To a warming pan & a lanthorne 6s two pewter drinking pots 5 Spoons 7s)	0 13 0
To a percell of Earthen Ware 10s to a percell of tin Ware 3s	0 13 0
to 2 brass kettles & a Skillet 20s to 2 Iron pot & frying pan 23	2 03 0
To a payre of tongues & a paire of hooks 4s	0 04 0
To one ox an old mill and Some Iron	0 08 0
To a Sadle pillion & Cloath all bad	0 08 0
To a Large gun 30s one ditto Small at 20s	2 10 0
To the bed and furneture given to his Nephew	3 00 0
To a Case of barbers Instruments at 10s	0 10 0
To 4 Chayres and 3 glass bottles at 3s	0 3 0

This Inventory Taken by ye us upon oath
Test our hands John Jagger Samuell Joanes Mathew Howell

[Page 51] Articles of Agreement made agreed and Concluded upon between Joseph Horten Senr of Rye brother to benjamin horten of Southold on Long Island Lately deceased and mary Horten the now widow of the [S^{d}] benjamin Horten deceased as followeth the Said Joseph Horten hath agreed with ye Said Mary Horten and promised and Engaged to give to her the one halfe of the neat Cattell of his brother benjamin that are In his Inventory: in the Inventory of his Estate [ ] two percells of meadow that was his Said brothers at [ ]
[Page 52] the one percell being at Carchauge Lying near the great Salt meadow it is Comonly Called by the name of ye Dam meadow and the other meadow it is in the said great Salt meadow towards the East or Southward of the Said great meadow not far from [] Rock Som doe Call the Same Devition the Rock meadow and also ye Said Joseph Horten doth give the Said Mary three Acres of that is by the barne it Lying to

ye Southward of his brother benjamin Hortens barne: which land is now in tillage and this Said Land and meadows above named the Said Mary is to have the use of the Same her Life time if Shee Remaine a widow or as Long Shee Remaine a widow and alsoe the Said Joseph doth give the Said Mary fr[ee] Liberty to dwell in one of his brother benjamins Houses as her owne all her Lifetime if Shee Remaine a widow Soe Long or Soe Long as Shee Remaines a widow but when She doth mary or dye the Said houses and Land above named and meadows Shall Returne to the abovesaid Joseph againe and his heyres also the Said Joseph is to give the Said Mary one third parte of all that is within the Said house Except the waring Cloaths made and Cut out and one fether bed and mens tools and Such Instruments and hats and neckcloaths and Linin Silk and Coverin[] and this gift and by ye vertue hereof it Shall put and End to all former Claimes of any gifts or premises or Engagement made by benjamin Horten his brother to the Said Mary by her husband to her the Said Mary and to her Children they Shall be voyd and Annull for Ever all former Engagements made between the Said benjamin Horten and the Said Mary Horten when Shee were Mary Mapham Shall no more be of any force but Shall be voyd and of no force and the Said Mary Ho[rten] doth Engage to pay one third parte of the debts that her husband did owe and benjamin Horten did owe as wittness our hands and Seales this 22^d of Aprill 1691
wittnessed In the presence of us Joseph Horten
Thomas tustin Sam[ll] Wines Mary Horten O her mark

Suffolk Southold the 2^d day of may 1691 then apeared before me the within written Joseph Horten and Mary Horten and acknowledged the within written Instrument of writing to be there act and deed

p Thomas Mapes Justice of the peace for the County of Suffolk //
[In the left margin] the Said Mary is to have a Mare

[Page 53] know all men whom it may Concerne that I mary Horten who was the wife of Benjamin Horten of Southold Latly deceased and now widow of the Said Benjamin I doe by these presents promis and Engage unto Joseph Horten of Rye to him who was brother to ye abovs[] Benja: Horten of Southold I doe ingage to the Said Joseph Horten to Secure him and his heyres from all former Covennats and Engagements made by the aboves[d] Benjamin Horten to mee and to all my Children and I will acquit him the Said Joseph Horten of the Same and I doe acknowledge that I have Received full Satisfaction of the Said Joseph Horten for the Same In Cattle and household goods and other things as wittnes my hand and Seale ye Six of may 1691
wittnessed in the presence of us the mark ~ of Mary Horten
Charles booth the mark ~ of Abigaile booth

Suffolk Southold ye 9th of may 1691 Then Apeared before me the above written Mary Horten and acknowledged this Instrument of writing to be her act and Deed

p me Thomas Mappes Justice of ye peace for the County of Suffolk

[Page 55] An Inventory and Aprizement of the goods and Chattells and moveable Estate of Leift Thomas Cooper of Southampton deceased November the 23 1692 Taken and Aprized by us Jonathan Rayner Samuell Clarke and Joseph Fordham all Sworne thereunto before Capt: Mathew Howell this 8th Day of December 1692 Equivolent to money &c

It: four oxen 12£ Six Cows 10£:10s two Steers 3 yearold 3£:10s	26 00 00
It: two 3 yearolds heifers 40s three Steer 2 yearold 3£:15s	05 15 00
It: two heifers 2 yearold 35s: one yearling 15s: twelve Calves 6£	08 10 0
It: one horse 7£ three horses 8£ one mare 30s one hors & mare yerling 12s	17 02 0
Item: 39 Sheep 9£:15 foure Swine & four pigs 44s	11 19 0
It: In the west Roome to a bedsted 15s the Curtaines & hangings 45s	03 00 0
It: to a bed & bowlster & 2 pillows 5£:9s a Coverled 30s & blanket 10s	07 9 0
It: one fourme 2s: two new tables 36s: Six leather Chaires 3£	4 18 0
It: a Chest of drawers new 3£ one Red trunk 16s one ditto Small 12s	4 8 0
It: 8 Small Chaires 12s two great Chaires 5s two Carpets new 25s	2 2 0

Item	£ s d
It: one Looking glass 18s one basket 2s:6 a Case with 5 knifes 3s-9d	1 4 8
It: one Sword Silver hilt 5£:6s and belt 15s: one Sadle 50s	8 11 0
It: two flower pots 4s one Cuberd Cloath 2s:6d Six glasses venice 7 bits	0 11 9
It: 16 yards of Raw Homespon karsey 48s two blancket 10s	2 18 0
It: a bested 13s: Sixteen yard of homspon karsey 3£:4s	3 17 0
It: a table 8s: one great Chest 16s) 40£ of powder 4£) 60£ Shot 18s	6 02 0
It: one grosse of pipes 8s: one bag of flints 8s: one Cradle 6s: 2 reeds 2s	1 04 0
It: 60 pounds Suger 20s: 20£ of flax 10s one negro bed 6s: a pr of old andIrons 13s	1 19 0
It: 50£ of feathers 37s:6d one negro bed 15s one bedsted & Curtain Rods 13s	3 5 6
It: 51 £ of pewter new 16d p £: 3£:8s a bed pan 8s	3 16 0
It: 5 Earthen platters 5s 4 Earthen pots 4s five basons 9s	0 18 0
It: two ditto 3s:9 Six porengers 12s one Candle Cup 3s) 4 pots 12s	1 10 9
It: one Small flaggon 4s 2 Cups 2s:3d: a paper box 3d: a great Lamp 3s	0 9 6
It: ½ pinte pot 1s: one Saltsellers 1s one duzen of Spoones 5s	0 7 0
It: 2 Small plates 2s one old porenger 9d 2 duzen trenchers 1s:9d	0 4 6
It: one barbours bason Eathen 18d one Case of pistolls & holsters 45s	2 6 6
It: one gun 36s: 1 ditto 30s one ditto musket 24s one Cartouch box 4s:6	4 14 6
It: one flask 18d one powder horne 18d: 3 bullet moulds 8s a Shutle 6s	0 17 0
It: a paire of Scales to weigh Silver 6s one tobacco box 3s: a kane 6s	0 15 2
It: one old Sword & belt 12s one old Cradle 3s one old table 6s	1 1 0
It: one p^{r} of Stillyards 6s one Iron ketle 40s two ditto potts 2£:9s:2d	4 15 2
It: one kittle ditto 12s:6 one pot ditto 8s:4d one kettle ditto 3s:4	1 4 2
It: one Iron kettle 30s one Iron ditto 12s:6 one Iron pot 6s	2 8 6
It: the Iron above at 5d p £: one grid Iron 5s one peele 6s	0 11 0
It: a paire of tongs 4s one Smoothing Iron 27d: on Chafing dish 3£	0 9 3
It: one brass kettle 3£ a brass pan 9s one brass kittle 10s	3 19 0
[Page 56] It: 2 belmetle Skellets 9s one old bras Skillet 2s	0 11 0
It: a frying pan 4s a warming pan 5s a tramell 6s	0 15 0
It: 3 barrells of beef 50s: 40£ of tallow 10s two Seivs 18d	3 01 6
It: one Chest 6s one bible 30s a percell of book 10s	2 6 0
It: one bedsted Curtaines & hangings 36s bed & boulster and pillows 3£:16	5 12 0
It: two blankets 20s two ditto old 12s a Rug old 6s old Carpetts 3s	2 1 0
It: one Chest 16s his wareing aparrell 16£ one Case 15s botles	17 11 0
It: one bed and beding 30s one old Sadle & bridle brest plate & Cruper 10s	2 00 0
It: one paire of boots 15s one Small trunk 4s one Chest 6s	1 5 0
It: one trunk 9s one Chest 12s one old glass & Curry Combe 1s	1 2 0
It: 4 glass bottles 1s 2 tunells 4s: 50 weight of warping 37s:6d	2 2 6
It: 111£ of Iron 1£:7s:9 25 gallons of Mallases 25s one Auger 1s	2 13 9
It: one gimlet 6d a broad ax 5s drawing knife 2s: 4 narrow axes 16s	1 3 6
It: beetle & wedges 10s hamer 18d 3 hows 6s: 2 Sieths & tacleing 10s	1 7 6
It: one harrow 15s one plow 15s 4 old Sicles 3s 1 Chaine 10s	2 3 0
It: 2 paire of Iron traces 18s one Cart Shelvens Clevis & pin 24s	2 2 0
It: one bed & furneture 3£:10 one old boat 5£ one fork 18d	8 11 6
It: one third In new boat 50s Craft to fit them out 4£ 13s	7 3 0
It: to hay wheat and oats 12£ two Small negro boys 25£	37 0 0
It: one negro man and woman 40£ to Ceder bouls 3£: 2 Spads 10s	43 10 0
It: 2 Shod Shovells 2s 2 yokes 10s one Cart rope 5s a halter 6d	00 17 6
It: 2 paire of Iron hopples 10s one Leather p^{r}: 9d	00 10 9
It: to wheels & pailes and milk vessells and other Lumber	02 0 0
It: to one ads & marking Iron 3s to book debts in good hands 35£	35 3 0
It: 12 paire of Sheets 12£ Six paire of pillow beers 18s 3 duz: napkins 2£:14s	15 12 0
It: 4 table Cloaths 30s by 60£:10s:6d In Cash	62 0 6

It: 100 weight of warping 9d p £: is 3:15s 03 15 0
It: 8 quoshings 8s: 20 Sheep Lost and now found 5£ a p^r Stilly^{ds}: 6s <u>05 14 0</u>
Totall is £: 420 16 4

Aprized according to money by us Jonathan Rayner Samuell Clark Joseph ffordham
A true Coppy p John Howell Clark

At a Court [ ] held at Southampton ye 28th day of March anno Dom 1693 Before ye honoured Isaac Arnold Esqr Judge of ye sd Court was proved & approved ye last Will & Testam^t of James Smith late of Huntington deceased at Huntington on y^e [ ] who while he lived & at ye time of his death had goods moveable & immoveable &c and the administration of ye same was then Committed to Jonas Wood of Hempsteed in Queens County (nominated in ye sd Testam^t) to exhibite a full & faithfull inventory of all & ye Goods & Chattells debts Rights & Credits of ye sd deceased as also to render a plaine & a true account of ye performance of his duty herein at or before ye 30th day of Sept ansuing before ye Judge of
[Page 57] The true Tenour of which sd Testamt ffolloweth in thes words.

The last Will and Testa[m^t] of James Smith in ye Province of Nyorke & County of Suffolke & of ye Towne of Huntington being sicke & weake in body but sound in memory & understanding, my worldly goods that God of his Mercy hath given me I doe dispose of as followeth. The one third parte of my whole Esttae I doe give unto my wife ye other two thirds of my Estate - Housing lands & meadows my will is that it shall be equally divided amongst my four Children as also ye two thirds of my Moveables to be equally divided amongst my four Children likewis my will is that my wife shall have the improvem^t of ye whole estate for ye bringing up of ye Children untill they Come to be of age to improve it themselves and my will is further that if it shall pleas God to take away any of my Children by death before they receive their portions that then their parts shall be equally divided amonst ye rest of my Children: My will is that Capt Epenetus Plat & my brother Jeremiah Smith & my brother in law Jonas Wood would be as overseers to se that this my will be performed This above written I doe declare to be my Mind & will as witnesse my hand & seale this 18th of Novemb in ye year of our Lord 1690 James Smith

Witnesses Thomas Wicks Jonas Wood who being sworne doe declare that ye testator James Smith deceased did acknowledge this to be his last will & that at ye making herof was of sound Memory & understanding. Tho. Helme Cler.

INDEX OF PERSONS

I

Y

Made in the USA
Monee, IL
05 March 2026

45505172R00195